MIKE ASHLEY is an author and editor of over ninety books, including many Mammoth titles. He worked for over thirty years in local government but is now a full-time writer and researcher specializing in ancient history, historical fiction and fantasy, crime and science fiction. He lives in Kent with his wife and over 30,000 books.

Other titles in this series

A Brief History of the Boxer Rebellion
Diana Preston

A Brief History of British Kings & Queens
Mike Ashley

A Brief History of the Celts
Peter Berresford Ellis

A Brief History of the Circumnavigators
Derek Wilson

A Brief History of Christianity
Bamber Gascoigne

A Brief History of the Druids
Peter Berresford Ellis

A Brief History of the Dynasties of China
Bamber Gascoigne

A Brief History of Fighting Ships
David Davies

A Brief History of the Great Moghuls
Bamber Gascoigne

A Brief History of the Hundred Years War
Desmond Seward

A Brief History of Napoleon in Russia
Alan Palmer

A Brief History of the Royal Flying Corps in WWI
Ralph Barker

A Brief History of Science
Thomas Crump

A Brief History of the Tudor Age
Jasper Ridley

A BRIEF HISTORY OF

KING ARTHUR

MIKE ASHLEY

ROBINSON

RUNNING PRESS
PHILADELPHIA · LONDON

Constable & Robinson Ltd
3 The Lanchesters
162 Fulham Palace Road
London W6 9ER
www.constablerobinson.com

First published in the UK by Robinson,
an imprint of Constable & Robinson Ltd
as *The Mammoth Book of King Arthur*, 2005

A copy of the British Library Cataloguing in
Publication Data is available from the British Library.

UK ISBN 978-1-84901-302-4

1 3 5 7 9 10 8 6 4 2

First published in the United States in 2010 by Running Press Book Publishers

9 8 7 6 5 4 3 2 1
Digit on the right indicates the number of this printing

Library of Congress Catalog Control Number: 2009935105
US ISBN 978-0-7624-3897-6

Running Press Book Publishers
2300 Chestnut Street
Philadelphia, PA 19103-4371

Visit us on the web!
www.runningpress.com

Printed and bound in the EU

CONTENTS

TABLES AND MAPS

Tables

Maps

ACKNOWLEDGEMENTS

So much has been written about Arthur and his world that it is easy to become influenced by the thoughts and findings of others, no matter how much you try to remain independent. For that very reason I have consulted few people during the course of this book. I have made full use of the scholarship available in the books and websites listed in the Bibliography at the end of this book and make specific acknowledgement here to the excellent work by Leslie Alcock, John Morris, Frank Reno and Richard Barber, as well as the contributors to Robert Vermaat's brilliant Vortigern Studies website.

However every author needs a lifeline and I must give special thanks to Peter Berresford Ellis. He read through the original manuscript and offered helpful comments and observations, and also responded to my frequent pleas for help on the Celtic languages and translations. In addition my thanks to Larry Mendelsburg who gave freely of his knowledge of Arthurian literature. I am exceedingly grateful to them both.

I must also thank Gary Kronk who kindly made available to me cometary data updated from his book *Cometography* (Cambridge University Press, 1999); and Antony Wilson of York Coins for confirmation of data on Danish minters.

And, of course, my thanks and gratitude to my wife Sue who puts up with my hours of isolation as I delve amongst "all those dead people", as she thinks of them, and then welcomes me back to the land of the living. To her I dedicate this book, with all my love and affection.

NOTE ON THE NEW EDITION

An earlier version of this book was published as the first half of *The Mammoth Book of King Arthur* in 2005. I have taken the opportunity to update the text and expand certain features as well as amplify some of my original thoughts in order to provide a more complete study and analysis of the sources relating to the original Arthur. This volume concentrates on the origins of the Arthurian story and not on the later medieval legends from Chrétien to Malory.

PREFACE:
PEELING BACK THE LAYERS

What's it all about?

This book is a quest back into history to find out what we can about King Arthur. It will test the evidence and question whether there ever was a real Arthur and, if there was, whether there is enough evidence to identify him.

There have been numerous books about Arthur and you may ask why we need another. However, most authors who claim to have identified Arthur focus on their specific theory and ignore the rest. Here, though, I want to keep an open mind and present all of the evidence to see what sense, if any, can be made of it. I'll even present a few theories of my own, and provide maps, family trees and a chronology. That way not only can you see how I arrive at my conclusions but it will allow you to draw your own.

The book looks at the world in which Arthur lived (roughly between 400 and 600AD), and explores what evidence has survived to prove or disprove his existence. It also looks at the many theories that have been put forward to identify Arthur and sets them against the historical background in the hope that the real Arthur will stand out. You might think it ought to be straightforward. If Arthur existed, if he was as famous as he's supposed to have been, whether under that name or another, then he'll appear in the historical record, just like Alfred the Great or Canute or Macbeth, other great kings from a thousand years ago whose existence is easily provable and not in doubt and whose exploits have become as much a part of legend as Arthur's. But it's far from straightforward and there's a lot of work needed to peel back the layers and reveal Arthur in all his glory.

The original Arthur dates back to those Dark Ages in the fifth and sixth centuries when the people of Britain were fighting for their lives against invaders, famine, plague and civil war. No one had much time to keep written records, and any that may have been kept have not survived the centuries. The single sobering fact is that there is not one single piece of genuine historical evidence to support the existence of someone called King Arthur.

Ironically, it is this lack of evidence that makes the search for the real Arthur so compelling, because there is a fair amount of circumstantial evidence to show that someone who was a great leader must have existed. That someone was the man who defeated the Saxons at the battle of Badon so decisively that the Saxon invasion was held at bay for at least a generation. Whoever did that – and for simplicity's sake I shall call him Arthur of Badon – had to exist because the one victory at Badon is that certain historical fact.

I believe that the original stories about Arthur are based on several historical people, at least three of whom were also called Arthur. Their lives, which only show dimly through the veils of history, soon became submerged into the oral tradition that created the Arthur of legend, a whole amalgam of historical and legendary characters spread across a wide period of history. That is one of the reasons why there are so many theories about the real Arthur and why he is so difficult to pin down.

The great puzzle

Arthur lived at that one period of British history when historians looked the other way. In fact, apart from a few Continental writers who commented briefly upon the state of Britain in the fifth century, there is only one possible contemporary of Arthur whose work survives – Gildas, who is discussed in detail in Chapter 5. Unfortunately, Gildas was not interested in recording history, and certainly not in noting dates, being more concerned with reprimanding the aberrant rulers whose waywardness had brought down the wrath of God by way of the Saxon invasion. Even more unfortunately for the Arthurian scholar, Gildas doesn't mention Arthur at all.

Nothing significant by any other contemporary writer survives, apart from a few church writings which tell us virtually nothing about the state of Britain. Even the surviving text of Gildas's work dates from the eleventh century, five hundred years after he wrote it. The same is true for other surviving texts, especially the Welsh Annals and the *Anglo-Saxon Chronicle*, as the copies we have were created several centuries later from long-lost sources. No matter how diligent the copyists were, mistakes could have crept in – in fact, some mistakes are all too obvious, as we shall see.

Then there is the problem of names – both personal and place names. Any individual could be known by a title, a personal name or a nickname. For instance, the name of the British king Vortigern is possibly not a name at all but a title meaning High King. Likewise the names of the Saxon chieftains, Hengist and Horsa, were probably nicknames; both names mean horse (or, more precisely in Hengist's case, stallion). This is more common than you might think. "Genghis Khan" was actually a title meaning "very mighty ruler"; the great Mongol ruler's real name was Temujin.

The real name of the Roman emperor we call Caligula was Gaius Julius Caesar Germanicus. "Caligula" was a nickname referring to the little boots he preferred as a child. He was never called that officially during his lifetime, but that name was circulating soon after his death.

Perhaps the same happened with Arthur. It's fine if we know the alternative names and titles for people, but hopeless if we don't. How do we know when we come across a new name that it isn't someone we already know? In the time of Arthur and in later writings about his period, the name could be recorded in Celtic (both British and the later Welsh variant), Latin or Anglo-Saxon. If these variants are also used for titles, real names and nicknames, then it means one individual could be called by nine different names, and that doesn't allow for misspellings, copyists' errors or mistaken identity. The same applies to place names, which are further complicated by their having evolved over time, and by many places throughout Britain having the same name. Just think how many rivers are called Avon or towns called Newtown. If original Celtic or local names have died out and been super-seded by Saxon or Norman names, and no documentation survives to identify the place, then tracking it down is as likely as winning the lottery.

The biggest problem is one of dates. The method of record-ing years from the birth of Christ may seem simple today, but it wasn't in the fifth century and had only really been introduced a few decades before. Copyists trying to update records from ancient documents encountered several problems. Firstly, they could not be sure whether the year recorded was calculated from the birth of Christ or from his baptism, usually treated as twenty-eight years later, or from his death and resurrection, variously thirty-three or thirty-five years later. Thus a year recorded as, say, 460 years from the "incarnation" of Christ could, by our reckoning, be 488, 493 or 495.

Some annals recorded events on an Easter cycle. The dates for Easter more or less repeat themselves every nineteen years. But it was entirely possible, if working from an incomplete manuscript, to lose track of which Easter cycle was being covered. The copyist would use his best judgement, but could be out by nineteen years. This is certainly evident in early entries in the *Anglo-Saxon Chronicle*, as we shall see.

Finally, the copyist might simply misread a figure, especially if working from a crumpled or charred document all but destroyed in a Viking raid. Years were usually recorded in Roman numerals, but it's easy to make a mistake, copying *ccclxviii* (368), for example, as, perhaps, *ccclxxiv* (374). Once the mistake is made and the original lost, who is there to correct it?

This problem about dates, which will keep resurfacing, is crucial to identifying Arthur, because we need to know when he lived and how his life related to other events. Imagine a future historian trying to understand events if the outbreak of World War II were placed twenty-eight years earlier, in 1911, or twenty-eight years later in 1967? How could you possibly relate it to individuals' lives?

The events of the fifth century were every bit as critical to those living then as World War II is to us. The Roman Empire, which had existed for over 400 years, was crumbling and so-called "barbarians" were taking over Europe. To individuals at that time the world was collapsing about them and chaos reigned. To help us interpret it and get back to what really happened, we need to understand the complete history and geography of those times. The secret to identifying Arthur is to find the right name in the right place at the right time, and it's those three criteria which we need to explore in this book.

Where do we start?

The search for the real Arthur will take us through a mass of material, some of it detailed and much of it complicated. Piecing together the Arthurian world is like trying to complete a jigsaw in which a lot of the pieces are missing. Many of those that remain may have only a partial picture, some may have the picture redrawn, and some belong to another jigsaw entirely. We have to look at each piece in detail and see what it is, whether it fits and, if so, where it fits.

First, let's start by looking at the big picture. It will help us keep things in perspective and give us a framework within which to fit the pieces.

If we are to find the real Arthur, we need to look somewhere in the two hundred years between the end of Roman administration of Britain, a date usually assigned as 410AD, and the emergence of the Saxon kingdoms, which were taking a strong hold by the start of the seventh century.

The traditional history of those two centuries can be described fairly easily. After the passing of Roman authority Britain sank into a period of decline. There was civil unrest, plague and famine, and Britain – i.e., the territory south of Hadrian's Wall – was constantly under threat of invasion by Germanic forces from the east, the Irish (Scotii) from the west and the Picts from the north. By the middle of the fifth century the Saxons and other tribes had gained a hold on territory in the east, and progressively, over the next hundred years or so, infiltrated Britain, pushing the British nobility west, primarily into Wales and Cornwall, and Brittany. The British, though weakened by their own strife, put up a resistance under various leaders. One Briton in particular managed to defeat the Saxons so significantly at Badon, sometime towards the end of the fifth century, that the Saxon advance was halted. For a period of perhaps forty years the British held their ground, and the Saxons did not advance further.

Historians are now less comfortable with this view. Growing archaeological and genetic research suggests that the Saxon settlement of Britain was less dramatic, with events drawn out over a longer period and with no sudden conquest, but rather a series of occasional conflicts, one of which would have been the battle of Badon.

From the middle of the sixth century, a new invader, the Angles, advanced and – presumably after the death of Arthur – began to win territory in the west. After the battles of Dyrham in 577 and Chester in 615, the British until then holding a unified territory in the west, were divided. Soon after 600 the powerful warlord Athelfrith established his own kingdom of Northumbria, stretching across northern Britain. The heartland of Britain, where a few Celtic enclaves struggled on, was also crushed by the Northumbrians and the next wave of Angles, who created the kingdom of Mercia under Penda. By 625, the territory later to be called England was under Angle, or "English" control.

During these two hundred years several British kingdoms emerged, based largely on the old tribal structure. We know some better than others, depending on what records have survived. Perhaps not surprisingly, the best known were those in Wales, which survived beyond the Arthurian age and well into the Middle Ages. The major kingdoms were Gwynedd (originally called Venedotia) in the north, Powys along the Welsh Marches, Dyfed (originally Demetia) in the south-west and Gwent in the south-east. There were several smaller Welsh kingdoms, such as Ceredigion, Builth and Brycheiniog, all of which will feature in our explorations, but the history of Wales is really the history of those four main kingdoms.

In the south-west of Britain was the kingdom of Dumnonia, primarily Devon and Cornwall but also, for much of the fifth century, covering parts of Dorset and Somerset.

There were also several kingdoms in the north. The Scottish Highlands remained the domain of the Picts, but between Hadrian's Wall and the Antonine Wall further north there were three main British kingdoms: the Gododdin (originally called the Votadini) in the east, with centres at Traprain Law and Din Eityn (Edinburgh), Strathclyde (originally Alclud) in the west, with its centre at Dumbarton, and Galloway in the south-west. At some stage Galloway seems to have become part of the kingdom of Rheged, which at its height stretched from Galloway, down through Cumbria and into Lancashire, probably as far as Chester, and thus bordering onto Gwynedd and Powys.

These were the main Celtic kingdoms to survive through the Dark Ages. There were further kingdoms in the east of Britain, but we know much less about these, because they were the first to be supplanted by the Saxons and the cultures soon merged. The main eastern kingdom in the north was York (originally

Ebrauc). To the north of York was Bryneich, in Northumbria; to the south was Lindsey (originally Linnuis), which covered much of Lincolnshire and the Fens. To the west of Lindsey was Elmet, based around Leeds, one of the last British kingdoms to survive in England. There were other smaller kingdoms north of Elmet, in the Pennines, but no formal record of them survives.

To the south was a kingdom stretching from London into Essex and parts of Suffolk. There was also a kingdom in Kent, though this hardly seems to have started before it was snuffed out. Beyond these it is probable that there were kingdoms based in the Chilterns, Oxford, Gloucester, Sussex and so on. The map opposite shows the approximate location of these kingdoms, but we do not know for certain their extent. Their boundaries remained fluid depending on the individual warlord's power.

The importance of these kingdoms is that if Arthur really was a king, then he must have ruled one of these territories. Not all the pedigrees survive; the best preserved are for the Welsh kingdoms and those of the North. We do not know the names of any of the rulers of London, for instance, and even the one name for a ruler of Kent is somewhat dubious. We will encounter several people with a name like Arthur in the pedigrees, all of whom I outline in the first chapter, but whether any of them is the real Arthur, or whether the real Arthur was a composite of them or of any other characters, is something that we need to explore.

At this stage we can think of Arthur solely as a British resistance leader. Whether he mustered that resistance from Cornwall, Wales or the North is something else we will have to consider. Whether he did this in the late fifth or early sixth century, or perhaps another time, we will also have to deduce.

There are plenty of clues, but none of them is straightforward, and some are very misleading. And it's dangerous to leap straight in and expect the clues to declare themselves. We have

1. British Kingdoms in the Fifth Century

to go looking for them, and we have to go armed with some basic information. First we need to consider the name Arthur itself.

I

AN INTRODUCTION TO ARTHUR – WHAT'S IN A NAME?

1. Myth, history and mystery

You will find in the course of this book that we encounter several Arthurs. There's not just one Arthur of legend, for a start, and there's certainly not one Arthur of history.

The Arthur we remember from our childhood reading is, for the most part, a fiction. Most of us know the basic legend from Sir Thomas Malory's *Morte Darthur*. Arthur was born of a deceitful relationship. With the help of the magician Merlin, Arthur's father Uther Pendragon, king of Britain, was able to take on the guise of Gorlois, Duke of Cornwall, and seduce Gorlois's wife Ygraine. After Uther's death, there was a contest to find the next king, who would be the one who could pull the sword out of the stone. All the champions and dukes tried and failed but young Arthur, still only fifteen, succeeded. Not all of the dukes and other rulers were happy about this, and Arthur had to fight for his kingdom. But he won and, for a while, ruled happily and wisely. Thanks to Merlin, Arthur acquired the sword Excalibur from the Lady of the Lake, the scabbard of which protected him from harm. He established the Round Table of brave and valorous knights, including Sir Kay, Sir Bedivere, Sir Gawain, Sir Bors, Sir Tristram and, of course, Sir Lancelot. We learn of the adventures of these knights, saving damsels and fighting villains, and we follow the quest for the Holy Grail. But there is a dark side. Arthur's queen, Guenevere, fell in love with her champion, Lancelot, and those knights who disliked Lancelot plotted against him. These included Arthur's illegitimate son Sir Mordred, whose mother, Margawse, was the wife of King Lot of Orkney and Arthur's half-sister. Mordred, caught up in the scheming of other knights, especially Sir Agravaine, revealed the truth about Lancelot to Arthur, and Guenevere was sentenced to burn at the stake. She was rescued by Lancelot, but in the fracas Gawain's brothers were killed. Lancelot exiled himself to France, but Arthur, urged on by Gawain, followed, allowing Mordred to usurp the kingdom. Arthur returned to do battle with Mordred and was mortally wounded at the battle of Camlann. The heroes of the Round Table not already killed in the war with Lancelot lay dead, all but Bedivere who returned Arthur's sword to the Lady of the Lake. Arthur was taken to the Isle of Avalon where his wounds would be cured, and one day he will return. Thus he is remembered as the Once and Future King.

That, in a nutshell, is how we remember Arthur.

Myth? Well, mostly. History? Well . . .

Malory took this story from earlier accounts, mostly from the so-called *Vulgate Cycle*, which drew on the work of Chrétien de Troyes. Chrétien got his stories from local tales and legends in France and Brittany, including some of the Welsh tales later collected under the title *The Mabinogion*. It was Chrétien who invented the name Camelot and created the character of Lancelot. In his stories we find much of the original of Malory's Arthur, but his sources, the Welsh tales, portray a different, earlier Arthur, an Arthur of legend, far removed from the world of Plantagenet chivalry. This Arthur's world is still one of fantasy and magic, but beneath that surface is a sense of history. The Celtic Arthur feels as if he really belonged in his own time, unlike Malory's Arthur who is rooted in a medieval Britain and the world of the Crusades.

But there is yet another Arthur of legend, the creation of Geoffrey of Monmouth. Three hundred years before Malory, Geoffrey set out to write (or, according to him, translate) a history of Britain from a mysterious and ancient book. The result, the *Historia Regum Britanniae* (*The History of the Kings of Britain*), contains a huge section on the exploits of King Arthur, which proved so popular that Geoffrey's *History* became a medieval best-seller. It was Geoffrey who created the fascination with Arthur and who created most of the myth, though his story differs in certain parts from Malory's later version and significantly from the Welsh tales. Yet both Geoffrey's and the Welsh Arthurs have some basis in history. Or at least a memory of history.

Geoffrey also had his sources. These included Nennius, a ninth-century collector of old documents and chronicles, and a sixth-century monk called Gildas. Both writers furnish some historical background to the story. Nennius provides a list of Arthur's battles whilst Gildas, without naming Arthur, refers to the most famous battle associated with him, Badon, and mentions Arthur's illustrious predecessor Ambrosius Aurelianus. When you dig around other ancient documents, like the Welsh Triads and the *Welsh Annals* (*Annales Cambriae*), and the various pedigrees of the ancient British kings, you find further references to Arthur.

Now you feel that you've moved out of legend into history, but Arthur doesn't quite fit into this history. A chronology proves difficult. By all accounts the original Arthur, that is, Arthur of Badon, ought to be living in the period between 490 and 520, but he's difficult to find there. The *Welsh Annals* place him a little later, around 510–540, but he's difficult to find there as well. Historical Arthurs pop up in the period 540–620, but these dates are too late for Badon. Does that mean that these later Arthurs became credited with the exploits of an earlier hero? Or does it mean that the chronology is all wrong and that Badon happened a century later? Or does it mean that these exploits, were really by a number of people spread over a much longer period of time?

That's what we need to unravel.

2. The historical Arthurs

You will encounter several Arthurs in this book and rather than introduce them one by one, which becomes confusing, I'll mention them now so you'll know who they are when they appear and how I shall refer to them.

(1) Lucius Artorius Castus, the Roman Arthur, who lived from about 140–197AD.

(2) Arthwys ap Mar, whom I shall call Arthur of the Pennines, who lived around 460–520.

(3) Artúir ap Pedr, known as Arthur of Dyfed, who lived around 550–620.

(4) Artúir mac Aedan, prince of Dál Riata, who lived around 560–596, but who never survived to become king.

(5) Athrwys ap Meurig, known as Arthur of Gwent, who lived around 610–680 by my calculations, but is given an earlier date by others. He may be the Arthur of *The Mabinogion*.

(6) Arthfoddw of Ceredigion, or Arth the Lucky, who lived about 550–620.

(7) Artúir ap Bicor, the Arthur of Kintyre, who also lived about 550–620.

(8) Armel or Arthmael, the warrior saint, who lived about 540–600.

(9) Arzur, the Arthur of Brittany, who may or may not be the same as,

(10) Riothamus, or Rigotamus, a military leader in Brittany last heard of in 470.

These are not the only contenders, but they are the primary ones called Arthur. As we explore the many old documents and pedigrees I shall frequently refer to these names as well as, of course, the original Arthur of Badon, who may be one, some or all of the above.

3. The name of Arthur

Much is made of Arthur's name, one argument being that there was a sudden flush of people in the late sixth century being named Arthur after some hero of the previous generation or two. In fact Arthur isn't that uncommon a name and it has its origins in two primary sources.

First and foremost, it is an Irish name, Artúr, derived from the common name Art, meaning "bear", which is well known from the Irish ruler, Art the Solitary, son of Conn of a Hundred Battles, and his son, the more famous Cormac mac Art, High King from 254–277. There are several diminutives (Artan, Artúr, Artúir), and these names passed into Wales with the Irish settlers during the fourth and fifth centuries. These were descendants of Art Corb, or Artchorp, the ancestor of the Déisi, a tribe who were exiled from Ireland and settled in Demetia, now Dyfed, in west Wales, and include the Artúir ap Pedr listed above. Other Irish, from the Dál Riatan kingdom in Ulster, settled in Kintyre and Argyll at around the same time, and Artúir mac Aedan is descended from them.

The other source is the Roman family name Artorius. It is not certain when or from where this family originated, but it may well have been Greece. The earliest known member was Marcus Artorius Asclepiades, physician to Octavian, the future Caesar Augustus. The Artorii lived in Campania in Italy, but also occupied southern Gaul and Spain. Apart from Lucius Artorius Castus, they seem to have had little impact in Britain, but the memory of his name may have lingered on, becoming adopted by the Celtic tribes in Gaul and gradually leeching into Britain. The name would have evolved to Arturius, and then to Artur, and would more likely have been used within the highly Romanised parts of southern Britain than in Wales or the North, where the name more probably came from the Irish.

There may be other sources. One is Artaius, a minor Romano-Celtic deity rather like Mercury, whose cult may have helped popularize a form of the name. Another slightly more tortuous derivation may be based on the Celtic for High King, *Ardd Ri*. The Brythonic *dd* is pronounced *th*, so that the title, pronounced *Arth-ri*, may later have been remembered as a name.

There is, though, a danger in looking at any name beginning with "Art" and assuming it has some Arthurian connection. It doesn't, and in any contemporary documents would otherwise be ignored, just as we would not confuse Tony with Tonto or George with Geoffrey. But we can't ignore the possibility that scribes working from inferior documents several centuries after the event might have misread, misinterpreted or miscopied names, so that an Arthwyr – a name which means "grandson of Arth" – became Arthur. The excitement in the press in 1998 over the discovery of a stone at Tintagel bearing the name Artognou, is a case in point. Artognou means "descendant of Art" and has no direct connection with Arthur, but because it was found at Tintagel, there was an immediate assumption that the two had to be connected.

Our quest is to find an Arthur whose credentials fit as much of the history as we know. In order to understand the world of Arthur, we have to understand the state of Britain from the arrival of the Romans, five hundred years before. So let us first explore Roman Britain and see what it has to tell us about the Arthurian world that followed.

2

BEFORE ARTHUR – THE ROMAN BACKGROUND

1. The first empire

When Julius Caesar took his first tentative and rather wet steps into Britain in 55BC, he learned that the native British were a challenging foe. He later wrote that there were separate tribal states in Britain between which there had been almost "continual warfare", but in order to oppose the Roman forces most of the states had united behind one king, the powerful Cassivelaunos, or Caswallon. Caesar eventually got the measure of the Britons, but his incursion into Britain was little more than that, and by no means a conquest. It would be nearly a hundred years before the emperor Claudius headed a successful invasion of Britain in 43AD and brought the island into the Roman Empire.

Even so, Britain remained an outpost. No one from Rome wanted to go there. It had a cold and forbidding reputation even though, by the second and third centuries, it had become a prosperous part of the empire, supplying much of the grain for

Rome. Those Romans who did live in Britain attained heights of luxury, although, in truth, they were Romans only by name. They were, for the most part, Britons, aspiring to the aristocratic lifestyle of the Romans, and seeing the benefits of working with the "enemy" rather than against them. This siding with Rome was evident even in Caesar's day. Mandubracius, son of the king of the Trinovantes, promised to give Caesar inside information to help the invasion. Likewise Cogidubnus, because of the aid he had given the Romans, became a client king and received the tribal territory of the Regnii in Hampshire, with a magnificent palace at what is now Fishbourne, near Chichester.

Other sympathetic tribal leaders included Prasutagus, ruler of the Iceni, and Cartimandua, queen of the Brigantes. Both retained their power and territory in return for aiding Rome. Cartimandua even turned over to Rome the rebel leader Caratacus, who had sustained a guerrilla-style opposition to the imperial forces for seven years.

Prasutagus may not be so well known today, but his wife certainly is. She was Boudicca (still better known as Boadicea), who, because of her treatment by the Romans after her husband's death, led a revolt, catching them unawares and destroying Colchester and London. But she was unable to defeat the might of the main Roman army under Suetonius Paulinus and died, probably by her own hand, in 61AD.

After Boudicca's revolt the process of Roman colonization continued but it was never simple and never straightforward. For a start, the Romans never got a firm grip on Scotland, despite the defeat of the chieftain Calgacus of the Caledonii in 84AD. In 122AD, the emperor Hadrian commissioned the construction of a wall across northern Britain, from the Solway Firth in the west to what is now Wallsend in the east. It contained the northern frontier, and recognized that it was not worth the effort to try and defeat the tribes to the north – the tribes that came to be known collectively as the Picts.

Roman occupation of Wales was also rather limited, and there was not the same civic development as in England. The Roman towns were mostly in the south, and Wales was held under control by several powerful forts. Relationships were not helped by the attempts of Suetonius Paulinus to annihilate the Druids in their retreat on the island of Anglesey, only halted by Paulinus being called to deal with Boudicca's revolt.

The rebellious nature of the British was one of the few facts known to the Romans at the core of the empire. Writing at the time that Claudius was planning his invasion, Pomponius Mela, who lived in southern Spain and probably knew the British, wrote in *De Chorographia* (43AD):

> It has peoples and kings of peoples, but they are all uncivilized and the further they are from the continent the less they know of other kinds of wealth, being rich only in herds and lands . . . Nevertheless, they find occasions for wars and do fight them and often attack each other, mostly from a wish for domination and a desire to carry off what they possess.

Tacitus, writing in 98AD about the campaigns of his father-in-law Agricola, saw these internecine struggles as an advantage:

> Once they paid obedience to kings, but now they are divided by warring factions among their leading men. Nothing has been more helpful to us in dealing with these powerful tribes than the fact that they do not co-operate. Seldom is there a combination of two or three states to repel a common danger; so, fighting separately, all are defeated.

This inability of tribes to live in harmony will re-emerge as a major factor in the Arthurian world. The number of hill forts throughout Britain is a testimony to how often the tribes fought each other, resulting in a need to build defences. Tacitus also recognized the impact upon the British of Roman civilization. Comparing the British to the Gauls in his *Life of Agricola*, he wrote:

... the *Britanni* display more fierceness, seeing that they have not been softened by protracted peace. For we know that the Gauls were once distinguished in warfare, but later sloth came in with ease and valour was lost with liberty. The same thing has happened to those [southern] *Britanni* who were conquered early; the rest remain what the Gauls once were.

This was the first recognition of a North–South divide in Britain.

There were over twenty different tribes in Britain. The Romans used the tribal divisions as the bases for their *civitates*, mostly in what is now England, each of which had a capital town. There were sixteen in total, mostly established within a century of the invasion in 43AD. These towns remained throughout the Roman occupation and into the early post-Roman period, and because they are relevant to the Arthurian story, it's worth noting them here. The following table lists them in sequence, from the southern coast of Britain rising north.

Table 1. The Roman *civitas*

Tribe (Civitas)	Capital	Present-day name
Cantii (*Cantiacorum*)	Durovernum	Canterbury (*Kent*)
Regnii (*Reginorum*)	Noviomagus	Chichester (*West Sussex*)
Belgae (*Belgarum*)	Venta Belgarum	Winchester (*Hampshire*)
Atrebates (*Atrebatum*)	Calleva	Silchester (*Hampshire*)
Durotriges (*Durotrigum*)	Durnovaria	Dorchester (*Dorset*)
Dumnonii (*Dumnoniorum*)	Isca	Exeter (*Devon*)
Trinovantes (*Trinovantium*)	Caesaromagus	Chelmsford (*Essex*)
Catuvellauni (*Catuvellaunorum*)	Verulamium	St Albans (*Hertfordshire*)
Dobunni (*Dobunnorum*)	Corinium	Cirencester (*Gloucestershire*)
Silures (*Silurum*)	Venta Silurum	Caerwent (*Monmouth*)
Demetae (*Demetarum*)	Moridunum	Carmarthen (*Carmarthenshire*)
Cornovii (*Cornoviorum*)	Viriconium	Wroxeter (*Shropshire*)
Iceni (*Icenorum*)	Venta Icenorum	Caistor St Edmund (*Norfolk*)
Coritani (*Coritanorum*)	Ratae	Leicester (*Leicestershire*)
Parisii (*Parisorum*)	Petuaria	Brough-on-Humber (*Yorkshire*)
Brigantes (*Brigantium*)	Isurium	Aldborough (*Yorkshire*)

These *civitas* capitals were rather like present-day county towns. They were essentially self-governing, run by elected magistrates. Although all too few of these magistrates' names survive, it is entirely likely that they came from the ruling families of the tribes and that the pre-Roman mini-kingdoms effectively continued, now reconstituted in Roman form (*see* Map 2).

The capitals were not the only important towns in Roman Britain. Of more significance were the *coloniae*. Initially these were independent towns with their own surrounding territory (separate from the *civitates*) and city council, occupied only by Roman citizens, usually retired soldiers and administrators. There were originally three *coloniae*: Camulodunum (Colchester), Lindum (Lincoln) and Glevum (Gloucester). Eboracum (York), one of the most important cities in Roman Britain, was later granted the status of *colonia* by the emperor Septimius Severus, who used it as his imperial capital from 208 until his death in 211, while he was involved in campaigns against the northern tribes.

York had been one of the three legionary fortresses at the start of the Roman occupation. It was home first to the IX Hispana Legion and then, from around 122, to the VI Victrix Legion. The other two fortresses were Isca (Caerleon), the home of the II Augustan Legion, and Deva (Chester) home, from around 87AD onwards, of the XX Valeria Victrix. Each became known as the City of the Legion. Before becoming a *colonia*, Lincoln had also briefly been a legionary fort, as had Wroxeter before it was developed as a *civitas* capital, but their legionary days were over by around 87AD.

Some large towns also acquired the status of *municipium*, in which the ruling magistrates and their families were all granted Roman citizenship. Each *colonia* must have been a *municipium* before rising in status. It is known that Verulamium (St Albans) was later granted this status, and it is likely that Londinium (London) and Venta Belgarum (Winchester) were similarly rewarded. There were other smaller towns and forts, but those listed above were the primary centres of Roman Britain. They gave their occupants a status in the Roman world, although

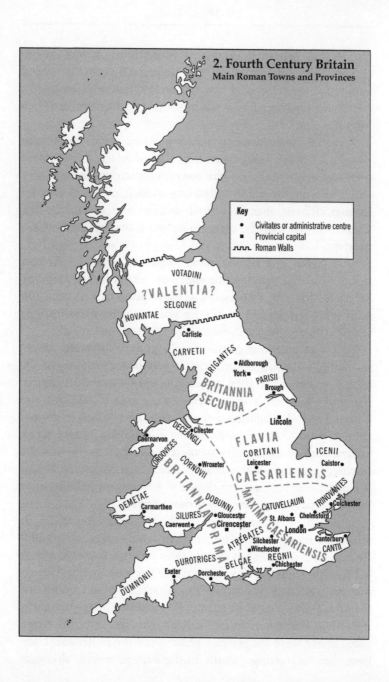

2. Fourth Century Britain
Main Roman Towns and Provinces

Key
- • Civitates or administrative centre
- ■ Provincial capital
- ᨠᨠ Roman Walls

VOTADINI

?VALENTIA?

SELGOVAE

NOVANTAE

Carlisle

CARVETII

BRIGANTES
• Aldborough
York ■
PARISII
Brough

BRITANNIA SECUNDA

Lincoln

DECEANGLI
• Chester
Caernarvon

FLAVIA

CORITANI
Leicester

ICENII
Caistor •

ORDOVICES
CORNOVII
• Wroxeter

CAESARIENSIS

DEMETAE
Carmarthen

DOBUNNI

CATUVELLAUNI

TRINOVANTES
Colchester •

BRITANNIA PRIMA

SILURES
• Caerwent

• Gloucester
Cirencester

St. Albans • Chelmsford

MAXIMA CAESARIENSIS

ATREBATES

Silchester •
Winchester •

London •

Canterbury •

CANTII

DUROTRIGES

BELGAE

REGNII
• Chichester

DUMNONII
Exeter •

Dorchester •

not all freeborn Britons were automatically granted Roman citizenship (that did not happen until 212, during the reign of Caracalla).

There were also countless villas dotted around the countryside. The majority were in the south, with concentrations around Gloucester and Cirencester, between Silchester and Winchester, and around London. Their number rapidly thinned to the north, and there were no substantial villas north of Vinovium, a fort near what is now Binchester, in County Durham. These villas, the Roman equivalent of stately homes, were also working farms, more suited to the soils of the southern lowlands.

North of Vinovium was essentially a military zone, running up to Hadrian's Wall and beyond to the Antonine Wall, an earth rampart with a series of forts built between the Forth and the Clyde. An advance under emperor Antoninus Pius in 139 was maintained for barely twenty years, and after Pius's death in 161 there was an effective withdrawal to Hadrian's Wall.

Between the walls lay the Scottish lowlands, inhabited by three major tribes (four if you count the Damnonii who lived in the area of what is now Glasgow with their "capital" at Dumbarton). To the east were the Votadini, whose territory stretched from what is now Edinburgh down as far as Newcastle. To the west, in the area of Galloway, were the Novantae. In the centre, inhabiting the vast wooded uplands, were the Selgovae. The Romans never conquered these tribes, but did reach a peace with the more amenable Votadini. The largest forts that the Romans established in the Scottish lowlands, at Bremenium (High Rochester) and Trimontium (Galashiels) were in the territory of the Votadini, and were as much to protect the Votadini as to serve the Roman advance.

Further north, beyond the Antonine Wall, was the heartland of the peoples who were to become known as the Picts. Writing at the start of the third century, the Roman historian and governor Cassius Dio recognized two main groupings of tribes: the Caledonii, far to the north, and the Mæatae, or Miathi, a

confederation of Pictish tribes who lived just north of the
Antonine Wall, near Stirling. In fact, both the Caledonii and
Mæatae were confederations of tribes who united against the
Romans, and in time they came to be ruled by separate Pictish
kings.

There were many fortresses along Hadrian's Wall, and at the
western end was the fortress town of Luguvalium (Carlisle). In
later years this was raised to the status of a capital of the *civitas*
of Carvetiorum, the homeland of the Carvetii tribe, an offshoot
of the Brigantes. Luguvalium remained a military town, and
was the largest of any administrative significance in northern
Britain.

All of these towns, fortresses and villas were linked by a
system of roads that remains the basis for the country's existing
network, fourteen centuries later (*see* Map 3). The roads were
kept in good repair by the army, certainly into the fourth
century, and would still have been in good condition in Arthur's
day. They were essential for Arthur's forces (and those of other
war leaders) in moving quickly across country. The Romans
regarded a day's steady march as twenty miles and as a consequence staging posts and refreshment establishments appeared
at roughly twenty-mile intervals along all of the major routes.
These did not vanish overnight at the end of the Roman era. As
archaeology is still rediscovering, Britain was a thriving society
throughout the Roman period and it was not until some time
afterwards that the major towns were abandoned and the native
Britons returned to their hill forts and encampments.

2. The first Arthur?

Despite the Romans having stamped their authority on Britain,
the undercurrent of rebellion was always there. After the
Boudiccan revolt, the southern tribes learned to adapt to the
Roman way of life, recognizing the benefits, though that did
not mean that they lost their individual identity. The creation
of the *civitas* perpetuated the original tribal structure, and this
remained throughout the Roman occupation.

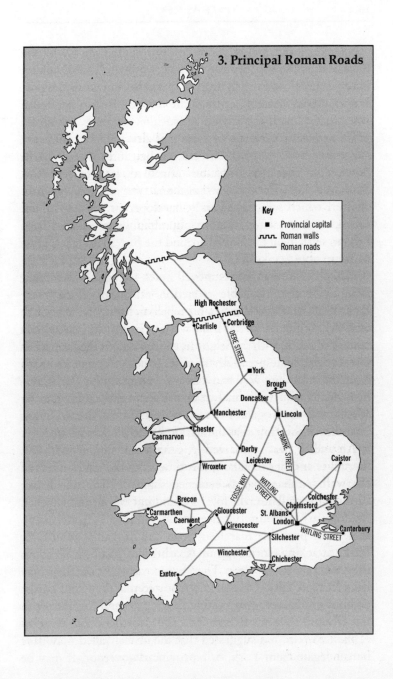

3. Principal Roman Roads

Key
■ Provincial capital
⌁⌁⌁ Roman walls
— Roman roads

High Rochester
Carlisle • Corbridge
DERE STREET
■ York
Brough
Doncaster
Lincoln ■
Manchester
Chester
ERMINE STREET
Caernarvon
Derby
Leicester
Caistor
Wroxeter
FOSSE WAY
WATLING STREET
Brecon
Colchester
Carmarthen
Chelmsford
Caerwent
Gloucester
St. Albans
Cirencester ■
London
Canterbury
Silchester
WATLING STREET
Winchester
Chichester
Exeter

The northern tribes were less compliant. Hadrian's Wall was built as much to separate the north's two main troublemakers, the Brigantes and the Selgovae, as it was to contain the empire. It was almost certainly at this time that the Brigantian *civitas* was created, with the capital at Isurium. At the same time a more extensive network of forts was developed in the west, suggesting that although the eastern Brigantes were calming down, the western Brigantes remained less trustworthy. Amongst these forts was Bremetennacum, modern-day Ribchester, which was significantly developed at the start of the second century. Over the next hundred years or so a large civilian settlement developed around the fort, making it a town of some note.

When the Roman forces moved north to man the Antonine Wall, with the inevitable reduction in troops along Hadrian's Wall, the equally inevitable rebellion happened. Although evidence is thin, it looks as if the western Brigantes, perhaps in a concerted action with the Selgovae, rose up against the Romans in 154AD, with widespread destruction, so that troops came back from the Antonine Wall and a new governor, Julius Verus, was brought in with additional troops. Verus regained control by 158AD, and the Brigantes were deprived of their *civitas*. It was probably at this time that the *civitas* at Carlisle was created.

An uneasy peace remained. A generation later, around 183, there was another rebellion, this time from the tribes north of the wall. Archaeological evidence suggests that they broke through the wall near the fort of Onnum (Halton) and attacked the forts at Cilurnum (Chesters) and Vindobala (Rudchester), their army probably marching down the Roman road of Dere Street, attacking Coriosopitum (Corbridge). Just how far south they reached is not clear. There's some suggestion they may have reached York. Cassius Dio reported that they "did a great amount of damage, even cutting down a general together with his troops". David Breeze, in *The Northern Frontiers of Roman Britain*, has suggested that the officer killed may have been a legate from York, or a provincial governor. It may be pertinent that the term of office of the governor, Quintus Antistius Adventus, ceased in 183, suggesting that he was either recalled to face the wrath of the emperor Commodus or was killed.

A new governor, Lucius Ulpius Marcellus, who had served in Britain ten years earlier, was despatched to Britain. Commodus must have felt it was important to have a man who knew the territory and was noted for his discipline and severity. According to Cassius Dio, Marcellus was "a temperate and frugal man and when on active service lived like a soldier . . . but he was becoming haughty and arrogant". Apparently Marcellus needed little sleep and was forever issuing commands and orders, ensuring that his soldiers also slept little. So although he might have endeared himself to some, he must have made many enemies. He inflicted major defeats on the Picts, but the soldiers were in disarray, and Marcellus was recalled. A new governor, Publius Helvius Pertinax, was sent to Britain in 185 to sort out the mess.

The army may not have rebelled solely against Marcellus. In Rome, Commodus, alarmed by an assassination attempt, had withdrawn into his palace, leaving the government of the empire to one of his favourites, Perennis, who instituted a number of unfavourable changes. The last straw seems to have been his meddling with the command structure of the legionary forces, replacing the senatorial command with one of lesser rank, called equestrians, similar to senior civil servants. This was so unpopular that the British army took the unprecedented measure of sending a deputation of 1,500 men to Rome in 185. Their ploy was to warn Commodus of another assassination attempt, this time by Perennis. It worked. Perennis was executed and it was then that Pertinax was sent to Britain to satisfy the troops.

Pertinax could be as severe as Marcellus, and the army mutinied against him, leaving him for dead. He recovered, however, and dealt with the army "with signal severity", as one chronicler recorded. Although he quelled the mutiny,

Pertinax never gained the full respect of the army, even though they wanted him as their next candidate for emperor. Pertinax refused and after two or three years of an uneasy relationship between him and the army, he asked to be relieved of his duties, and became governor of Africa. When Pertinax was governor of Britain, a conflict erupted in Armorica (Brittany). Pertinax turned to a soldier who has since been swept into the debate as a possible candidate for Arthur: Lucius Artorius Castus.

Lucius Artorius Castus (140–197) had served as a centurion in four different legions. When the Sarmatian tribes from Hungary invaded the empire in 170, a five-year war, in which Castus would have been involved, ensued. In 175, as part of the peace deal, 8,000 Sarmatian cavalry were handed over to serve in the Roman army; 5,500 of these were sent to Britain, and settled at Bremetennacum (Ribchester). Castus oversaw the transfer and returned to Rome, but returned to Britain in 181 as prefect of the VI Victrix Legion, based at York. Linda Malcor and C. Scott Littleton have suggested that it was Castus who led his legion, perhaps including the Sarmatian contingent, against the Caledonii in 183, chasing them back north of the border. These battles, they suggest, could equate to the series later attributed to Arthur by Nennius (*see* Chapter 7). Castus was promoted to the rank of *dux* in about 185, almost certainly as a reward for his service in Britain. After being sent back to Armorica by Pertinax in the same year for another campaign, Castus retired from the army and spent his last days as a procurator of the province of Liburnia, in Dalmatia. Malcor has speculated that Castus may have been called back from retirement by the new emperor Septimius Severus at the time of the revolt by Clodius Albinus, and may have died in battle at Lugdunum (Lyon) in 197. He would then have been about fifty-seven years old. Castus's sarcophagus has been found at Stobrec, near Split, on the Adriatic coast.

3. The revolting British!

Over the next ten years there was an uneasy peace in Britain, but in 207 rebellion erupted again of sufficient magnitude that the emperor Septimius Severus came to Britain with his sons Caracalla and Geta. Cassius Dio records that Severus was determined to conquer the whole of Britain once and for all, but as ever the tactics of the enemy north of the wall made this impossible. Cassius Dio reports that Severus lost up to 50,000 men, which, though surely an exaggeration, shows the scale of the problem.

The campaign stretched out over three years until Severus's death in York in February 211. His son Caracalla, who had hated this enforced stay in Britain, was anxious to return to Rome to secure the transfer of power. Somehow he reached peace terms with the Caledonii. The exact nature of this is not known, but he was able to secure a handover of more territory, possibly the area of Fife, where a new fort was secured at Carpow. The area between the walls seems to have come under Roman command even if it was never formally part of the empire. It was probably patrolled by the Votadini, who remained loyal to Rome.

Caracalla also enacted plans prepared by his father to divide Roman Britain in two. This meant there were now two governors rather than one, with less power and fewer troops at their command. Severus had been determined not to see a repetition of the Albinus affair. From 211 onwards Britain was divided into Britannia Superior in the south, with its capital at London, and Britannia Inferior with its capital at York. The dividing line ran from the Wash to the Dee, skirting south to avoid the Pennines. Britannia Superior was the larger area, as well as the more wealthy and peaceful, and had two legions, whereas Britannia Inferior was essentially a military zone with a minimum of settled civilian life, and had one legion augmented by many auxiliary troops. Although Caracalla has passed into history as a brutal and wayward emperor, his peace arrangements in Britain were effective, allowing Britain to develop and prosper over the next seventy years.

We can skim over the next fifty years or so, pausing only to mention that whilst Britain experienced a period of unusual calm, the rest of the Roman Empire was plunged into turbulence with a succession of minor and short-lived emperors. During this period there was an offshoot Gallic Empire, which included France and Britain, and which lasted from 260–274. A brief stability was restored under the dual control of Diocletian and Maximian, from 285, but soon after the empire faced another rebel who used Britain as his base. This was Carausius.

During the third century, and especially from 260 onwards, the Roman borders became subject to raids and incursions from Germanic tribes. It led to several British cities being walled, and stronger defences created around the British coast, with new forts at Reculver in Kent and Brancaster in Norfolk. This was the start of what later became known as the "Saxon shore". The port of Dover was also rebuilt and the Roman fleet was strengthened to patrol the Channel against Saxon and Frankish pirates. Carausius, based in Gaul, at Boulogne, was placed in charge of that fleet, and was thus the prototype of a later official post called the Count of the Saxon Shore. He was a canny individual, popular with his troops, and not averse to a little piracy of his own. He often waited until after the barbarian raid and then captured the ships, keeping the booty for himself. When Maximian learned of this he ordered Carausius's arrest, but Carausius used his popularity and declared himself emperor in 286, shifting his base to Britain. Carausius seems to have been readily accepted by the British, even though he was not a true Celt but was from a Germanic tribe, the Menapii. In any case the British had by now built a reputation for supporting any rebel against Rome. Carausius may well have intended to restore the Gallic Empire, since he kept a hold on Boulogne for as long as he could.

Archaeological evidence seems to suggest that Britain prospered during Carausius's reign. He not only completed the fortification programme already initiated but built further forts and castles, such as Portus Aderni (Portchester) and Cardiff

Castle, and probably started work on the massive fort at Anderida (Pevensey). He also established the first mint in London. Unfortunately, he also apparently withdrew troops from Hadrian's Wall to defend the Saxon shore and the Welsh coast, allowing the Caledonii to take advantage for the first time in nearly a century.

Because of his defences and his fleet, attempts to capture Carausius proved difficult, and Maximian suffered heavy losses. In 293 he delegated the problem to his new caesar, Constantius. After a long siege, Constantius regained Boulogne and was able to blockade Britain. Though still popular, Carausius became weakened and was murdered by his second-in-command Allectus, who proclaimed himself emperor. Allectus had been Carausius's treasurer, ensuring that the troops were paid, and thus was able to retain their support. He remained independent for a further three years until Constantius mounted a major invasion on two fronts. Allectus was killed in battle, either near Farnham in Surrey, or near Silchester, by Constantius's second-in-command Asclepiodotus. Allectus's troops fled to London where they met Constantius's army and were defeated. Legend has it that many were executed and their bodies thrown into the Walbrook.

Both Carausius and Asclepiodotus left their mark in British myth, though in reverse. By the time Geoffrey of Monmouth produced his *History*, Carausius had become the enemy of the British, an invader and usurper, who killed Bassianus (Caracalla's original name) and ruled in his place. Geoffrey correctly has him killed by Allectus and then Allectus murdered by Asclepiodotus, but identifies the latter as a Briton and Duke of Cornwall. Geoffrey states that Asclepiodotus reigned for ten years before being in turn killed by King Coel, the Old King Cole of the nursery rhyme. Coel will feature again in our history, though in his rightful place, but this story serves to show how soon oral history and legend transmute facts into pseudo-history. With Carausius we are, in fact, a little over a hundred years away from the start of the Arthurian period, yet that is sufficient time for history to mutate into myth. Such mutation is something we have to bear in mind throughout this book.

The truth is that Carausius's rebellion had a more significant impact upon Britain. The caesar, Constantius, having rid Britain of Allectus, undertook a lightning tour to check defences, especially on the northern frontier. Contemporary accounts refer for the first time to the tribes as the Picts, though there's little reason to believe they are any other than the Caledonii and other northern tribes. Constantius ordered some refurbishments and then returned to Rome to celebrate his triumph.

He returned to Britain ten years later, in 305, this time as emperor. He was later joined by his son Constantine. The intervening decade had seen Diocletian introduce a series of sweeping reforms to the administration of the empire, though precisely when they were enforced in Britain is not clear. Diocletian divided the empire into twelve dioceses, each with a *vicarius* in charge. Every diocese was divided into provinces, each with its own governor. Britain was one diocese and now had four provinces. The former northern province of Britannia Inferior was divided in two from the Mersey to the Humber. The northernmost province became Britannia Secunda, with its capital at York, whilst the southern half became Flavia Caesariensis, with a capital at Lincoln. The former southern province of Britannia Superior was also split in half by a line heading almost straight north from Southampton. The west, including Wales and the south-west, became Britannia Prima, with the capital at Cirencester. To the east was Maxima Caesariensis, with the capital at London. London also seems to have been the overall diocesan capital. This further division was to have consequences a century later with the re-emergence of British kingdoms. These reforms also separated the civic administration from the military. Whilst Britain was administered by a *vicarius* based in London, the northern forces were controlled by the *dux Britanniarum*, based in

York. Diocletian was going to have no more rebellious usurpers able to call upon vast armies though, as we shall soon see, this did not work in Britain.

Diocletian also issued a violent edict against Christianity. It was probably at this time that Britain saw its first martyr in Alban, who was executed at Verulamium (St Albans). Christianity had a strong hold in Britain, and was a factor in how the provinces developed distinct from the rest of the empire.

Constantius undertook a series of campaigns in northern Britain against the Picts. Little is known about this, but it seems to have been successful as there was comparative peace for another fifty years. For Constantius, alas, there was little time to appreciate his achievement. He was seriously ill, possibly with leukaemia (his nickname was Constantius the Pale), and he died in York in July 306, aged fifty-six.

Under Diocletian's reforms, Constantius should automatically have been succeeded as emperor by his nominated caesar, Flavius Valerius Severus. In fact, Constantius had not selected his successor; it had been done for him by Galerius, his co-emperor in the east. Not everyone wanted Severus as emperor, least of all the British, and true to tradition the British troops promptly nominated their own successor, Constantius's son Constantine. Galerius begrudgingly made Constantine the successor to Severus, but it was a far from simple succession, and it would be eighteen years before Constantine became sole emperor.

Because Constantine became such a great emperor and, most significantly, made Christianity the official religion of Rome, and because his cause had been promoted by the British, he was well remembered in Britain and entered popular folklore.

Constantine's mother Helena was a native of Bithynia (in present-day northern Turkey) and never, apparently, came to Britain. Later beatified, Helena became a devout Christian and undertook a pilgrimage to Palestine in 326, founding several churches. She is supposed to have found the True Cross in Jerusalem, though dates conflict; she died in about 330 whilst the legend of the discovery of the Cross dates from about 335, during the construction of Constantine's basilica. At some stage the legend grew that Helen was British, the daughter of King Coel of Colchester, whom we have already met in myth as the murderer of Asclepiodotus. This legend took a firm hold in Britain, because it made Constantine a Briton and the grandson of Coel. It is probable that later chroniclers, especially Geoffrey of Monmouth, confused Helena with Elen, wife of a later British usurper-emperor, Magnus Maximus, who also had a son called Constantine. Elen was the daughter of the British chieftain Eudaf (of whom more later).

But the legend refuses to die. As we have seen, myths have a habit of ousting history, and we have to be on our guard.

4. The end of empire

By good organization, strength of character and sheer charisma, Constantine kept the Roman Empire together, but thereafter the empire was on the decline. His successors fought each other, weakening the empire at its heart and crumbling it at its frontiers, making it vulnerable to barbarian attack. This was as evident in Britain as elsewhere in the empire.

One mystery related to Britain at this time is worth mentioning, as it may have later relevance. By the 340s the empire was split between Constantine's two surviving sons: Constans, who ruled the west, including Britain, and Constantius II who ruled the east. In 343 Constans made an impulsive visit to Britain. His visit remains a mystery, yet the fact that he risked crossing the English Channel during the winter suggests that it was something serious. The contemporary chronicler Libanius, who recorded the visit (but seemed equally at a loss to explain it), noted that "affairs in Britain were stable", thereby ruling out the likelihood of a rebellion.

So what prompted it? Was it a religious matter? We shall see later that Britain was one of the rebel nations when it came to Christianity, supporting pagan worship and later encouraging dangerous interpretations of Christian teachings such as Pelagianism. Would this be enough to tempt Constans across the waves at such a dangerous time? Possibly, but I am not convinced.

Further incursions by the Picts in the north is a possible explanation, but the winter was not a great period for warfare, and although British defences to the north were not as thorough as they had been, they were still sufficient to cope with any activity that had not come to the notice of the chroniclers.

Was it, perhaps, an enclave of support for Constantius against Constans, or perhaps a lingering support for their dead brother Constantine II, who had ruled Gaul and Britain until his murder just three years earlier?

This seems more likely. Diocletian had set up an extremely efficient intelligence agency, known as the *agentes in rebus*, who were good at sniffing out areas of unrest. Britain was always a hotbed of rebels, and the fact that Libanius reports that Britain's affairs were "stable" might only mean that word had not got out and any rebellion had been nipped in the bud by Constans's surprise visit.

Support for this interpretation comes from events just a few years later. In 350 Constans was murdered following an uprising in support of his army commander Magnentius. Although Magnentius was born in Gaul, his father was believed to be British and was probably a high-ranking official. Did Constans learn of a plot, perhaps by Magnentius's father in 343, which he was able to stifle? Magnentius had a brief but mostly successful period as rival emperor until a series of defeats led him to commit suicide in 353. Constantius lived to fight another day, and sent the heavies into Britain to root out any remaining supporters of Magnentius. His envoy was an over-zealous martinet from Spain called Paul who tortured, killed and imprisoned many British officials, regardless of their guilt or innocence. So vicious were Paul's measures that the *vicarius* of Britain, Flavius Martinus, tried to assassinate him but, when he failed, killed himself.

Soon after Paul's inquisitorial rampage another usurper rose in Britain, the mysterious Carausius II. Continental writers seem to know nothing about him, not even the ever-vigilant Ammianus Marcellinus, whose *History* is one of the best records of this period. Unfortunately, most of the early part of his work has been lost, so we know of the existence of Carausius II only from surviving coinage. Some historians have even dismissed the very existence of Carausius. However, he has been adopted into Welsh legend as the son-in-law of the patriarchal Eudaf Hen ("the Old"), from whom most of the British kings claimed descent.

Even more mysteriously, amongst the British coinage is a record of someone called Genceris, who may have ruled elsewhere in Britain at the time of Carausius. Analysis of these coins can only tell us so much, but it suggests that rival rulers did emerge in Britain in the period 354–358. They were seeking not to proclaim themselves rival emperors but, like Carausius I, to rule Britain independently. Britain in the fourth century was at its wealthiest. Profits from grain exports and other native industries, plus unprecedented periods of comparative peace, had allowed the Romano-British to become comfortable, and to think thoughts of independence. Constantine's successors were fighting so much amongst themselves, and drawing troops away from the borders, that Britain was becoming increasingly vulnerable. Saxons were continuing to harry the eastern coasts, the Irish were raiding the west, and the Picts were once again invading from the north. The Romano-British aristocracy did not feel that the empire was providing sufficient protection.

From 360, Roman Britain was overrun by a massive Pictish invasion, with further uprisings in 364 and 367. Ammianus Marcellinus, who lived through these times, recorded the 367 revolt with dramatic effect in his *Res Gestae* in 378:

> At this time, with trumpets sounding for war as if throughout the Roman world, the most savage tribes rose up and poured across the nearest frontiers. At one and the same time the Alamanni were plundering Gaul and Raetia, the Sarmatae

and Quadri Pannonia; the Picts, Saxons, Scots and Attacotti harassed the Britons with continual calamities.

The Attacotti (or Attecotti) were another tribe in the far north of Britain. The Scots, or Scotii, were in fact the Irish. Later in his narrative, Ammianus provides amplification of the above:

> . . . at the time in question the Picts were divided into two tribes, the Dicalydones and the Verturiones. These, together with the warlike Attacotti and the Scots, were ranging over a wide area causing much devastation, while the Franks and their neighbours the Saxons ravaged the coast of Gaul with vicious acts of pillage, arson and the murder of all prisoners . . .

We also learn that the *areani* who, rather like present-day police informants, were relating intelligence of barbarian activities back to the military, had turned traitor and allied themselves with the Picts and Scots in revealing troop movements. As a consequence, the barbarians captured the *dux Britanni-arum* Nectaridus, and killed the Count of the Saxon Shore, Fullofaudes.

The new emperor, Valentinian, sent a general to deal with the problem, but he was soon recalled because of the enormity of the situation. Eventually, a much bigger force was despatched, under the command of the brilliant general and tactician Theodosius. Upon his arrival, he discovered bands of marauding barbarians as far south as Kent and London. The Roman army was also in disarray, many having deserted or forsaken their posts. The remaining force was demoralized and lacked co-ordination. The barbarians had by now no central command, and it was easy for Theodosius and his troops to pick them off. He arrived at London in triumph and soon restored morale, pardoning deserters and encouraging the return of others. He spent the next two years not only recovering the diocese, but undertaking a major programme of repair and refortification. Old forts were strengthened, towns were rebuilt and fortified, and a new series of watch-towers and signal stations was built along the north-east coast to serve as advance guard against sea-borne attacks. Theodosius also nipped one possible revolution in the bud when he arrested one Valentinus, a criminal exiled to Britain from Pannonia, who was apparently planning some sort of takeover in Britain. Most interestingly, Ammianus refers to Theodosius recovering an existing province, which had fallen into the hands of the enemy, and restoring it to its former state, renaming it Valentia in honour of the emperor. Unfortunately he does not say where Valentia was, presumably having described it in one of his earlier, lost, books. The fact that Theodosius restored a former province means either that one of the four existing provinces had been lost to Roman control and was now recovered, or that a fifth province had previously been created. Evidence that it was a fifth province comes from the glorious document of the Roman civil service, the *Notitia Dignitatum*, a compendium of the various offices of state throughout the empire, which lists Valentia separately. Although this document came into being during the reign of Constantine the Great, it was continually amended and updated and the version in which we know it today dates to some time around the end of the fourth century. Therefore we don't know exactly when Valentia was created or where it was.

In the *Notitia*, Valentia is grouped with Maxima Caesariensis, the south-eastern province based around London, as being governed by a consul rather than a *praesides*. This could suggest either that Valentia had been created by dividing Maxima Caesariensis in two – though then giving both halves consular governors was perhaps a little top-heavy – or that Maxima Caesariensis had been renamed Valentia. If that is the case, it means that one of the more senior provinces had somehow been wrested from Roman control, and the chances of this being in the south are remote. We do not know if this was related to the rebel Valentinus, or where he was located, though in all likelihood he would have been in one of the southern provinces. Ammianus states that "it had fallen into the hands of the enemy", which probably means it had been taken over by the barbarian Picts. This would suggest it was a province in the north, the most obvious one being Britannia Secunda, based at York. It may well be, therefore, that Valentia was a province split from Britannia Secunda. As we have seen in the past, the most difficult area to control had been the western Pennines, and it has been suggested that Valentia could have been created in what is now Cumbria and which, in Arthurian times, was part of Rheged.

It is just possible that Valentia was the territory between the Walls, not strictly a "province" but a buffer zone, and was the easiest province to lose to the Picts.*

The separate reference to Valentia in the *Notitia Dignitatum* rules out the suggestion that Valentia was the name given to the whole of the diocese of Britain, an interpretation that could be read into Ammianus's text, and which would certainly have made sense. The fact that it was either a renamed fourth province or a new fifth province that was, albeit briefly, taken away from Roman control, makes identification important, because it shows the abilities of the Picts, perhaps in collaboration with any rebellious indigenous population. This becomes important when mapping out the Arthurian world in the next century.

Theodosius confirmed a number of new officers in various posts at this time. It's possible that some of the people who were ancestors of the British kings may have been installed now, such as Paternus, the grandfather of Cunedda, as a commander of the Votadini. One other appointment is worth mentioning. A short while after these events, Valentinian transferred a Germanic king, Fraomar, to Britain as a military tribune in command of an existing contingent of Alamanni troops. It is not recorded where he was placed but it is a reminder that a high-ranking Germanic commander was in

* For a full discussion of Valentia see Salway (1981), pp. 392–6 and "The Province of Valentia" by Ann Dornier, *Britannia*: 13 (1982).

Britain in the fourth century, in charge of Germanic troops, and he may well not have been the only one. DNA analysis has shown that there were many Germanic settlers in Britannia at this time, especially along the eastern coast.

Theodosius's campaign and reforms were successful in improving British morale and restoring Roman command and also, as a consequence, improving the quality of life in Britain. Archaeological evidence, especially in the south, has identified plenty of places where high-quality villas were extended or rebuilt at this time. Theodosius did not, however, stop continued attempts by the Picts to undermine control in the north. This was especially so after the death of Valentinian in 375. He was succeeded by his two sons, Valentinian II, who was only four, and Gratian, who was sixteen. Though Gratian grew into a passable soldier, he was no good at government and soon lost the confidence of the army. Once again the time was right for another usurper.

This came in the shape of Magnus Maximus, the "greatest of the great". He was of Iberian descent and had served in Britain with Theodosius in 367. He had remained with Theodosius, serving in Raetia from 370, against the Alamanni, and in Africa from 373, before returning to Britain in 380, possibly as *dux Britanniarum*. In 382 there was another incursion by Picts and Scots which Maximus repulsed, bringing him great acclaim. He was popular amongst the troops and knew how to use this to his advantage, especially in denigrating the work of Gratian. In 383 the ever-rebellious British soldiers declared Maximus their emperor.

Maximus took his army into Gaul and defeated Gratian after a protracted skirmish outside Paris. Gratian fled, but was murdered. Maximus knew better than to go after Valentinian, who was still only thirteen. An agreement was reached with Theodosius whereby Valentinian remained emperor in Italy, but Maximus controlled the western empire north of the Alps.

And so it remained until Maximus became too sure of himself. His fate was an early example of the Christian faith being used by rulers to further their own ends. Valentinian, heavily influenced by his mother, had passed an act legitimizing Arianism, a creed that held Jesus to be human and not divine. Maximus, who purported to be a devout Christian, and who had been the first to have a non-orthodox Christian bishop executed for heresy, used Valentinian's act as a cause to invade Italy and confront the young emperor. He took with him a large army, including further troops from Britain. It was a foolish act. Maximus found himself trapped by the army of Theodosius, who had come to Valentinian's aid, and he was killed. Maximus's son, Flavius Victor, whom he had appointed as caesar and left behind in Gaul, was also killed.

Maximus was bad news for Britain. He could have been a good emperor, but his belief in his own importance got the better of him and he drained many troops from Britain, seriously weakening its defences. These troops did not return. Many settled in Armorica (Brittany) and became the core of a British settlement.

Curiously, however, Maximus has entered British legend as something of a hero, and his march upon Rome has become subsumed into Arthurian myth, as we shall later see. To the Celts he was Macsen Wledig – *wledig* means "leader". They claimed he was the grandson of Constantine the Great, through a daughter. This would fit into the chronology – Maximus was born about 330 – though there is much uncertainty about his father. It is also claimed that Maximus was married twice: firstly to Ceindrech ferch Rheiden, who claimed descent from Caswallon, and secondly to Elen, daughter of Eudaf. By his first wife he had two children – the unfortunate Victor, and Owain, who will feature again shortly. By his second wife he had five children, including Constantine, a name which becomes drawn into the Arthurian legend, and Severa, who is identified as the wife of Vortigern, the future ruler of Britain though was more likely his mother or grandmother. There is no reason to doubt that these children of Maximus existed. A tomb, which may be Constantine's, has been found near

Segontium (Caernarvon), a place strongly associated with Maximus. Future kings and usurpers all liked to claim descent from Maximus, especially as he himself claimed descent from Constantine the Great, but one has to treat these genealogies with caution. I shall discuss all of them in much detail later. All we need note at the moment is that despite having weakened Britain's defences, Maximus was hailed a British hero and his life is a prelude to the story of Arthur.

Following the death of Maximus, Roman control over events in Britain was virtually lost. As Gildas later expressed it, "The island was still Roman in name, but not by law and custom." Maximus's son Victor was killed by a soldier called Arbogast, who set up his own puppet emperor, Eugenius, and sought to make himself king of France. Arbogast, a pagan, encouraged the return to pagan worship in Britain and Gaul. Theodosius's two sons, Honorius and Arcadius, were both too young to rule so the Vandal general Stilicho governed the western empire as regent for Honorius. Stilicho prevailed and, after the deaths of Eugenius and Arbogast, sought once again to shore up defences in Britain. Around the years 395–396, Stilicho sent a force against the Picts, but it was too little too late. Soon after, in 401–402 Stilicho withdrew further troops from Britain to help fight against Alaric, the Visigoth governor of Illyria, who had invaded Italy.

Hadrian's Wall was now undefended and all troops had been withdrawn from Wales. Only one legion remained in Britain, at Chester. The Irish now secured a grip on the fringes of Britain. The chieftain Eochaid, ruler of the Déisi in present-day Waterford, established a base in south-west Wales, in the territory then known as Demetia (later Dyfed). Meanwhile the descendants of Cairbre Riata, founder of the territory of the Dál Riata in Northern Ireland, had established settlements in what are now Argyll and Kintyre.

No new Roman coinage entered Britain after 402. Feeling abandoned, and having lost all hope in any further support from Rome, Britain once again chose its own emperors. The first two – Marcus, a Roman official, and Gratian, a British official – scarcely lasted a few months before both were murdered. This was between December 406 and May 407. The third choice was more promising, even though he was apparently an ordinary soldier from the ranks. This was Flavius Claudius Constantine, later Constantine III. Constantine marshalled what few troops remained in Britain and marched on Gaul, winning over the troops both there and on the Rhine. The latter desertion was a disaster for Rome, as the barbarian armies had already crossed the borders of the empire and the defences were crumbling. Nevertheless Constantine proved a surprise. His presence seemed to deter the Vandals and other armies, and there was a brief respite in hostilities.

The problem for Britain, though, was that Constantine was now in Gaul. He seemed to have lost interest in Britain, and once again Britain became subject to increasing attacks from Picts and Saxons. By 408 Constantine had lost his grip on affairs, and the Vandals were again on the move. Britain had enough, and, in 409, expelled all Roman officials. The Greek historian Zosimus, who lived only a few years after these events, tells the story in his *Historia Nova* (c500).

> The barbarians beyond the Rhine, attacking in force, reduced the inhabitants of Britain and some of the Celtic tribes to the point where they were obliged to throw off Roman rule and live independently, no longer subject to Roman laws. The Britons therefore took up arms and, braving the danger on their own behalf, freed their cities from the barbarians threatening them. And all Armorica and the other Gallic provinces followed their example, freed themselves in the same way, expelled their Roman rulers and set up their own governments as far as lay within their power.

But it proved difficult. There were continued attacks, and in 410 the British wrote to the emperor Honorius (son of Theodosius) pleading for help. Honorius, however, had enough to contend with, what with the barbarians overrunning the empire and Constantine III seeking to destroy him. According to Zosimus, he replied telling them to look to their own defence. A.L.F. Rivet and Colin Smith, in *The Place-Names of Roman Britain*, have suggested that Zosimus somehow mistook the town of Bruttium in southern Italy for Britannia – the names in Greek are very similar – which may mean that Honorius did not officially dismiss the British. However, the British had certainly dismissed the Romans, and Honorius was in no position to respond. Whether by design or default, and no matter how temporary it may have seemed at the time, Britain was no longer under direct Roman rule.

It now had to defend itself and needed strong men to do so. The Age of Arthur was about to begin.

3

THE DARKNESS DESCENDS

1. British authority

I have dwelt for some time on the Roman background to the
Arthurian age because it is important to understand the state of
Britain at the start of the so-called "Dark Ages". We have seen
that the British had increasingly sought independence during
the third and fourth centuries and, as troubles beset the rest of
the Roman Empire, had grown wealthy and financially resi-
lient. Though Germanic, Irish and Pictish invaders continued
to trouble the periphery of Britain, even in the late fourth
century, the Romano-British lived in style, in grand villas with
expensive goods imported from elsewhere in the empire.

The years 409/410, with the apparent end of Roman control
in Britain, were part of a process of independence that stretched
for over a century. It should not be seen as Britain being
abandoned by Rome, with the sudden desertion of the army
leaving Britain at the mercy of the Saxons waiting to pounce.
Britain had been steadily deprived of its forces at intervals over

the last thirty years or more. The native British had been well trained and conditioned in Roman ways for nearly four centuries, and British officials would have ensured continuity with the training of their own troops. The British forces, which no doubt included Germanic mercenaries, may not have been as disciplined as the Roman legions, nor as numerous, but we cannot discount them.

Moreover, there were already plenty of Germanic settlers and retired soldiers in Britain. The Roman Empire was multicultural, allowing the free movement of people throughout Europe. Many of the soldiers stationed in Britain were not of strict Roman stock, but from Germanic and other tribes, as we have already seen with the Sarmatians at Bremetennacum. There were many Friesian cavalry units posted in northern Britain, such as at Vinovia (Binchester) and Derventio (Papcastle). They even feature in the Arthurian legends.

The researches of Stephen Oppenheimer, in *The Origins of the British*, reveal that the genetic bloodstock of the tribes in eastern Britain – in particular the area later to become England – was Germanic, mostly from the area of Saxony and Frisia. Although they are historically identified with the "British", they were genetically different to the Celts of Wales, Ireland and northern Britain.

The dismissal of the Roman administration was no doubt part of a power struggle in Britain, both secular and religious. The British appeal to Honorius had come from the heads of the *civitates*, not the provincial heads or the *vicarius*. Some historians believe this means that the British usurpation of power had come from the provincial governors who had overthrown the *vicarius*, leaving the *civitates* in a degree of confusion. With no overall diocesan control it meant that after 409 Britain was no longer one single diocese but four provinces, each with its own governor.

Before the Roman occupation, the tribal structure within Britain had caused continuous rivalry and conflict between the British. The Roman administration had stifled this to a degree, particularly in the south, but it was always there, and would have reasserted itself after the Romans left. In our own time we have seen a similar resurgence of tribalism in Eastern Europe following the fall of Communism.

To this must be added a conflict in religious views. The Christian faith was still evolving and various sects were emerging throughout the Roman world. At the dawn of the fifth century, the strongest voice of Christian understanding, and the one regarded as orthodox, was that of Augustine of Hippo. His interpretation of doctrine, including the concept of predestination (that mankind's fate is controlled by God and that original sin is inherited) was upheld by Pope Innocent, the most powerful pope of the period. As a consequence, any opposing views were seen as heretical. One such came from the British monk Pelagius, who had studied law in Rome but turned to the Church around the year 386. Pelagius's strong opinions apparently made ready enemies. He held the viewpoint that individuals had free will and could have a one-to-one relationship with God, not requiring the channel of a priest. Pelagius and Augustine were vehemently opposed, and it was Augustine whose doctrine held sway. Pelagius was first condemned by the Pope in 411, again in 416, and threatened with excommunication by Innocent in 417. Pelagius did not reform and, in 418, solely through the forcefulness of Augustine, was excommunicated. Pelagius died soon afterwards, in 419, but his views lived on, especially in Britain, where they seem to have found favour with the aristocracy.

So, not only were there pro-Roman and pro-British views of governance, there was also a pro-Catholic/pro-Pelagian divide in Britain. Effectively Britain would have split into two political factions, whilst various military leaders established themselves to repel invaders and take over control in their own territories. Combine this with external threats from hostile forces and you have a Britain where, over a period of time, the social structure cracked through the lack of strong central control.

It is that central control which is so fundamental to the Dark Age history of Britain and where the Arthurian legend has its roots. Even though the British had dismissed the Roman administrators, it does not mean that the system of administration in Britain ceased overnight. The existing officials, except perhaps the dismissed *vicarius* and his retinue, were probably already British, being part of the original tribal aristocracy.

In the pre-Roman days, at times of civil upheaval, the tribes would have looked to a High King, usually the most powerful of the tribal rulers. In effect, whoever might take on the role of the *vicarius* in Britain would become the equivalent of a High King.

You might wonder what role the usurper emperor Constantine III played in this, and the answer is very little. Constantine had effectively been dismissed along with all the other Roman officials after 409. Despite his British origins, he had virtually turned his back on Britain by trying to establish himself within the empire from his base in Gaul, at Arles. The British officials must have held a dim view of Constantine as they had appealed not to him, but directly to Honorius. Evidently the appeal was from the pro-Roman faction. In 410, soon after the British expelled the Roman officials, Rome was itself entered and sacked by the Visigoths under Alaric. The empire was in turmoil. Constantine's general, Gerontius, an able man who might have been a capable leader in Britain, deserted him and changed his allegiance. He killed Constantine's son Constans, and raised another general, Maximus, as a rival emperor. Maximus and Gerontius took control of Spain and parts of Gaul and Constantine found himself isolated. Unable to function, Constantine surrendered and was executed in September 411. Gerontius, unable to capitalize on events, was betrayed by his troops and forced to kill himself.

With no help from Europe, Britain was left to its own devices. The approach within each of the four provinces was probably different. With no surviving written record we do not know what happened and can only surmise from a vague knowledge of later history, all too much of which has to be viewed through the haze of myth. It becomes apparent, however, from the archaeological record, that every effort was made to continue with Roman life as much as normal. The area most affected was the heavily militarized zone in the north, in Britannia Secunda. Never really acquiring the civilized benefits of the south, it had been occupied and run by the legions and settled by legions' families, who dominated and controlled the local British. If there was anywhere where the old native rivalries would surface, it was going to be in the north.

2. Northern Britain

Britannia Secunda contained the tribes of the Carvetii, Parisii and Brigantes, the last of which was the biggest and most rebellious. This was also the area under the control of the *dux Britanniarum* who would need to stamp his authority, not only in marshalling troops to fight back the Picts, but also to quell any internal rebellions. We do not know the name of the *dux Britanniarum* at this time, but a name that rapidly comes to the fore is Coel, or "Old King Cole". The real Coel is so wrapped in legend that it is difficult to get at the truth.

If Coel was not formally appointed as the Northern *dux Britanniarum* – and he might have been by Constantine III before the latter's departure for Gaul – he almost certainly filled that role. His official base was at York, but the flimsy evidence that survives, most of it circumstantial, suggests that he operated primarily from Carlisle. It's quite possible that Coel took over control of the old Roman province of Valentia if, as has been surmised, this was based in the northwest around Carlisle. Valentia had already shown a strong disposition to independence in the late Roman period, and would certainly have sought to re-establish itself as an independent state soon after the end of Roman authority.

Genealogists would establish a pedigree for Coel, identifying descent from the early pre-Roman kings, with a line direct from Caswallon (*see* Table 3). Some genealogies identify his father as Guotepauc or Godebog, but most authorities now believe that Guotepauc was an epithet. In the old Brythonic tongue it means "protector" or "defender", a title that fits the role of *dux* admirably.

We do not know Coel's tribal affiliations. Regardless of the genealogies, which suggest a descent from the pre-Roman Catuvellauni tribe, his forefathers could have come from any-where, having been posted to help command Hadrian's Wall. Coel, if not from the local Brigantes, may have been a seventh- or eighth-generation settler along the Wall. Coel is also associated with Kyle in Galloway – indeed some believe Kyle's name comes from Coel, though really it comes from the Gaelic word *caol* meaning 'strait'* – so he may have been from the Novantae tribe.

By all accounts Coel had rivals in the area between the walls. This area had never been under direct Roman control (unless it was Valentia), though the Votadini had been friendly towards Rome and probably provided a policing role. The territory of the Votadini stretched around the eastern coast from the Forth estuary to Hadrian's Wall. The north-western part of their lands was known as the Manau Gododdin. Gododdin was, in fact, a Brythonic variant of the name Votadini, and later the whole tribe became known as the Gododdin. Over time, they became divided between the Manau in the north and the southern Gododdin, later Bryneich.

The earliest known ruler of the Manau is Cunedda, grandson of Paternus, who may have been a commander placed in control of the territory by Magnus Maximus. Cunedda was evidently something of a thug. An elegy to him, *Marwnad Cunedda*, attributed to Taliesin, calls him a "relentless raider", and implies that he had control of all the lands between the walls and per-haps even south into Cumbria. At some stage Coel and Cunedda must have reached a treaty. The elegy describes how Cunedda's warhounds "will constrain the Coeling in a

---

* Mills (1991), p. 285.

truce of peace". The genealogies state that Cunedda married Coel's daughter Gwawl, which doubtless sealed the treaty. The rivalry between the Coelings and Cunedda is hinted at in another poem, *Y Gododdin*, which I will discuss in more detail later. This poem describes how the Gododdin "used to defend their land against the sons of Godebawc, wicked folk". A picture of open and continuous warfare in the north with Coel seeking to stamp his overall authority becomes apparent.

One other name emerges in the north via the writings of St Patrick. He refers to a king Coroticus, who was slave trading with the Irish. Coroticus is believed to be Ceretic, who became a ruler of Strathclyde, the old tribe of the Damnonii, at about the same time that Cunedda ruled in the Manau. The genealogies suggest that Ceretic, like Cunedda, was descended from Romano-British who were probably military commanders in northern Britain (*see* Table 5).

We do not know Coel's precise dates, but it is probable that he was dead by the year 430. His territory was divided between his "sons" (if the genealogies are correct), though some of these may have been military deputies whom Coel appointed as successors. One of these, Germanianus (called Garbanion by the British), although identified as a son, was almost certainly a high-ranking military commander, whose name suggests either a Germanic origin or that he was a commander of Germanic troops. He probably received command of territory east of the Pennines, including York and the southern Gododdin, whilst another "son", Ceneu, received the land west of the Pennines, including the territory of the Carvetii, later known as Rheged and which may have been Valentia.

At some stage, perhaps as part of a treaty with Coel, Cunedda went south, to North Wales, to lead the resistance against the Irish raiders. Cunedda's son Tybion remained in the Manau but did not establish a dynasty, and it is probable that his territory was fought over by the sons of Coel. Cunedda's shift to Wales is mentioned by Nennius in an infuriating section which has rankled scholars ever since.

We will discuss Nennius's *Historia Britonum* in detail later, but this part is best discussed here. In Section 62 he says:

> Maelgwn the Great King ruled the British in Gwynedd, for his ancestor [*atavus*] Cunedda, with his eight sons, had come from the North, from the country called Manaw Gododdin, 146 years before Maelgwn reigned and expelled the Irish from these countries with immense slaughter, so that they never again returned to inhabit them.

If the 146 years runs from the start of Maelgwyn's reign, usually regarded as 534, then it takes us back to 388AD. This means that Cunedda came down from the North to fight the Irish in Wales at the same time as the death of Maximus, and while Britain was still part of the empire. We know that Eochaid had established a base in south-west Wales, in Demetia, at around this same time and it may be that, with a power vacuum left by Maximus's death and that of his eldest son, the officials in Britain brought further troops down as a defence. This would make Cunedda a contemporary with Coel, but the likely dates of his descendants means that this date is too early.

The genealogies list Maelgwyn as Cunedda's great-grandson. If we allow twenty-five and thirty years to a generation (see page 51 for explanation), that means that if Maelgwyn was at the height of his powers in the 530s, then Cunedda was probably most active in the 450s. This could be stretched back to the 430s. The alternative is that the genealogies are wrong. The word used to describe Cunedda's relationship with Maelgwyn is *atavus*. As Leslie Alcock explains in *Arthur's Britain*, this word can be used loosely to describe an ancestor, or more precisely to describe a great-great-great-grandfather. This adds two further generations, or another fifty to sixty years, exactly what is needed to fill the gap.

The time span of 146 years is so precise that whoever first calculated it clearly had something specific in mind. It cannot be a copyist's error because the years are written out in full –

centum quadraginta sex. It could, of course, just be a false figure to reinforce the authority of Cunedda's descendants over North Wales in their rivalry with the rulers of Powys and Gwent. If it is, then we have no real guidance.

But as we have seen, errors exist elsewhere relating either to the Easter cycle of nineteen years, or to the gap between the incarnation and passion or death of Christ. The 146 years could have been calculated with a built-in error. The likeliest is the difference between the birth and passion of Christ, noted by Nennius as thirty-five years. Deducting this brings the gap to 111 years which, if deducted from 534, gives 423. This might suggest that Cunedda moved south after reaching an agreement with Coel. There might also have been an arrangement with Ceretic of Alclud, because by the mid-fifth century there is a clear spread of control. Ceretic and his descendants ruled the land between the walls, the Coelings ruled northern Britain (sometimes called Brigantia), and Cunedda ruled Venedotia, with its base at Anglesey but spreading across North Wales.

3. Southern Britain

The position in the south was far less clear. There were three provinces: Maxima Caesariensis, the original base for the *vicarius*, with its capital at London; Flavia Caesariensis, with its capital at Lincoln, and the first (from the archaeological record) under major threat from the Saxon settlers; and Britannia Prima, which included Wales. North Wales was not unlike northern Britain. It was primarily a militarized zone with minimal Roman settlement, despite the legionary fortress at Chester and another major fort at Segontium (Caernarvon). This had been the area of the Deceangli and Ordovices tribes, both of whom, like the Brigantes in northern Britain, had been hostile to Rome. South-west Wales, the area of the Demetae, was the main focus for Irish settlement, and it is evident that with the withdrawal of troops by Magnus Maximus the Irish had succeeded in settling in Demetia and had established what became the kingdom of Dyfed. It is interesting that the name in

the pedigrees at about the time of the Roman withdrawal is
Tryphun, a Brythonic version of "tribune", which may have
been a rank and not a name.

This arc, from Demetia through west and north Wales,
rapidly shifted away from centralized Roman control. When
Cunedda came down from Manau Gododdin to North Wales
in the 420s, he was able to establish various territories for
himself and his sons, that subsequently became the kingdoms
of Gwynedd (Venedotia), Ceredigion and Meirionydd plus the
smaller chiefdoms of Rhos and Dunoding. The tables at the end
of this chapter show the emergence of these kingdoms and
attempt to provide a chronology of their rulers.

South Wales was another matter. Despite the original hosti-
lity of the Silures to the Romans, South Wales had become
heavily Romanized as had the area later known as the Welsh
Marches. This territory included the Severn basin and was the
rich heartland of Roman Britain. Here were the towns of
Gloucester, Worcester and Wroxeter, plus Cirencester, the
biggest city in Britain after London.

Just what happened here, both within this territory and
between it and Maxima Caesariensis, is not entirely clear
but, according to the accounts left by Gildas and Nennius,
there was discord between various factions. Two names become prominent, Vitalinus and Ambrosius. Vitalinus, according to Nennius's genealogies, came from the city of Gloucester,
but is described by Geoffrey of Monmouth as the archbishop
of London. Whether Geoffrey meant archbishop or someone
in a senior magisterial role is not clear, but it may well be that
Vitalinus made himself head of the province of Maxima Caesariensis, whilst Ambrosius took control of parts of Britannia
Prima. Vitalinus, though, may have belonged to the Cornovii
civitas as his grandson, whom we shall come to know as
Vortigern, was regarded as the ancestor of the rulers of Powys,
the kingdom that grew out of that *civitas*. Ambrosius, on the
other hand, may have belonged to the Dobunni tribe which
occupied the Severn estuary and parts of Somerset and

Wiltshire. Their power struggle seems to have had consequences for both the provinces of Britannia Prima and Maxima
Caesariensis and, in due course, for Arthur.

The leading official in the *civitas* of Caerwent, out of which
would emerge the kingdoms of Gwent and Glywysing, was
probably Owain Finddu, another of the sons of Magnus
Maximus. His name is given in one of the Welsh Triads,
ancient triplets of verse used to memorize people and events
(*see* Chapter 8). Triad 13 lists the "Three Chief Officers of the
Island of Britain":

Caradawg son of Bran
And Cawrdaf son of Caradawg
And Owain son of Macsen Wledig.

Owain was not Maximus's eldest son – that was Victor, who
was murdered soon after Maximus's death in 388. Owain was
Victor's younger brother and, though we do not know his age,
he may still have been quite young at the time of his father's
death, perhaps only in his early teens. This means he would
have been in his thirties around the year 410 and, because of his
parentage and seniority, may well have been appointed as
deputy by Constantine III when he left for Gaul. The very
phrase "chief officer", rather than king or ruler, suggests a
senior administrative role, such as provincial governor or
possibly vicarius.

We can dismiss any suggestion that Owain, which is the
British version of Eugenius, was the same as the puppet
emperor set up by Arbogast in 392 because Zosimus recorded
the execution of Eugenius in 394, an event he is not likely to
have got wrong.

Through his mother, Owain was a grandson of Eudaf Hen,
who could claim descent from Caratacus. Eudaf, the Brythonic
version of Octavius, was almost certainly a high-ranking
Romano-British official, who had held command in Gwent
in the fourth century. Geoffrey of Monmouth calls him a duke

of the Gewisse, and I shall explore what that means in more detail later. According to tradition, Eudaf married the daughter of the usurper Carausius, which is unlikely, as that would push his lifetime back to the dawn of the fourth century. His own daughter is supposed to have married the shadowy Carausius II, which may well be how the Carausius connection arose, and places Eudaf more satisfactorily in the middle of the fourth century. He was almost certainly dead by 410, but his power and influence had been strong, and many of the later rulers of southern Britain, including Arthur, would claim descent from him (*see* Table 2).

Table 2 The Arthurian Patriarchs

So it is possible that, in the decade after 410, the three leading officials in Britain were all based in Britannia Prima: Vitalinus in Wroxeter (though bishop of London), Ambrosius in Gloucester or Cirencester, and Owain in Caerwent.

Eudaf's own sons and grandsons were also active at this time, though not necessarily in Britain. Two of his sons, Cynan and Gadeon, had apparently supported Maximus in his bid for empire in the 380s. In reward, Maximus made Cynan leader of the British who settled in Brittany around the end of the fourth century. The earliest known chieftain of Brittany was Cynan Meriadoc, and there is some confusion between him and Cynan ab Eudaf. Meriadoc is usually assigned dates towards the middle of the fifth century, whereas Cynan ab Eudaf must have been born in the mid-fourth century, and was perhaps in his forties when he fought alongside Maximus.

Gadeon joined Cynan in Brittany, and the two brothers may have ruled jointly. Almost certainly Cynan was dead by 410, and Gadeon may have been too. His successor Saloman has been accorded the dates 405–412 for his reign. Gadeon was old enough to have a daughter, Ystradwel, who allegedly married Coel, and if he had also fought alongside Maximus in the 380s, he must have been in his sixties by 405. Geoffrey of Monmouth, who frequently gets his facts back to front, reports animosity between Cynan and Eudaf over the crown of Britain, with Cynan believing he was the rightful heir. This may mask a real tension that developed between Owain and Cynan.

Legend remembers Owain as a strong, virile man, who fought the giant Eurnach, with both wielding tree trunks. The same legend records that although Owain defeated Eurnach the giant fell on Owain, killing him. This may all be fanciful, but at the core it may be a folk memory of Owain struggling against a greater authority whom Owain weakened, but who ultimately defeated him. That greater authority could well have been Vitalinus (or Vitalinus's grandson Vortigern) who was also Owain's brother-in-law, having married Maximus's daughter Severa. Owain's tomb is recorded as being at Beddgelert in Snowdonia, which was near one of Vortigern's strongholds. There is no further reference to Owain after Vortigern's rise to power.

As we have seen, the British gave their military leaders the title *wledig*. Magnus Maximus, for instance, was Macsen Wledig, and the title was also applied to Ceretic of Strathclyde, Cunedda of the Manau and Ambrosius the Younger (son of Vitalinus's rival), who was called Emrys Wledig. There were

about a dozen *wledigs* from the fifth and sixth centuries, some
of whom are remembered only in later tales and legends, and it
is difficult to know what part they played in the emergence of
these kingdoms. One in particular stands out – Amlawdd
Wledig. I shall discuss him in more detail later, but because
he married a daughter of Cunedda, he must also have been
fairly active around this period. Legend makes him the grandfather of Arthur's wife Guinevere. He is associated with
territory in South Wales and it is possible that he filled the
vacuum left by Owain.

There is no reason to believe that any other kingdoms
emerged in the south at this time. Both the archaeological
evidence and, to a degree, the written record – primarily that
left by Gildas – suggest that Roman life continued much as
before for at least a generation. Whilst northern Britain and
parts of west Wales were the scenes of fighting and increasing
devastation, it was not until the 430s and 440s that the south
began to be threatened by the more serious incursion of the
Saxons. It was then that the seeds were sown for the Arthurian
legend with the stories of Vortigern, Ambrosius and Uther
Pendragon.

In order that we can see how this legend emerged I want to
follow through all of the surviving ancient documents that
cover this period, no matter how dubious.

The principal documents are the *De Excidio et Conquestu
Britanniae* (*The Ruin of Britain*) by Gildas, the *Welsh Annals*
(*Annales Cambriae*), the *Historia Brittonum*, usually credited
to Nennius, and the *Anglo-Saxon Chronicle*. There are also the
genealogies, a few ancient poems such as the *Y Goddodin*, and
the lives of the saints, none of which is contemporary and few
of which are reliable.

There may well have been more documents at some stage.
When Geoffrey of Monmouth wrote his *History of the Kings of
Britain* in the 1130s, he referred to a "certain very ancient
book" which he had consulted. But such chronicles as may
have been kept in the fifth or sixth centuries would mostly have

been compiled and retained in monasteries, and these were subject to regular attack from the Vikings for over two hundred years, let alone the ravages of time and other dangers such as fire and flood. The library at Glastonbury Abbey was all but destroyed by fire in 1184 and one can but weep at what irreplaceable documents were lost both then and during the dissolution of the monasteries under Henry VIII.

The Venerable Bede, regarded as the father of British history, was a dedicated researcher and may have had access to some of these lost documents, but he relied heavily on Gildas for his coverage of the fifth and sixth centuries and, like Gildas, makes no mention of Arthur. That may by itself seem significant, but Bede was not that interested in events before the arrival of St Augustine, and would not have looked further into ancient British history. He was, however, the first to provide the name Vortigern. His primary research relates to later years, which means that England's foremost historian of the Dark Ages can provide no help with the story of Arthur.

One can live in hope that some long-lost document may surface in an ancient archive, but until then we have to work with what we've got and hope that archaeology may help substantiate or further define the world in which the events took place. I shall look at each of these sources over the next few chapters, which will also help flesh out a chronology so we know where in time to place Arthur.

Before doing that, though, it is worthwhile listing here the various pedigrees that survive in the ancient records. These are far from reliable – in fact at times they are wholly misleading – and they are almost impossible to date. But we will encounter many of these people as we travel through the other documents so it is worth acquainting ourselves with them and trying to get at least a rough chronology. This will also show where the various individuals named Arthur or Artúir or Arthwyr appear.

Genealogies and king lists

One of the key essentials to identifying Arthur is to place him in a specific period of time, along with his contemporaries. Without that we will get nowhere. In the next few chapters I will go through the various chronicles and see what timeline they suggest. Here, in order to acquaint ourselves with the names and territories that later emerged in Britain, I shall set out the various "royal" pedigrees and make some attempt to date them. Several authorities, not least Dr David Dumville, one of the undisputed experts on the Dark Ages, have demonstrated the difficulty in trying to get any chronology from the pedigrees for reasons I shall cover in a moment. So I start with a huge caveat that of all the sources covered in the next few chapters, these are amongst the most unreliable. But it seems to make sense to start with the data which are the least in focus and fine tune them as we go along.

The British pedigrees and regnal lists are extensive and survive in a wide variety of ancient documents, though none contemporary with Arthur's period. There are three major sources and many minor. The major ones are known as the Harleian MS. 3859, Jesus College MS.20 and *Bonedd y Saint*. The Harleian manuscript is part of the text which also includes Nennius's *Historia Brittonum*, but the oldest surviving copy with the genealogies dates from about 1100. The name Harleian comes from the original collection, now housed in the British Library, established by Robert Harley (1661–1724), first Earl of Oxford. The surviving copy of Jesus College MS.20 (now in the Bodleian Library in Oxford) has been dated to around 1340, and was probably drawn from a copy completed about a century earlier. The *Bonedd y Saint*, or "Lineage of the Saints", survives in many copies and versions, but the oldest dates from the end of the thirteenth century. This is held in the National Library of Wales and is known as Peniarth MS.183. Both the *Anglo-Saxon Chronicle* and Nennius also provide a number of pedigrees.

The pedigrees start with a contemporary descendant and work backwards through the generations. For instance, the first genealogy of the kingdom of Gwynedd listed in Harleian MS.3859 begins:

Uen map iguel map catell map Rotri map mermin map etthil . . .

. . . "Owen son of Iguel son of Catell" and so on. For the purposes of this book I want to reverse them into the order we usually understand genealogies, reading from earliest to latest.

Clearly these genealogies are so far removed in time from the Arthurian period that their accuracy is spurious. This is not simply because they may have been corrupted by scribal errors, but because there has been ample time for genealogies to have been fabricated. The primary reason for producing a pedigree is to identify a priority of descent, and thereby a claim to a title or land, and later rulers would have no compunction in having their scribes create a false genealogy. It is only by comparing the many hundreds of documents that survive that we can identify variances and attempt to correct them.

The other problem is that all too few of these genealogies contain identifiable dates. The only way to create a chronology is by working backwards or forwards from known dates and for that reason I take many of the following lists beyond our period of 400–600AD in order to get a firm footing. But dating pedigrees has an inherent problem. There is a general rule of thumb that a generation covers twenty-five to thirty years.* We can easily test that. We can trace the descent of the present Prince William back to William the Conqueror. This spans thirty-four generations and approximately 940 years, which is an average of just over 27.5 years per generation. However, it is a very approximate yardstick. We do not always know if a name in a genealogy is a first born or last born, and a man could father a son at any time from, say, age fifteen to sixty-five. It is

* See Donn Devine, "How Long is a Generation", *Ancestry Magazine* 23:5, September/October 2005.

quite easy to have a youngest son who is younger than his own nephew. Unless we have some corroborating dates it is easy to be out by an entire generation but, generally, over a span of a few centuries the average will not be far out.

In the following pedigrees I alternate generations by twenty-five and thirty years to keep the average to around twenty-eight. I use the term *floruit* to denote the period of an individual's prime of life, from about age twenty to fifty The dates given for *floruit* therefore are not birth–death. Where any real dates are known I provide them. In some cases I list generations from brothers and because you have to allow ten or more years between a range of brothers I have extended the generational span accordingly from thirty to forty years. Clearly all of this is very approximate but, if the pedigree itself is in any way accurate, it will give us a bearing on an individual at least to within thirty to forty years. Even so, some displacements in time do occur, which suggests corruption within the pedigree.

I am indebted to the work of P.C. Bartrum who has collected and assimilated many of these surviving pedigrees in *Early Welsh Genealogical Tracts* (1966) and explored them further in *A Welsh Classical Dictionary* (1993). Without his work the following would have been extremely difficult. However I have not always followed the dates that Bartrum has assigned to individuals, preferring to follow my own logic as consistently as I can.

Following the sequence I discussed above, starting with the kingdoms in the north, the following charts begin with the ancestry of Coel and Cunedda and work through the Men of the North to Wales, the south-west and finally Brittany. I also include the Saxon pedigrees, such as they are.

Table 3 lists the two pedigrees in Harleian MS. 3859 that show the descent of both Cunedda and Coel through collateral lines from Beli. The names given are first the Latin names, as per the pedigree, followed by their Celtic equivalent, as per Bartrum.

Table 3 The ancestors of Cunedda and Coel

	Beli	Floruit BC/AD	Key events
Beli	Beli	1–30	Son of Bran the Blessed and husband of Anna, cousin of the Virgin Mary
Amalech/Aballac	Aballac	25–55	Also known as Afallach or Evelake
Eugein [Owain]	Eudelen	55–85	* also called Prydein, the original Celtic name for the Picts
Brithguein [Brychwain*]	Eudos	80–110	
Dubun [Difwng]	Ebiud [Eifudd]	110–140	
Oumun [Onwedd]	Outigirn [Eudeyrn]	135–165	
Anguerit [Amwerydd]	Oudecant [Euddigan]	165–195	Lucius Artorius Castus in Britain 181–185
Amguoloyt [Afloyd]	Riitigirn [Rhydeyrn]	190–220	
Gurdumn [Gwrddwfn]	Iumetel [Rhifedel]	220–250	
Dumn [Dwfn]	Grat [Gradd]	245–275	
Guordoli [Gwrddoli]	Urban	275–305	revolt of Carausius, 286
Doli	Telpwyll	300–330	Constantine the Great declared emperor, 306.
Guorcein [Gwrgain]	Teuhant [Deheuwaint]	330–360	Constans visits Britain, 343
Cain	Tecmant [Tegfan]	355–385	Time of Carausius II and Genceris; Pictish invasion, 360; Magnus Maximus emperor, 383–388
Tacit [Tegid]	[Guotepauc] (probably an epithet for Coel and not a separate generation)		
Patern [Padarn]	Coel Hen	385–415	Roman administration ends, 410
Atern [Edern]	Garbanion	410–440	
Cunedda	Dumnagual Moilmut	440–470	

The table shows the limitations of the twenty-five to thirty year average for each generation, especially when the starting point is also vague. If we assume that Amalech in the first column is a duplication of Aballac, then there are fifteen generations to Coel and seventeen to Cunedda, which gives us roughly 410 and 465 respectively. That gives a reasonable mid-life *floruit* for Coel, but the extra generation places Cunedda too late. Since Cunedda is supposed to have married Coel's daughter, he must have lived a generation earlier, in the 420s. Although Coel's dates seem about right, if the name listed as his father, Guotepauc, was really the title "Protector", it would push Coel back a generation, making him too early.

It shows that though the generation calculation may get you to roughly the right period, you need other data to fine tune it, albeit still approximately. The more we work through the pedigrees, the more the chronology will come into focus.

Table 4 introduces the second "Arthur" after Artorius. Because Coel's descendants are so numerous, I have grouped them by generation, giving an idea of their territories. I have excluded Coel's daughter Gwawl who married Cunedda, who appears in a later chart, and Coel's third son Dydrwr, whose descendants are not known. Because each line includes older and younger sons, I've lengthened the prime-of-life "floruit" to forty years, and averaged the generation span to about thirty years.

This table is a synthesis of several pedigrees, not all of which concur. Presenting them in a chronological form opens up even more queries. For instance, the few certain dates we know are the life of Kentigern and the fall of Ceredig, last king of Elmet, who was expelled by Edwin of Northumbria around 619/620. Ceredig is usually regarded as the son, or successor, of Gwallawg, who was involved in battles with the early kings of Bernicia (northern Northumbria and the southern territory of the Gododdin) in the 580s. But Gwallawg is recorded as the son of Llenauc, great-grandson of Coel, and thus could only have lived around the early 500s. It is possible that the sons

Table 4 The descendants of Coel

Floruit												
385–415	Coel. *Married Ystradwel, daughter of Gadeon ap Eudaf Hen.*											
410–450	Ceneu											Garbanion
440–480	Maeswig the Lame	Mar *(Mar and Maeswig may be the same person. He and his descendants may have ruled the Southern Pennines.)*		Pabo, Pillar of Britain *(He and his descendants may have ruled the Borders and Northern Pennines)*					Gwrwst the Ragged			Dyfnwal Moelmud *(Dumnagual Moilmut)*
470–510	Llenauc	Arthwys *(this would give a life-span of roughly 450–520AD)*		Einion		Samyl the Humble *(daughter married Maelgwyn; had sister called Arddun)*	*(missing generation?)*	Moryd	*(missing generation?)* Merchiaun the Lean. *He and his descendants ruled Rheged*			Cyngar *(and brother Bran Hen)*
500–540	*(missing generation?)*	Ceidyaw	Eliffer of the Great Host	Cynvelin	Rhun the Wealthy	Guticern	Dunod *(died 590)*	Madog Morfryn	Cinmarc or Cynfarch the Dismal	Elidyr the Stout		Morcant Fwlch
530–570	Gwallawg *(fought Bernicians in 580s)*	Gwendolau *(died at Arfderydd 573)*	Peredur and Gwrgi *(both died 580)*	Cynwyd	Perweur *(married Rhun ap Maelgwyn)*		Deiniol *(died 584)*	Myrddin	Urien of Rheged *(killed c590)*	Llywarch Hen	*possibly* Lleuddun *(Loth)*	Coledauc or Clydog
560–600	Ceredig *(last king of Elmet died c620)*		Cadrod and Cynfor Host-Protector				Cadwallon		Owain *(killed c592)* and Rhun *(alive in 620s)*		*possibly* Gwrfan *(Gawain?)*	Morcant *(possible assassin of Urien)*
590–630											Kentigern *(lived 550–614)*	Rhoeth

were born in their father's older years, but that raises the
question of older sons more likely to succeed (or, if they were
killed in battle, to be remembered in the poems). It suggests
there may be a missing generation. The same applies to Dunod,
who is always listed as a son of Pabo, yet the annals give his
death as 590, suggesting either that he lived a very long time or
that there is a generation missing.

The most confused genealogy belongs to the children of
Mar (or Mor) and Maeswig, grandsons of Coel. Bartrum
conjectures that Mar and Maeswig may have been the same
person, as they feature commonly in the ancestry of their
descendants. Mar's son Einion is sometimes listed as a son
of Arthwys, but we know that Einion's son Rhun must have
been contemporary with Maelgwyn Gwynedd (i.e. 500–540)
because Rhun's daughter married Maelgwyn's son. Eliffer is
sometimes listed as a son of Gwrwst, but the earlier pedigrees treat him as a son of Arthwys and this best suits the
chronology.

This table should not be set in stone. It is an approximation
of descendants and chronology but it is unlikely to be out more
than twenty-five or thirty years either way. It places Arthwys
somewhere in Yorkshire, possibly in the area of Leeds, which
was the kingdom of Elmet, in the period 470–510 which, as we
will see, ties in with the probable dates of Arthur of Badon. It
does not mean that he is the same as King Arthur, but it raises
the question as to whether some activities attributed to
Arthwys in now-lost ancient records were picked up by
Nennius and Geoffrey. We have tentatively recognized a part
of the jigsaw.

Besides the descendants of Coel and Cunedda there were the
British rulers of Alclud (Strathclyde), with their capital at
Dumbarton. Only one of the ancient records lists their pedi-
gree, so we have no corroboration. Some of the other Men of
the North, who ruled amongst the Votadini at Din Eidyn
(Edinburgh) belong to this pedigree, through Dyfnwal Hen

rather than Coel, so I have amalgamated all of them below. The only change I have made is that, in the pedigrees, Neithon is listed as descended from Dyfnwal's son Gwyddno, but that is impossible according to the time scale. I believe this was a scribal error mistaking his descent from a later Gwyddno, grandson of Garwynwyn. This is supported by the later Gwyddno having another son called Alpin who is recorded as a contemporary of Neithon.

Table 5 The descendants of Ceretic of Strathclyde

						Floruit
Cluim [Clemens]						340–370
Cinhil [Quintilius]						365–395
Cynloyp [Cynllwyb]						395–425
Ceretic guletic [Ceredig wledig]						420–450
Cinuit [Cynwyd]						450–480
Dumnagual Hen [Dyfnwal Hen] (*whose daughter married Brychan of Manau*)						475–505
Clynog	Cynfelyn	Cedig		Garwynwyn	Gwrwst	500–540
Tutagual	Clydno Eidin (*ruled Votadini*)	Serwan	Senyllt	Cawrdaf	Elidir the Wealthy (*killed c555*)	530–570
Rhydderch (*ruled Alclud c580–c614*)	Cynon (*may have survived Catraeth*)	Mordaf the Generous	Nudd the Generous	Gwyddno "Long-shanks"		560–600
Constantine				Neithon (*ruled Alclud 614–621*)		590–630

Table 6 The rulers of Dál Riata and the Picts

Picts	Dál Riata
Talorc (400–424)	
Drust (424–453)	
Talorc (453–457)	
Nechtan Morbet (457–468)	
Drest (468–498)	
Galanan (498–513)	Fergus (498–501)
Drest mac Drust (513–516 and 521–529)	Domangart (501–507)
Drest mac Girom (513–521 and 529–533)	Comgall (507–538)
Gartnait and Cailtram (533–541)	Gabhran (538–558)
Talorg (541–552)	
Drest (552–553)	
Cennalath (553–557)	
Brude (556–584)	Conall (558–574)
Gartnait (584–602)	Aedan (574–608) and his son
Nechtan/Neithon (602–621) (*same as Neithon of Alclud in Table 5*)	**Artúir** (*c560–596*)

Table 6 completes the North with the Picts and the rulers of
Dál Riata in Argyll. The chronology of the Picts at this time
is confusing and is further aggravated by their kingship
passing through the female line, making paternity difficult
to track. The table shows both sets of rulers as a list of
kings, rather than a pedigree. This includes our third
"Arthur".

We now move our attention to Wales. Table 7 lists the
pedigree of the kings of Dyfed. They were descended from the
Irish tribe of the Déisi, who were driven out of Leinster in the
fourth century and settled in Demetia in south-west Wales,
under Eochaid mac Artchorp.

Table 7 The rulers of Dyfed

Irish pedigree	Welsh pedigree	Floruit	Notes
Artchorp	[Cyngar]	320–350	
Eochaid Almuir	[Ewein]	350–380	may be first to settle in Demetia
Corath	[Cyndwr/Kyndeyrn]	375–415	
Aeda Brosc	[Ewein "the Stout"]	405–435	
[Tryffin]	Tryphun	430–460	contemporary with Vortigern
Aircol	Ayrcol	460–490	contemporary with Ambrosius
	Erbin	485–515	may be a brother of Vortipor
Gartbuir [Vortipor]	Gwrdeber/Guortepir	490–520	Gildas noted was old in the 530s
Congair [Cyngar]	Cyngar	515–545	
Retheoir [Pedr]	Peder	545–575	
Artúir	**Arthur**	570–600	this suggests a life-span of 550–620
Nowy	Nennue/Nougoy	600–630	also ruled Brycheiniog
Cloten [Gwlyddien]	Clothen	625–655	also ruled Brycheiniog
Cathen	Cathen	655–685	also ruled Brycheiniog
Cadwgan	Catgocaun/Gwgawn	680–710	also ruled Brycheiniog
Rhain	Regin/Rein	710–740	lived when Seisyll of Ceredigion conquered part of Dyfed in c730

This is a rare example where there is both a Welsh pedigree and an independent Irish one. The latter, from the *Book of Uí Maine*, is listed in the first column, as reprinted by Bartrum from a twelfth-century document held in the Bodleian Library (MS. Rawlinson B.502). The second column is the Welsh version from Jesus College MS.20. The Welsh list is dubious for the first five generations where at some stage a different pedigree has been fused on to Tryphun to create a descent from Magnus Maximus. I have placed those names in brackets but they are best ignored. From Tryphun on the two pedigrees agree. This pedigree is important because the third Arthur is our first real "Arthur".

The chronology looks reliable. It allows for Eochaid to settle in Demetia in the mid- to late fourth century, which fits in with known events. It allows Vortipor to be an old man at the time of Gildas (the above would give Vortipor's life-span as 470–540), and it terminates at the known dates assigned to Rhain. Allowing for an error of maybe no more than twenty years, we can fix Arthur of Dyfed firmly in the late sixth century.

The pedigree of the rulers of Gwent and Glywysing (Table 8), which includes our fourth "Arthur", is both complicated and confusing. Unlike Gwynedd (Table 9), where a strong hereditary kingship became established early on, in Gwent this proved harder to do. Leslie Alcock, who undertook a major archaeological study at Dinas Powys in Glamorgan, has suggested that because Gwent and Glamorgan had been strongly Romanized, Gwent clung more tenaciously to the Roman way of life and no single hereditary kingship emerged for some time. Instead, there were competing administrators and governors, no doubt many from the old Silurian nobility, all of whom sought overall authority but few of whom achieved it. When chroniclers tried to piece this back together two or three centuries later the key records were lost. The position is not helped by Gwent incorporating three or four small kingdoms, which began independently and at various times merged or regained independence. Gwent and Glywysing were the two main kingdoms. Part of Glywysing was originally called Cernyw and became Gwynllwg. In later years when Glywysing merged with Gwent it was called Morgannwg. To the east of Gwent was Ergyng, which later became a sub-kingdom of Gwent.

The following table depicts all of these parallel and sometimes overlapping dynasties, and tries to rectify some of the obvious errors in the old genealogies. For instance, the Jesus College manuscript shows a descent from Caradog Vreichfras, placing him so far back as to be contemporary with the emperor Constantine. Yet other sources we will encounter show him as a companion of King Arthur. A study of the pedigree shows that two recurring names (Meurig and Erb) have become repeated, conflating two pedigrees into one and doubling the span of time.

Table 8 The rulers of Gwent and Glywysing

Glywysing	Gwent	Ergyng	Floruit	
Owain Finddu			385–415	son of Magnus Maximus
Nor		Caradog	410–440	
Solor [Filur]	Ynyr [Honorius]		440–470	
Glywys		Caradog*	465–495	* may be *Vreichfras*
Gwynllyw (*married Brychan's daughter*)		Erb	495–525	
Cadog	Nynnio	Peibio	520–550	Cadog gave the kingship of Glywysing to Meurig
Meurig ab Enhinti	Llywarch or Teithfall	Cynfyn and Gwrgan	550–580	
Erbic	Tewdrig (*killed at Tintern in mid-620s*)	Caradog*	575–605	* more likely to be *Vreichfras*
Glywysing merged with Gwent	Meurig	Cawdraf	605–635	
	Athrwys	Medrawd	630–660	equates to a life-span of 610–680
	Morgan (*died 665?*)	Gwrfoddw	660–690	
	Ithel [Einudd]		685–715	
	Ffernfael (*died 775*)		715–745	
	Athrwys		740–770	

Dates for some of the reigns are more reliable by the eighth century, and the death of Ffernfael ap Ithel is recorded as 775 in the *Welsh Annals*. We also know that Meurig's father, Tewdrig, died after the battle of Tintern when he was already of an advanced age. That battle has been variously dated between 577 and 630, with around 626 being the most likely. However, Morgan ap Athrwys is believed to have died in 665, which is too early for his position in the chart. We know that many of these kings lived to an advanced age, even the later ones not listed here. Hywel ap Rhys died in around 885, well into his eighties; Tewdrig ap Llywarch was also into his eighties. So we may find a twenty-five to thirty-year generation span insufficient in this instance. However, that makes it even more difficult to count back from Tewdrig, as it would push Owain Finddu, son of Magnus Maximus, back too far. Meurig's mother Enhinti is identified as either the daughter or sister of Urien of Rheged, so I have placed him in the mid-sixth century, even though he was probably of the same generation as Cadog.

The table is nevertheless within a reasonable degree of accuracy and provides a life-span for Arthur of Gwent of around 610–680, perhaps slightly earlier to accommodate his son and the known longevity of his grandfather. This will seem late for those who have theorized that he is the Arthur of Badon. This Arthur's primary advocates are Alan Wilson and Baram Blackett and, in *Artorius Rex Discovered*, they give Arthur's dates as 503–575, or a *floruit* of 525–555, a century earlier than the above. I find it difficult to accept such a date if the above pedigree is even approximately accurate. I suspect we may be missing a generation or two, even assuming the lines of succession are correct.

One of the curiosities of this table is that it identifies a person called Medrawd (or Mordred) as a grandson of Caradog, contemporary with Arthur.

In order to set these chronologies against the main power-base in Wales, it will be useful here to set out the ruling dynasty of Gwynedd, where the chronology is better understood. It will help us understand who else was active at the time of Badon, and during the lifetimes of the other Arthurs so far identified.

Table 3 provided dates for Cunedda of 440–470 but, as discussed, he almost certainly belonged to an earlier generation which I have adjusted here. These pedigrees are taken from Harleian MS.3859, though I have modernized the names where possible for easier understanding. Also, as with Table 4, because I am charting brothers and cousins, I have allowed a forty-year *floruit*, rather than thirty, and used an average generation span of thirty years rather than twenty-five to thirty.

The chronology throws up a few anomalies, especially in the line of Ceredigion. We know that Seisyll conquered parts of Dyfed sometime in the eighth century, probably in 730. To accommodate this I have had to move Seisyll, his father and descendants down by two generations. However, as we have no independent dates to confirm Clydog's ancestors it is impossible to know when these missing generations occur. Something has to be adrift. There are nine generations from Cunedda to Arthwen, who died in 807. Taking the average twenty-five to thirty years per generation, that gives 250 years, which would put Arthwen's mid-life at around 675, suggesting we are missing four generations. It means we cannot be sure where to place Arthfoddw, which may prove important later.

In the house of Gwynedd, we find that around the time of Cadwallon and Cadwaladr, the chronology shifts out of sync, suggesting an earlier date. This may mean that they were descended from the older sons and thus the generation span should be reduced to twenty to twenty-five years. However, by the time of Cynan this has righted itself, suggesting that some younger sons must have inherited, perhaps through the deaths of older brothers in conflict.

We know virtually nothing about the rulers of the other three kingdoms to be able to corroborate their dates although the death dates for Idris of Meirionydd and Cadwal of Rhos, taken from the Annals, do fit the pattern. There is a legend about the giant Idris, after whom the mountain Cader Idris is supposed to be named, that says he was killed by Arthur. The

Table 9 The rulers of Gwynedd and other descendants of Cunedda

Floruit	Gwynedd	Rhos	Ceredigion	Meirionydd	Dunoding
410–440	Cunedda		Ceredig	[Tybion, *stayed in Manau*]	Dunaut
440–480	Einion the Stricken		Usai	Meirion	Eifion
470–510	Cadwallon Longhand		Serwyl	Cadwaladr	Dingad
500–540	Maelgwyn (*died c549*)	Owain White-tooth / Cynlas the Red (*the Cuneglasus of Gildas*)			
530–570	Rhun the Tall	Maig	Boddw	Gwrin Cut-Beard	Meurig
560–600	Beli	Cangan or Aeddan	**Arthfoddw**	Clydno	Eifion
590–630	Iago (*died c615*)	Cadwal (*possibly killed at Chester c615*)	Arthlwys	Gwyddno	Isaac
620–660	Cadfan	Idgwyn	*missing generation?*	Idris (*died 632, allegedly killed by Arthur*)	Pobien
650–690	Cadwallon (*died 634*)	Einion	*missing generation?*	Sualda or Yswalt	Pobddelw
680–720	Cadwaladr (*died 664 or 682*)	Rhufon	Clydog	Brochwel	Eifion
710–750	Idwal the Roebuck	Meirion	Seisyll (*conquered part of Dyfed in c730*)	Einudd	Brochwel
740–780	Rhodri the Bald (*died 754*)	Caradog (*killed 798*)	Arthwen (*died 807*)	Ednyfed	Eigion
770–810	Cynan (*died 816*) / *His daughter Essyllt married Gwriad of Man*	Hywel (*died 825*)	Dyfnwallon	Brochwel	Ieuanawl

Table 10 The rulers of Powys, Gwrtheyrnion and Brycheiniog

Floruit	Powys (primary line)	Powys (subsidiary lines)		Gwrtheyrn [Vortigern]	Builth and Gwrtheyrnion	Brycheiniog
420-450					Pascent	Brychan
450-480	Cadell Gleaming-Hilt	Categirn (*died c455*)	Britu [Brydw]		Riagath/Riocatus	Rhain the red-eyed
480-510	Cyngen the Famous		Camuir		Idnerth	Rhigeneu
510-540				Thewer *married* Casanauth Wledig		
540-570	Brochwel of the Tusks		Millo	Cynan	Pawl	Llywarch
570-600	Cynan of the White Chariot		Cynan	Cenelaph	Elaed	Idwallon
600-620	Eiludd		Elfoddw	Rhun	Morvo	Rhiwallon
			Llemenig (Lancelot?)			
630-660	Beli		Gurhaiernn [Gwrhearn]	Madog	Gwyddaint	Ceindrech *married* Cloten of Dafyd, *fl* 625-655
660-690	Gwylog		Hesselis	Merin	Pascen	Cathen, ruled Brycheiniog and Dyfed
690-720	Elisedd			Tudwal	Gloud	Cadwgon
720-750	Brochwel			Sandde	Brawstudd, *wife of* Arthfael ap Rhys	Rhain
750-780	Cadell (*died 808*)			Madog	Rhys	Tewdwr
780-810	Cyngen (*died 855*)			Noë	Hywel	Nowy

ruler Idris was called Idris the Tall, and the date of his death would be roughly contemporary with Arthur of Gwent, or just possibly Arthur of Dyfed.

The two other major Welsh kingdoms are related, so I have listed their rulers together in Table 10. These are Powys and Brycheiniog. Hemmed between the two was the small but historically significant kingdom of Buellt and Gwrtheyrnion, whose later rulers inherited Glywysing and Brycheiniog.

The pedigrees for Powys are highly corrupted and virtually no two agree. Bartrum has, however, detected a reasonable pattern which may reflect the original. There is still much confusion over the immediate descendants of Vortigern, and, although the general consensus is that Cyngen the Famous was the son of Cadell Gleaming-Hilt, there are sufficient other pedigrees that show an additional generation between them. However, we know that Eiludd survived the battle of Chester in 615 in which his brother Selyf was killed. It is also fairly certain that Elisedd, whose memory is commemorated in Eliseg's Pillar, erected by his great-grandson Cyngen, was active in the early 700s.

Table 10 includes a secondary but otherwise unknown cadet line of Powys, descended from Brittu, variously treated as a son of Vortigern, Categirn, or Cadell. I've shown him here as Cadell's brother because otherwise his descendants shift too far out of sync.

The pedigrees of Armorica are also vague and frequently confused with the pedigrees of Dumnonia. Part of the problem is that when the Britons migrated to Armorica in the fifth century, they took local names with them, and two of the principalities of Armorica were called Domnonée and Cornouaille. The latter should not be confused with Cernow, which later became Cornwall, or Cernyw which, as we shall see, was part of Glywysing. Just to add to the confusion, the Welsh name for Armorica was Llydaw, and it seems that name also had its equivalent in south-east Wales, probably on the borders of Brycheiniog and Gwent, and perhaps bordering

Ergyng.* Caradog Vreichfras was associated with Llydaw, which is usually interpreted as meaning that he ruled Brittany, but which probably meant he ruled territory from Brycheiniog to Ergyng, including Llydaw.

Most of these pedigrees trace their descent from Eudaf Hen. However, unlike the Welsh pedigrees, the Breton and Cornish ones have become greatly corrupted and merged with legend, to the point that the two have become almost indistinguishable. The following presents one interpretation whilst recognizing the non-historicity of much of it. The dates for Dumnonia are the most suspect and maybe a generation or two earlier for all the names or Mayeren overlap.

Not all the names in the line of Armorica are related. Cynan's line was interrupted after Budic when the kingdom was usurped by Canao, whose descendants ruled until Cynan's line was restored under Alanus.

Table 11 The rulers of Dumnonia and Armorica [Brittany]

fl 340–370	Eudaf Hen (*his daughter Elen married Magnus Maximus*)		
fl 370–395	Cynan and Gadeon (*sons of Eudaf*)		
fl 395–425	Gwrfawr or Morfawr (*son of Gadeon*)		

	Dumnonia	Armorica	Domnonée	Cornouaille
fl 425–455	Tudwal	Cynan Meriadoc		
fl 450–480	Cynfor	Grallo/ Gradlonus		Iahann Reeth (*possibly Riothamus*)
fl 475–505	Custennin Fendigaid	Saloman	Riwal	Daniel
fl 505–535	Erbin and Meirchion (*cousins*) *ruled separately*	Aldroenus	Deroch	Budic
fl 530–560	Geraint ab Erbin and Mark ab Meirchion *ruled separately*	Budic ——————— *Kingdom usurped by Canao*	Riatham then his brother Ionas *Conmor seized power during his rule*	Meliau or Macliau *Title usurped from his brother Rivold*
fl 560–590	Cadwr	Macliaw	Iudwal or Judhael	
fl 585–615	Peredur	Waroch	Iuthael	
fl 615–645	Tewdwr	Canao (II)	Haelog	
fl 640–670	Erbin	Alanus		
fl 670–700	Geraint (*who fought the Saxons in 710*)	Budic		

---

* Bartrum (1993), p. 420.

Table 12 The ancestors of the Saxons

Floruit	Kent	West Saxons	Bernicia	Deira	East Angles	East Saxons	Mercia	Lindsey
360–390		Freawine	Beornic	Saebald	Tytmon	Gesecg	Wermund	Finn
390–420	Wecta	Wig	Gechbrond (*ASC reverses Beornic and Brond*)	Saefugl	Trygils	Antsecg	Offa	Friodulf
415–445	Witta	Gewis	Alusa (*ASC has Aloc*)	Soemil (*not in ASC*)	Rothmund	Swebba	Angengeot	Frealaf
445–475	Wihtgils	Esla	Ingui (*ASC adds extra generation Angenwit*)	Swaerta (*Nennius*) Westerfalca (*ASC*)	Hryp	Sigefugel	Eomer	Woden
470–500	Hengist	Elesa	Esa *ASC* Athelbert (*Nennius*)	Wilgsil	Wilhelm	Bedca	Icel	Winta
500–530	Octa	Cerdic	Eobba	Wyscfrea	Wehha or Guechan	Offa	Cnebba	Cretta
525–555	Ossa or Oisc	Cynric or Creoda	Ida	Yffi	Wuffa	Aescwine	Cynewald	Cueldgils
555–585	Eormenric	Ceawlin	Athelric (*died c593?*)	Aelle (*died c599*)	Tytill	Sledda	Creoda (*died c593*)	Cædbad
580–610	Athelbert (*died c618*)	Cutha	Athelfrith (*died 616*)	Athelric (*died 604*)	Redwald (*died 625*)	Saebert (*died c616*)	Pybba (*died c606*)	Bubba

The above has covered the Welsh pedigrees, but we also need to consider the early Saxon royal pedigrees, as listed in Nennius and the *ASC*. The *ASC* takes its ancestries back to the god Woden, but though we can ignore that, that is not a reason for treating the whole of the ancestries as fabrication. They are equally as reliable or suspect as the British ones. The *ASC* pedigrees do not always agree with those in Nennius, so where they vary I have noted accordingly. Nennius provides no pedigree for the West Saxons, East Saxons, South Saxons or Lindsey. Indeed the *ASC* is also silent on the South Saxons, yet their chieftain, Aelle, was regarded by Bede as the first Bretwalda, or overlord of the Saxons.

Nennius identifies Soemil as the first to separate Deira from Bernicia, and with his *floruit* of around 440, he must remain the earliest named Angle in Britain. Nennius also credits Wilhelm as being the first to rule over the East Angles, showing that in those two generations the Angles had moved from being mercenaries and invaders, to settlers with established territories. Icel and Hengist both fall into that same generation, and although logic would suggest that Hengist must have reigned earlier, if he really was the first Saxon to be invited over by Vortigern, the record suggests something different. We will explore this in more detail later.

The purpose of exploring these pedigrees in such detail has been to try and ascertain an approximate chronology as a backcloth against which we can paint in some detail. Now we can start our exploration for Arthur amongst the ancient chronicles.

4
THE CHRONICLERS

1. The early chronicles

Now that we have some idea of who lived when, it would be helpful to explore the few relevant chronicles that exist in relation to Britain to see what they can tell us about what was going on. In order to fix a date for Arthur we need to chart the events leading to Badon.

A good starting place is not in Britain, but in Gaul, with the *Gallic Chronicle*, one of the few contemporary documents that give us a firm, if contestable, date. We do not know who compiled the *Chronicle*, but it was a continuation of an earlier chronicle established by the scholar Jerome, finished in 378AD. In fact there are two *Gallic Chronicles*, one of which stops at the year 452, whilst the other continues to 511. The 452 *Chronicle* was once attributed to Prosper of Aquitaine, who also produced his own continuation of Jerome's *Chronicle*, but whoever compiled the 452 *Chronicle* – and there is a surprising candidate somewhat closer to home whom we shall encounter later – held ecclesiastical views that differed from Prosper's. Prosper's work shows him as a supporter of the views of Augustine of Hippo, whilst the Gallic chronicler was sympathetic towards the Pelagians. His *Chronicle* is important because it was a contemporary record by someone who knew Britain.

The dates within the *Gallic Chronicle* are not without their problems as the compiler used more than one system. However, the supporters of the *Chronicle* have, to a large degree, reconciled the dates, especially in the later years, and the two that interest us are accurate to within a year or two.

The *Chronicle* has two entries relating to Britain in the post-Roman period.

> *Honorius XVI* [410AD]. At this time the strength of the Romans was completely reduced by [a host of enemies] who were gaining strength. The British provinces were devastated by the Saxons. The Vandals and the Alans devastated part of Gaul; what remained the tyrant Constantine occupied. The Sueves occupied the better part of Spain. Finally, Rome itself, the capital of the world, suffered most foully the depredations of the Goths.

> *Theodosius XVIII* [441AD]. The British, who to this time had suffered from various defeats and misfortunes, are reduced to the power of the Saxons [i.e. the Saxons held sway].

The 511 *Chronicle* records the last event in similar words, though with one interesting addition: "Britannia, lost to the Romans, yields to the power of the Saxons."

These two entries are of great significance. The first makes clear that the Saxon incursions into Britain were of some strength, sufficient to "devastate" the provinces, though whether it means some or all four (five?) provinces, is not clear. Some authorities have preferred to treat this entry as relating to the year 408, suggesting a build-up of Saxons within Britain and that the lack of help by Rome against the Saxons is what caused the British to eject the Roman administration. It also adds reason to why, around this time, the British were so keen to appoint their own emperor. As the record shows, though, "the tyrant Constantine" (Constantine III) moved away from Britain to occupy Gaul, leaving Britain further bereft of forces.

The second entry is the more remarkable. The wording "yields to the power" implies that by 441, Britain was under the control of the Saxons, an event usually placed in the second half of the century. Likewise, the 511 *Chronicle*'s phrase "lost to the Romans" implies that it was not until the year 441 that Britain formally passed from Roman control to Saxon. Even though Honorius had apparently told the British to look to their own defences in 410, he had probably not meant to sever Britain from the empire. For thirty years it remained in limbo.

Another entry of interest appears in the chronicles maintained by Prosper of Aquitaine, which ran parallel to the *Gallic Chronicles*. Prosper lived throughout this period, about 390–465, and had a keen awareness of events, especially during his role as notary to Pope Leo the Great. He records the following event for the year 429:

> Agricola, a Pelagian, the son of the Pelagian bishop Severianus, corrupted the British churches by the insinuation of his doctrine. But at the persuasion of the deacon Palladius, Pope Celestine sent Germanus, bishop of Auxerre, as his representative and, having rejected the heretics, directed the British to the catholic faith.

Prosper is the only source for the date of Germanus's visit to Britain, placing it right in the middle of that period from the end of Roman administration in 409 to the apparent domination of Britain by the Saxons in 441. Germanus was a native of Auxerre, in north-central Gaul, and came from an aristocratic family. Trained in law, he became a governor of Armorica and was raised to the rank of *dux*. In 418, he was appointed Bishop of Auxerre.

Constantius of Lyon wrote a "life" of Germanus, *Vita Sancti Germani*, around the year 480. Although it was written while those who knew Germanus were still alive, the *Vita* shows little evidence of research. Any factual reliability is buried beneath a welter of hyperbole and hagiophily.

Constantius confirms Germanus's visit, saying that it had arisen following "a deputation from Britain". We do not know who in Britain sent the deputation, but it shows that Britain was not isolated, and that there was traffic to and from Gaul, and probably the rest of the Mediterranean world.

Constantius tells us that Germanus, with Bishop Lupus, crossed the Channel during winter. They were beset by a great storm, but through prayer arrived safely in Britain. We do not know where Germanus landed, but it was probably at Richborough in Kent, where there was a strong Christian community. Constantius reveals that they were met by "great crowds" who had come "from many regions", and that news of their arrival spread far and wide. Eventually the Pelagians, who had gone "into hiding" for fear of Germanus, reappeared, "flaunting their wealth" and prepared for a debate at a "meeting place". Constantius does not tell us where this was, but as he tells us that soon after the debate Germanus visited the shrine of St Alban, we may presume that they met at the Roman amphitheatre at Verulamium. Verulamium was the third largest town in Britain and remained fully functioning throughout the fifth century.

During the debate, Germanus, through his inspired responses, out-manoeuvred the Pelagians and received the accolades of the crowds. Constantius goes on to say that a man "of high military rank" gave his young blind daughter to the bishops to heal. Germanus suggested that the tribune take his daughter to the heretics, but the heretics blanched at the idea and begged the bishops to cure the girl, which they did. Germanus and Lupus won the day and "this damnable heresy had been thus stamped out".

After visiting the shrine, Germanus tripped, injuring his foot, and had to be taken to a house where he was confined to a bed for several days. A fire broke out, burning several houses "roofed with reeds", and the wind carried the flames towards the house where Germanus lay. Although the flames engulfed the surrounding houses, Germanus's was spared.

What Constantius tells us next is most revealing:

> Meanwhile, the Saxons and the Picts had joined forces to make war upon the Britons. The latter had been compelled to withdraw their forces within their camp and, judging their resources to be utterly unequal to the contest, asked the help of the holy prelates. The latter sent back a promise to come and hastened to follow it.

Constantius does not tell us where this "camp" was situated, but does say that it was during Lent and that upon the arrival of the bishops the soldiers eagerly sought baptism. A small chapel was built out of branches, and Easter was celebrated. In the absence of any other military leader, Germanus offered himself as their general. Constantius continues:

> He chose some lightly-armed troops and made a tour of the outworks. In the direction from which the enemy were expected he saw a valley enclosed by steep mountains. Here he stationed an army on a new model, under his own command.
>
> By now the savage host of the enemy was close at hand and Germanus rapidly circulated an order that all should repeat in unison the call he would give as a battle-cry. Then, while the enemy were still secure in the belief that their approach was unexpected, the bishops three times chanted the Alleluia. All, as one man, repeated it and the shout they raised rang through the air and was repeated many times in the confined space between the mountains.
>
> The enemy were panic-stricken, thinking that the surrounding rocks and the very sky itself were falling on them. Such was their terror that no effort of their feet seemed enough to save them. They fled in every direction, throwing away their weapons and thankful if they could save their skins. Many threw themselves into the river, which they had just crossed at their ease, and were drowned in it.

This became known as the Alleluia victory and entered legend. For Constantius, writing fifty or so years later, it would have been a noted event, and therefore it is all the more surprising that he does not say where it took place. Indeed, throughout his biography of Germanus, Constantius's description of Britain is woefully lacking, suggesting he had not visited Britain himself. There is a site in what was north Powys, called Maesgarmon, just outside Mold in Flintshire, where the River Alun runs through a steep valley. If this was the site then the combined Pict/Saxon army had sailed along the River Dee, suggesting the army may also have included Irish warriors. This area has several Arthurian sites, including Moel Arthur and particularly Moel Fenlli (*see* Chapter 6).

What is perhaps most surprising about this account is that the British forces had no competent battle leader of their own. Germanus was a *dux* in his own right and could have been the most senior official at the "camp", and been offered the command through respect. Or it could have been a purely nominal gesture, with Germanus being the spiritual leader of the troops, whilst the temporal commander is conveniently forgotten. It may even be that this battle had nothing to do with Germanus, who may have become confused with the British holy man Garmon, of whom more later.

We may wonder, though, whether by the year 429 the British troops had become demoralized and lacked training, even though this was not long after Cunedda's forces had been restationed in North Wales. Gildas has some comments on the state of the British defences, as we shall see in the next chapter.

In summing up the victory Constantius remarks:

> Thus this most wealthy island, with the defeat of both its spiritual and its human foes, was rendered secure in every sense.

No matter how much Constantius embellishes this text, he was writing within only a generation or two of the real events and his readers would know exactly how Britain had fared over those years. Thus we must give some credence to his account that at this time Britain was wealthy and still unconquered by the Saxons.

Constantius reveals that some years after this visit there was a resurgence of Pelagianism, and Germanus was again called upon to visit Britain, this time accompanied by Severus, Bishop of Trier. The decision to return to Britain must have been sudden (despite another synod of bishops) because British officials were unaware of it. An official called Elafius, described as "one of the leading men in the country", hurried to meet Germanus. Otherwise the visit is all too similar to the earlier one. The resurgence of Pelagianism seems to have been restricted to just a few, who were quickly identified and condemned. In order to prevent any further growth of Pelagianism, the leading heretics were taken by Germanus into exile on the Continent.

There is no separate record of Elafius in the pedigrees, but that would not be surprising if he were a church, rather than civic, official. Amongst the descendants of Coel is the Latinized name of Eleutherius (Eliffer in British), and although he lived a century later, in northern Britain, the name was not uncommon. I conjecture more on Elafius later.

Constantius does not provide a date for this second visit or give any indication of how long it was after the first. The only clue is that Germanus died soon after his return. His death is usually dated to around 448, but that contradicts other known events. Most significant is that upon his return to Gaul, Germanus was sent to Ravenna to plead with the emperor about the rebellious Bretons, but the 452 *Chronicle* records the downfall of their leader Tibatto by the year 437. This would place Germanus's second visit in the year 436, a date which has growing support.

At the core of Constantius's account is a picture of a wealthy Britain, at least in the south. It was subject to surprise attacks from the Saxons and Picts but, by 436, the officials had regained some level of control and Britain was, perhaps, in a period of relative calm.

2. The *Welsh Annals*

The *Welsh Annals*, or *Annales Cambriae*, is a list of events, recorded year by year, which was kept by the British chroniclers. Over the years copies were made of copies and none of the original documents survives. The earliest copy (Manuscript A) dates from the end of the tenth century, but the earliest date entered relates to the year 447. Another version (Manuscript B) is of a later date although the entries go back far earlier. They are believed to have been copied from another document, most likely one of the Irish Annals, which runs until 1203, as does a third version (Manuscript C). Where A, B and C overlap, they are fairly consistent, with just an occasional variance of a few years.

Unfortunately, there are only six entries for the fifth century and eighteen for the sixth century. Clearly either the original *Annals* were in such a poor state that later copyists were unable to interpret records against certain years or, more likely, the records were not commenced until much later. In fact a regular sequence of dates does not start until the year 807. The Welsh ruler Merfyn the Freckled, whose reign began in 825, encouraged the study of British history, and it is likely that during his reign the *Annals* as we know them were brought together from a variety of earlier documents. Therefore none of the fifth- and sixth-century records is likely to be contemporary. Moreover, it is impossible to tell whether entries were copied correctly from originals, or were distorted by error.

There is an added problem in knowing which dates apply. The *Annals* do not record a standard date. Written in Latin, and thus recorded in Roman numerals, the entries begin from Year 1. Assuming that each individual year is accurately recorded, we need to find a year in which the event is recorded against a verifiable timeline, and count back. The usual event selected is against Year 9, "Easter altered on the Lord's Day by Pope Leo". This happened at Easter 455, which makes Year 1 equal 447, the generally accepted date. Originally it was believed Leo had adjusted Easter earlier, in

452. Therefore, some sources list the *Annals* as starting in 444. There are other entries which help us identify dates, especially in relation to St Columba (Columcille), whose life was written by Adomnán, one of his followers, and who was excommunicated from Ireland in 561 and died on 9 June 597. The following *Annals* concur with this timeline, which allows some degree of confidence.

Listed below are the relevant entries from the fifth and sixth centuries. The key dates are those for 518, 539 and 575.

447 Days as dark as night

459 St Patrick raised to the Lord

460 St David born thirty years after Patrick left Menevia

518 The battle of Badon in which Arthur carries the Cross of Our Lord Jesus Christ for three days and three nights on his shoulders and the Britons were the victors

523 St Columcille born. The death of St Brigid

539 The battle of Camlann, in which Arthur and Medraut fell: and there was plague in Britain and Ireland

549 A great plague in which Mailcun king of Venedotia died

560 The death of Gabran son of Dungart

564 Columcille leaves for Britain

565 The voyage of Gildas to Ireland

572 Gildas, the wisest of Britons, died

575 The battle of Armterid between the sons of Eliffer and Guendoleu, son of Keidiau, in which battle Guendoleu fell; Myrddin became mad

581 Gwrgi and Peredur, sons of Eliffer, died

591 The conversion of Constantine to the Lord

594 Edilburt reigned in England

597 The death of Columcille. The death of king Dunaut, son of Pabo. Augustine and Mellitus converted the English to Christ

Apart from the references to Arthur and Myrddin (Merlin), what strikes me most about these *Annals* is what little reference is made to other secular rulers. You would expect entries on such major church figures as Patrick and Columba, for example, but the only individuals actually designated as king (*rex*) are Mailcun (Maelgwyn) and Dunaut, and the Saxon ruler Edilburt (Athelbert). There is no mention of such well-attested rulers as Cadwallon or Rhun, let alone the more shadowy figures of Vortigern or Ambrosius Aurelianus. Most amazing of all, there is no mention of the domination of the Saxons. The monks may not have wanted to record the activities of pagan invaders, but it is surprising that there is no mention of Hengist or Cerdic or Aelle, names that figure strongly in Arthurian history. All of this suggests that not only were the *Annals* compiled at a later date, when the only reliable dates available to the chroniclers were a few well-remembered events in church history, but that they came from a source, such as the Irish Annals, for which these secular British events were of no interest.

With this in mind, one wonders just where the entries for Arthur and Merlin came from. Are these genuine or merely added by a later scribe who enjoyed the heroic tales? All the other entries are brief references to births, deaths and disasters, but the Arthurian and Myrddin entries are longer. The Badon entry almost feels like an echo of Germanus's Alleluia victory (which is conspicuously missing), as if there were a folk memory of some distant battle of religious significance. We will encounter a similar reference amongst the list of Arthur's battles rescued by Nennius.

I do not believe that a monk would deliberately invent a record, though I believe he could include one in good faith. The other entries are known from other records, and no one would doubt their existence. To believe that the Arthur and Merlin entries were the only fabricated ones is to suggest a conspiracy, and there is no reason to suspect that of a ninth-century annalist. However, they could have been copied from a document, now lost, which was erroneous, suggesting that both the names and the dates must be suspect.

We may accept that the *Welsh Annals* provide hearsay evidence that someone called Arthur achieved a major victory at Badon, and that another Arthur (not necessarily the same one) "fell" at the battle of Camlann. They provide similar evidence for the existence of Merlin, even though this Merlin lived over thirty years after Arthur's passing.

3. The *Anglo-Saxon Chronicle*
As with the *Welsh Annals*, there are no copies of the *Anglo-Saxon Chronicle* (*ASC*) contemporary with the fifth or sixth centuries. The oldest surviving copy, known as the Winchester Manuscript, seems to have been compiled during the reign of King Alfred, around 890, and continued by others into the tenth century. There are other variants of the *ASC*, most of much later date. As a consequence the reliability of the early entries is always open to question. It is evident that the compilers of the *ASC* drew upon other sources such as Bede for the entry for 449. Bede himself had relied heavily on Gildas for the early part of his history, so much of the *ASC* information is third-hand. Unlike the *Welsh Annals*, however, the *ASC* tends to include more complete entries, sometimes adding anecdotes not available elsewhere.

Once again I've selected records from the period 410–600, focusing on areas of importance. The translation comes primarily from Manuscript A, the oldest of the surviving versions of the *ASC*, but I've included any additional or variant data from the other versions within [square] brackets. I've kept place names in the original Saxon and show them in italics. Any brief interpretations by myself are in [*square*] brackets and italics.

418 The Romans gathered all the gold-hoards there were in Britain; some they hid in the earth, so that no man might find them, and some they took with them to Gaul.

443 The British sent men over the sea to Rome, and asked for help against the Picts, but they never got it, because [the Romans] were on an expedition against King Attila the

Hun. They sent then to the Angles, and the Anglian Aethelings, with the same request.

449 Mauricius [Martianus] and Valentinian succeeded to the kingdom and ruled seven years. And in their days Hengist and Horsa, invited by Vortigern, king of the Britons, came to Britain [in three ships] landing at the place which is named *Ypwines fleot*, at first to help the Britons, but later they fought against them. [The king Vortigern gave them land in the south-east of this land on condition that they fought against the Picts.] They did so and had victory wherever they went. They then sent to Angeln, requesting more aid, and commanded that they should be told of the Britons' worthlessness and the choice nature of their land. They soon sent hither a greater host to help the others. Then came the men of three Germanic tribes: Old Saxons; Angles; and Jutes. [. . .] Their war-leaders were two brothers, Hengist and Horsa, who were Wihtgil's sons. First of all, they killed and drove away the king's enemies; then later they turned on the king and the British, destroying through fire and the sword's edge.

455 Hengist and Horsa fought against Vortigern the king in the place which is called *Ægælesþrep*, and his brother Horsa was killed. And after that Hengist, and Æsc his son, succeeded to the kingdom.

456 Hengist and Aesc fought against the Britons in the place called *Crecganford*, and there killed 4,000 men [4 troops]; and the Britons then abandoned *Centlond* and in great fear fled to *Lundenbyrg*.

465 Hengist and Aesc fought against the Welsh [i.e. British] near *Wippedesfleot*, and there killed 12 Welsh chieftains and one of their thegns, whose name was Wipped, was killed there.

473 Hengist and Aesc fought against the Welsh and seized countless war-loot, and the Welsh fled from the English like fire.

477 Aelle and his three sons came to Britain with three ships at the place which is named *Cymenes ora*, and there killed many Welsh and drove some to flight into the wood which is named *Andredes leag*.

485 Here Aelle fought against the Welsh near the margin of *Mearcrædes burnam*.

488 Here Aesc succeeded to the kingdom and was king of the inhabitants of *Cantwara* 24 years [34 years].

491 Here Aelle and Cissa besieged *Andredes cester* and killed all who lived there; there was not even one Briton left there.

495 Here two ealdormen, Cerdic and Cynric his son, came to Britain with five ships at the place called *Cerdices ora*, and on the same day fought against the Welsh [and were victors in the end].

501 Here Port and his two sons, Bieda and Mægla came with two ships to Britain at the place which is called *Portesmuþa* [and immediately seized land] and killed a certain young British man – very noble.

508 Here Cerdic and Cynric killed a certain British king, whose name was Natanleod [Nazanleod] and five thousand men with him, after whom the land as far as *Cerdices ford* was named *Natanleag*.

514 Here the West Saxons came to Britain with three ships at the place called *Cerdices ora*, and Stuf and Wihtgar fought against the Britons and put them to flight.

519 Here Cerdic and Cynric succeeded to the kingdom of the West Saxons; and the same year they fought against the Britons at the place they now name *Cerdices ford*. And the royal family of the West Saxons ruled from that day on.

527 Here Cerdic and Cynric fought against the Britons at the place which is called *Cerdices leag*.

530 Here Cerdic and Cynric took the Isle of Wight and killed a few [many] men at *Wihtgaræsbyrg*.

534 Here Cerdic passed away and his son Cynric continued to rule 26 years; and they gave all Wight to their two *nefa [*i.e. *nephews or grandsons]* Stuf and Wihtgar.

538 Here on 16 February the sun grew dark from early morning until *undern [9.00 a.m.]*.

540 Here on 20 June the sun grew dark and the stars appeared for well-nigh half an hour after *undern*.

544 Here Wihtgar passed away and they buried him at *Wihtgaræsbyrg*.

547 Here Ida, from whom originated the royal family of the Northumbrians, succeeded to the kingdom and ruled twelve years. And he built Bamburgh which was first enclosed by a stockade and thereafter by a wall.

552 Here Cynric fought against the Britons at the place which is named *Searo byrg* and put the Britons to flight.

556 Here Cynric and Ceawlin fought against the Britons at *Beran byrg*.

560 Here Ceawlin succeeded to the kingdom in Wessex, and Aelle succeeded to the kingdom of the Northumbrians, Ida having died, and each of them ruled 30 years.

565 Here Columba the priest came from Ireland to Britain to teach the Picts, and made a monastery on the island of Iona. Here Athelberht succeeded to the kingdom of Kent and held it 53 years.

568 Here Ceawlin and Cutha [Ceawlin's brother] fought against Athelberht and drove him into Kent; and they killed two ealdormen, Oslaf [Oslac] and Cnebba, on *Wibbandun*.

571 Here Cuthwulf [Cutha] fought against the Britons at *Biedcanford* and took four settlements: *Lygeanburg* [Limbury], *Ægelsburg* [Aylesbury], *Benningtun* [Benson?], *Egonesham* [Eynsham]; and in the same year he passed away.

577 Here Cuthwine and Ceawlin fought against the Britons and they killed three kings, Coinmail, Condidan and Farinmail, in the place which is called Dyrham; and took three cities, Gloucester, Cirencester and Bath.

584 Here Ceawlin and Cutha fought against the Britons at the place which is named *Fetham leag*, and Cutha was killed; and Ceawlin took many towns and countless war-loot.

588 Here King Aelle passed away and after him Aethelric ruled for five years.

591 Here Ceol ruled for five [six] years.

592 Here there was great slaughter at *Woddes beorge* and Ceawlin was driven out. Gregory succeeded to the papacy in Rome.

593 Here Ceawlin and Cwichelm and Crida perished; and Aethelfrith succeeded to the kingdom of the Northumbrians.

595 [596] Here Pope Gregory sent Augustine to Britain with very many monks who preached God's word to the English nation.

597 Here Ceolwulf began to rule in Wessex and he continually fought and strove either against the Angle race or against the Welsh or against the Picts or against the Scots.

601 Here Pope Gregory sent the pallium to Archbishop Augustine in Britain and very many religious teachers to help him [and among them was] Paulinus who turned Edwin, king of Northumbria, to baptism.

603 Here Aedan, king of the Scots, fought with Dæl Reoda and against Aethelfrith, king of the Northumbrians, at *Dægsanstan* and they killed almost all his raiding army; [there Aethelfrith's brother, Theobald, was killed with all his troop. After that no king of the Scots dared lead a raiding army into his nation. Herin, son of Hussa, led the raiding army there.]

There is no mention of Arthur, but that is perhaps not too surprising. The Saxons liked to record their victories and ignore their defeats. It is a shame that the *Welsh Annals* are not as complete, so that we had a more adequate view of both sides of the same story, although, arguably, the two chronicles are not telling the same story. The *Welsh Annals* are primarily church history with some secular references, whilst the *ASC* concentrates on the conquest of Britain. The only events to appear in both lists are the start of Columba's mission and that of Augustine's. Fortunately, both dates agree.

If we assume, for the moment, that the dates in both chronicles are correct, then we can see that at the time of the battle of Badon in 518 Cerdic was in the thick of his conquest of what would become Wessex, establishing himself as king the following year, in 519. These two records raise a serious question. Arthurian legend has it that Arthur's victory at Badon was so complete that the Saxons had to retreat and that for at least twenty-five years there was a relative peace. The *ASC* does show this to some extent. We get a significant

increase in the West Saxon offensive from 552 onwards, and
arguably from 547 if Ida's rise to power also involved conflict,
though this was in the North. There is a gap of around thirty
years in which the *ASC* records no Saxon conquest except for
the exploits of Cerdic.

Cerdic is one of those fascinating enigmas. His name is not
Saxon but British, the same as Caradoc or Ceretic. Because of
this he is regarded as possibly a renegade British chieftain who
might have fought against Arthur, perhaps with Saxon mercenaries. Alternatively, if he came to power after Badon, he
might previously have fought on Arthur's side and benefited
subsequently with lands in Wiltshire. Some even go so far as to
suggest that Cerdic *was* Arthur. I won't go that far, but he is
crucial to fixing a date for Arthur's life.

If we look closer, the entries relating to Cerdic raise further
questions. The entry for 495 seems to duplicate that of 514,
except that Cerdic and Cynric have become Stuf and Wihtgar.
The 501 entry also appears to be a repetition of the same event,
whilst 501 and 508 also have some elements in common – the
"very noble young Briton" of 501 might be the same as the
Natanleod of 508.

It's as if there were a standard story, known to all West
Saxons: that the founder of their kingdom had arrived with his
son and fought against the British, and that places involved
with that arrival and battle are named after them.

If we look elsewhere in the *ASC* we find two further pieces
of information that help us unravel this. Not surprisingly for a
Chronicle brought together at the time of Alfred the Great, the
ASC includes a genealogy of Alfred. Manuscript A incorporated this in a "Preface", which begins by saying:

In the year when 494 winters had passed since Christ's birth,
Cerdic and Cynric his son landed at *Cerdices ora* with five
ships. [. . .] And 6 years after they landed, they conquered the
West Saxons' kingdom; and these were the first kings who
conquered the West Saxons' land from the Britons. And he held

the kingdom 16 years, and then when he departed his son
Cynric succeeded to the kingdom and held it 26 years . . .

The other surviving manuscripts for the *ASC* place this note
under the year 855, and insert the name Creoda between
Cerdic and Cynric.

This Preface tells us that Cerdic arrived "after 494 winters"
[the year 495], took six years to attain the kingdom and then
ruled for sixteen years, which brings his death to the year 517 –
just before (maybe even *at*) the battle of Badon. But let's not
jump to conclusions. In the Introduction I discuss the problems faced by annalists copying from old records in which
entries may be grouped by the Easter cycle, which repeats itself
every nineteen years.

If we look again at the near-duplicate entries for 495 and 514,
we find that these are nineteen years apart. The "Preface" to the
ASC notes that Cerdic "obtained the kingdom after six years".
519 is the sixth year after 514 (if you count the years as
inclusive), and the adjacent entries between 495 and 501 and
508 and 514 are also six years apart. There is a pattern here,
suggesting that the annalists knew certain time spans and
perhaps an end-date, but did not quite know how to get there.
Entries thus became duplicated.

The problem we have is determining which dates are
correct. We cannot know, because the only way we can
verify it is to rely further on the dates within the *ASC*. If,
for the moment, we accept that the dates closer in time to the
final compilation of the *ASC* are more likely to be accurate,
particularly in relation to the length of reigns of the later
rulers, then we can work backwards. The "Preface" lists
the rulers and years down to King Aethelwulf. His father
Egbert died in 839, a date well attested by other documents. If
we add up the total lengths of the reigns of all the West Saxon
kings from the start of Cerdic's to the end of Egbert's, we get
310 years. Deducting this from 839 gives 529 as the start of
Cerdic's reign. This clearly contradicts the entry for 534

which records Cerdic's death after, we are told, a reign of sixteen years.

This total of 310 years does not include Creoda, who is not otherwise mentioned. However, the *ASC* also gives two different reign lengths – seventeen years or thirty – for Cerdic's grandson Ceawlin. The missing thirteen years could belong to Creoda without disrupting the grand total.

At present, therefore, we have three possible dates for Cerdic's reign. The Preface states 501–517, the individual entries support 519–534, whilst the total reign lengths give 529–545. Table 12, based on the pedigrees, supports a later date, suggesting a death around 550.

It is important to confirm Cerdic's reign because of its implications for Arthurian history, but how do we resolve this problem? Various people have tackled the matter. In *The Historic King Arthur* Frank D. Reno undertook an exercise similar to mine, but added Creoda's reign, allocating him seventeen years (on the basis that Creoda's reign is wrongly assigned to Ceawlin) and resolving some other anomalies. He determined that the Preface dates of 500–516 were accurate. In "The West Saxon Genealogical Regnal List" (1985), the most detailed study of this issue, David Dumville analysed all the surviving documents of the *ASC* and other supporting data and concluded that the West Saxon regnal list had been corrupted with the purpose of pushing back the founding of the West Saxon line as far as possible. He believes that the annalists compiling the *ASC* in Alfred's time recognized this but could do little about it, so fudged the issue, which is why so many contradictions arise. He produced his version of the regnal list which has Cerdic's reign starting in 538, a date that I also used when I compiled my *Mammoth Book of British Kings & Queens* though, curiously, I arrived at it by a different method based on the Easter cycle (two cycles of nineteen years from 500). This agrees with Table 12. It also means that if the *Welsh Annals'* date for Camlann is correct then Cerdic may have benefited from the death of Arthur. This date would support a period of peace during Arthur's reign – a *Pax Arthuriana* – and may therefore suggest an end-date of 538/9. We need other evidence to confirm this, but it's something to orientate upon.

So, setting dates aside for the present, let us reflect on what the *ASC* tells us. We learn that the Britons first appealed to Rome for help against the Picts, and, when that was not forthcoming, turned to the Angles for help. There seems to be a distinction between this first appeal and that of Vortigern six years later, though this frequent leaping of six years is further evidence of uncertainty. Following Vortigern's invitation, the Angles arrived, led by Hengist and Horsa, and in payment for fighting the Picts Vortigern gave them land in the "south-east". This is usually interpreted as being in Kent, more specifically the Isle of Thanet, but this is not necessarily accurate. I explore this in more detail in Chapter 6.

Hengist and Horsa were successful and brought more mercenaries over, comprising Saxons, Angles and Jutes. Trouble brewed, Hengist and Horsa fought against Vortigern, and the British were defeated, fleeing to *Lundenbyrg* (usually interpreted as London but more on that later). A series of conflicts now occurred, spread over several years, whilst further waves of Saxons arrived, including those led by Aelle and Cerdic. The Saxon victories were not decisive and, as mentioned above, apart from the Cerdic anomaly, the Saxons made no further significant advances until after 547, but from then on the writing was on the wall, especially following the victories of 571, 577 and 584. It is evident from this that Arthur's victorious days must have been before 547, to allow for his twenty-one years (or more) of peace. Even though these dates remain suspect, they do not contradict the *Welsh Annals'* dates of 518 for Badon and 539 for Camlann. In fact they fit into the sequence rather neatly, especially if we have resolved the Cerdic question.

One other date from this period is worthy of further thought. The entry for 540 refers to the sun growing dark, as does the entry for 538. These could simply refer to solar eclipses. Chroniclers frequently record eclipses and they are very useful for confirming dates, as eclipses can be precisely calculated. Unfortunately there was no solar eclipse in 538 or 540 visible from Britain.* However, research has shown that these records refer to something far more significant. David Keys, in *Catastrophe*, has demonstrated that the decade starting in 535 saw the consequences of a worldwide catastrophe, with cold summers, freezing winters, crop failures and plague. It is recorded in virtually every ancient civilization. He believes the cause was a volcanic eruption in 535, pointing the finger at Krakatoa. Mike Baillie, however, in *Exodus to Arthur*, is more convinced that the disaster arose following a near collision with a comet, resulting in cometary debris in the atmosphere.

Whatever the cause, it remains clear that there was a major catastrophe, maybe two, that led to a decade or more of suffering, a scenario which sounds remarkably like the Waste Land of Arthurian legend. Moreover, Keys notes that "great natural catastrophes often induce political instability, administrative dislocation and the consequential collapse of regular record keeping in affected societies". Be it a comet or volcano, it could well have been a disaster such as this that tipped the balance in Britain after 540, with the battle-hardened Saxons taking the upper hand, being better able to endure the plague and pestilence than the now weakened Romano-British.

A period for Arthur's "reign" between 516 and 539 seems to be appearing, but we have a long way to go, and the comparative simplicity of the above is about to become very complicated.

---

* See Williams, Sheridan, *UK Solar Eclipses from Year 1 to 3000* (Clock Tower Press, 1996).

5

GILDAS – THE MAN
WHO KNEW ARTHUR

1. Gildas

We have already encountered Gildas via the *Welsh Annals*. The year 565 lists his voyage to Ireland and his death is recorded under the year 572. Whether these dates are correct is something we'll need to consider. Gildas's writings are perhaps the most important in relation to the authenticity of Arthur, and yet they are annoyingly vague and obtuse.

We know few genuine facts about Gildas. His life became the subject of two books, one by a monk of Rhuys in Brittany, where Gildas is believed to have died, and another by Caradog of Llancarfan. The first was written at least five hundred years after Gildas's death and the second another sixty years or so after that. What's more, Caradog was a close friend of Geoffrey of Monmouth, so the fact that Arthur features prominently in Caradog's *Life of Gildas* and not once in the earlier biography, speaks for itself.

The two biographies have only a few events in common. According to these sources, Gildas was born in Alclud

(Dumbarton), one of the many children of Caw or Caius, who was probably a Romano-British official. When he was born is crucial, in fact the most important date in all Arthurian studies, as we shall see. In his youth in South Wales, Gildas studied under Illtud, whom legend makes a cousin of King Arthur. Gildas also studied in Ireland. According to Caradog, while Gildas was in Ireland several of his brothers rebelled against Arthur. During the confrontation, Arthur killed one of the brothers, Huail, leading to a rift between Arthur and Gildas, although they later made peace. Later, Gildas apparently travelled to Rome, and lived in Brittany for several years, where he probably died.

The many tales about Gildas have led some to believe that there were at least two people of this name, Gildas son of Caw, and the Gildas who wrote *De Excidio Britanniae* (*The Ruin of Britain*), but this only confuses the issue. It may, though, explain why the *Welsh Annals* chose to describe him as Gildas the Wise, as if to distinguish him from another, but we may simply accept that as an endearment written by one who knew him.

What makes Gildas important is that his writings, principally *De Excidio*, are the only works that survive from the sixth century, providing a first-hand witness to the events of the preceding fifty years, the period, if the *Welsh Annals* are correct, when Arthur was alive. In other words, here is a book by someone who would certainly have known Arthur, or known of him. However, Gildas chose not to write about Arthur. And although his work does include a history of Britain, it was not Gildas's intention to write a history. *De Excidio* takes the form of a very long letter, most of which is filled with complaints about the church and about the wicked rulers of Britain. Gildas believed that the fate of Britain at the hands of the Saxons was directly due to the corruptness of the British, their laziness and inability to fight for themselves. It was a sentiment picked up by the *ASC*, which refers to the "worthlessness of the Britons" (year 449). Gildas was thus something of a Jeremiah, bewailing the fate of the British, and quoting events and scriptures as appropriate to make his case. He worries little about dates or historical characters, which is what makes his *De Excidio* so infuriating. Here was the one man who could have told us exactly what happened, but instead he chose to moan – probably from the safety of Brittany – about the corruptness of the British.

2. *De Excidio*

Despite his moaning, as the lone voice from that time we must pay attention to what he says. I won't quote *De Excidio* in full, but will refer to the relevant sections set after the fall of Roman authority in Britain and will also quote his complaints against the British kings who were his contemporaries. Hidden in the following should be further clues about Arthur, provided we can find them.

In Sections (§) 18 and 19 Gildas provides a graphic picture of the horrors of Britain after the Romans left. He gives the impression that before the Romans departed they did what they could to improve the island's defences and train the people. He seems to believe that the Wall (presumably Hadrian's) was built at this time, rather than nearly 300 years earlier, which shows how poor the surviving records in Britain were. He may be recounting a memory of the strengthening of the Wall during the fourth-century struggle with the Picts. He also refers to the Saxon shore defensive forts, and he may be remembering other defences built at this time, such as the Wansdyke in Somerset and Wiltshire, which dates from the mid-fifth century.

He tells us that the British forces were "too lazy to fight and too unwieldy to flee". The men were apparently "foolish and frightened", and they "sat about day and night rotting away in their folly". Leaving aside Gildas's hyperbole, his comments could support the problem Germanus had faced of a wealthy country where the people were unprepared for the horrors to come. And come they did. He talks of the "foul hordes" of

Scots and Picts who massacred the British. Death was apparently preferable to the "miserable fate" (possibly slavery) of those that were snatched away. St Patrick became a victim of the slave trade (probably in the 440s, though some say the 470s). He wrote to Ceretic (usually treated as the ruler of Alclud), complaining about the slave trade between Ireland and Britain, which had clearly been prevalent for many years.

At the end of §19 Gildas tells us:*

Our citizens abandoned the towns and the high wall. Once again they had to flee; once again they were scattered, more irretrievably than usual; once again there were enemy assaults and massacres more cruel. The pitiable citizens were torn apart by their foe like lambs by the butcher; their life became like that of beasts of the field. For they resorted to looting each other, there being only a tiny amount of food to give brief sustenance to the wretched people; and the disasters from abroad were increased by internal disorders, for as a result of constant devastations of this kind the whole region came to lack the staff of food, apart from any such comfort as the art of the huntsman could procure for them.

§ 20. So the miserable remnants sent off a letter again, this time to the Roman commander Agitius, in the following terms: "To Agitius, thrice consul: the groans of the British." Later came this complaint: "The barbarians push us back to the sea, the sea pushes us back to the barbarians; between these two kinds of death we are either drowned or slaughtered." But they got no help in return. Meanwhile, as the British feebly wandered, a dreadful and notorious famine gripped them, forcing many of them to give in without delay to their bloody plunderers, merely to get a scrap of food to revive them. Not so others: they kept fighting back, basing themselves on the mountains, in caves, heaths and thorny thickets. Their enemies had been plundering their land for many years: now for the first time

---

* All excerpts from Gildas are adapted by the author from previous translations by J.A. Giles (1891) and Hugh Williams (1901).

they inflicted a massacre on *them*, trusting not in man but in God, for, as Philo says, "when human help fails, we need the help of God". For a little while their enemies' audacity ceased, but not our people's wickedness. The enemy retreated from the people, but the people did not retreat from their own sins.

§ 21. It was always true of this people that it was weak in beating off the weapons of the enemy but strong in putting up with civil war and the burden of sin: weak, I repeat, in following the banners of peace and truth, but strong for crime and falsehood. So the impudent Irish pirates returned home (though they were shortly to return); and for the first time the Picts in the far end of the island kept quiet from now on, though they occasionally carried out devastating raids or plunder. So, in this period of truce the desolate people found their cruel scars healing over. But a new and more virulent famine was quietly sprouting. In the respite from devastation the island was so flooded with abundance of goods that no previous age had known the like of it. Alongside there grew luxury. It grew with a vigorous growth, so that to that time were fitly applied the words: "There are actually reports of such fornication as is not known even among the Gentiles."

Up until now Gildas has only been telling us about the onslaught of the Picts and Scots, and that after an appeal to Rome, which brought no help, some of the British fought back. They inflicted such a "massacre" that there was a respite. The Picts and Irish went "home". Now Britain prospered, and there was an abundance of wealth, as Germanus witnessed. But with it came civil war:

Kings were anointed not in God's name, but as being crueller than the rest; before long, they would be killed, with no enquiry into the truth, by those who had anointed them, and others still crueller chosen to replace them. Any king who seemed gentler and rather more inclined to the truth was regarded as the downfall of Britain: everyone directed their hatred and their weapons at him, with no respect.

Amidst this political strife Gildas tells us that rumours reached the British of "the imminent approach of the old enemy, bent on total destruction and (as was their wont) on settlement from one end of the country to the other". Yet the British did nothing and, as if by way of punishment:

§22 [. . .] . . . a deadly plague swooped brutally on the stupid people and in a short period laid low so many, with no sword, that the living could not bury all the dead. But not even this taught them their lesson . . .

Gildas emphasizes how hopeless the British were and how that sealed their fate. Now he comes to the crucial part:

§22 [. . .] And they convened a Council to decide the best and soundest way to counter the brutal and repeated invasions and plunderings by the people I have mentioned.

§23. Then all the members of the Council, together with the *superbo tyranno* "proud tyrant", were struck blind. As protection for our country, they sealed its doom by inviting in among them, like wolves into a sheep-fold, the ferocious Saxons, hated by man and God, to beat back the peoples of the North. Nothing more destructive, nothing more bitter has ever befallen the land. How utter the blindness of their minds. How desperate and crass the stupidity. Of their own free will they invited under the same roof a people whom they feared worse than death even in their absence.

Then a pack of cubs burst forth from the lair of the barbarian lioness, coming in three keels, as they call warships in their language. The winds were favourable; favourable too the omens and auguries which prophesied, according to a sure portent among them, that they would live for three hundred years in the land towards which their prows were directed and that for half that time, a hundred and fifty years, they would repeatedly lay it waste. On the orders of the ill-fated tyrant they first of all fixed their dreadful claws on the east side of the island, ostensibly to fight for our country, in fact to fight against it. The mother lioness learned that her first contingent had prospered and she sent a second and larger troop of satellite dogs. It arrived by ship and joined up with the false units. [. . .] The barbarians who had been admitted to the island asked to be given supplies, falsely representing themselves as soldiers ready to undergo extreme dangers for their excellent hosts. The supplies were granted and, for a long time, "shut the dog's mouth". Then they again complained that their monthly allowance was insufficient, purposely giving a false colour to individual incidents, and swore that they would break their agreement and plunder the whole island unless more lavish payment was heaped upon them. There was no delay: they put their threats into immediate effect.

§24. In just punishment for the crimes that had gone before, a fire heaped up and, nurtured by the hand of the impious easterners, spread from sea to sea. It devastated town and country round about and, once it was alight, it did not die down until it had burned almost the whole surface of the island and was licking the western ocean with its fierce red tongue. [. . .] All the major towns were laid low by the repeated battering of enemy rams, laid low too all the inhabitants – church leaders, priests and people alike – as the swords glinted all around and the flames crackled. It was a sad sight. In the middle of the squares the foundation-stones of high walls and towers that had been torn from their lofty base, holy altars, fragments of corpses covered with a purple crust of congealed blood, looked as though they had been mixed up in some dreadful wine press. There was no burial to be had except in the ruins of houses or the bellies of beasts and birds – [. . .].

§25. So a number of the wretched survivors were caught in the mountains and butchered wholesale. Others, their spirit broken by hunger, went to surrender to the enemy; they were fated to be slaves forever, if indeed they were not killed straight away, the highest boon. Others made for lands beyond the sea [. . .]. Others held out, though not without fear, in their own land, trusting their lives with constant foreboding to the high hills, [. . .] to the densest forests and to the cliffs of the sea coast.

After a time, when the cruel plunderers had gone home, God gave strength to the survivors. Wretched people fled to them from all directions, as eagerly as bees to the beehive when a storm threatens, and begged whole-heartedly that they should not be altogether destroyed. Their leader was Ambrosius Aurelianus, a gentleman who, perhaps alone of the Romans, had survived the shock of this notable storm: his parents, who had certainly worn the purple, were slain in it. His descendants in our day have become greatly inferior to their grandfather's excellence. Under him our people regained their strength, and challenged the victors to battle. The Lord assented and the battle went their way.

§26. From then on, victory went now to our countrymen, now to their enemies, so that in this people the Lord could make trial of his latter-day Israel to see whether it loved him or not. This lasted right up to the year of the siege of Badon Hill, pretty well the last defeat of the villains, and certainly not the least. That was the year of my birth; as I know, one month of the forty-fourth year since then has already passed.

But the cities of our land are not populated even now as they once were; right to the present they are deserted, in ruins and unkempt. External wars may have stopped, but not civil ones. For the remembrance of so desperate a blow to the island and of such unlooked for recovery stuck in the minds of those who witnessed both wonders. That was why kings, public and private persons, priests and churchmen, kept to their own stations. But they died; and an age succeeded them that is ignorant of that storm and has experience only of the calm of the present.

At this point Gildas launches into his tirade against the present-day kings, but before considering that, let us reflect upon what Gildas has told us so far. It's wrapped up in hyperbole, but tucked away in these nine sections is a history, and most of it we can match to the chronicles already noted.

The start of §20 is a rare moment when Gildas gives us the opportunity to verify a date. He refers to a letter written to the Roman commander Agitius, referring to him as "thrice consul".

Although Agitius would more accurately translate as Aegidius, most historians believe that Gildas meant Aëtius, who did indeed hold the consulship three times. In fact, he was the only Roman (excluding emperors) to have done so for over three hundred years. Aegidius (d. 464), on the other hand, was never consul. He was a Roman general, who was appointed the *magister militum* of northern Gaul by the Western Roman emperor Avitus in 457, and later became king of the Franks, establishing a small kingdom around Soissons.

Aëtius became consul for the third and fourth times in 446 and 453, so the letter, if Gildas remembered it correctly, had to be written between 446 and 452. The *ASC* records this as happening in 443, and notes that the Romans were coping with Attila the Hun and thus could not help the British. In fact the first major confrontation between Aëtius and Attila was in 451, which could be the date the letter was sent.

As Gildas quotes from the letter, it is possible that a copy may have survived to his day, although of course it's easy to reconstruct an apparent text from hearsay. This means that the previous section, concerning the conflict with the Picts and Scots, covers a period of over thirty years, from 410 to at least 446AD.

Even when we get to the letter to Aëtius, an apparent moment of certainty instantly becomes uncertain. Gildas tells us that no help came from the Romans and that a famine descended upon Britain until at last the British fought back and achieved a major victory. At this stage, Gildas is still referring to the Picts and Scots, not the Saxons.

The period 446 to 454 seems a bit short for the British to weaken, lapse into famine, fight back against the Picts and Scots and, as we learn in §21, become "flooded with abundance". Evidently Gildas has become confused again. The British may well have written to Aëtius in 446 or soon after, but that would almost certainly be in relation to the Saxon incursions. The victory over the Picts and Scots is more likely to be the Alleluia victory of Germanus. Gildas, bewailing the wretched-

ness of the British in §19, is recalling the decline into Pelagianism, and the appeal he refers to in §20 was probably the one to
the church leaders in Gaul that resulted in Germanus's visit
to Britain. It is noticeable that when Constantius referred to
Germanus's second visit, he described Britain as a "wealthy
island", precisely as Gildas recalls it here. What probably
happened was that Gildas knew of the appeal to Aëtius, but
confused it with the earlier appeal, so that the events in §19
really relate to 410–429, a far more probable period, whilst §20
and §21 relate to 429–446, or perhaps 441. The *Gallic Chronicle*
had referred to Britain "yielding to the power of the Saxons" in
441. This is close enough to 446 (though one might hope it
could have been closer) to suggest that from the late 430s the
Germanic incursions had grown stronger, and that by 441,
insofar as was apparent to the chronicler in southern Gaul, the
Saxons had taken hold of Britain.

This would also explain why the British should write to
Aëtius. After all, if they had been independent of Rome for
thirty years, why should they suddenly write to a Roman
commander and expect help? Admittedly they got none,
perhaps a sign that Rome had no further hold on Britain. It
seems to confirm what I suggested earlier, that Britain was not
really "expelled" in 410, but that Honorius and the empire
simply had rather too much to contend with. Technically
Britain remained in the empire, appointing their own officials,
but by 441–446 those final slender threads were cut. Aëtius sent
no help, the Saxons were overrunning Britain, and Britain now
regarded itself as independent. This would explain why, in §21,
Britain anoints "kings". Evidently the turnover was rapid as
"before long they would be killed".

Once again, Gildas is probably recording a tradition of a
great number of petty rulers, suggesting that by the 440s the
old provincial boundaries had broken down. The British,
fleeing from the Saxons, had taken refuge in the mountains.
The archaeology shows a resettling of a number of ancient hill
forts, mostly in the west and south.

In Gildas's eyes all kings were usurpers, hence his term "tyrants". There was a particular outbreak of them from the 440s onwards, once the first generation of leftover Romans, like Ambrosius, had died out.

In §21, therefore, Gildas records his account of the rise of a series of lawless usurper kings, whose successors are to become the subject of his later condemnation. This is the central point of *De Excidio*, namely that this lawlessness was to be punished by God and the form of that punishment is shown in §22 with the return of the "old enemy", the Picts and Scots. Gildas tells us that the British did not learn from the return of these enemies but continued to sink into further corruption until laid low by a plague. Europe was regularly devastated by plagues during the fifth and sixth centuries, and although there is not a specific record of one in Britain around this time, it is known that in 452 the Huns were struck by plague, one which could have spread to Britain.

In §23 Gildas refers to the most crass decision the British could have made. The Council, "together with the *superbo tyranno*", chose to seek help from the Saxons to fight the Picts. This is recorded in the *ASC* as happening sometime between 449 and 455, which ties in with 451–452 suggested above. Gildas does not name his "proud tyrant", but the *ASC* tells us it was Vortigern, so it's likely that's who he meant. The name Vortigern means "supreme king", and Gildas's *superbo tyranno* is a pun on that. Nennius (*see* Chapter 6) has much more to say about Vortigern, so I shall save my comments about him until then.

Gildas reports that the Saxons soon turned upon the British, and those Britons who were not enslaved retreated into the mountains or fled abroad. There was another wave of refugees from Britain to Armorica about this time. It is about now that records note the mysterious character of Riothamus, a "king of the Britons" fighting in Gaul, and who has been suggested as another candidate for Arthur (*see* Chapter 6). Gildas paints a desolate picture of abandoned Roman towns and the British hiding in their hill forts, cut down wherever they met the Saxons. The archaeological record also shows that many Romano-British cities were deserted by this time. Only St Albans, Wroxeter, Silchester, Chester, Gloucester, London and Caernarvon show signs not only of continued occupation, but also of new development. It also shows that several pre-Roman hill forts were reoccupied, the major ones being South Cadbury, Cadbury-Congresbury, Glastonbury, Tintagel, Deganwy, Dinas Emrys, Dinas Powys, Dumbarton and the Mote of Mark.

Interestingly, in §25 Gildas comments, "after a time, when the cruel plunderers had gone home . . .", the implication being that this wave of Saxon invaders was out for plunder and not for settlement. The *ASC* makes no reference to the Saxons returning home, but does state that they sent for reinforcements, after which successive waves of Saxons invaded Britain over the next sixty years. But then perhaps the *ASC* would not want to record a retreat. There are sufficient gaps in the years to allow a return, such as between 456 and 465. There is something a little suspicious about the *ASC*'s record of events from 449 to 477. It drags on too long. For a period of twenty-eight years we only learn about Hengist and his son fighting the Britons, or the Welsh. In fact the change in terminology from Britons (456) to Welsh (465) itself gives pause for thought. The Saxons began to call them the Welsh, or *Welisc* (later *Wealhas*), meaning "foreigners", which is rather audacious for an invader. (The British, incidentally, called the Saxons the *Sais*, which in Gaelic became *Sasunnach*, or Sassenach.)

It is as if the records after 465 come from a genuine Saxon source whereas the earlier entries were derived from a British, or at least non-Saxon, source. Could it be that the later chroniclers were embarrassed by a gap in the record from, say, 456 to 477, and so pushed back some events to fill the gap? They could not push back entries relating to Aelle or Cerdic, but they could add extra events for Hengist, or extend the time during which he really was in Britain. The events recorded against 465 and 473 may have taken place in the late 450s, after which the majority of the "plunderers" returned to Saxony and Angeln. The British were able to regroup under a new leader and drive the Saxons back to their settlements along the east coast. For a time, until around 477, the British could breathe again.

Gildas is discussing a period that would have been remembered clearly by his parents, certainly his grandparents, and be well known amongst the older churchmen with whom Gildas associated. Although his history may be weak on the events and chronology of a century earlier, there is no reason for him to get more recent history wrong. We therefore have to accept that perhaps during the early 460s most of the Saxon marauders returned home (presumably to Germany, though by "home" Gildas may mean the Saxon settlements along the east coast), allowing the British to regain control. This was when Britain rallied under a new leader.

And who was the new leader who rallied the British? For once Gildas names him, and it isn't Arthur. It's a man whom Gildas clearly reveres, Ambrosius Aurelianus. Gildas calls him a "gentleman" and refers to him as a *"duce"*, a senior official. What's more, his parents, who had been slain during the hostilities, had "worn the purple". Gildas really does mean "parents", not forebears, as he refers to their deaths during the recent hostilities. Ambrosius's father may not have literally worn the purple, in terms of the rank denoted by his toga, but the phrase itself would certainly have meant that he had held a very senior position. In the later Roman Empire consuls were also allowed to wear the purple, usually a purple-fringed toga. In the previous chapter I referred to the *Notitia Dignitatum*, a catalogue of official posts which was still valid at the time of Britain's "departure" from the empire. This listed the four or five provinces of Britain, two of which had governors of consular rank, Maxima Caesariensis, based on London, and the mysterious Valentia. We do not know the name of the consular governors in Britain at the start of the fifth century, so it is entirely possible that one might have been Ambrosius's father.

Incidentally, it is worth noting here that the venerable Ambrose (339–397), Bishop of Milan, later canonized as St Ambrose, was himself a consular governor in Italy, based at Milan. His father, who was the Praetorian Prefect of Gaul, at Arles, and to whom the *vicarius* of Britain reported, was also called Ambrosius Aurelianus. He was descended from a notable senatorial family possibly related to the emperor Aurelian (215–275), one of the more successful emperors of his day, who earned the title *Restitutor Orbis* ("Restorer of the World") for reuniting the empire in 274AD. If Gildas's Ambrosius Aurelianus could count these amongst his antecedents and be the son of a consular governor, no wonder Gildas emphasized his name, and regarded him as special.

So, if my deductions are correct §25 of Gildas would seem to take place during the 470s when Ambrosius led the British in a series of battles against the Saxons, which eventually led to the momentous victory at Badon. This was the battle recorded in the *Welsh Annals* as the "victory of Arthur" in 518. It does seem a little surprising that, having named Ambrosius and sung his praises, Gildas chooses not to name Arthur, whose victory over the Saxons he describes as "pretty well the last defeat of the villains and certainly not the least". Gildas does not mention Arthur anywhere in *De Excidio*. Why not?

There are at least six possible reasons:

(1) Arthur didn't exist. We have to consider that the reference in the *Welsh Annals* might have been added by a later chronicler, based on the growing Arthurian legend, and that the victor was someone else, possibly Ambrosius himself.

(2) Gildas had no need to mention Arthur. As we have seen, Gildas does not mention many names at all, not even Vortigern's. He mentions Ambrosius Aurelianus because he was clearly one of Gildas's heroes, the man who turned the tide against the Saxons during Britain's darkest days.

(3) Arthur's name was superfluous. Gildas is referring to events within living memory, only forty-three years in the past.

If Badon was such a glorious victory, everyone would remember who the victor was.

(4) Gildas disliked Arthur and did not want to glorify him. If Caradog's life of Gildas has any basis of truth, Arthur was responsible for the death of Gildas's brother Huail. Whilst having to admit that Badon was a crucial victory, he did not see fit to go further and name him as the victor. It's even possible that Arthur is named, but as one of the "tyrants" Gildas later castigates. He would not want to praise him whilst also vilifying him.

(5) Arthur was not yet born. It could be that the real Arthur, to whom the various legends and triumphs became attached, lived later than the time Gildas was writing. Someone else was the victor at Badon, but Arthur was retrospectively given the credit.

(6) Gildas did not know who the victor was. This seems the unlikeliest of reasons, but although Arthur seems such a major character to us today, he may not have been in Gildas's day. His legend had yet to grow, and despite the triumph of Badon, the victor's name may not have been that well remembered.

Whatever the reason, Gildas's omission of Arthur's name is not proof that Arthur did not exist, but the onus is on us to find that proof elsewhere.

Gildas's account tells us that the siege of Badon happened in the year of his birth, forty-three years and one month before the time of writing. Such precision, so unusual for Gildas, might have helped us date Badon and provide corroboration for the year 518 in the *Welsh Annals*. Unfortunately, we don't know when Gildas wrote *De Excidio*.

There are, however, clues within *De Excidio* itself. Most telling is the final paragraph quoted from §26, in which he refers to the "calm of the present". He is writing in a time when external wars have stopped, and a whole generation has grown up that is now ignorant of the "storm" with the Saxons. He makes no mention of plague or famine, and yet if the evidence presented by David Keys in *Catastrophe* and Mike Baillie in

Exodus to Arthur is true – and there is no reason to doubt it – from 535 onwards Britain was subject to bitterly cold winters and summers. A plague swept through Europe during the 540s, one of the worst ever. Had Gildas experienced this at the time of writing *De Excidio* there is little doubt that he would have referred to it, because it was further support for his argument – another punishment from God for the wicked ways of the kings. This suggests that Gildas must have written *De Excidio* before 540, possibly even before 535. If so, then forty-three years earlier would place Badon at 492–497 at the latest, suggesting that the entry in the *Welsh Annals* is wrong. The gap from 497 to 518 is twenty-one years, and we have seen already that later annalists, copying from earlier documents, may have confused entries dated only by Easter cycles of nineteen years.

A date of 497 for Badon is more consistent with Gildas's narrative. We deduced earlier that Ambrosius led the resistance to the Saxons during the 470s, and Gildas tells us that victories went both ways until the time of Badon. If Badon took place in 518, then the Saxon war continued for some forty years. Not impossible, of course, but Gildas's narrative does not suggest that long a period. Also, in §25, Gildas remarks that Ambrosius's descendants "in our day" were greatly inferior to their "grandfather's" excellence. He would not have used the term "grandfather" unless he genuinely meant two generations. This gives us some 60 years from the 470s, which brings us to the 530s. On this basis *De Excidio* was written in the mid- to late 530s; thus Gildas was born in the early 490s, placing Badon between 492 and 497.

An alternative translation of Gildas §26 by Bede appeared in his *Ecclesiastical History of the English People*, completed in 731. Bede's research was impeccable, his understanding of Latin first-class and, living just two centuries after Gildas, he was close enough to have had access to an original or early copy of Gildas's work, one less prone to error. The following extract, from Chapter 16 of Bede's *History*, is clearly lifted from Gildas:

When the army of the enemy had exterminated or scattered the native peoples, they returned home and the Britons slowly began to recover strength and courage. They emerged from their hiding places and with one accord they prayed for the help of God that they might not be completely annihilated. Their leader at that time was a certain Ambrosius Aurelianus, a discreet man, who was, as it happened, the sole member of the Roman race who had survived this storm in which his parents, who bore a royal and famous name, had perished. Under his leadership the Britons regained their strength, challenged their victors to battle and, with God's help, won the day. From that time on, first the Britons won and then the enemy were victorious until the year of the siege of Mount Badon, when the Britons slaughtered no small number of their foes about forty-four years after their arrival in Britain.

Bede has read Gildas's reckoning of forty-three years and one month as being from the arrival of the Saxons, the so-called Saxon *adventus*, and not related to Gildas's birth at all. Bede actually gives a year for the *adventus*, 449, a date later adopted by the *ASC*. This gives us a date of 492–493 for Badon which, remarkably, fits into the time frame cited above.

If Arthur was the battle leader at Badon, and not someone simply added by an overzealous annalist, then he was in his heyday at the end of the fifth century. And, if the *Welsh Annals* have the date for Badon wrong, then the date for Camlann may also be out by the same degree. Instead of 539 it could have been during the 510s, certainly no later than the year 520. However, we must not assume that the victor of Badon and the victim of Camlann are the same "Arthur", and thus the *Annals* entry for Camlann might still be accurate.

There is one other reference in this first part of Gildas's work which is easily overlooked, but which will prove crucial to our later research. In his earlier discussion about Britain under the Roman Empire, he refers to Britain's martyrs: "St Alban of Verulam, Aaron and Julius, citizens of the City of the Legions, and the others of both sexes who, in different places, displayed the highest spirit in the battle-line of Christ". In referring to their shrines, Gildas says, in §10:

> Their graves and the places where they suffered would now have the greatest effect in instilling the blaze of divine charity in the minds of beholders, were it not that our citizens, thanks to our sins, have been deprived of many of them by the unhappy partition with the barbarians.

In other words, in the time that Gildas was writing, the mid- to late 530s, there was a partition between the British and the Saxons which denied the British access to these sites. These shrines must have been in the east, because we know from both written and archaeological records that the Saxons had not advanced far to the west by this time. Verulam (St Albans) was north-west of London. The City of the Legions, as we will discuss in Chapter 7, could apply to at least three sites, but as two of those, Caerleon and Chester, were in the west, Gildas must have meant York. York was part of the Angle kingdom of Deira, later part of Northumbria, and Nennius tells us (*see* Chapter 6) that the start of this Saxon colony was in the mid-fifth century under Soemil. By Gildas's time presumably Yffi, father of Aelle, was established as the ruler.

The two big questions are where this partition ran and when it came into being. Fitting York into the division is less of a problem than St Albans. It is known that there were significant British enclaves in both London and St Albans throughout most of the fifth century, with no evident Saxon infiltration until the late sixth century. The battle of *Biedcanford* entered in the *ASC* for 571 shows that Cuthwulf succeeded in capturing the towns of Limbury, Aylesbury, Benson and Eynsham. If those locations are correct, then Cuthwulf captured a small British kingdom known as Calchvynydd, usually treated as covering the Chilterns, mostly Bedfordshire and Oxfordshire (*see* Map 1). Limbury, now part of Luton, was within 20km of St Albans, suggesting that St Albans must have been right on this frontier. The resident population may have remained primarily British, hence the archaeological evidence, but under Saxon control, hence the access problem.

Normally one might expect divisions to be decided by rivers, but few rivers in eastern England flow north–south. However, there is another obvious boundary. The Roman road of Dere Street ran from the eastern end of the Antonine Wall, past Hadrian's Wall near Corbridge, continuing just west of York and on to Lincoln. From there, now renamed Ermine Street, it ran direct to London. A confluence of roads there allows a switch along the Lower Icknield Way to St Albans, and from there south, skirting London to the west and terminating, presumably, at the Thames (*see* Map 3).

This boundary, which follows the route of today's A1 trunk road, would contain all the nascent Anglo-Saxon settlements along the east coast. The kingdom of Kent, tucked away at that time in the far south-east of the island, was to a large extent separated by the natural boundary of the Weald.

The boundary may have run slightly to the west of these roads but there is little evidence to suggest any significant Anglo-Saxon settlement further west than around Leicester or Rugby in the Midlands, so that the boundary may have followed part of Watling Street and the Fosse Way. Such a boundary was sufficiently far away from the border of Britannia Prima to feel "safe" yet still close enough for Saxon and Angle armies to have harried the British during any pre-Badon battle campaign.

As to when, the obvious answer must be the battle of Badon. That victory allowed the British to contain the Saxons within a fixed area, just as Alfred's victory over the Danes resulted in the same division, the Danelaw, four centuries later.

We will return to this partition in Chapter 7.

2. The tyrants

We have not yet finished with Gildas. Having presented us with his understanding of the history of Britain, he then launches into an attack on five kings whom he sees as wicked and the enemies of God. I will not transcribe these in full, colourful though they are, as his lengthy condemnation of their lives and actions adds little to our quest for Arthur. But there are some factors that are relevant.

"Britain has kings, but they are tyrants," Gildas begins (in §27). The first he castigates is Constantine, "tyrant whelp of the filthy lioness of Dumnonia" (§28). Constantine is evidently alive at this time, as Gildas writes: "This same year after taking a dreadful oath not to work his wiles on our countrymen . . . he nevertheless, garbed in the habit of a holy abbot, most cruelly tore the tender sides of two royal children and their two guardians." Constantine apparently killed these children in a church, with sword and spear, whilst they clung to the altar. Gildas also accuses Constantine of adultery and sodomy. Constantine appears in the Arthurian story as Arthur's appointed successor, and he is described as the son of Cador, Duke of Cornwall. Dumnonia was the Celtic kingdom in south-west Britain, including Cornwall and Devon, although just to add to the confusion it was also the name of a province in Brittany. When Gildas states that Constantine had sworn not to act against "our countrymen", he could be talking about the men of Brittany. However, this Constantine does not feature in the Welsh pedigrees and thus is not in Table 11, although he would be a contemporary of Geraint and Mark.

Geoffrey of Monmouth repeats this story, making the princes that Constantine kills the sons of Mordred. This happened soon after the battle of Camlann, which, as Gildas tells us, had happened only within the last year. If Gildas was writing in the period 535–540, perhaps Camlann's date really was 539, and not subject to the nineteen–year error. This heightens the idea of an Arthurian Golden Age lasting from 500 to 540. Gildas seems to support this as in §26 he speaks of the "calm of the Present" and of "an age" ignorant of past violence. This seems more like forty years than twenty.

*   *   *

The next king to be excoriated by Gildas is Aurelius Caninus, who, according to Geoffrey, later murdered Constantine. Gildas states that Caninus is "engulfed by the same slime" as Constantine, and accuses him of "parricide, fornications, adulteries" and of being a warmonger (§30), but does not say where he ruled. Some authorities have equated him with Cynan Garwyn (Cynan of the White Chariot, or Cynan the Cruel), a prince of Powys who was noted for his battles. However, this Cynan ruled towards the end of the sixth century and would not be a contemporary of Gildas. There is also no indication that Cynan Garwyn killed his father, the famous Brochwel of the Tusks. Another Cynan appears in the genealogies, five generations in descent from Vortigern, but he was a contemporary of Cynan Garwyn and was thus unlikely to have been born when Gildas was writing.

The name Caninus is more likely an epithet applied by Gildas. He was fond of nicknames, calling all of the kings he identified after animals. "Caninus", or "little dog", would mean "the whelp", and the king's name was therefore Aurelius, suggesting that he may have been one of the grandchildren of Ambrosius Aurelianus, whom Gildas had described as "greatly inferior" to their forebear. If this is so, the father that Aurelius Caninus killed was either Ambrosius's son or son-in-law. Such an action would be sure to raise Gildas's wrath.

Aurelius may not have inherited a kingdom, but usurped one through murder. If so, this is likely to have been in the south, possibly in the Severn Valley.

It's possible that Caninus is the same as Conmor, sometimes called Comorus, or Conomorus, the ruler of Leon in Armorica and later usurper of the whole territory. Conmor had killed the ruler, Ionas, forcibly married Ionas's widow, and imprisoned their son, Iudwal. Conmor was an exact contemporary of Gildas – indeed the usurpation had happened while Gildas was deliberating over writing *De Excidio* (he put it off for ten years). Conmor is sometimes identified with Mark (or March), a king of Dumnonia associated with the Tristan legend. This may explain Gildas's remark than Caninus was "engulfed by the same slime", meaning that Caninus and Constantine ruled in the same territory. Interestingly, Conmor called for a holy man, Paul, a pupil of Illtud, to spread the Christian faith through Brittany. This Paul is called Paul Aurelian, and though the epithet is believed by some to refer to the fact that Paul's remains were later moved to Orleans, it is possible that Paul was related to the Aurelian family.

The next to feel the bite of Gildas's tongue was Vortipor, "tyrant of the Demetae" (§31). We know something about him because his tombstone was discovered in 1895 in the churchyard at Castelldwyran in Dyfed. It bore the inscription MEMORIA VOTEPORIGIS PROTICTORIS. "Protector", the title also given to Coel, was a genuine title bestowed on barbarians who, in the latter days of the Roman Empire, helped patrol the empire's frontiers. Vortipor appears in the genealogies of Dyfed/Demetia as the son of Aircol Lawhir ("the long-hand"). Aircol is the Brythonic version of Agricola, suggesting that Vortipor's father was a Romano-Briton. Gildas clearly thought well of Aircol, calling Vortipor the "bad son of a good king". Vortipor is charged with having divorced and possibly even murdered his wife and then raping her daughter (presumably by a previous marriage, though Gildas does not say). Vortipor may not have been all bad. Gildas calls him "spotted with wickedness", and it is likely that he was a once strong king who descended into wickedness in his final years. Gildas remarks that "the end of your life is gradually drawing near" and that his "head is already whitening", so we may presume Vortipor was well into his sixties. This is borne out by the analysis of the Demetian pedigree in Table 7, which suggests a lifetime for Vortipor of 470–540. If so then Vortipor would have been a young man at the time of Arthur's triumphs and his father, Agricola, would certainly have known, and possibly fought alongside Ambrosius Aurelianus.

Incidentally, the name by which Vortipor is known in the Irish pedigrees is Gartbuir. If a later chronicler came across this written in Gaelic script as *Garthuir*, might he have misread the 'b' as an 'h' and read *Garthuir*? A thought.

The fourth of Gildas's kings is Cuneglasus, the "tawny butcher" (§32). Cuneglasus's sin, in addition to waging war "with arms special to yourself", was to reject his wife and lust after her sister, a widow who had retired to a convent. This king is most likely Cynlas Goch, a cousin of Maelgwyn and ruler of the small cantref of Rhos (Table 9). Gildas reports that Cuneglasus had been a wicked man ever since his youth, and refers to him as "driver of the chariot of the Bear's Stronghold". Knowing Gildas's delight in puns, we can interpret "Bear's Stronghold" into Welsh as "Din-arth" (*din* for fortress and *arth* for bear); Dinarth is a small village near Llandrillo in North Wales. Others* have taken the reference to "the Bear" as relating to Arthur, as the prefix *Arth* means "the Bear", and have suggested that Cuneglasus was Arthur's charioteer or even Arthur himself.

What did Gildas mean by referring to Cuneglasus as having "arms special to yourself"? What did he have that no one else did? A specially trained army, perhaps, or a huge arsenal of weapons? Yet Gildas's phrase sounds more personal, as if Cuneglasus had his own particular weapon. It makes one think of Excalibur. Would a sword that invoked awe and wonder, and which the owner believed protected him, be "special"? Probably, but unless Cuneglasus had somehow acquired Arthur's own sword, I find it hard to believe that Cuneglasus, a violent, psychotic despot, could ever be remembered as the heroic Arthur.

Gildas saves the worst for last: Maglocunus, better known as Maelgwyn, whom Gildas refers to as "first in evil". The catalogue of Maelgwyn's crimes takes up as much space as all the others put together. In his youth, Maelgwyn murdered his uncle, the king. This might have been Owain Danwyn

* See website www.angelfire.com/md/devere/urse.html.

("white-tooth"), ruler of Rhos and father of Cuneglasus, but according to Peter Bartrum in *A Welsh Classical Dictionary*, the word used for uncle, *avunculus*, means strictly "his mother's brother". We do not know who his mother's brother was, so cannot be sure which kingdom Maelgwyn usurped. He seems to have repented and sought penance in a monastery. But this was short-lived. He subsequently murdered his wife, and, determined to marry his nephew's wife, had his nephew murdered as well.

Gildas must have felt very sure of himself. Castigating one or other of the first four kings was risky enough, but to take on Maelgwyn was like Thomas More taking on Henry VIII. As Gildas describes him, Maelgwyn was "dragon of the island", the Pendragon or High King. Arthur was also described as the Pendragon, a title steeped in historical lore which I shall explore later. Maelgwyn was the most important ruler in Britain, although Gildas did not see it this way: "The King of all kings has made you higher than almost all the generals of Britain, in your kingdom as in your physique." (§33). Maelgwyn was called "the Tall", and we can imagine him as a well-built, powerful man, towering over all others. Gildas does not say what he means by "almost all the generals", but he clearly believed that there was one more powerful than Maelgwyn in Britain. Gildas had decried most of the kings of Wales and the West and had made no comment on the kings of the North. Perhaps he is alluding to one of them. Or perhaps this is Gildas's one cryptic reference to Arthur. We know the names of most of Maelgwyn's contemporaries, and possibly only Eliffer of the Great Host or his sons Peredur and Gwrgi might otherwise be classified as great generals. Once again Gildas masks his facts.

As the best-attested ruler mentioned by Gildas, Maelgwyn's reign has been used to help date when Gildas wrote *De Excidio*. I have already used other factors to deduce that it must have been written in the mid- to late 530s. The *Welsh Annals* note the death of "Mailcun" in 549, and Maelwgyn's reign is usually allocated to 534–549. This suggests that Gildas was writing early in Maelgwyn's reign, but the catalogue of crimes Gildas lists, including three marriages, suggests a good few years have passed. However 534 relates to the death of Cadwallon and that date is far from certain, and Cadwallon could have died in the 520s. Also the throne Maelgwyn usurped by murdering an uncle relates to a smaller chiefdom, not the main line of Gwynedd that he later inherited. In all probability, Maelgwyn's post-monastic catalogue of crimes began in the 520s, perhaps even earlier, allowing plenty of opportunity for Gildas to vilify him in the late 530s.

Gildas was the major witness to early sixth-century events, and if Arthur existed he would have known about him. The fact that he does not name him is frustrating but in itself proves nothing. What Gildas does do is prove that a battle of Badon took place, but he also casts doubt on the dating in the *Welsh Annals*, forcing us to consider an earlier date, during the 490s. He also provides useful details on Ambrosius, Vortigern and Arthur's contemporaries, but any other clues about Arthur, despite ingenious interpretations, are very circumspect. We must continue our search, but now we enter the murky waters of Nennius's *Historia Brittonum*.

6

NENNIUS'S OLD PAPERS

1. *Historia Brittonum*

Nennius is both the saviour and the curse of Arthurian research. The works attributed to him provide considerable background to early British history that is missing from other sources. Nennius claimed to "heap" together those records that other historians and church fathers had rejected. Like a jackdaw, he assembled a miscellany of writings known as the *Historia Brittonum*, which, on the surface, seems a goldmine of information, but on close analysis poses more questions than it answers. After working our way through Nennius, the path we have carved with the help of the *Welsh Annals*, the *ASC* and Gildas will have lost some of its definition.

Nennius tells us in his opening section that "from the passion of Christ 796 years have passed; from the Incarnation 831 years". In fact, the date, as evident from various references within the papers, was closer to 828/9. Nennius's figures show that he believed the life of Christ was thirty-five years, whereas most scholars treat it as thirty-three, and we will need to bear this in mind in the computations arising from Nennius's work.

Nennius benefited from that flowering of research at the court of King Merfyn "the Freckled" of Gwynedd, which also encouraged the compilation of the *Welsh Annals*. However, it is evident that there were several revisions to the original *Historia Brittonum*, and only one of these incorporates a preface ascribing the work to Nennius. Whilst there's no reason to doubt it, we must consider that the attribution may have been a guess by a later scholar. Nevertheless, for the sake of convenience, I will continue to refer to Nennius as the author.

That same preface refers to extracts found by Rhun. If this is accurate then it is significant, for it means that amongst the papers found by Nennius were some going back to the century following Gildas. The son of Urien of Rheged, Rhun was alive in the 620s (*see* Table 4), and entered the church in his later years, retiring to live in Powys. He was on good terms with the Angles (even credited with baptizing King Edwin of Northumbria), and is a logical candidate for producing a Northern Chronicle.

Nennius's papers go back to the settlement of the Roman consul Brutus, a story told in greater detail by Geoffrey of Monmouth. We need not concern ourselves with his prehistory, but there are occasional chronological references. For instance, §16 states*

> From the year when the Saxons first came to Britain to the fourth year of king Mervyn, 429 years are reckoned; from the birth of the Lord until the coming of Patrick to the Irish are 405 years. From the death of Patrick to the death of Saint Brigit are 60 years; from the birth of Columba to the death of Brigit are 4 years. 23 cycles of 19 years from the Incarnation of the Lord

---

* All extracts from Nennius are adapted by the author from the translation by J.A. Giles (1891).

until the coming of Patrick to Ireland; these years number 438. From the coming of Patrick to the present 19 year cycle there are 22 cycles, that is 421 years, two years in the Ogdoad until this present year.

Clearly Nennius – or the author of the paper he was editing – had access to a set of annals, but not the same as those from which the *Welsh Annals* were compiled, as the latter cite the birth of Columba and the death of St Brigid in the same year (523). The key date noted here is the first one, relating to the coming of the Saxons. King Merfyn's reign is generally accepted to have begun in 825. His fourth year, therefore, is 828/829, the date believed to be when Nennius compiled his *Historia*. That makes the first Saxon *adventus* the year 400, loosely tying in with the entry in the *Gallic Chronicle* under 410 when the British provinces were "devastated" by the Saxons, but clashing with another date I shall come to shortly.

The start of his next paragraph contradicts the previous one, though in fact the year cited for the mission of Patrick to Ireland, 438, is close to the traditionally accepted date of 432. The gap between 438 and 405 is thirty-three years, the generally accepted lifetime of Christ. Adjusting the number 405 to running from the death of Christ, rather than from his incarnation, reconciles the dates. Moreover, if we add the 405 years in the first paragraph to the 421 in the second and then add on the two years of the ogdoad (an ogdoad is a set of eight years), that gives us 828, consistent with the reference to Merfyn's reign. This kind of confusing consistency runs throughout Nennius.

The next inconsistency appears between §28 and §30. First Nennius says:

Hitherto the Romans had ruled the British for 409 years. But the British overthrew the rule of the Romans and paid them no taxes and did not accept their kings to reign over them and the Romans did not dare to come to Britain to rule any more, for the British had killed their generals.

The year 409 at first seems fairly accurate, close to Zosimus's date of 410, when the British expelled the Roman officials. However, the Claudian conquest of Britain was in 43AD, meaning that Nennius's 409 years begins then, bringing us to the year 452, which seems far too late. Before contesting this further, let's see what it says in §30:

> The Romans came with a great army to help them and placed emperors in Britain; and when the emperor was established with his generals the armies went back to Rome, and came and went in alternation over 348 years. But the British killed the Roman generals, because of the weight of the empire, and later asked their help. The Romans came to bring help to the empire and defend it, and deprived Britain of her gold and silver and bronze and all her precious raiment and honey, and went back in triumph.

Adding 348 years to 43AD gives 391, soon after the death of Magnus Maximus. It is, however, worth noting that the gap from 391 to 409 inclusive is nineteen years – one Easter cycle. Nennius's source may simply have missed (or lost) one set of records.

Elsewhere in his Miscellany, in §66, Nennius has this to say:

> From the reign of Vortigern to the quarrel between Vitalinus and Ambrosius are 12 years, that is Guoloppum, or *Catguoloph* [the battle of Wallop]. Vortigern, however, held the empire in Britain in the consulship of Theodosius and Valentinian, and in the fourth year of his reign the English came to Britain, in the consulship of Felix and Taurus, in the 400th year from the incarnation of our Lord Jesus Christ.

The first joint consulship of Theodosius and Valentinian was in 425AD, although they also held the title jointly in 426, 430 and 435. However, Felix and Taurus held the consulship only once, in 428, which was indeed the fourth year after 425. Nennius, though, equates that year to the 400th since Christ's birth, but may have meant from the baptism of Christ, at age twenty-eight, when he received the Holy Spirit, sometimes referred to as Christ's true "incarnation".

Thus we can see that Vortigern came to power in 425, that the Saxons first arrived in 428 and that in 437 there was a battle between Ambrosius and Vitalinus, which I shall explore in more detail shortly.

All this gives the impression that the information is there, but one has to work hard to find it. With that in mind, let us run through the *Historia Brittonum* from §31 onwards, which follows from the death of Magnus Maximus:

> It came to pass that after this war between the British and the Romans, when their generals were killed, and after the killing of the tyrant Maximus and the end of the Roman Empire in Britain, the Britons went in fear for 40 years. Guorthigirnus [Vortigern] then reigned in Britain. He had cause for dread, not only from the Scots and Picts, but also from the Romans, and a dread of Ambrosius.
>
> In the meantime, three ships, exiled from Germany, arrived in Britain. They were commanded by the brothers Horsa and Hengist, sons of Wihtgils. [. . .] Vortigern received them as friends, and delivered up to them the island which is in their language called Thanet, and, by the Britons, Ruym.
>
> Gratianus Æquantius at that time reigned in Rome. The Saxons were received by Vortigern, three hundred and forty-seven years after the passion of Christ [and, according to the tradition of our ancestors, from the period of their first arrival in Britain, to the first year of the reign of king Edmund, five hundred and forty-two years; and to that in which we now write, which is the fifth of his reign, five hundred and forty-seven years].

The opening paragraph is ambiguous. It could be interpreted as meaning that the fearful forty years occurred directly after the fall of Maximus in 388AD, during which time Vortigern ruled, or that Vortigern came to power at the end of the forty-year period. If the latter, then Vortigern's rule began in 428, close to the date of 425 extrapolated from §30.

It is pertinent that Nennius records Vortigern as afraid not only of the Picts and Saxons, but also of the Romans, specifically Ambrosius. This reference to the Romans may mean that Vortigern feared they might try to reclaim Britain for the empire, but I believe it has to be read in conjunction with the reference to Ambrosius, namely that Vortigern was in fear of the Roman faction in Britain, led by Ambrosius. Can this be the same Ambrosius that led the British rally against the Saxons in the 460s? It seems unlikely, especially when we check §66, which refers to Ambrosius's battle with Vitalinus in 437. If we read this in conjunction with Gildas's description of Ambrosius's parents as having "worn the purple", and therefore being Roman, we can more logically deduce that Vortigern was in dread of Ambrosius the Elder. But who was Vitalinus?

This brings us to the matter of Vortigern's real name. The name Vortigern, as mentioned earlier, means "supreme king", hence Gildas's pun on "superb tyrant". It may well have been the name by which Vortigern was always known. In §49 Nennius provides a genealogy for Vortigern, telling us that "Guorthegirn Guortheneu was the son of Guitaul, son of Guitolion of Gloui." Latinized, this reads "Vortigern, son of Vitalis, son of Vitalinus of Gloucester". Vitalinus was thus Vortigern's grandfather and it is possible that Vortigern's real name was also Vitalinus or Vitalis.

There is, however, more to Vitalinus. An ancient list of archbishops of London, believed to have been compiled by the twelfth-century Jocelin of Furness and incorporated by John Stow into his *Annales of England* (1580), includes the name Guetelinus as the twelfth to hold that office. No date is attached to him, but intriguingly Geoffrey of Monmouth, in his *History of the Kings of Britain*, also mentions this Guetelinus as the archbishop of London at the time of the Roman withdrawal. He attributes to Guetelinus the writing of the letter, which we know to have been written in about 446, to the Roman commander Aëtius, seeking help against the invaders. Although it is entirely possible for Guetelinus to have survived that long, I believe that both Geoffrey and Nennius's sources were confusing father and son, or grandson. The elder Vitalinus would have been bishop in 410, and either Vitalis or Vortigern fought Ambrosius the Elder at Guoloph in 437, and wrote the appeal in 446.

Nennius tells us that Vortigern granted Hengist and Horsa territory on Ruym, which in other copies of the manuscript is spelled Ruoichin. *Ruoichin*, or *Ruithin*, is sometimes translated as "river-island", and is taken to mean the Isle of Thanet in Kent, separated from the mainland by the Wantsum Channel, and long regarded as the landing place of the Saxons and their first settlement in Britain. But this does not wholly accord with Nennius's record. In fact, there is no reference to Kent in this paragraph. For a start he states that Ruym is called "Tanet" in "their [the Saxons'] language", but the Isle of Thanet's name is of Celtic origin, *Tanat*, meaning "fire island", perhaps because there was a beacon there.

Ruym, on the other hand, is more likely derived from *rhwym*, meaning a bond or obligation. In other words, this land, wherever it was, was granted to the Saxons in return for their services. The town of Bonby in the North Lincolnshire Wolds, though its name is of Scandinavian origin, has a similar meaning, *Bond-by*, usually interpreted as "peasant's farmhouse", but meaning literally "farmland worked under bond". Bonby is on the edge of the Ancholme river valley which was regularly flooded until extensive drainage works were built in the seventeenth century. Moreover, just north of Bonby is Saxby, "Saxon's farmhouse", and just north of that, near Barton on Humber, is Beacon Hill, which was almost certainly an island in Saxon times and may also have been called Tanet by the British. This is not to say that the site of Bonby was the original Saxon settlement, but its location is significant for two reasons. Directly across the Ancholme valley from Bonby are the villages of Winteringham and Winterton, the names of which are both from an Angle, Winta. J.N.L. Myres has suggested in *The English Settlements* that this is the same

Winta as in the ancestry of the kings of Lindsey (*see* Table 12), a contemporary of Hengist and Icel, and thus one of the first settlers after the initial forays. Additionally, the archaeology has identified early Saxon settlements with mixed British and Saxon burial customs throughout this area.

Sections 32–35 of Nennius's *Historia* tell a story about Germanus's visit to Britain, a story that does not relate to any other life of Germanus of Auxerre. It tells how Germanus tries to seek audience with the wicked king Benli, who refuses to see him. He is welcomed instead by one of Benli's servants, Cadell. Germanus warns Cadell to leave the fortress, and that night it is destroyed by a bolt from heaven. Cadell was the grandson of Vortigern and became the forefather of the kings of Powys. Table 10 assigns him the dates 460–530, which is too late for St Germanus. Most scholars believe that Nennius has confused Germanus with the Irish-born St Garmon, who may have been a nephew of St Patrick, and who preached throughout Wales, especially Powys, in the late fifth century. The hill fort of Moel Benlli is near Maesgarmon, the suggested site for the "Alleluia" victory. It is possible that both sites should be associated with St Garmon.

In the next section Nennius returns to the Saxon invasion of Britain, although, as with the Cadell episode, he seems now to be recounting folklore rather than true history.

In §36 he tells us that after the Saxons had been settled on Thanet for "some time", Vortigern promised to supply them with provisions if they would fight the enemy, the Picts and Scots. But as the barbarians had "greatly increased in number", the Britons could not keep up with demand and told the Saxons they were no longer needed and could go home.

We don't know how long Nennius meant by "some time". It could mean an entire generation, possibly suggesting two different folk memories that have become jumbled. The first Saxon *adventus*, around 428, led to them being granted land at

Ruym. The next stage may be after that settlement has grown through children and fresh settlers. We could now have moved on to the period described in the *ASC* as starting in 449.

In §37 Nennius contradicts himself. He reports Hengist as saying, "We are indeed few," and promising that if Vortigern agrees, Hengist will go home and return with more men. He returns with sixteen ships and his daughter, with whom Vortigern becomes besotted. Hengist agrees that Vortigern can marry her in exchange for the "province" of Kent. Vortigern grants Kent to the Saxons, much to the annoyance of the native ruler Gwrangon. Hengist continues with his grand plan and, in §38, says to Vortigern:

> If you approve, I will send for my son and his brother [cousin], both valiant men, who at my invitation will fight against the Irish, and you can give them the countries in the north, near the wall called Guaul.

Vortigern agrees, and Octa and Ebissa arrive with forty ships. The two sail to the land of the Picts, lay waste to the Orkneys and take possession of territory "beyond the Frenessican Sea", a contrived name for the Solway Firth.

One other point to note from this section is that Nennius says Vortigern had an interpreter called Ceretic. This was a common Celtic name, so one should not jump to conclusions, but one wonders why Nennius (or his chronicler) should name the interpreter at all, as he appears nowhere else but here. It suggests a connection with Cerdic, the later West Saxon leader, but since we have already determined that Cerdic's reign may not have started until 538, he is unlikely to be with Hengist in the 440s.

Nennius's narrative turns to another reason to condemn Vortigern. In §39 he reveals that Vortigern married his own daughter. As he had only just married Hengist's daughter this seems to be another folktale inserted well out of sequence. Nennius tells us that Vortigern has had a son by his daughter whom he tries to deny, and that Germanus (or St Garmon) condemns Vortigern for this. It may be that Vortigern married a widowed daughter-in-law or step-daughter. The child of this union is believed to have been called Faustus, of whom more shortly.

The next section takes us into the legend of how Vortigern first met the young Ambrosius. Vortigern seeks the counsel of his wise men who tell him to retire to the "remotest boundaries of your kingdom", and there build a city to defend himself from the Saxons who, they say, intend to slay him. Vortigern sets off, and, reaching the province of "Guined" (clearly Gwynedd), finds a suitable site on the summit of Hereri, or Snowdon.

Building work commences, but each morning the previous day's work is found to have vanished overnight. Vortigern again consults his counsellors, who tell him he must find a "child born without a father", who can be sacrificed to satisfy the gods. Despite Vortigern's professed Christianity, certain pagan rituals had clearly resurfaced. Excavations at several hill forts have found evidence of human sacrifice.

Vortigern's men search the land and we learn that:

41. [. . .] they came to the field of Elleti, in the district of Glevissing, where a party of boys were playing at ball. And two of them quarrelling, one said to the other, "O boy without a father, no good will ever happen to you." Upon this, the messengers diligently inquired of the mother and the other boys, whether he had had a father. Which his mother denied, saying, "In what manner he was conceived I know not, for I have never had intercourse with any man"; and then she solemnly affirmed that he had no mortal father. The boy was, therefore, led away, and taken before King Vortigern.

The next day the boy asks Vortigern why he has been taken. Vortigern reveals the problem with his citadel and the boy, as if by inspiration, reveals the reason for the problem.

42. [. . .] "There is," said he, "a pool; come, dig and you will find." They did so, and found a pool. "Now," he continued, "tell me what is in it", but they were ashamed, and made no reply. "I," said the boy, "will show you. There are two vases in the pool." They looked, and found it so. Continuing his questions the boy said, "What is in the vases?" They did not know. "There is a tent in them," said the boy. "Separate them, and you shall find it so." This being done by the king's command, there was found in them a folded tent. The boy, going on with his questions, asked the wise men what was in it. But they did not know what to reply. "There are," said he, "two serpents, one white and the other red; unfold the tent." They obeyed, and two sleeping serpents were discovered. "Consider attentively what they are doing," said the boy. The serpents began to struggle with each other; and the white one, raising himself up, threw down the other into the middle of the tent, and sometimes drove him to the edge of it; and this was repeated thrice. At length the red one, apparently the weaker of the two, recovering his strength, expelled the white one from the tent; and the latter being pursued through the pool by the red one, disappeared.

Then the boy, asking the wise men what was signified by this wonderful omen, and they expressing their ignorance, said to the king, "I will now reveal to you the meaning of this mystery. The pool is the emblem of this world, and the tent that of your kingdom: the two serpents are two dragons; the red serpent is your dragon, but the white serpent is the dragon of the people who have seized many lands in Britain, almost from sea to sea. At length, however, our people shall rise and drive away the Saxon race across the sea, whence they originally came. But you must depart from this place, where you are not permitted to erect a citadel. I, to whom fate has allotted this mansion, shall remain here; whilst to you it is incumbent to seek other provinces, where you may build a fortress."

"What is your name?" asked the king: "I am called Ambrosius (in British Embreis Guletic)," returned the boy; and in answer to the king's question, "What is your family?" he replied, "A Roman consul is my father."

> Then the king gave him that city, with all the western provinces of Britain; and departing with his wise men to the sinistral district, he arrived in the region named Guunnessi, where he built a city which, according to his name, was called Cair Guorthegirn.

This story is best remembered in the version retold by Geoffrey of Monmouth, in which he transforms Ambrosius into Merlin. The important matter here is that despite being called a boy without a father, Ambrosius reveals he is the son of a consul. Perhaps by now the elder Ambrosius was dead, killed, as Gildas wrote, in the Saxon wars or in the battle of Guoloph in 437. If the younger Ambrosius was at his height in the 460s, he was perhaps born in the 430s, and therefore still a child at the time of the Saxon settlement.

The fortress is usually taken to be Dinas Emrys, in Snowdonia, one of the major hill forts of North Wales. The name has obvious associations with Ambrosius, who was also called Emrys Wledig. Though it is unlikely that he lived here, it is possible that he (or his father) ordered that it be rebuilt as a safe retreat from Segontium during the raids by the Irish and Picts.

It is interesting that Ambrosius is found in Glevissing (Glywysing), one of the early Welsh kingdoms in Gwent, the territory of the Silures. This area was heavily Romanized, but also clung steadfastly to its British roots. Glywys, the traditional founder of Glywysing, was the great-grandson of Owain, son of Maximus. We do not know the precise dates of Glywys but, as shown in Table 8, they were probably around 445–515. This means he was active throughout the Arthurian period.

The name *Glywys* means "a man of Glevum", the Roman name for Gloucester. Vortigern was descended from one of four brothers credited with founding Gloucester. Though Gloucester is not in Glywysing, it is close to the borders of Gwent, in the territory of the Gewisse. Glywysing itself was not established until around 470, so although Nennius records

Ambrosius as having been found there, the chronicler was simply using a later name for a traditional site. This ties in with the theory that the Ambrosius family was connected with Gloucester.

Glywys is sometimes called Glewys Kerniw, or Glywys Cernyw, and some commentators have connected him to Cornwall (Cernow). However, Cernyw is also the name of a place in South Wales, a strip of territory along the coast between Chepstow and Cardiff. Glywys founded a church here towards the end of his life and the name lives on in the present-day Coedkernew, four miles south-west of Newport.

Finally, Nennius tells us that, unable to build his original fortress, Vortigern sets off to the "sinistral" part of Wales, where he establishes his citadel at Caer Gwrthegirn. "Sinistral" means "left", and Vortigern evidently moved west from Snowdonia towards the Lleyn Peninsula. There is still today a Nant Gwrtheyrn on Lleyn, in the extreme west of Gwynedd, and Lleyn Peninsula has several sites of Arthurian interest. However, Vortigern is also associated with Gwrtheyrnion, which later formed part of Brycheiniog and southern Powys, whilst Geoffrey places his final fortress at Ganarew in Gwent.

After this detour about Vortigern and the young Ambrosius, Nennius returns to the main story about the Saxons, and for once we may have some real history.

> 43. Meanwhile Vortimer, the son of Vortigern, valiantly fought against Hengist, Horsa, and his people; drove them back to the Isle of Thanet, and thrice enclosed them within it, and besieged, attacked, threatened and frightened them on the western side. The Saxons despatched envoys to Germany to summon reinforcements, with an additional number of ships with many men: and after he obtained these, they fought against the kings of our peoples and princes of Britain, and sometimes extended their boundaries by victory, and sometimes were conquered and driven back.

44. Four times did Vortimer valorously encounter the enemy; the first has been mentioned, the second was upon the river Derguentid, the third at the Ford, in their language called Episford, though in ours Rithergabail, there Horsa fell, and Categirn, the son of Vortigern; the fourth battle he fought was near the Inscribed Stone on the shore of the Gallic sea, where the Saxons, being defeated, fled to their ships and were drowned.

Soon after Vortimer died; before his decease, anxious for the prosperity of his country, he charged his friends to bury his body at the entrance of the Saxon port, viz. upon the rock where the Saxons first landed. "For though," said he, "they may inhabit other parts of Britain, yet if you follow my commands, they will never live again in this island." They imprudently disobeyed this last injunction, and neglected to bury him where he had appointed [for he is buried in Lincoln].

This episode of Vortimer's battles against the Saxons sounds like the precursor to the campaign of Ambrosius as told by Gildas, and could explain Gildas's account that the Saxons had returned home. It also echoes the *ASC*'s description of the battles between Vortigern and the Saxons, although only one seems to be specifically cited in both accounts. Nennius records that Horsa was killed in the battle of Episford, which would seem to equate with the *ASC* entry under the year 455, which notes that Horsa was killed at *Ægælesþrep*. The name *Ægælesþrep* has long been translated as Aylesford on the River Medway in Kent, though a proper translation would be Aylesthorp. Because it has long been believed that all these battles were fought in Kent, antiquarians have looked for likely Kentish names. In fact *Ægælesþrep* would more likely evolve into Addlethorpe or Althorp, both villages in Lincolnshire. The first is near Skegness, but Althorp is on the Trent, almost within site of Bonby, where I suggested the Saxons may have first settled (*see* Map 4).

Nennius, who calls this battle Episford, says its British name is *Rithergabail*, or *Rhyd-yr-ceffyl* in modern Welsh, the "ford

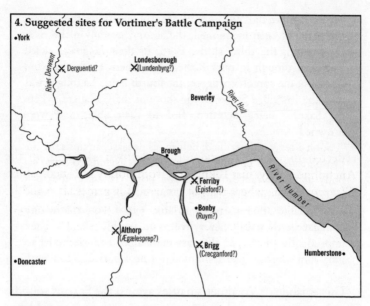

4. Suggested sites for Vortimer's Battle Campaign

- York
- River Derwent
- ✗ Derguentid?
- Londesborough ✗(Lundenbyrg?)
- Beverley
- River Hull
- Brough
- ✗ Ferriby (Episford?)
- River Humber
- • Bonby (Ruym?)
- ✗ Althorp (Ægæelesprep?)
- ✗ Brigg (Crecganford?)
- Humberstone •
- • Doncaster

of horses". As *epi* means horse, Nennius may have believed that the name Episford commemorated the death of Horsa, rather than simply signifying a ford where horses gathered. However, in the *Brut Tysilio* (*see* Chapter 9), Episford is treated as Fishford, which is apparently a literal translation of the original Welsh version, *Rhyd y pyscod*. *Pyscod* is sufficiently similar to Episford to suggest an error in translation or copying. But the translator of *Tysilio*, Peter Roberts, maintains that Nennius's source did not state *Rithergabail* but *Sathnegabail*, more properly *Syddyn-y-ceubal*, "the station of the ferryboat". This is still reflected in the towns of North and South Ferriby, on either side of the Humber, just north of Bonby.

The river *Derguentid* is usually translated as the Darent in Kent, and is therefore equated with the battle at *Crecganford* in 456. *Crecganford* itself is usually translated as Crayford, in north-west Kent, though this is not on the Darent, but the neighbouring River Cray. Though Darent is an accurate translation of *Derguentid*, which means "river where oak trees grow", that name must once have applied to scores of rivers, and is still plentiful in such modern names as Derwent, Darwen, Dart or Derwen. Of these the Yorkshire Derwent joins the Ouse just at its estuary with the Humber, only 25km (16m) from Althorp. As for *Crecganford*, whilst it might conceivably be Crayford, there may be another explanation. The name may be derived from the original Celtic word *chrecwen*, meaning laughter and revelry. The same word in Saxon is *gleam*, as reflected in Glanford Bridge, now known as Brigg, in the Ancholme Valley, just 10km (6m) from Bonby in Lincolnshire. *Gleamford* was where people gathered for games. It could be that this is also the location of Arthur's first battle in Nennius's battle list (*see* Chapter 7).

The *ASC* entry says that after their defeat the British fled to *Lundenbyrg* from *Centlond*, usually treated as London and Kent. However if this battle was at Brigg or along the Derwent the British must have fled elsewhere. Ten kilometres east of the Derwent is Londesborough (*Lodenesbyrg* in the Domesday Book). Near here was the Roman town of Delgovitia, an ideal haven. Kent was usually rendered as *Cantwara* not *Centlond*, but just east of Doncaster is Cantley and though its name is Saxon (*Canteleia*) that may be how Nennius knew it.

Finally, the Gallic Sea was the standard name for the sea between Gaul and Britain, which continued round the coast of Essex and East Anglia until it merged with the Germanic Sea somewhere around Lincoln. No inscribed stones survive in this area. In fact, they are extremely uncommon in eastern England and are found mostly in the west, but this is because so many of these stones were destroyed and plundered by generations of farmers and settlers. However, at the point where the Humber enters the sea is a town called Humberston where there used to be a boundary stone.

Vortimer's victory over the Saxons was short-lived because, as Nennius tells us, they did not bury him where he requested. Nennius recounts the consequences in §45 and §46. With

Vortimer dead, Hengist regathers his strength. He knows he now has Vortigern under his thumb, and asks Vortigern and his nobles to come to a meeting to ratify a treaty. When they have been wined and dined, Hengist's men draw their knives and murder all 300 of Vortigern's noblemen. Only Vortigern is spared, and, in return for his life, grants the Saxons the territories of Essex, Sussex and Middlesex, as well as others of their choosing.

The story of how Hengist killed Vortigern's men is the stuff of legend, and similar tales appear in other countries' myths. It may well have a basis in fact, but the nub of it suggests that the Saxons had overrun south-east Britain by this time, probably in the 460s before Ambrosius's counterattack.

According to Nennius (§47), Vortigern flees to his fortress in Gwrtheyrnion, where Germanus prays for his sins. Curiously, it is at this point that Nennius recounts the story of the Alleluia battle, with Germanus leading the army and driving the "enemies" back into the sea.

Vortigern now flees to his castle of Caer Gwrthegirn in Demetia, followed by Germanus. But after three days and nights the castle is destroyed by fire from heaven, killing Vortigern, his wives and all the inhabitants. This sounds like a repetition of the Benli episode, in reverse. It could have been Vortigern and not Benli who died by fire and allowed Cadell to succeed to the throne of Powys.

After providing a summary of Vortigern's wickedness, Nennius tells us:

48. [Vortigern] had three sons: the eldest was Vortimer, who, as we have seen, fought four times against the Saxons, and put them to flight; the second was Categirn who was slain in the same battle with Horsa; the third was Pascent, who reigned in the two provinces Builth and Guorthegirnaim, after the death of his father. These were granted him by Ambrosius, who was the great king among the kings of Britain. The fourth was Faustus, born of an incestuous marriage with his daughter, who was

brought up and educated by St Germanus. He built a large monastery on the banks of the river Renis, called after his name, and which remains to the present period.

Categirn is a variant of Catotigirn which, according to Peter Bartrum, means "war-lord" or "battle-king". This Categirn is recorded as being the father of Cadell. With their deaths it is the

Table 13 The Family of Vortigern

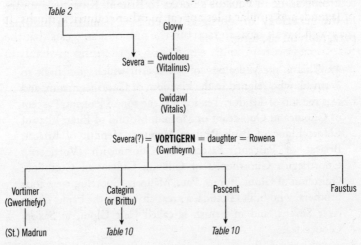

third son, Pascent, who becomes king, ruling the territories of Builth and Gwrtheyrnion as vassal to Ambrosius.

The final reference is to the fourth, incestuous son, who was educated by Germanus and established a monastery at Renis. This sounds very similar to Faustus, Bishop of Riez, who is usually accorded the dates 405–490, though if he really were a later son of Vortigern he must have been born in the early 410s and would have been an adolescent when Germanus visited Britain in 429. Faustus was known as "the Briton", and accounts of his life make much reference to his mother but none to his father. If Nennius's account is true, then we may believe that Faustus and his mother were sent by Vortigern to Armorica, where he was taken into the care of Germanus.

Faustus was probably sent to Armorica when he was a young child, perhaps soon after the end of Roman administration in 410. Germanus was then the governor of Armorica. Faustus trained as a lawyer but entered the monastery at Lérins in the 420s, becoming head of the monastery in 433, and Bishop of Riez around 462. What is intriguing about Faustus is that in a surviving letter his friend, the Roman aristocrat Sidonius, refers both to "your Britons" and to a friend of Faustus called Riocatus, who is returning some of Faustus's books to Britain. Riocatus appears in the genealogy of Vortigern given by Nennius in his final paragraph on the king:

> 49. This is the genealogy of Vortigern, which goes back to Fernvail, who reigned in the kingdom of Guorthegirnaim, and was the son of Teudor; Teudor was the son of Pascent; Pascent of Guoidcant; Guoidcant of Moriud; Moriud of Eltat; Eltat of Eldoc; Eldoc of Paul; Paul of Mepurit; Mepurit of Briacat; Briacat of Pascent; Pascent of Guorthegirn (Vortigern); Guorthegirn Guortheneu of Guitaul; Guitaul of Guitolion; Guitolion of Gloui. Bonus, Paul, Mauron, Guotelin, were four brothers, who built Gloiuda, a great city upon the banks of the river Severn, and in British is called Cair Gloui, in Saxon, Gloucester.

Riocatus is the name copied in error as Briacat, from the original *map Riacat* ("son of Riocatus"). This makes Riocatus the son of Pascent, and nephew of Faustus. The name Riocatus means "king of battles" which strikes a chord with Arthur's title as "duke of battles". Table 10 gives Riocatus the dates 460–530, making him an exact contemporary of Arthur of Badon. However, Sidonius's letter refers to Riocatus as an "Overseer", suggesting a senior church rank and therefore probably older. The letter was written in 475 so Riocatus may have been in his 30s and so born in the 440s. He could still have been present at Badon, especially given the religious connection. The connection, though raises the tempting idea that Faustus could have been the anonymous compiler of the *Gallic Chronicles*. He certainly would have had knowledge of events in Britain at that time and a clearer understanding of their import than his contemporaries.

Since we have touched on Armorica and mentioned the like-sounding Riocatus, it is appropriate here to consider Riothamus and his Arthurian connections.

2. Riothamus

In 1019, a Breton monk called William wrote a life of St Goeznovius, *Legenda Sancti Goeznovii*, in which he refers to Vortigern and Arthur, "King of the Britons". William stated that his information came from a now lost book called *Ystoria Britanica*, the only known reference to this source:

> In due course the usurper, Vortigern, to strengthen the defence of Britain, which he held unrighteously, summoned warriors from the land of Saxony and made them his allies. Since they were pagans and possessed by Satan, lusting to shed human blood, they brought much evil upon the Britons.
>
> Presently their pride was limited for a while through the great Arthur, king of the Britons. They were largely expelled from the island and reduced to subjection. But when this same Arthur, after many glorious victories which he won in Britain and in Gaul, was summoned at last from human activity, the way was open for the Saxons to again enter the island and there was great oppression of the Britons, destruction of churches and persecution of saints. This persecution went on through the times of many kings, Saxons and Britons fighting back and forth.

In spirit this agrees closely with Gildas's passage in §25 and §26, but without mention of Ambrosius. In William's summary Arthur follows on from Vortigern, separated only by the key word "presently". In the original language this was *postmodum*, meaning "soon afterwards" or "shortly", certainly not after twenty or thirty years. William is unlikely to have confused Arthur and Ambrosius as they must have been identified by name in the original document. In fact it was Vortimer, Vortigern's son, who led the campaign which rid Britain of the Saxons, and perhaps William's source had identified Vortimer as Arthur. If so, Vortimer cannot have been the victor of Badon as Vortimer was killed during his campaign. It is also difficult to bring Badon forward in time much earlier than the 490s because we know it came after Ambrosius's campaign and he followed Vortimer.

This summary is significant because it identifies Arthur as "king", not *dux*, and states that Arthur won victories in Britain and Gaul, possibly the source for Arthur's European campaign against Rome that we will find in Geoffrey's account. This could suggest that there were two major campaigns, one by Ambrosius and a separate one by Arthur, which brought him to Gaul.

This is where the shadowy figure of Riothamus rides briefly into the light. During the mid-fifth century Gaul, like Britain, was subject to attacks from Germanic tribes and after 466 was under threat by the new Visigoth king Euric. The newly appointed emperor, Anthemius, was determined to restore order. He brought in mercenaries, including a a sizable force under the command of Riothamus. The account of this is recorded by the sixth-century historian, Jordanes, in *De Rebus Gothicis*.

> Euric, king of Visigoths, aware of the frequent change of Roman Emperors, endeavoured to take Gaul by his own right. The Emperor Anthemius, hearing of this, asked the Brittones for aid. Their king Riotimus came with 12,000 men into the state of the Bituriges by way of the Ocean, and was received as he disembarked from his ships. Euric, king of the Visigoths, came against them with an innumerable army and, after a long fight, he routed Riotimus, king of the Brittones, before the Romans could join him. So, when he had lost a great part of this army, he fled with all the men he could gather together and came to the Burgundians, a neighbouring tribe then allied to the Romans. But Euric seized the Gallic city of Arverna, for the emperor Anthemius was now dead.

Anthemius was killed in 472, so Jordanes's account must take place between 467 and 472. Ian Wood in *The Merovingian Kingdoms* dates the battle in 469.

Riothamus is called "king of the Brittones", which probably means the British in Armorica. This is supported by the fact that the Roman senator Sidonius had written several letters to Riothamus appealing for help over some rebellious Bretons. Yet, if Riothamus was in Armorica, why did Jordanes say that he arrived in ships "by way of the Ocean"? Riothamus travelled into the "state of the Bituriges" (now Bourges) which is near the River Arnon, a tributary of the Loire which marked the southern border of Armorica. Twelve thousand troops is a large force and it is likely that Riothamus brought in reinforcements from others fleeing Britain, who would have sailed around Armorica and down the Loire valley.

It seems that William's Arthur is Riothamus. But if that is so, why did William call him Arthur, a name he presumably took from the *Ystoria Britanica*? Like Vortigern ("supreme ruler") Riothamus is an epithet, meaning "great king". Arthur, in the Brythonic, as *Ardd-ri*, also means "High King". The author of *Ystoria Britanica*, knowing the meanings of both *Rio-thamus* and *Ardd-ri*, may have assumed they related to the same ruler.

Somehow this explanation feels unsatisfactory. If Riothamus's real name was Arthur, we might have to recognize that someone old enough to be king and to command troops – let us say twenty-five – in 469 could still have been victorious at Badon in around 493x497 – aged about fifty – and perhaps have fought at Camlann in 514x518 at the age of seventy. The bigger question, though, is: why would a king in Armorica, already defeated by the Goths, re-emerge in Britain over twenty years later? And, if he were a king of Armorica, why does his name not appear in the king lists? The names of the rulers of Armorica (*see* Table 11) during the fifth century are confusing because there were waves of settlers whose chieftains claimed princedoms in various parts of Armorica, in particular Dumnonée in the north and

Cornouaille in the south. However, there are some clues that may help clarify the problem over names.

The Cartulary of Quimperlé lists four early *comes* or counts of Cornubia [Cornouaille], amongst whom is Iahann Reeth. As P.C. Bartrum explains in *A Welsh Classical Dictionary*, Reeth or Reith is the Breton adaptation of *Regula* derived from *Rex* or *Lex* for king. Iahann is an early version of Jean or John. In the medieval text, *The Life of St Melor*, there is a passage which Bartrum quotes:

> A certain nobleman from beyond the seas, whose name was *Lex* or *Regula*, a man of royal race and great wealth . . . after the desolation wrought by the Frisians and duke Corsoldus, fitted out a fleet, crossed the sea and came to our desolate Cornugallia with a great company, took the kingdom and settled there.

This would be dated to the 450s so we can imagine that one of the first British princes of Cornouaille was a man later known as John *Regula*. He was succeeded in turn by his son, Daniel, and his son Budic, who lived around the year 510. Budic's daughter married the notorious Cunomor. His wife had previously been married to the prince of Dumnonée, in the north, whose name was Ionas, another version of John. This Ionas is sometimes called Ionas Riotham, another designation meaning king. So, within the space of four generations you have two rulers both of whose names mean John the King. The second one, who died in 540AD, bears the title Riatham. The first one, Iahann Regula, had come to Armorica with a large fleet of ships in the 450s. He could easily have been the king who fought against Euric and whose name became confused with Ionas Riotham who lived soon afterwards. The connection with Arthur may have arisen because of the link with Tristan. It leaves open the question of who this original Iahann, a man of "royal race", really was and where he fits in the time of Vortigern and Ambrosius.

3. A tentative chronology

So we come back full circle to the lifetime of Vortigern. By all accounts he was banished and killed soon after the death of his son Vortimer, which means he must have died around the year 460. Into the vacuum, so Gildas tells us, stepped Ambrosius, who rallied the British and fought against the Saxons, leading to the major British victory at Badon. In studying these events, it seems increasingly likely that Badon had to come at the end of the fifth century, most likely around 493–497 and not the later date (518) listed in the *Welsh Annals*. According to the annals, it was Arthur who was the victor at Badon. By now Ambrosius must have been an old man, and a new general was leader.

This appears to be the background to Arthur, and it is only now in Nennius's miscellany that Arthur appears. Nennius provides a battle list which is one of the most discussed and analysed sections in all Arthurian lore. It appears as a separate section and I discuss it fully in the next chapter.

Nennius makes only two other brief references, both in his catalogue of the wonders of Britain and both of which really belong in the section of Welsh tradition. He tells of a stone at Carn Cafal, in the province of Builth, that apparently bears the imprint of Arthur's hound. The other is a tomb in the province of Ergyng, which is called Llygad Amr. According to legend, Amr (or Amhar) was Arthur's son, whom he killed and buried there. These two sites, along with the statement in the battle list that Arthur alone had cut down over nine hundred men, show that already Arthur's status had taken on the trappings of legend. The sites also help us locate associations with Arthur in both Builth and Ergyng, territories in south-east Wales already linked with events we have discussed. A pattern is emerging of activities linking Arthur to South Wales and to earlier connections with Vortigern and Ambrosius, stretching across southern Britain, especially around Gloucester and Hampshire. But we also have to recognize the conflicts in the north, especially in Lindsey, and that Ambrosius's and Arthur's theatre of operations was far broader than southern Britain.

From the last few chapters, we can attempt to piece together a provisional chronology which gives us a framework to fifth-century Britain, and see where Arthur fits.

Table 14 Chronology from Roman withdrawal to Badon

410	Britain secedes from Roman Empire. Incursions by Picts and Saxons on the increase.
410–425	Coel serves as *dux*. Wars in North. Remaining Romans hide their wealth. Rise to power of Vitalinus in rivalry with Ambrosius the Elder. Clergy support Pelagianism.
425–430	Treaty reached between Coel and Cunedda. Cunedda moves south to Wales. Vortigern rises to power. Conflict with Ambrosius the Elder continues.
428	Possible first major Saxon *adventus*. Perhaps under Gewis.
429	Visit of Germanus of Auxerre. Possible date for the Alleluia victory over the Picts and Saxons.
436	Possible second visit of Germanus, though this may be confused with mission of Irish monk Garmon.
437	Conflict between Vortigern/Vitalis and Ambrosius culminates in battle of Guoloph. Vortigern now takes on full power and becomes *superbus tyrannus*.
441	Saxon infiltration into Britain now so complete that Gallic chronicler (Faustus?) believes Britain has fallen to the Saxons. Continued civil wars and plague lead to poor harvests and famine. Further waves of British settle in Armorica.
446–452	Vortigern appeals to Aëtius to send reinforcements to Britain. None is forthcoming.
449–455	Vortigern negotiates with Saxons to provide mercenaries to help fight Picts.
455–460	Saxons under Hengist revolt against Vortigern and mount campaign to win territory in Britain. Vortigern is expelled. Vortimer leads British resistance but is killed in battle, as is his brother Categirn. Horsa killed. Saxons are driven back and there is a brief respite. Further waves of settlers in Armorica, amongst them Iahann Reeth/Riothamus.
460s	Saxon forces return. Massacre of British nobles. Vortigern flees and is killed. Start of counter campaign, perhaps initially by Garmon and then Ambrosius the Younger, supported by Aircol of Dyfed. Rise to power of Pascent and Brychan.
469/470	Riothamus and army of "Brittones" fight the Visigoths. Defeated, Riothamus survives the battle but disappears from recorded history.
470s–485	Further waves of Saxon warriors. Ambrosius's campaign has mixed results. Main opponents are Octa and Aelle.
480s	Dyfnwal Hen, Lord of Strathclyde and Arthwys, Lord of the Pennines.
485	Aelle fights British at *Mearcraedes burn*. Start of possible new campaign under Arthur. Rise to power of Cadell and Riocatus.
488	Octa succeeds to the kingdom of *Cantwara*.

491	Massacre at Anderida by Aelle. Rise to power in Dyfed of Vortipor.
493–497	Victory of Arthur at Mount Badon. Death of Aelle and perhaps of Octa. Partition of Britain.
495–516 or 538	Arthur's reign, *Pax Arthuriana*.
514–518 or 535–539	Battle of Camlann; Cerdic assumes power over West Saxons.
536–540	Gildas writes *De Excidio*.

7

ARTHUR'S BATTLES –
SEEKING THE SITES

1. Nennius's battle list

One of the most discussed items in all Arthuriana is Nennius's list of twelve battles. It is a list which seems to offer so much, and yet reveals so little. Clearly identifying the battle sites should enable us to pinpoint Arthur's theatre of operations, and ultimately identify him. Unfortunately the sites almost defy interpretation. Despite valiant and ingenious efforts by scholars over two centuries there is not a single site on which there is universal agreement. It is yet another mystery within a web of mysteries, making it all the more fascinating.

As we shall see, suggested locations are scattered the length and breadth of Britain. One might imagine that if Arthur were fighting a common foe such as the Saxons, then the battles would be along a frontier. Alternatively, if he were a ruler of a specific territory then those battles might be within or around its borders. However, if Arthur were fighting several enemies, either as High King or *dux bellorum*, the scattering of sites would be more random. We also have to consider whether or not the list is of the battles of several kings, which might reveal a different pattern.

Nennius's battle list is his first and – bar the two items in his "wonders" – only reference to Arthur. Here is what he says:

56. At that time, the Saxons grew strong by virtue of their number and increased in power in Britain. Hengist having died, his son Octha came from the northern part of Britain to the kingdom of the Kentishmen and from him are descended the kings of Kent. Then Arthur, with the kings of Britain, fought against them in those days, but Arthur himself was the *dux bellorum*. The first battle was at the mouth of the river which is called Glein. The second, third, fourth, and fifth battles were above another river which is called Dubglas and is in the region of Linnuis. The sixth battle was above the river which is called Bassas. The seventh battle was in the forest of Celidon, that is Cat Coit Celidon. The eighth battle was at the fortress of Guinnion, in which Arthur carried the image of holy Mary, the everlasting virgin, on his shoulders [shield]; and the pagans were put to flight on that day. And through the power of our Lord Jesus Christ and through the power of the blessed Virgin Mary his mother there was great slaughter among them. The ninth battle was waged in the City of the Legion. The tenth battle was waged on the shore of a river which is called Tribruit. The eleventh battle was fought on the mountain which is called Agned. The twelfth battle was on Mount Badon in which there fell in one day 960 men from one charge by Arthur; and no one struck them down except Arthur himself, and in all the wars he emerged as victor. And while they [the Saxons] were being defeated in all the battles, they were seeking assistance from Germany and their numbers were being augmented many times over without interruption. And they brought over kings from Germany that they might reign over them in Britain, right down to the time in which Ida reigned, who was son of Eobba. He was the first king in Bernicia, that is, in Berneich.

As many commentators have noted, Arthur is called not a king but a *dux bellorum*, a "duke of battles". We are in a

Britain being carved up by petty kings, but they still look towards an overall military command. However the phrase may simply be hyperbole.

This happens, according to Nennius, after Hengist dies (in 488, according to the *ASC*). Octha [Octa] comes down from northern Britain, probably either from Lindsey or the territory by the Wall, triggering the start of a campaign of twelve notable battles between the British and the Saxons, culminating, as Gildas also cites, in Badon. We have already dated Badon to around 493–497, allowing Arthur's campaign to last for five to ten years, a believable span of time for twelve battles which are unlikely to have been crammed into one season.

There were probably other battles. Nennius's list almost certainly comes from a now lost battle-song commemorating the victories and ignoring the defeats. John Koch, in *The Celtic Heroic Age*, believes that it is possible to reconstruct the rhyming scheme of the original poem. He adds that the reference to Badon fits into that rhyme, and therefore was part of the original list and not added later due to Arthur's prestige. Arthur was associated with Badon from whenever this poem was first told, possibly during his lifetime. However, if it was composed a century or two later, the memory of Badon and the other battles may have become blurred.

We know that Gildas wrote of Ambrosius's campaign, so we cannot discount the possibility that the battle list belonged primarily to Ambrosius. Or it may have been a catalogue of major victories over the Saxons, regardless of commander, and thus could include Vortimer's campaign. One factor in favour of this theory is the reference to four battles taking place in one area, which suggests a concentrated campaign like Vortimer's.

The third sentence seems to suggest that all of Arthur's battles were against the Saxons, and, more specifically, against Octha and the men of Kent. It may, however, be that this sentence did not originally follow on from the previous two, but began a new section. "Them" may not refer solely to the

Saxons, but to a more general enemy. The list does not suggest a civil war.

The title *dux bellorum* has been discussed extensively. Although its literal translation is "duke of battles", a tremendous amount has been read into it. Firstly, because Arthur fought "with the kings of Britain", many have suggested he was not a king himself, but a military commander. The title *dux*, of course, was one previously owned by the *dux Britanniarum*, the commander based in the north but having control over all of Britain's military. It was doubtless appropriated by Coel and possibly passed on through his descendants, one of whom was Arthur of the Pennines.

Does Nennius's phrasing preclude Arthur from also being a king? Clearly he is set apart; fighting alongside kings suggests equal, or superior, rank. *Dux Britanniarum* was a very senior role, almost equal to *vicarius*, and if that role had continued in some form the rulers of the smaller kingdoms would certainly have looked up to the *dux* as their senior commander. He may not have held the title of High King, but he could have wielded the same authority.

Perhaps we should not take the title *dux* too literally. By Nennius's day, the understanding of the role of *dux* may have been lost, so only the title survived. It may have had some vestigial prestige attached, so that any military commander who brought various kings together to fight a common foe might have been given this title without it meaning anything specific. This means Arthur need not have been stationed in the north (where the battle-hardened Men of the North probably didn't need a commander), but may have been based in Wales or in the south. Indeed, if the southern factions had had no kings of stature since the old Roman provinces crumbled, they probably needed a commander to bring them together.

Having said the Arthur had fought alongside kings, it was he who was "lord of battles", meaning the champion and hero.

In some ways it does not matter. The *dux* would have to be of royal blood in order to command kings, as they would not serve alongside someone whom they regarded as inferior. We might not find Arthur ruling a kingdom, but he'll be in the pedigrees. So if Nennius's battles provide us with locations and we can fine tune the time, we should be able to identify him.

1. *The first battle was at the mouth of the river which is called Glein*

The name Glein is derived from the Celtic *glan*, meaning "pure" or "clean". No river is called Glein today, but two are called Glen, in Lincolnshire and Northumberland. The Lincolnshire Glen flows through the Fens and today joins the River Welland near Spalding, but in the fifth century Spalding was on a hard ridge of land virtually on the shoreline of the Wash, which then reached further inland. Interestingly, the origin of the name Welland is uncertain, but it is also a Celtic word and could mean "good" or "holy" stream, thus the names Glen and Welland may be connected and the mouth of the Glen may, at one time, have been at the mouth of the Welland. This is a possible site, because the area to the north, in Lindsey, was one of the first to be settled by the Angles. The Fens do not lend themselves to major battles but, as Hereward the Wake proved five centuries later, they are suited to a covert guerrilla operation in territory which would be known by the British but highly dangerous to the unwary invader. There is, however, no significant base nearby from which Arthur could have launched his attack. There may be another appropriate site in Lincolnshire at Brigg, originally Glanford Bridge, which I discussed in the last chapter. The river, now called the Ancholme, was a major estuary, before drainage works reduced much of the surrounding marsh.

The Glen in Northumbria also flows into another river, meeting the Till near Doddington. This confluence is close to Yeavering Bell, the largest Iron Age hill fort in Northumberland. It was a significant site of over a hundred dwellings, and a major archaeological dig in 1960 showed that it had been reoccupied after the Roman period. Yeavering has an unspoilt view down to Bamburgh and Lindisfarne and would have been a major defensive site against the early Germanic invaders in the fifth century. The site was of such importance that after the conquest of the area by the Angles, Edwin of Northumbria established his own palace here at the foot of the hill. If Nennius's list is in chronological order, Yeavering Bell is also a suitable location for the first conflict. However, considering how important this site would have been to the British and Saxons, it is surprising the battle list refers to the river and not to the fort.

There are other suggestions. In 1867, in *Chronicles of the Picts and Scots*, W.F. Skene suggested Glen Water, a small stream running down to the River Irvine at Darvel in Strathclyde, near Kilmarnock. His suggestion was based on local legend, which even supplies a date for the battle, 542AD. However, since that was the year that Geoffrey of Monmouth said Arthur of Badon died, it would seem an unlikely date for the first of his battles.

Josephus Stevenson suggested, in notes to his 1838 translation of Nennius, either the River Lune, in Westmorland, or the Leven in Cumberland. The Lune is of special interest. The name is derived from *glein*, likewise meaning "pure and healthy". The river has a major estuary at Lancaster where there was a small Roman fort, strengthened in the 340s as a coastal defence against the Irish. Of all the *glein* rivers it is the only one with a mouth to the sea and a significant fortification.

Other suggestions include the River Glyme in Oxfordshire, Glynch Brook near Bewdley, and Gleiniant near Llanidloes, in west Wales. The Glyme is an intriguing possibility. The name means "bright one", so is not immediately related to *glein*, but its confluence, where it joins the River Dorn at Wootton, north of Oxford, is at the southern end of the little-known British enclave of Calchvynydd, which ran up through the Chilterns between Oxford and Northampton. Nearby is Ambrosden, a town which is suggestive of Ambrosius Aurelianus, and a likely spot for one of his battles.

Gleiniant has the distinction of retaining the name *glein*. The stream at Gleiniant meets the Trannon at Trefeglwys in present-day Powys, close to the old borders with Gwynedd and Ceredigion. It is also close to one of the suggested sites for Camlann. Gleiniant would suit an internal struggle, but is far out of the conflict zone for the Saxons.

It's just possible that Glein was a corruption of *Cluain*, the Brythonic for pasture and which today appears as Clyne or Clun. There is a River Clyne on the Gower Peninsula in South Wales and a River Clun a few miles east at Pontyclun. This site is of interest as the river runs by the Iron Age hill fort of Caerau, the alleged site of a battle against the Saxons in 873, though this may be a folk memory of an earlier battle.

One final possibility is the Glynde Reach in Sussex, one I'm not aware has previously been suggested. This small stream was originally the Glynde Bourne – indeed it flows right below the famous Glyndebourne Opera House – and Glynde is derived, according to some etymologies, from the Celtic for valley, *glen*. Others say it comes from the Saxon *glind*, for enclosure. Either way it has a striking similarity to the first in Nennius's list, made all the more intriguing as this could be the site of one of Aelle's battles listed in the *ASC* as happening at *Mearcrædes burnam* in 485, exactly when I have suggested that Arthur's battle campaign may have started.

Of all the suggestions the best possibilities are the Northumbrian Glein, the Cumbrian Lune, the Oxfordshire Glyme and the Sussex Glynde.

2–5. The second, third, fourth, and fifth battles were above another river which is called Dubglas and is in the region of Linnuis.

Dubglas is the original of the name Douglas. It is usually translated as meaning "black water", but a more strict interpretation is "black-blue" or even "black-green" (*dub+glas*). *Glas* means that blue-green colour seen in glass – the name Glasgow means "green hollow". So we're really looking for a dark, probably deep, river that reflected blue-black, or green-black. Unfortunately, that could apply to many, not helped by the fact that the name Douglas survives as one English river, two Scottish rivers and twelve called Dulas in Wales. Doubtless there would have been plenty more called Dulas in England, which changed their name under Saxon domination to such variants as Dawlish or even Blackwater (there's a tempting site in Hampshire that I discuss separately on page 177). It was probably because of this abundance of names that the original chronicler qualified the description by adding that it was in the region of Linnuis.

In 1945, Kenneth Jackson, in an article in *Modern Philology*, determined that *Linnuis* derives from *Lindenses*, meaning "the people of Lindum", or Lincoln. This at first seems promising, because we know that the area around Lincoln, which was Lindsey, was one of the earliest areas settled by the Angles. Unfortunately, no river in that area has a name remotely like Douglas. The primary river is the Witham, and some have suggested that the Witham might originally have been called the Douglas, on the assumption that Witham is a Saxon name, derived from "Witta's ham". However, Kenneth Cameron, in *English Place Names*, states that the Witham is probably one of a group of rivers the names of which go back before Celtic times into unrecorded history, so it was probably never known as the Dubglas.

There is another candidate for Linnuis. The Roman geographer Ptolemy used that word to describe the area now known as Lennox, covering the territory north of the Clyde and Firth around Loch Lomond. Just east of Loch Lomond is Glen Douglas, where the Douglas Water gushes down through the glen to enter the loch at Inverbeg. Beyond, across Loch Long, but still clearly visible from Glen Douglas, is the strangely shaped peak of Ben Arthur, which may well be connected with the Dál Riatan king's son, Artúir mac Aedan. The old road from the Dál Riatan capital at Dunadd, in Argyll, skirts the southern fells of Ben Arthur before descending into

Glen Douglas. There could certainly have been a battle here
involving Artúir mac Aedan, probably against the Picts. Otherwise it is far too distant for a battle of a southern or even a
northern British Arthur against the Saxons.

Leslie Alcock has suggested that *Linnuis* may have been
copied wrongly and that the original word was *Lininuis*, which
would have derived from the peoples known as the Lindi-
nienses, who lived in Dorset and parts of Wiltshire, Somerset
and Hampshire, the area that later became Wessex. The Roman
name for Ilchester was Lindinis. Here the River Divelish runs
from Bulbarrow Hill at Woolland, to Sturminster Newton in
Dorset. Just south of Bulbarrow Hill is the Devil's Brook,
running south to Burleston where it enters the River Piddle. En
route it passes through Dewlish, a village which also means
"dark stream". Although these two watercourses are minor,
they do form a north–south barrier. Bulbarrow Hill is the site
of a Celtic hill fort, and the rivers run through a triangle formed
by Cadbury Castle, the Badbury Rings and the Cerne Giant, all
significant Celtic landmarks. This could certainly be a location
for a confrontation between the British and the West Saxons.

August Hunt on the Vortigern Studies website draws attention to the Devil's Water, a stream in Northumberland that
passes through Linnel Wood and joins the River Tyne near
Corbridge, at Dilston. Linnel is probably derived from *llyn-
elin* ("lake-elbow"). It is an interesting combination of the two
names in an area that would have been rich for conflict during
the fifth and sixth centuries.

Of the many Dulas rivers in Wales, Steve Blake and Scott
Lloyd in *Pendragon* suggest the Dulas that flows into Liver-
pool Bay at Llandulas, just east of Colwyn Bay. Another Dulas
worth noting is now called Dulas Brook, and runs parallel to
the Golden Valley in northern Ergyng, eventually joining the
River Dore at Ewyas Harold. This is in the same area as part of
Arthur's hunt of the giant boar Twrch Trwyth, as told in the
story of *Culhwch and Olwen* (*see* Chapter 8). That story, as we
shall see, may well represent a series of battles conducted by

Arthur across southern Wales and it is possible that at least some of the battles in Nennius's list equate to it. We shall encounter another later.

One other Dulas, or Dulais, worthy of note flows through Pontarddulais in Glamorgan, where it joins the River Neath. Near its source it flows through Cwm Dulais, above which is Craig y Bedw, or Bedwyr's Crag. This area was known for its groves and bushes. The Welsh for grove is *llwyn*, and there are places called Llwyngwenno, Llwynadam, Llwyn-y-domen, and so on. The area might have been known locally as the land of groves, or Llwyni, which might have evolved into *Linnuis*.

There is one other River Douglas worth considering. This is in Lancashire and runs from Wigan to join the sea near Preston at the estuary of the Ribble. The Roman name for Lancaster is not known but it may have been Lunium ("the people of the Lune"), based on a reference to an unidentified Roman fort at Calunium,* which might have corrupted to Linnuis. If this river was to be the site of four battles against the Saxons and Angles it would have to be late, at the time of Edwin's advance across north Britain in the early 620s. But it was a frontier against the Picts who certainly did advance this far south in the early 400s. Equally, it would have been a barrier against the Irish. We have already seen that the Lune, to the north, is a possible site for the first of Arthur's battles, so that the Douglas may have been the next frontier against a concerted Irish attack which led to four battles. This locale is also only a few miles north of Chester and a similar distance to the west of the Roman fort at Bremetennacum (Ribchester).

6. *The sixth battle was above the river which is called Bassas.* This is one of the more baffling locations and even the most dedicated Arthurians have declared it impossible to identify.

---

* See www.roman-britain.org/places/lancaster.htm.

The more intrepid have suggested sites as far afield as Bass
Rock off North Berwick in the Firth of Forth, and the
River Loddon in Old Basing in Hampshire, suggesting
that the Loddon was once known as the river of Basa's
people. The etymology for Basing is Saxon, and though this
makes it unlikely to appear in what was originally a Celtic
battle song, it may refer to an area so long occupied by the
Saxons that their name had superseded the original.

The same problem affects Basford, the name of three places
in Cheshire, Staffordshire and Nottinghamshire. All seem to be
derived from the Angle *Basa's ford*. Blake and Lloyd's suggestion, Basingwerk, in Shropshire, is also of Saxon origin ("Basa's
stronghold"), and its Celtic name was *Maesglas* ("Green
field"). Equally frustrating is Bassingbourne in Cambridgeshire, for although of Angle origin, it does at least mean
"Bassa's stream". It is, however, in an area long occupied
by the Saxons.

In the 1860s, Skene suggested Dunipace, the site of two
hillocks at Falkirk in Scotland, near the Roman fort of Camelon. He proposed that the name was originally *Duni-Bass*,
meaning "two mounds". However the origins of Dunipace are
not clear, with suggestions that it came from *Dun-y-pax* ("hills
of peace") or *duin-na-bais* ("hills of death"). John Stuart
Glennie, writing in *Arthurian Localities*, whilst recognizing
this as a possibility, felt there was an even better site across the
river where a huge rock precipice may be the *bass* (or rock).
Neither of the rivers in the area (the Bonny and the Carron) is
called Bassas, but there is a ford across the Carron, and the
Celtic name for ford, or shallows, is *bais*. But all this seems to
be clutching at straws. The same concept of *bais* for shallows
would work even better at the Fords of Frew on the Tribruit,
discussed under battle 10.

The most likely suggestion is Baschurch in Shropshire, put
forward by Graham Phillips and Martin Keatman in *King
Arthur, the True Story*. The name derives from the churches
of Bassa, mentioned in a poem by Taliesin as the burial place of

the kings of Powys. Situated near the Welsh Marches, Baschurch could well have been the site of forays by the West Saxons. It is within a day's march of the Gewisse territory to the south, and close to the site for Badon (Caer Faddon) given in the Mabinogion story *The Dream of Rhonabwy* (*see* Chapter 8). The nearest river is the Perry, but this name may be of Norman origin, derived from the Peveril family who controlled the area after the Norman conquest. We do not know the original Celtic name.

One other possibility concerns the Roman cognomen Bassus. One of the consuls at the time of Julius Caesar was Ventidius Bassus, and there were two noted poets at the time of Nero, Caesius Bassus and Saleius Bassus. Several inscriptions have been found in Britain, mostly in the north, bearing the name Bassus. One at Black Carts, halfway along Hadrian's Wall, notes that part of the wall here was built by "Nas . . . Ba[ssus] of the First Cohort". Most significantly, at the fort of Alavana at Kendal in Cumbria, there is a tombstone to the centurion Publius Aelius Sergius Bassus Mursa of the Twentieth Legion. Alavana stood on what is now the River Kent, though the original name for this river is not known. Might Publius Aelius Bassus have earned such a reputation that the area around his burial would be remembered by his name?

7. *The seventh battle was in the forest of Celidon, that is Cat Coit Celidon.*
Unlike Bassas, most scholars pounce on this site as straightforward and unchallenged. Leslie Alcock says it is the battle "about which we can have the most confidence", adding that "there is full agreement that this was in Scotland". But if there was full agreement when he wrote that, there isn't now.

Cat Coit Celidon means "battle in the forest of Celidon", which Nennius had already said in Latin. It seems strange that he should restate it in Celtic unless he wished to emphasize the original Welsh name as something specific, rather than another Forest of Celidon which had become better known in the intervening years. If so, then it suggests there are at least two Celidons, which immediately complicates the matter.

The usual interpretation is that this refers to the Caledonian Forest, which is a very widespread location. Caledonia was the Roman name for Scotland. Sometimes it was used to specify the Highlands, north of the Antonine Wall, but generally it applied to the whole country. Stories about the bard Myrddin record that after the battle of Arderydd he fled into Coed Celyddon, where he ran wild and went mad. Arderydd is the modern Arthuret, a few miles north of Carlisle. Just beyond, up Liddesdale, is the start of the present-day Border Forest, which runs through to the Kielder Forest in Northumbria. There is no specific spot within this forest called Celidon, so if this is the same forest where Arthur's seventh battle occurred it could have happened almost anywhere across the north-west, perhaps as far as High Rochester, where the Roman fort of Bremenium stood. Nikolai Tolstoy, following clues in the Scottish Arthurian romance *Fergus of Galloway*, has determined that the battle probably took place near Hart Fell.

There is an ancient inscribed stone here, near the village of Yarrow. Dating from the early sixth century, it commemorates the burial of two princes, Nudus and Dumnogenus (Nudd and Dyfnwal), sons of Liberalis. *Liberalis* may be a Roman cognomen but it is as likely an epithet suggesting he was generous, a nickname that appears as *Hael* in British. It is tempting to think this refers to Nudd Hael, the grandson of Dyfynwal Hen (*see* Table 5), but he lived in the late sixth century, too late for this inscription. Nudd/Nudus was involved in a raid on Anglesey against Rhun ap Maelgwyn to avenge the death of Elidir the Wealthy. Rhun retaliated with a march across Britain to York, and up as far as the Clyde, so he would have passed through this area. Possibly Nudd was killed in this show of force, which might have been the real battle of Celidon.

The Caledonian Forest is too generalized a description to pinpoint Nennius's battle, and yet he seems to be trying to be specific. He does not say the "Caledonian Forest" but the "Forest of Celidon", which may be something different, even personalized. In the Mabinogion story *Culhwch and Olwen*, we learn that Culhwch is the grandson of Celyddon Wledig, an important local chieftain. The story is set chiefly in Gwent. Celyddon is not otherwise identifiable, so we cannot verify his territory, but it would not be far removed from Gwent. This is the area of Arthur's capital, Gelliwig, as we will explore later. There are several towns and localities in this area bearing the prefix *gelli-*, derived from *celli* for a woodland grove, including Gellideg, Gelligaer and Gellinudd. Though no Gelliddon survives, the other names are testament to a special wood around Caerphilly, and it is quite possible that the Forest of Celyddon was once there. Blake and Lloyd have used similar logic but different etymological trails to fix Celidon in North Wales, between the Rivers Clwyd and Conway.

Frank Reno follows a different route, reminding us that *coed* is a contraction of *Argoed*, the proper Brythonic word for forest, and that the phrase "Men of Argoed" was a phrase used to describe the Men of Powys. The main forest in Powys is the Clun, in present-day Shropshire, and is relatively close to Baschurch and Caer Faddon.

Earlier in his *History* Geoffrey refers to the Forest of Calaterium, where one of his pre-Arthurian kings, Archgallo, wanders dejectedly after being deposed. Archgallo is almost certainly based upon Arthwys ap Mar (Arthur of the Pennines), and I'm convinced that Geoffrey had access to a Northern Chronicle which covered the exploits of Arthwys, some of which he may have confused with Arthur of Badon's. Calaterium is sufficiently similar to Celidon to cause possible confusion. Some experts, including J.A. Giles, have suggested that Calaterium was the old Royal Forest of Galtres, north of York, around Sutton-on-the-Forest and Easingwold. This was a rich area much treasured by the later kings of Northumbria. We will see in Chapter 9 that, according to Geoffrey, Arthur pursued the Saxons from Lichfield to the Forest of Caledon. It is over 300km to the Caledonian Forest, but about half that to the Forest of Galtres.

8. *The eighth battle was at the fortress of Guinnion, in which Arthur carried the image of holy Mary, the everlasting virgin, on his shoulders [shield]; and the pagans were put to flight on that day*.

This is the only battle that carries a description and is not unlike the *Welsh Annals* reference to Badon, suggesting that the reference to the Virgin Mary must be significant. Why did Arthur carry the image of the Virgin Mary at this battle rather than any of the earlier ones? The usual answer is that the battle occurred at a church or other holy place, and that Arthur may have been protecting a church from the heathen invaders. We should not overlook the fact that the Celts were Christians whilst the Saxons and Angles were pagans. One legend attached to Arthur, but linking him to the Crusades, tells that Arthur brought back with him from Jerusalem a splinter of the Holy Cross, which was kept at Wedale. Wedale is in the Scottish Borders and the main town is Stow. Stow is the Saxon for "holy place" and the church there is dedicated to St Mary.

Connecting Stow with a fort called Guinnion is not straightforward. Skene and others simply based it on the fact that a Roman fort was known to be nearby, and that this must have been Guinnion ("White Fort"). The nearby Gala Water tumbles at high spate along the valley and is sometimes called the "White Strath" or *Gwen-y-strad*, though this seems rather convoluted. Alistair Moffat, in *Arthur and the Lost Kingdoms*, follows a more convincing route. He reminds us that *gwen*, or more properly *gwyn*, means not only "white" but also "holy", in the sense of "pure". Thus the name Stow may simply have been a Saxon translation of an earlier Celtic name. Some etymologists suggest that Wedale was originally Woe-dale, or "dale of woe", remembering a Saxon defeat, whilst Moffat suggests the name derived from *Guidh-dail*, the Valley of Prayer, but had previously been the Holy Valley or *Gwyn-dail*, possibly corrupted into *Gwyn-ion*. This all seems rather tenuous to me.

In fact as Gwynion the name is quite common in Wales. There are at least four noted hills, or crags, called Carreg Gwynion, near Pembroke, Rhayader, Rhos and in the Berwyn Mountains at Llanarmon. This last is the site of a well-preserved Celtic hill fort, which seems more likely to have been the "fortress of Guinnion" than at *Guidh-hail*. This locale would better suit a battle between Welsh factions, but it is less than a day's ride from Chester and cannot be ruled out. There is also Castell Gwynionydd near Llandysul in Dyfed, though the history of this place is uncertain before the thirteenth century. The fact that the name is fairly common in Wales suggests that at one time it was probably equally common across the rest of Britain. If so the name may have adapted to Wenbury or Winbury or Whitsbury, near Fordingbridge, a site I discuss later in relation to Cerdic's battles.

A more intriguing possibility is Wanborough, just outside Swindon. The name was once *Wenbeorge*, which is usually treated as "wenn beorge", meaning the "place at the tumour-shaped mounds", as *wenn* is Saxon for tumour. However, *wen* could as easily be derived from the Welsh *gwyn* for "white", a theory strengthened by the fact that nearby are two sites, White Hill, renowned in Roman times for its pottery production, and Whitefield Hill, near the site of some ancient earthworks. The surrounding hillsides are covered by the many famous chalk carvings, such as the White Horse at Uffington. Wanborough was the site of the Roman fort Durocornovium, the Fort of the Cornovii, and this may well have been known locally as the White Fort. What adds to the intrigue of this site is that a little way to the south is Liddington Castle, one of the most favoured sites for the battle of Badon.

There have been other suggestions, including Burgh Castle (Gariannonum) in Norfolk, Winchester (Caer Guinn), and the Wrekin (Caer Guricon) in Shropshire, but the only other one that has some merit is Binchester, near Durham. Here was the

Roman fort of Vinovium, one of the earliest in Britain which was later refortified and remained in use until the early fifth century. The origin of the fort's name is uncertain, most suggesting "the Way of the Vines" or similar. The Celtic spelling of Vinovium is *Uinnouion*, becoming *Gwinnouion*. It was the largest fort in the north-east and held a contingent of Germanic soldiers. Its location must have been important to later settlers because they also buried their dead here, showing that it became a sustained community. At nearby Escomb is the oldest surviving Saxon church in England, and it may be that, once converted, the Saxons were drawn to what had long been a holy and venerated area, as Arthur's battle in the name of the Virgin Mary might imply.

9. *The ninth battle was waged in the City of the Legion.*
This ought to be reasonably straightforward but unfortunately isn't. There were three main legionary towns, Caerleon, Chester and York. With the construction of Hadrian's Wall, Carlisle also became a legionary town but not in the conventional sense, and, unless it was the capital of Valentia and its status changed, not at the end of the Roman period. Although Caerleon remained a legionary base, the legion was seldom there, beyond a skeletal force. It was involved in the construction of Hadrian's Wall, but by the third and fourth centuries was assigned elsewhere, including Richborough in Kent. So whilst Caerleon can rightly claim the name City of the Legion, it was far less significant than either York or Chester.

York was not only the home of the VI Legion, it was the military capital of Britain, and the fortress remained permanently manned and strengthened throughout the Roman period. The headquarters of the fort was such a major building that it remained in use well into the ninth century.

Like Caerleon, Chester's XX Valeria Victrix Legion was often stationed elsewhere, especially during the third century, but Chester was refortified in the fourth century and remained so until the end of the Roman period. Nennius refers to the city in the singular, as *urbe Legionis*, "city of *the* Legion", as if by the time of this battle all but one legion had left Britain. Gildas, in describing York, used the plural *Legionum urbis cives*, "the city of the Legion*s*". Unless this was too subtle for Nennius's source we are evidently talking about a different place. The XX Valeria Victrix was the last legion to leave Britain.

So whilst York was the major legionary fortress, and more likely to have been a focus for Anglo-British confrontation, Chester was the centre of the last legion, and is known to have been the site of a major Anglo-British battle in about 615. Both therefore have an equal case to argue. Which one Nennius meant can only be solved by identifying the other localities in the list.

10. *The tenth battle was waged on the shore of a river which is called Tribruit.*

Like Bassas, this river has almost defied analysis, and most authorities admit defeat. The early analysts, Skene and Glennie, considered the Celtic version of Tribruit, *Tryfrwyd*, a name which also appears in the poem *Pa Gur* (*see* Chapter 8), where it is spelled *Trywruid*. In a study of Scotland written in 1165, they found that the old British name for the Firth of Forth was *Werid*, derived from *Gwruid*, meaning "men of the forth". The word "shore" is significant as it suggests more of a sea-shore than a river bank. The Celtic word is *traeth* and the word *Tribruit* or *Trywruid* may have originally been a combination of *Traeth* and *Gwruid*, with the "g" dropped, becoming *Traewruid*. It sounds plausible, albeit tortuous, and the site suggested is the Links of Forth between the river and the heights of Stirling Castle, a site better known for the battle of Bannockburn in 1314.

O.G.S. Crawford, the pioneer of aerial surveys in archae-ology, also suspected that this battle was waged on the Forth, but further east at the Fords of Frew, between Gargunnuck and Kippen. This was one of only two safe crossing places on the Forth, used most notably by Bonnie Prince Charlie in 1745.

Two other streams join the Forth at the point of the Fords, the Boquhan Burn to the west and the Goodie Water to the east. Crawford believed that the old name for the Frew was the *Bruit*, so that the Fords of Frew, marking the stretch of three streams, was the *Tribruit*. The site seems more likely than its explanation, as it was a key crossing point, regarded as the gateway between the Lowlands and the Highlands. It was doubtless a frontier for many engagements between the British and the Picts.

Others who reject this derivation, including Kenneth Jackson whose essay "Once Again Arthur's Battles" (1945) is considered one of the cornerstones of Arthurian research, do not necessarily reject the location. He notes that *tryfrwyd* could be used to describe something pierced or broken, and that Nennius's location is not necessarily a river's name but a description of a shoreline as "the broken place". This could still refer to a ford, particularly one where the river is very shallow, leaving sandy and stony banks breaking the surface of the river.

For another possible location, Barber and Pykitt looked to the story of *Culhwch and Olwen*, which tells of the hunt for the Irish Boar, the Twrch Trwyth. They suggest that this tale involves a play on words with the River Twrc (also called the Troggy) and *trwyth* as a variant of *traeth*. Twrch Trwyth therefore not only meant the Irish Boar, but the "shores of the Twrc", becoming, over time, *Try-Troit*, and later *Try-wruid*. They also believe that the story of the Irish Boar hunt is the retelling of a battle between the British and the Gewisse with the final decisive battle at the mouth of the River Twrc on the Severn estuary near Caerleon.

One other suggestion of interest is the River Ribble. The Ribble is known as the "roaring river", a name adopted by the Roman fort at Ribchester, known as Bremetennacum. The *Bre*-prefix comes from the Celtic *breffw*, which means "to bellow". The original river name may therefore have been something like *Breffwrd*, from which the "b" was eventually dropped, becoming *Reffwrd*. The Ribble meets the Douglas from the south and the Dow from the north at what is now called Hutton and Longton Sands. Because of this confluence of three rivers it has been conjectured that the locality may have been known as *Trireffwrd*, which could easily mutate into *Tryfrwyd*. With the Lune and Douglas in this vicinity, this might suggest a series of battles against the Irish marauders.

11. *The eleventh battle was fought on the mountain which is called Agned.*
This battle has the added confusion that there is an alternative entry. A later version of the Nennius manuscript calls this site Breguoin, and other manuscripts have other spellings, including Bregnion and Bregomion. One manuscript even combines the two as *Agned Catbregomion*, implying that the two names mean the same site: that is, the battle (*Cat*) of Bregomion on Mount Agned. Just as with Dubglas and Linnuis, bringing the two together is not easy, though the fact that Breguion and Agned are such rare names means that if we can identify the two we would almost certainly have a unique site.

Mount Agned is referred to by Geoffrey of Monmouth, though not in connection with Arthur's battles. He says that the British ruler Ebrauc founded the cities of Kaerebrauc, Alclud and Mynydd Agned. John of Fordun, in his fourteenth-century *Scotichronicon*, states that Agned was an old name for Edinburgh. Edinburgh was usually called Eidyn and the fortress there, on top of what is now called Arthur's Seat, was Din Eidyn. It would require some philological contortions to convert Eidyn into Agned, and even more to make it convincing. August Hunt suggests the two are a play on words. Eidyn could relate to the Greek *eidon*, meaning "to behold or envision", similar to the Latin *agnitio*, which means "recognition or understanding". Both would suggest that Din Eidyn might have been called Mount Agned because both could mean the "Mount of Understanding". It's a romantic notion, but one not even hinted at in folklore.

Geoffrey of Monmouth says that Mount Agned was known as

"The Castle of the Maidens". This relates to the Picts. The right
to kingship passed through the female line, and, according to
legend, the Picts kept all the eligible royal maidens in the castle
for their security and education. However, Eidyn was a British
stronghold and though it was briefly captured by the Picts, it was
never settled by them. The Picts had several strongholds along
the Forth in the area of the Manau, especially at Myot Hill to the
west of Camelon. Their territory was at Stirling and one might
imagine the rock of Stirling Castle being an equally suitable site
for a "Castle of the Maidens". However, in the Middle Ages, the
Castle of Maidens was always believed to refer to Edinburgh,
regardless of any historical accuracy.

Geoffrey also called Mount Agned the Dolorous Mountain,
which may be appropriate as one understanding of the word
agned is that it is related to the Welsh *ochenaid* meaning
"sigh". This makes an interesting connection to the possibility
of Wedale as the eighth battle at Guinnion, since the Eildon
Hills near Wedale are referred to as the Dolorous Mountains in
the Arthurian romance *Fergus of Galloway*. This may link with
the location of Breguoin, which has been shown to derive from
Bremenium, the Roman fort at High Rochester, a day's ride to
the south, perhaps suggesting a continuation of the first battle.

The philologist Alfred Anscombe demonstrated that had
Breguoin been spelled *Breguein*, it would have derived from
Bravonium, the Roman fort at Leintwardine, in Herefordshire.
This is just west of Ludlow and within hurling distance of the
Clun Forest, one of the candidates for the Celidon battle.
Bravonium appears in one Roman itinerary as Branogenium.
Kenneth Jackson has suggested that Branogenus means "born
of the raven", but it can equally mean "born of the king" or,
taking *genus* in its more general sense, "people of the king".
This could suggest that the original Celtic site of Bravonium/
Branogenium was a hill fort occupied by royalty or descen-
dants of royalty.

Linda Malcor has shown that Bremetennacum, the name of
the fort at Ribchester which has the same prefix as Bremenium,

would also adapt to Breguoin. Bremetennacum was the fort at which Lucius Artorius Castus was based, and would be a natural candidate during the period when the Picts were attacking the forts south of the wall.

One other intriguing suggestion arose from a marginal note in the Cotton Library copy of Gildas found by Joseph Ritson in 1825,* suggesting that the site was Cathbregion, in Somerset. Barber and Pykitt identified this as Catbrain in Bristol, now at one end of Filton airfield. It has also been suggested that this might be Cadbury, where the Saxon *Caddesbyrig* was derived from the Celtic *Cat-bregyon*. Cadbury has long been associated with Arthur, as a possible site for Camelot, but not with this battle. There are two other proposals for the origin of the name Cadbury, that it is either *Cat-byrig* meaning "Battle Fort" or, more likely, *Cada-byrig* meaning Cada's Fort, possibly named after Cadwr the sixth-century ruler of Dumnonia.

12. *The twelfth battle was on Mount Badon in which there fell in one day 960 men from one charge by Arthur; and no one struck them down except Arthur himself, and in all the wars he emerged as victor.*

This is the one battle for which we have irrefutable historical support because Gildas mentioned it, and said that it happened in the year of his birth. We have already tentatively dated it to some time in the 490s, probably between 493 and 497. We have also seen that both the original battle poem and the *Welsh Annals* connect Badon with Arthur. Unfortunately Gildas does not tell us who the commander was at Badon, or where it was fought. Why did he need to? In his day, the audience for his *De Excidio* would have remembered Badon or have heard of it, and the location was well known.

The fact remains that Badon was the decisive battle which forced back the Saxons, resulting in a period of comparative

* See Riton (1825), p. 73.

peace in Britain. Whoever was the victor at Badon became the Arthur of legend. Tying Badon into the landscape is thus vital in helping identify Arthur.

Gildas would have referred to the place by its British name, and *Badon* or *Baddon* is British for "bath". Nennius had the same view. In his historical miscellany is a reference to "the Hot Lake, where the baths of Badon are, in the country of the Hwicce" (§67). The passage then describes what are clearly Roman baths, and the obvious assumption is that the reference is to Bath itself.

The territory of the Hwicce centred upon Worcester and its main town Winchcombe, but included Gloucester and Cirencester, and thus were the lands opened up to the Saxons following the battle of Dyrham in 577. Bath was tucked in at the southern end of the Hwicce, and the southern boundary follows the River Avon to the coast and along part of the Wansdyke defensive earthwork. However, the Hwicce people must have roamed because their name is remembered as far afield as Whiston (formerly *Hwiccingtune*), east of Northampton.

Bath continued to be known as the city of the "Hot Baths" long after the Roman period and into the Saxon. It was called *aet Badum* in the foundation charter for Bath Abbey in 676AD. Just when the original of Nennius's list of wonders was compiled is not known. The baths would have to have survived in sufficiently useable condition to be regarded as a "wonder". Barry Cunliffe, in his excavations at Bath in the 1980s, confirmed that whilst there was considerable stone-robbing in the post-Roman period, efforts were made to maintain other buildings well into the fifth and even sixth centuries. The likelihood is that Bath was still a functioning British city at the time of the battle of Dyrham, and the baths there must still have been held in awe.

This would seem to prove that Badon must be Bath, but we need to be cautious. To begin with, Gildas does not refer specifically to the town of Bath. His phrase is *obsessionis Badonici montis*, "the siege of Mount Badon" or "Badon Hill".

Bath isn't on a hill – quite the contrary. The area of the hot spring which fed the baths was originally in a marshy valley. Bath is, however, surrounded by hills, and most authorities assume that Gildas meant one of those, but which one?

All other references to Badon date from several centuries later, and they give us three other pieces of dubious information. Firstly, that Arthur fought at Badon carrying the Cross of Jesus on his shoulder, or shield. This presumably refers to an emblem, unless it is meant figuratively, in that Arthur is defending a church, or fighting in the name of Christ, as at Guinnion. Secondly, Nennius tells us that the siege lasted for three days and nights. Thirdly, Nennius also states that Arthur killed 960 of the enemy. This does not mean Arthur killed them single-handedly, but that he led the charge that resulted in such wholesale, and doubtless exaggerated, slaughter.

If Badon Hill is one of the hills surrounding Bath, it could be one of several. The most favoured are either Bannerdown Hill or Little Solsbury Hill, both at Batheaston. Analysis by John Morris, for instance, suggests that the Saxon forces were almost certainly infantry, perhaps no more than a thousand strong, whilst the British forces were probably cavalry. Little Solsbury Hill has a major hill fort on its plateau-like summit, which was certainly large enough to house a cavalry unit, but a difficult site for a cavalry charge. It is unlikely that the Saxons would take the hill fort and then be besieged by the British from below. However, the Saxons could have been hemmed in on Bannerdown Hill, less than a mile to the east, which has no hill fort.

Such speculation, however, takes us no nearer to identifying the location precisely. There are certainly many who do not believe that Badon does equate to Bath and presume that Badon Hill is a specific location. Kenneth Jackson demonstrated that if Badon was the site of a hill fort, and therefore known as Din Badon to the British, it would convert into the Saxon *Baddanbyrig*, evolving into the English Badbury. Badbury in Wiltshire, Badbury Rings in Dorset and Badby in

Northamptonshire are all recorded as *Baddanbyrig* in tenth-century records. There is also Badbury Hill in Oxfordshire, near Faringdon.

All of these sites except Badby have Celtic hill forts associated with them. That at Badbury, in Wiltshire, is now called Liddington Castle, a name I shall use to avoid confusion. Although an interesting case could be made for each of the sites, Liddington seems the most suitable by virtue of its location. It stands just above the Ridgeway, the ancient British trackway that runs through the Chilterns to the Marlborough Downs, and towers above the neighbouring land. Over 277m (900 feet) at its highest point, it had a strong vantage point over the neighbouring territory, and was within sight of other major hill forts, including Barbury Castle. Liddington stands as the frontal defence against a northern or eastern attack, with its back line of defence at the Wansdyke. It allows for greater flexibility than Solsbury Hill at Bath, which would not only have to have conceded a significant Saxon advance, but is also a highly restricted site.

Like Liddington, Badbury Rings in Dorset is an open site, and would have been a primary focus for any Saxon advance from the coast around Poole Bay. However, it is not a focal point for a major breakthrough. Badon was decisive because it repulsed the Saxons in their advance into the west. The Saxon target would have been the rich territories of Cirencester and Gloucester, and their advance would have been either from the south, where Aelle had established his base in Sussex, or from the east, around Lindsey. Aelle's base after 491 was at Pevensey, but there were no major Roman roads in that area. So if Aelle were to strike towards Cirencester he would have had to move along the coast to Chichester, then follow the Roman road to Silchester and from there to Cirencester. That road goes right past Liddington. This is far more likely than working all the way along the coast as far as Badbury Rings, and then striking north for Bath along the Ackling Dyke, with the intention of taking the Fosse Way up to Cirencester.

A Saxon advance from Lincoln towards Cirencester would have taken a direct route along the Fosse Way. However, the *ASC* tells us that though the Saxons had been making steady territorial gains in the south, and archaeological evidence reaches the same conclusion for East Anglia, Lindsey and further north along the coast, central Britain was untamed territory. The Angles would have needed to make far more gains towards the Midlands before risking an assault on the golden lands of the Cotswolds. The alternative would have been to march from East Anglia down Icknield Street to Verulamium (St Albans), and then either follow Ackeman Street to Bicester and then to Cirencester, or follow the Ridgeway to Swindon and up to Cirencester. The latter route would, again, take them right past Liddington. There are no other logical routes that would take them past the alternative sites of Badbury Rings or Badbury Hill, and certainly not to Badby in Northamptonshire.

It would of course have been possible for the Saxons to sail round the coast and up the Severn Estuary, a daring tactic considering the treacherous currents around Land's End, though one of which they were capable. Then they would either strike directly at Gloucester or divert along the Avon towards Bristol and Bath. But why go to such lengths when they could have marched to Bath from the south anyway?

Not everyone accepts that Liddington is Badon, or that Badon need necessarily be in the south. Alternative suggestions run from Dumbarton in Strathclyde and Bowden Hill in the Lothians, to the Wrekin in Shropshire or Caer Faddon near Welshpool. Dumbarton is a difficult one to accept if we believe that the battle was between the British and the Saxons in the 490s. The Gaels, the Irish Scotii of Dál Riata, called it *Din Brithon* (the "Fortress of the Britons"), certainly not Din Badon. In any case Gildas, who allegedly came from this area, would call it by its British name, Alclud.

Bowden Hill, near Linlithgow, relies on little other than the similarity of the name and the fact that, like Bath, it is on a

River Avon. In 1710, the antiquarian Sir Robert Sibbald
identified it in his *Account of Linlithgowshire* as having been
the site of a major battle, and thereafter fancy took over. There
is another Bowden in the Scottish Borders, a village on the
southern slopes of the Eildon Hills. Since a possible site for the
previous battle at Agned is also in the Eildon Hills, and since
this held the major British hill fort in the area, it begs closer
inspection, although it would seem strange for such a notable
battle to be named after Bowden and not Eildon.

There is also a Bowden in County Durham, between the
towns of Willington and Crook. It has all but vanished today,
and the location is only worth noting because it is close to
Vinovium/Binchester.

Caer Faddon is the locale for Badon given in the Celtic tale
The Dream of Rhonabwy (*see* Chapter 8) but its tradition as the
site for a key battle may have derived from later conflicts.

The Wrekin is championed by Frank Reno, who also draws
upon *The Dream of Rhonabwy*, but interprets the directions
differently. The Wrekin was a major hill fort outside present-
day Telford, near the old Roman town of Viriconium. This was
the fourth largest town in Roman Britain and continued to be
occupied, in various stages of disintegration and repair, well
into the seventh century. What is significant about Viriconium
is that it had a major set of baths which almost certainly
survived into the seventh century. Indeed, part of the outer
wall, known now as the Old Work, is still standing after 1,800
years. Though it seems scarcely credible that Gildas would
refer to Viriconium as Badon, it is possible that in his delight
for word-play he would nickname the Wrekin as the Hill of the
Baths. He may also have been alluding to the Breidden Hills,
one of the probable sites for Caer Faddon, which can be seen
from the Wrekin.

Another suggestion is Mynydd Baidan in mid-Glamorgan,
south of Maesteg. Alan Wilson and Baram Blackett suggest that
the name *baidan* is derived from the Celtic for "to dare", which
is *beiddio* in modern Welsh. North of Mynydd Baidan is

Maescadlawr, which they translate as the "area of the battle field". They believe this may be the site of the second battle of Badon in the year 667, but it's one worth considering for the original battle.

For completeness I should mention Laurence Gardner's suggested site at Dun Baetan, near Carrickfergus in Ulster. In *Bloodline of the Holy Grail*, Gardner refers to the conflict between the Scotii kings of Dál Riata and their Irish overlords. In their battle for independence, the Scots defeated the Irish at Dun Baetan in 516, but were defeated there in 575. It was this second battle, according to Gardner, at which the young Artúir mac Aedan was present. Despite the internal logic and consistency of Gardner's argument, there is an inherent problem in accepting that the British would celebrate a victory in Ireland by Irish settlers in Britain, and Gildas specifically states that the victory at Badon was against the Saxons, not the Irish.

Before plotting the locations, let us turn to Arthur's final battle.

2. Camlann

Camlann is not included in Nennius's list. This may be because the original compiler did not want to sing of a defeat but of Arthur's victories, ending at the triumph of Badon, or because the original list was compiled during Arthur's reign, and therefore before Camlann. Its absence from the list is not necessarily critical, although it will inevitably raise doubts about whether it was fought by the same Arthur who fought the others. Curiously, Camlann is not mentioned anywhere else by Nennius, nor is it referred to by Gildas. Its first appearance is in the *Welsh Annals* under the year 93 (539AD), the year "in which Arthur and Medraut fell". It also appears in several of the Welsh Triads, where the clear implication is that it arose out of a quarrel between Gwenhwyfar, Arthur's queen, and Gwenhwyfach, Gwenhwyfar's sister and the wife of Mordred, and, in the way of such things, a quarrel led to a battle. Geoffrey of Monmouth typically took it out of

all proportion and has Mordred abduct and seduce Gwenhwyfar and seize the kingdom while Arthur is away. The Triads
regard it as one of the "Three Futile Battles", emphasizing that
it mushroomed out of nothing. This has the feel of authenticity,
a memory of Britain's greatest hero brought low by a pointless
quarrel.

Geoffrey of Monmouth places the battle at Camelford
in Cornwall, based on no more than the name – the river
Camel was known as Cambla – and possibly the proximity to
Tintagel. The bridge over the Camel here is known as Slaugh-
terbridge, though this probably refers to a battle between the
British and Saxons during the reign of Egbert of Wessex in 823.
In fact, the name may not refer to a battle at all as it could be
derived from the old Saxon word *slaggy* for muddy, as in
Slaggyford in Northumberland. In 1602 the antiquarian
Richard Carew, one time High Sheriff of Cornwall, developed
the Arthurian connection in his *Survey of Cornwall* by identifying a stone near the Camel as being the spot where Arthur
died. This stone, however, bears the inscription *Latini ic jacit
filius Mogari*, recording the burial of Latinus, son of Mogarus,
and was probably brought to the site years before to form part
of a footbridge across the river. Although many Arthurian
legends have developed in this area, it is difficult to find any
basis for them.

The word Camlann means either "crooked bank" (*cam glan*)
or "crooked enclosure" (*cam llan*), a phrase which must describe thousands of locations across Britain. The River Cam in
Somerset is a likely contender. It is a tributary of the Yeo and
flows from the hills near Yarlington to join the Yeo just outside
Yeovilton, near Ilchester. En route it passes by the impressive
hill fort of Cadbury Castle, long believed to be the original
Camelot. Excavations by Leslie Alcock in the late 1960s
showed that Cadbury Castle was significantly refortified from
470 onwards, for at least two generations. It was both a
defensive fort and an inhabited village right through the
Arthurian period. If it were occupied by Arthur then Camlann

may have been fought right on his doorstep. The Cam twists through a vigorous series of bends about a kilometre away at Sparkford.

In 1935 O.G.S. Crawford proposed that the name was originally *Camboglanna*, a Roman fort along Hadrian's Wall at what is now Birdoswald. It is certainly true that here the River Irthing twists its way around the site in a very crooked glen but, as Geoffrey Ashe has highlighted, the name Camboglanna, in evolving towards Camlann, would for centuries have been known as *Camglann*, and that ought to be how it is recorded in the *Welsh Annals* and any other near-contemporary sources. The fact that every source records it as Camlann suggests a much older name. Nevertheless, Camboglanna has another connection of interest. Some thirty kilometres to the west, at what is now Burgh-by-Sands, was the fort of Aballava, which became Avalana by the sixth century. The legend has Arthur taken to Avalon to heal his wounds after Camlann. Intriguingly, there are dedications at several of the forts along Hadrian's Wall, including Aballava, to Latis, the goddess of lakes and water. August Hunt has suggested she may be the basis for the Lady of the Lake legend.

Another northern site frequently suggested is Camelon, near Falkirk in the Lothians, just north of the Antonine Wall. It has also been suggested as the original for Camelot, most recently in David Carroll's *Arturius, a Quest for Camelot*. Laurence Gardner has Artúir mac Aedan fight at both Camelon and Camboglanna, in his battles against the Picts. Camelon was a significant Roman fort which had been strengthened in the 140s at the time the Antonine Wall was built. The Roman name of the fort is no longer known, although the village that grew up around it gained the British name of *Caermawr* ("Great Fort") so is unlikely to be confused with Camelot. It is difficult to know when it was abandoned, because the site was substantially robbed and subsequently built over. The presence of a nearby Romano-British temple, now called Arthur's O'en, suggests a stable period of occupation. Nevertheless, the fort was almost certainly abandoned by the mid-third century and steadily fell into ruin.

There are several locations in Wales still called Camlan today. Two of these are near Dolgellau, near the village of Mallwyd, a name which may mean "battle ground". This is the area advocated by Blake and Lloyd in *Pendragon* and by Alan Wilson and Baram Blackett in *Artorius Rex Discovered*. It is close to other locations connected with Vortigern and Ambrosius, and to several of the suggested sites from the battle list, especially the Rivers Glen and Dubglas. It is also close to one of the suggested sites for Llongborth (discussed below), showing that it might fit a pattern of struggles within the Welsh princedoms. There is also a stream called Afon Gamlan just north of Dolgellau, emphasizing how common the name is in the area.

Another site is also associated with the battle. This is Cwm Llan, a valley on the southern flanks of Snowdon, close to the fort of Dinas Emrys. Peter Bartrum draws attention to the legend about this battle as recorded in *Y Brython*. It tells how Arthur and his men were heading from Dinas Emrys towards the pass over Snowdon at Cwm Tregalan, and met the enemy in Cwm Llan ("the Valley of the Lake"). Arthur was able to push the enemy back but at the top of the pass they were ambushed in a hail of arrows. Arthur was killed and buried where he fell at a cairn called Carnedd Arthur, and the pass is still called Bwlchysaethau, "The Pass of the Arrows". A steep climb down from the pass takes you to Llyn Llydaw, supposed to be the home of the Lady of the Lake. Nearby is supposed to be Ogof Llanciau Eryri ("The Cave of the Young Men") in which, rather like the Christian legend of the Seven Sleepers of Ephesus, the seven who survived Camlann are supposed to be sleeping, awaiting their call to fight again for Arthur.

The Welsh sites are tempting because of the continuity of the name, but we should not forget that the name would have been just as common throughout Britain before the Saxon settlement. Nevertheless, the Welsh sites suggest a link with Arthur of Dyfed, who probably had conflicts with Gwynedd in this region. These sites do not, however, fit comfortably with any for Badon, raising again the question of whether the battles were fought by two or more different Arthurs.

3. The Saxon sites

Before we map out all of the above locations, we need to remind ourselves of the known Saxon battles during the Arthurian period. If Arthur's twelve battles were all against the Saxons or Angles then, although the *ASC* was not given to recording defeats, there may yet be some hints.

We have determined that the Arthurian period ran from about 480–520, and the *ASC* lists these battles during and around those years.

477 Aelle fought Welsh at *Cymenes ora*, [who] fled into the wood *Andredes leag*.

485 Aelle fought Welsh near the margin of *Mearcrædes burnam*.

491 Aelle besieged *Andredes cester*.

495 Cerdic fought Welsh at *Cerdices ora*, which is on or near the coast.

501 Port landed at Portsmouth and killed a noble young Briton.

508 Cerdic killed the British king Natanleod, after whom the land as far as *Cerdices ford* was named Netley.

514 Stuf and Wihtgar fought the Britons at *Cerdices ora*.

519 Cerdic fought the Britons at *Cerdices ford*.

527 Cerdic fought the Britons at *Cerdices leag*.

530 Cerdic took the Isle of Wight at *Wihtgaræsbyrg*.

Only a few of these provide much help, especially since we know that some of the names may arise retrospectively, such as Port and Portsmouth. However, even though the individual's names may be suspect, the locations are probably more accurate, if they can be traced. Thankfully a few are easier to identify than others.

Cymenes ora (*ora* meaning shore) appears in a charter of Selsey Abbey as *Cumeneshore* relating to a grant of land by Caedwalla, king of Essex, to the abbey in 673. The surviving copy is not contemporary, leading some authorities to term it a forgery, but regardless of whether or not the abbey owned the land, the description must still be accurate. It states that *Cumeneshore* was a stretch of coast between Pagham and Selsey Bill, now known as The Owers, much of which has long since eroded away. The *Andredes leag* is taken as the vast forest of Anderida, the Weald, which at that time densely covered much of Sussex and west Kent. Its western extremity was just north of Selsey, around Midhurst and Petersfield, so the *ASC* entry does hold together. In 491 Aelle besieged *Andredes cester*, the Roman fort at Anderitum [Pevensey]. Pevensey, some 80km east along the coast from Selsey, is the same spot that William the Conqueror chose to land nearly six hundred years later.

These first three entries seem to make clear the spread of Aelle's territory. The archaeology, however, does not wholly support this. The Saxons made little inroad into what became Sussex, and certainly not in the area around Selsey. One would expect a successful landing there to result in Aelle capturing the Roman town of Noviomagus [Chichester], but not only is there no mention of this, there have been no archaeological discoveries of any fifth-century Saxon sites there. The main area of Saxon settlement in the fifth century was between the Rivers Ouse and Cuckmere, and by the sixth century it had expanded westward into the area between the Ouse and the Adur. There must be some significance in the battle of 485 "near the margin of *Mearcrædes burnam*". This name has been interpreted as "the river of the frontier agreed by treaty", suggesting that Aelle had an agreement with the British that the Saxons could settle on one side of a river only. We do not know which river, but it must be either the Cuckmere or, more probably, the Ouse. A major hill fort, Mount Caburn, rises above the Ouse where it is joined by the Glynde Reach.

Caburn is one of the few Celtic names surviving in Sussex, originally *Caer Bryn*: "strong fort". It seems likely that the original Saxon settlers, despite their initial victory at Cymen's shore, must have settled between the Ouse and the Cuckmere, where they were guarded on the west by the fort at Caburn and on the east by the fort at Anderida. In 485 the Saxons sought to break out across one of the rivers, probably the Ouse at Caburn. Unusually for the *ASC*, this is not recorded as a victory. It simply says, "they fought the Welsh". No doubt they were contained and pushed back across the river and later, in 491, broke out across the Cuckmere and slaughtered the British at Pevensey.

What it most interesting about Mount Caburn is the Glynde Reach. This small stream was originally the Glynde Bourne, thus bearing a striking similarity to the first battle of Nennius's list at the River Glein. If it is the same battle, then it may have been the first Arthurian victory. We do not know how accurate the date is, but 485 fits perfectly with the likely date for the start of the Arthurian campaign, culminating in Badon in 493 or so. It appears that Aelle was contained by the defeat at *Mearcrædes* until he defeated the British at Anderida. After that he was able to move further west. It is perhaps telling that the hill that faces Mount Caburn, just to the north, is now called Saxon Down, possibly a memory of where the Saxons gathered in readiness for their battle against the British.

Aelle is something of a mystery amongst the early Saxon settlers. The earlier Hengist and his successor Octha have been remembered in the story of Vortigern and Ambrosius, whilst the later Cerdic became the founder of a dynasty. Aelle exists between these two almost as an aside, as if he were battling away in Sussex whilst the main action was happening elsewhere. He doesn't appear in any of the Arthurian foundation stories, and after his passing we know nothing more about Sussex for over 150 years. Yet Bede cites Aelle as the first of the Saxons "to rule over all the Southern kingdoms". He was the first to be regarded as the *Bretwalda*, a form of High King, to whom all the other chieftains offered their loyalty. We have no reason to doubt Bede. He tells us that he gathered his information about Sussex from Bishop Daniel of Wessex who knew the people of Sussex intimately. Somehow Aelle, although seeming to have been confined to the shores of Sussex, became paramount chief of the Saxons.

This suggests that whilst his people may have remained closeted in Sussex, Aelle was in contact with the British leaders, almost certainly with Ambrosius and probably with Arthur. The evidence has shown that the Saxons had been held in check by the resistance under Ambrosius and that for nearly a generation the Saxons and Angles remained in their coastal settlements. This peace had become strained by the late 480s, and then broke, perhaps when Ambrosius was too old to govern, and Aelle led a Saxon revival. The assault on Anderida may have been the start of this revival, which culminated at Badon.

Thus it would seem that Aelle was the Saxon leader at Badon, even though tradition names Octha. Octha may have been the commander under Aelle. The British victory at Badon would seem to be a suitable retaliation for the slaughter at Anderida, wiping out the Saxon army. In all likelihood Aelle and his sons were killed in the battle, which is why we hear no more of him, and why he left no dynasty to rule Sussex. Thereafter Sussex survived as a small insignificant enclave, hemmed in by the British in the Weald. If this is true – and Aelle's high rank would strongly suggest it – then it would argue that Badon, and probably most of Arthur's battle campaign, was in the South.

Octha may also have been killed at Badon or, if he survived, it was now that he was assigned a small territory in Thanet in the far east of Kent, keeping the Saxons at arm's length from the British heartland. Octha is sometimes equated with Aesc, but we cannot be sure they are the same individuals. Aesc is supposed to have ruled the *Cantwara* for thirty-four years, from 488 to 522, which almost parallels the Arthurian period, but we cannot accept those dates without question. I am not convinced that the Octha who fought at Badon, according to the story in *The Dream of Rhonabwy*, is the same as Aesc (or Oisc) from whom the rulers of Kent were descended.

The remaining battles listed at this time all relate to Cerdic and his nephews, Stuf and Wihtgar. We have already discussed the uncertainty of Cerdic's reign (*see* Chapter 4) and that his arrival in Britain could have been any one of a series of dates – 495, 514, 523 or 532. Remember that the *ASC* states that Cerdic "succeeded to the kingdom" six years after his arrival, so that he could have assumed the kingship in 501, 520, 529 or 538. Intriguingly, two of those dates show that he could have arrived either at the time of Badon (493–497) or at the time of Camlann (*circa* 520).

It is hard to imagine that Cerdic's rise to power is not in some way connected to either Arthur's triumph or his downfall. Badon was supposed to have instigated a period of peace, a *Pax Arthuriana*, in which all conflicts with the Saxons ceased. Indeed, Gildas still recalled this remarkable calm while writing *De Excidio* in the 530s. If Cerdic arrived in 495, then his sequence of battles would have disrupted that calm unless they were confined to an area not under Gildas's consideration. Alternatively, if Cerdic did not arrive until 532 and his battles fell into the period 532–538, Gildas may not have considered them worth commenting on, especially as Cerdic was British. Cerdic's rise to power must have come as a consequence of Arthur's fall, unless he was in league with Arthur. But because Cerdic was British, Gildas might have regarded his battles as yet another of the civil wars that continued in Britain through this period of peace. However, if Cerdic was alive and ruling when Gildas was writing, he would have seen him as the greatest traitor of them all, and would undoubtedly have mentioned him. This means Cerdic was either already dead or not yet in power. Thus we have two scenarios:

(1) Cerdic was a young Briton, born around the time of the major Saxon revolt in the 440s. He may well have had a Saxon mother and thus knew the language and became an interpreter.

He sought personal gain during the subsequent British retaliation, but failed and retreated to Gaul, possibly Armorica,
returning in 495 to curry favour with Arthur and, as a consequence, was granted command of the Gewisse. Wanting
more power he fought against the British and took control
of land in Hampshire and Wiltshire, setting himself up as king
in 501 and ruling to 517. His death is close to the probable date
for Camlann and we might conjecture that Cerdic was involved
in the wars with Arthur and was a supporter of Medraut/
Mordred. Cerdic's usurpation would thus fit into the category
of Gildas's civil wars but because Cerdic was dead by the 530s,
Gildas did not single him out for comment.

(2) Cerdic fits into the later wave of chieftains who established control in the 540s. Cerdic's campaign ran from 532 to
538 when he assumed control of the West Saxons. This makes a
stronger case for Cerdic being the military commander of a
group of confederate Saxons and Britons. The West Saxons
were not yet a unified whole, and during the mid-sixth century
were a number of separate units carving out territory across the
south and the Thames Valley. After a few battles Cerdic
managed to unify an area of Saxons and Britons. Gildas would
doubtless dismiss Cerdic's initial forays as part of the continuing civil unrest and not see it as a re-emergence of the Saxon
onslaught which gathered pace in the 540s. What's more, if
Camlann did occur just before Gildas wrote De Excidio (as
suggested by his comments about Constantine), then Cerdic
may have benefited from Arthur's death, taking territory in the
inevitable chaotic aftermath. If he did not already have control
of the Gewisse, he certainly took command now.

Of these two options (2) best fits the overall time frame for the
chronology of the rulers of the Wessex; (1) has a romantic appeal
that makes Cerdic an ally and then an enemy of Arthur, and has
some substance in some of the later tales that claim Cerdic was a
friend of Arthur's until they argued. However, as we have seen,
there were so many people called Ceredig/Ceretic/Cerdic that
the tradition probably relates to someone else – most likely

Caradog Vreichfras – and was later identified with Cerdic. This solution concurs with our earlier analysis based on the *ASC*, and convinces me that Cerdic was not contemporary with Arthur but rose to power in the vacuum left by Arthur's death.

If we look at Cerdic's battles as listed in the *ASC*, regardless of other chieftains such as Port or Stuf, we find only four sites mentioned – *Cerdices ora*, *Cerdices ford*, *Cerdices leag* and *Wihtgaræsbyrg*. No firm location is known for any of these. It has been suggested that *Cerdices ora* may be the same as Calshot, a spit of land that juts out at the end of Southampton Water, though other sources suggest this was named after the chalky deposits in the area – *celces ora*. O.G.S. Crawford puts forward a theory that the Saxons landed at Totton, at the head of Southampton Water, based purely on a logical route rather than any philological data.* However, Crawford believed that the Saxons followed an ancient trackway known as the Cloven Way, which passes through two other possible sites. The *ASC* tells us that *Cerdices ford* was on the far side of Netley Marsh, and if we assume this reference to be correct, it would place it somewhere just north of the New Forest. The chronicler Athelweard identified it as being on the River Avon, but since *afon* is the Celtic for any river this does not necessarily help. The Hampshire Avon flows through Charford, just north of Fordingbridge, and Crawford suggested that this was *Cerdices ford*. However, most etymologists believe the name Charford (and there are several villages with that name) is derived from either *Ceorl's-ford*, named after another individual, or *cyric forda* meaning "ford by the church". Interestingly, just to the east of Charford is the source of the River Blackwater, which flows into the Test near Netley Marsh (*see* Map 5). These four battles (*Cerdicesora*, *Cerdicesford*, *Cerdicesleag* and *Wihtgaræsbyrg*) could be the four fought on the *Dubglas* if the British were fighting Saxons arriving via Southampton Water.

* See Crawford, O.G.S. "Cerdic and the Cloven Way", *Antiquities*, Volume 5, December 1931.

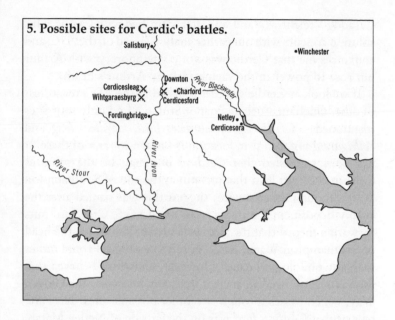

5. Possible sites for Cerdic's battles.

Continuing along the Cloven Way, Crawford identifies a site to the west of Charford, near the ancient earthworks known as Grim's Ditch, listed in a charter as *fyrdinges lea*. Fyrding refers to an army on full war footing, and he suggests this could have been the site of *Cerdices leag*. There is a logic to this route. It may also be significant that at Downton, the village that adjoins Charford to the north, is a feature called The Moot, or Moot Hill, believed to have been a meeting place for Saxon councils. It would seem only natural that, if the Saxons under Cerdic first established themselves in this area, they would have a meeting place for their *witan* which, as the first in that area, would have become held in high esteem. Perhaps even more intriguingly, the part of the Moot that abuts the River Avon has been called for centuries Natanbury, and is believed to have been the burial mound of Natanleod.

It is worth noting that if Cerdic's confederates did establish themselves in the basin of Southampton Water around Charford, they were within striking distance of both Badbury Rings and Liddington, which would have made Cerdic a contender for fighting at Badon if his arrival could be satisfactorily dated to 495. The chronology, however, best suits a later arrival. If it were possible to prove that one of Cerdic's battles equated to Camlann, it would bring the Arthurian world into much sharper focus. Unfortunately, no amount of research can detect any trace of an early Celtic name like Camlann for any of the locations along the Avon valley in which Cerdic's early battles may have taken place. One can look longingly at the twists and turns in the river and think that maybe somewhere here was called the 'crooked enclosure' or something similar at one time, but that could apply to almost any river.

Intriguingly, the *Mort Artu*, part of the early Vulgate Cycle of Arthurian legends on which Malory based his famous work, has Camlann take place on Salisbury Plain. There is no evidence for this at all. Possibly this reflects some distant folk memory, but that could be a dim recollection of any major battle near Salisbury, such as that in 715 between Ceolred of Mercia and Ine of Wessex.

Despite these suggestions, no firm location can be made for any of Cerdic's battles. That also applies to *Wihtgaræsbyrg*, presumed to be a hill fort on the Isle of Wight. The only such fort is at Carisbrooke, but neither archaeological nor linguistic evidence can show any relationship between this and *Wihtgaræsbyrg*. The obvious place, based on the other Cerdic locales, is Whitsbury, less than 10km (6m) west of Charford, and set amongst a maze of valleys and ancient earthworks. However, most etymologies note that Whitsbury evolved from *Wiccheberia*, from *wice* for "wych elm", thus meaning the "fort where wych elms grow."

Trying to identify any other possible places associated with Cerdic is complicated by the abundance of the name Cerdic/Ceretic, and also, being a Celtic name, it was doubtless superseded by a Saxon name in due course. In this sense Cerdic is unusual amongst the early Saxon leaders in that he did not have places named after him. Creoda of Mercia, for example, is

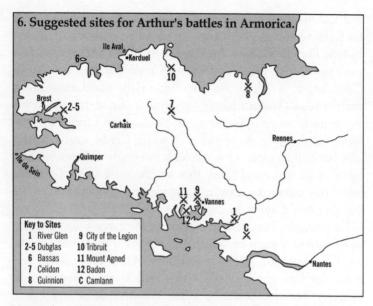

6. Suggested sites for Arthur's battles in Armorica.

Key to Sites
1 River Glen
2-5 Dubglas
6 Bassas
7 Celidon
8 Guinnion
9 City of the Legion
10 Tribruit
11 Mount Agned
12 Badon
C Camlann

remembered in Credenhill in Herefordshire, and Icel, his forebear, in Ickleton near Cambridge. For some reason Cerdic did not leave his mark on the landscape as much as he did on history.

4. The Breton angle

Ronald Millar, in *Will the Real King Arthur Please Stand Up?* (1978), has enterprisingly managed to find sites for all of Arthur's battles in Brittany (*see* Map 6, and below). Some people have dismissed this book as a spoof, or simply as a humorous read, but it raises some interesting points.

Millar reminds us that the Arthurian story also thrived in Brittany, and indeed much of the Arthurian story as we now know it developed there. In later centuries Arthur's name had mutated to Arzor, perhaps remembered in the name of the town Arzal, in the south near the mouth of the River Vilaine. Further along the coast is Arzon, which looks over the Golfe du Morbihan to the cliffs at Baden.

Below is a list of the possibilities identified by Millar:

1. At the mouth of the river Glein
   River Vilaine (formerly Gwilen), at Arzal

2–5. On the River Dubglas in the region of Linnuis
   River Daoulas, near Brest, in Leon (called Linnuis or Lyonesse)

6. On the River Bassas
   The Ile de Batz off North Finisterre

7. In the Caledonian Forest, that is Cat Coit Celidon
   The Forest of Quenecan (formerly Guerledon or Gerlidon)

8. In Fort Guinnion
   Castel Guennon at Tregon, near Dinard

9. The City of the Legion
   Vannes, the legionary capital in Armorica

10. On the bank of the River Tribruit
    The River Trieaux (formerly Trifrouit) at Lanleff

11. On the Mount of Agned, at Breguoin
    Ste-Anne (formerly Ste-Agned) near the village of Brech

12. Badon Hill
    Baden, near Vannes, on the Golfe du Morbihan

and Camlann
    Camerunn, near St-Nazaire

Millar is able to get a compellingly close similarity with most of the battles, except Bassas, Badon and Camlann. Perhaps this should not be too surprising. It is known that when the British migrated to Armorica and established new settlements, they brought their old names with them, such as Cornouaille. What this demonstrates is that place names in Brittany have remained relatively unchanged. Millar's research is an interesting snapshot of how names might have been identifiable in Britain had not so many changed under successive settlers.

Having identified a name is one thing, but are they necessarily appropriate settings? Millar himself admits that Baden, atop the cliffs overlooking the massive estuary of the river Vilaine, does not really fit the description of a *Mons Badonicus*.

The monastery of St Gildas is only the other side of this bay, near Arzon, so one would expect Gildas's description of it to be more accurate. Likewise, Millar's suggestion of Camerunn in the marshland near St-Nazaire is really a throwaway at the end of his book, and not a serious proposal.

The Breton dimension, however, raises the question of whether Arthur's battles started in Armorica and he then came to help the British at Badon. The Breton historian Léon Fleuriot, in *Les Origines de la Bretagne* (Librairie Payot, 1980), suggested that one reason why the British were able to maintain a resistance against the Saxons around the turn of the fifth/sixth centuries was partly due to "the support of continental Bretons" and that the collapse of the British defence in the late sixth century was because the Bretons were involved in their own war against the Franks. If the British saviour was Arthur then possibly he either came from Armorica or he was able to command Breton mercenaries, a concept that Geoffrey of Monmouth utilizes in his own story of Arthur. It is also the basis of Geoffrey Ashe's case for proposing Riothamus as Arthur though, as we have seen, the dates undermine this.

A variant on this idea comes from Chris Barber and David Pykitt in *Journey to Avalon* where they suggest that Arthur survived Camlann and retired to Brittany as a religious hermit, adopting the name Arthmael or Armel. Barber and Pykitt believe that he was Athrwys of Gwent, whom they date from 482–562. Little is known about Arthmael. He is believed to have been born in Gwent, near Llantwit Major, but no one knows when. He was a contemporary of and probably related to St Samson and St Cadfan. He appears in Armorica around the year 538, the same year as Camlann according to the *Welsh Annals*. He died sometime between 552 and 570. The church of Saint-Armel-des-Boscheaux is on the Golfe du Morbihan, close to the monastery of St Gildas.

Barber and Pykitt's dates coincide with those in the *Welsh Annals* for Badon and Camlann, but are too early for Athrwys of Gwent who I believe lived from around 600–660. The name change from Athryws to Arthmael also seems strange. Arthur of Badon is hardly likely to have kept his identity hidden after Camlann, not with Gildas living nearby.

All the evidence suggests that Badon was in Britain – that's where Gildas set it. The battle campaign that ended in Badon was therefore also going to be in Britain. The commander might have previously fought in Armorica. He might even have been a son of Riothamus, and so could have retired to Armorica afterwards. But otherwise we can exclude Armorica from our battle zone.

5. The overall picture

Map 7 brings together the distribution of battles. Apart from a few isolated proposals in Lincolnshire and Cambridgeshire the concentration of sites is in the North, the West, the South and North Wales. This may be an accident of language, in that old names survived longer in these areas and thus can be made to fit the sites, whereas sites in the East and Midlands have been too long influenced by later settlers and the old names have been lost. Nevertheless, they suggest three possible frontiers, as well as an agglomeration in North Wales. Nor should we ignore a possible eastern frontier, to include the partition mentioned by Gildas.

Table 15 groups the more likely sites for these battles by those five areas. In plotting these sites (*see* Map 8) several patterns emerge. The southern, eastern and western sites form clear frontiers. The northern frontier is more problematic. The pattern suggests a focus around the territory of the Gododdin, with the eastern line presenting a barrier to the Angles whilst the northern and western lines are a barrier against the Picts or Britons of Strathclyde. The southern line more or less follows Hadrian's Wall and would also be a frontier against the Angles and the Coelings.

The North Welsh sites plot a fluctuating border between Gwynedd and Powys. These sites could be interpreted as

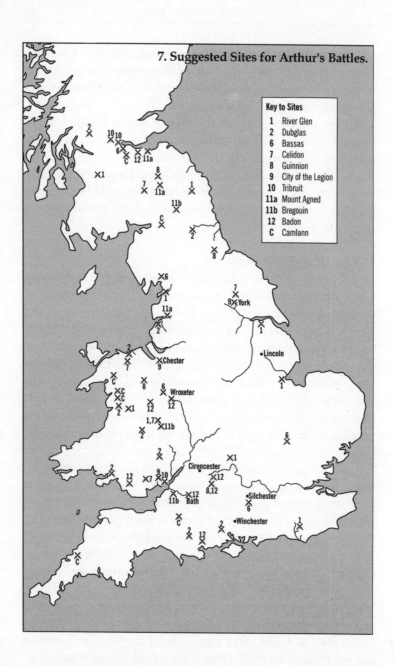

7. Suggested Sites for Arthur's Battles.

Key to Sites

1	River Glen
2	Dubglas
6	Bassas
7	Celidon
8	Guinnion
9	City of the Legion
10	Tribruit
11a	Mount Agned
11b	Bregouin
12	Badon
C	Camlann

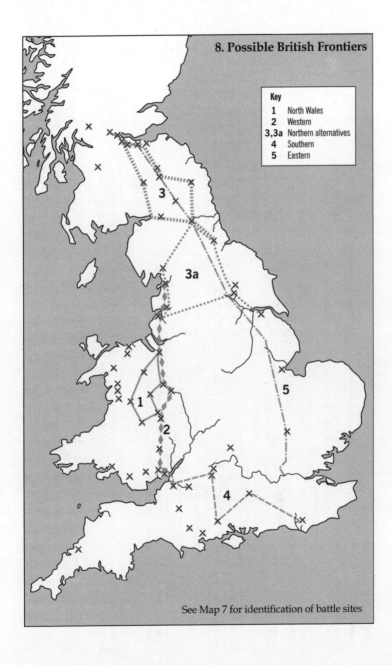

8. Possible British Frontiers

Key
1 North Wales
2 Western
3,3a Northern alternatives
4 Southern
5 Eastern

See Map 7 for identification of battle sites

Table 15 Nennius's Battle Sites

Nennius's site	Southern frontier	Western frontier	Northern frontier	Eastern Frontier	North Wales
Mouth of River Glein	Glynde Reach, Glyme, Oxford; Lewes, Sussex	Lune, Lancaster; Clun, Shropshire	Glen, Northumberland	Glanford Brigg, Lincolnshire	Gleiniant, Trefeglwys, Powys
River Dubglas in Linnuis	Divelish/Devil's Brook, Dorset; Blackwater, Hants	Douglas, near Preston, Lancashire	Devil's Water, Corbridge, Northumberland	Devil's Water, Corbridge, Northumberland	Dulas, Llandulas, Colwyn Bay, Gwynedd
River Bassas	Old Basing, Hampshire; or Bassingbourne, Cambridge	Baschurch, Shropshire	Dunipace, Camelon, Falkirk	Bassingbourne, Cambridgeshire	Baschurch, Shropshire
Forest of Celidon	Gellideg, nr Caerphilly, Gwent	Clun Forest, Shropshire	Hart Fell, Ettrick Forrest, Borders	Galtres Forest, York	between Clywd and Conway, Gwynedd
Fort Guinnion	Wanborough, Swindon, Wiltshire	The Wrekin, Wroxeter, Shropshire	Binchester, Durham; or Stow-in-Wedale, Borders	Stow-in-Wedale, Borders	Gwynion, Llanarmon, Powys
City of the Legion	Caerleon	Chester	York or Carlisle	York	Chester
Bank of River Tribruit	Twrc estuary, near Caerleon, on Severn	Ribble estuary, Lancashire; or Twrc estuary, near Caerleon	Links of Forth, Stirling; or Fords of Frew, Kippen	Links of Forth, Stirling; or Fords of Frew, Kippen	?
Mount Agned at Breguoin	Catbrain, Bristol	Leintwardine, Herefordshire; or Ribchester, Lancashire	Edinburgh; or Eildon Hills; or High Rochester, Borders	Edinburgh; or Eildon Hills; or High Rochester, Borders	Leintwardine, Herefordshire
Mount Badon	Solsbury Hill, Bath; Liddington Castle, Swindon; Mynydd Baidan, Glamorgan	The Wrekin, Shropshire; Caer Faddon or Breidden Hill, Welshpool	Bowden Hill, Linlithgow	Bowden Hill, Linlithgow; or Liddington Castle, Swindon	Caer Faddon or Breidden Hill, Welshpool

dealing with Irish raiders, but if that were so you would expect a stronger distribution in Dyfed, yet few sites have been proposed for Nennius's list in either Ceredigion or Dyfed. Whilst accepting the limitations imposed by a selective interpretation of battle sites, the sparsity of other options somewhat speaks for itself.

There is always the possibility that the battle sites did not follow a frontier but were opportunist strikes against local threats. If so, this would suggest that the battles were fought by local chieftains and not one overall commander. No sensible commander would stretch his resources across Britain, even if the capability were there, but would focus them against the main threats. These were Aelle in the south or the Angles in the North, suggesting that the campaign could have been in two halves.

We have deduced from our earlier chronology that Arthur's battle campaign, leading up to Badon, probably fell between 485 and 497 so if Nennius's battle list genuinely relates to Arthur and is not an amalgam of heroic battles, this map will help us focus more closely. We have five options. And we need to know who was ruling, or was the likely premier battle commander, in these locations during those years.

North Wales

The pattern of battles suggests conflict either between the territories of Gwynedd and Powys, or within Gwynedd, between the successors of Cunedda. The Saxons were still many years away from reaching the borders of Powys, and the threat from the Irish raiders, though still present, was no longer of such significance as to require so consolidated a campaign.

At this stage Gwynedd was not the united power it later became but was ruled by the sons and grandsons of Cunedda who governed from their hilltop forts in Anglesey and across the north of Wales. The principal ruler was Cadwallon Lawhir ("Longhand"). Early in his reign he was involved in a series of battles, where he combined forces with his uncle Ysfael against the Irish, who had settled on Anglesey in previous generations. Cadwallon took part in a famous battle called *Cerrig-y-Gwyddyl* ("Stones of the Irish"), where they hobbled their horses' front legs together so that they could only charge straight ahead. This was remembered in a Welsh Triad as one of the "Three Fettered Warbands".

Cadwallon appears in Geoffrey's story of Arthur as one of the four kings who bore golden swords at Arthur's coronation. This confirms that at least some tradition makes Cadwallon and Arthur contemporaries, but otherwise there is no firm evidence that Cadwallon fought either against or alongside Arthur.

Another candidate is Cadwallon's cousin Owain Danwyn, "White Tooth". Ruler of Gwynedd at Din Arth, he was the father of Cynlas the Tawny (Cuneglasus the Butcher), one of Gildas's tyrants, and was possibly murdered by his nephew Maelgwyn, son of Cadwallon, another of the tyrants. Graham Phillips and Martin Keatman, in *King Arthur, the True Story*, suggest that Owain is Arthur, noting that Owain was a contemporary of Arthur of Badon, that Arthur was murdered by his nephew, and that the rulers of Gwynedd were known as the "Pendragons" (head dragons) of Britain.

The title Pendragon, whilst closely associated with Arthur and, more specially, his father Uther, was not held solely by the rulers of one territory. According to Laurence Gardner in *Bloodline of the Holy Grail*, the Pen Dragon or "Head Dragon" was the "Guardian of the Celtic Isle". The Pendragon was appointed by a council of Druid Elders, and the earliest recorded was Cunobelinus (Cymbeline). During the Roman occupation the title must have been little more than honorific, but once the Roman yoke was lifted the Pendragon was able to re-emerge. The holder would also be a powerful ruler of his own kingdom but, as the Pendragon, was also the personification of Celtic authority. He was not a battle commander, who, rather like the Roman *dux*, was the *guletic*, or *wledig*.

Gardner provides his list of the Pendragons in *Realm of the Ring Lords*. Those relevant to our period of scrutiny are listed below. Their dates are drawn from my own assessments in Chapter 3. I have added the names of the relevant *wledig*, according to Gardner, as well as other known *wledigs* [in brackets] not specified by Gardner.

Table 16 British Pendragons and Wledigs

Pendragon	Wledig
Eudaf Hen, c330–400	Macsen [Magnus Maximus] 383–388
Coel Hen, c355–425	[possibly also Coel Hen]
Vortigern, c400–455	Cunedda, c390–460
Cunedda, c390–460	Ceretic of Strathclyde, c400–470
Brychan of Brycheiniog, c430–500	Ambrosius, c425–495
Dyfnwal Hen, c455–525	[Amlawdd, c440–510]
Brychan of Manau, c480–550	[Casanauth, c480–550]
Maelgwyn of Gwynedd, c480–550	[Celyddon, c500–570]
Aedan mac Gabhran of Dál Riata, c534–608	Artúir, 559–596

Gardner shows that although the Pendragon inheritance follows a bloodline, this can pass through daughters as well as sons, and thus may not stay within one kingdom. For instance, Aedan mac Gabhran, of Irish descent, inherited the title because his mother was the daughter of Brychan of Manau, whose wife was the daughter of Dyfnwal Hen.

The Pendragon at the time of Badon, in the 490s, may have been Brychan of Brycheiniog, though he would have been old and unlikely to be present at the battle. Since we cannot be precise about individuals' life-spans, it's possible Brychan was dead by then and that Dyfnwal Hen, whom we shall meet later, was the Pendragon. It was not Owain White-tooth.

Phillips and Keatman treat Owain as a ruler of Powys, with his capital at Wroxeter, but the genealogies do not support this. Powys at this time was almost certainly ruled by Cadell (*see* Chapter 6), the servant of King Benli, who with the help of Germanus (or Garmon) assumes the kingship. Powys was still a single kingdom, as inherited from Vortigern, though it later split into North and South. Bartrum conjectures (based on the Benli story) that Cadell's fortress was in North Powys, at

Llanarmon. Another suggestion, dating back to the seventeenth century, was that the descendants of Cadell (the Cadellings) lived at Gaer Fawr (the Great Castle), a massive hill fort just north of Guilsfield (Cegidfa), near Welshpool.* Intriguingly, if you plot the likely Welsh sites for Arthur's twelve battles, all but one of them (the Twrc estuary for Tribruit) form a defensive square surrounding Guilsfield. It is a compelling thought that these battles might represent a campaign by Cadell to defend and rebuild the boundaries of Powys. Unfortunately, though archaeological evidence shows that this hill fort was restrengthened at the end of the Roman period, there is not much support for its continued occupation in the fifth or sixth centuries. If it was reoccupied it may have been only as a short-term defensive strategy.

A site nearby, though, holds more intriguing possibilities. Phillips and Keatman believe that Wroxeter was, at least for some time, the most important city within Powys, and the archaeology supports this. Ken Dark, in *Civitas to Kingdom*, states that "the evidence from Wroxeter does encourage us to suppose that this was, if not *the* political centre of the Powysian kingdom on the fifth century, at least one of them". Wroxeter was occupied through to the mid-sixth century, but soon afterwards the population moved to the refuge of the hill fort at the Wrekin, just outside the Roman town. Wroxeter has long been proposed as Vortigern's town. Graham Webster confirms that in the centre of Wroxeter, in the mid-fifth century, something like a grand country mansion was built for a "powerful character".

There is also a memorial stone, dating from this time, commemorating a king called Cunorix. It reads CUNORIX MAQUS MAQUI COLONE, and is usually translated as "Cunorix, son of Maquicoline". It has been dated as most likely of the late fifth century, probably 460–475. It is usually presumed to be a

---

* See Owen, George, *The Description of Penbrokeshire* (1603) edited by Henry Owen (London, Cymmrodion Society, 1892), vol. 1, p. 187.

memorial to a visiting king, possibly one of the rulers of Dyfed, who was the guest of the head man in Wroxeter.

Cun- is a frequent prefix in Celtic names, such as Cunedda and Cunobelinus. The name Cunorix means "Hound King", and would convert into Welsh as Cynwrig, strikingly similar to Cerdic's son Cynric, suggesting the possibility that Cynric was named after one of Cerdic's relatives, perhaps an uncle, who might be commemorated here because he was one of the defenders of Wroxeter.

Maquicoline is an unusual compound name. It translates as "Son of the Holly". The equivalent word in Welsh for holly was *celyn*. Celyn was an occasional name, sometimes corrupted to Cuhelyn or Celynin. One of Gildas's brothers was called Celyn, but the name is not known for any king. Curiously, in the *Brut y Brenhinedd*, the name of Vortigern's grandfather, Vitalinus (Guethelinus), is copied as Cuhelyn. If we follow this fancy a little further, then Cunorix, as "the son of the son of" Cuhelyn, could be Vortigern himself. Vortigern means "supreme king", which could also be an interpretation of Cunorix.

Regardless of who Cunorix was, it is evident that Wroxeter was not only a major town in the fifth century, but one that was fit for a king who entertained kings. Someone would have succeeded to this estate after the death of Vortigern and his sons, and this can only have been the successor to the territory of Powys. Initially it may have been Ambrosius himself, ruling Powys from Wroxeter from the 460s to the 470s before Cadell took over.

This all rather temptingly makes Cadell a candidate for Arthur, one I have not seen previously suggested. One could even fancy Viriconium as the mythical Camelot, not by name, but as the most impressive surviving town in sub-Roman Britain. The archaeologists at Wroxeter stated that the town contains "the last classically inspired buildings in Britain". Christopher Snyder, in *An Age of Tyrants*, writes, "sub-Roman Wroxeter was a town worth protecting, with new structures and imported goods, worthy of a local lord and his guests".

This suggests something of far wider consequences than
Cadell protecting Powys from the young upstart Maelgwyn.
It suggests that Viriconium, in the hands of Cadell, served as a
protection not just for Powys but for the whole of Wales,
which brings us to the next option.

Western frontier

The most remarkable aspect of the line connecting these battles
is that it runs almost vertically north–south, much of it following what later became Offa's Dyke. It thus forms a natural
frontier between Wales and beyond, reaching up into the old
British kingdom of Rheged. It could easily be held from three
forts – Caerleon in the south and Chester and Ribchester in the
north, with Viriconium as the administrative centre. It would
require a consortium of only three rulers, as in the 480s and
490s Chester was probably part of Powys. If we accept Cadell
as the principal ruler in Powys, the ruler in Rheged was most
likely Merchiaun (Mark) the Lean. The ruler in Gwent is more
problematic as data are confusing. Table 8 suggests it would be
Erb, one of those individuals who is no more than a name in a
pedigree. The power in the area was either Brychan of Brycheiniog, or more likely Erb's predecessor Caradog, who was
probably still alive.

Caradog is one of many with that name, but some believe
that this is the real Caradog Vreichfras, not the descendant of a
century later. Caradog was Arthur's senior counsellor whom
we will discuss in more detail in the next chapter. Meirchion
may have been the father of King Mark of the Tristan legend.
This frontier would thus be held by four powerful rulers:
Cadell, Brychan, Caradog and Meirchion. All of them could
have been involved in battles holding the line in the name of the
Ardd Ri, who at that time was Brychan.

The biggest problem with this proposal is why the frontier
was here. Although today it runs remarkably close to the
present border between Wales and England, there was no such
division in the late fifth century. If there was any border, it was

that between Britannia Prima and the other two southern provinces, which ran about thirty miles to the east. If, as we have suggested, Maxima Caesariensis had still sought to continue a Roman style of administration, whilst Flavia Caesariensis was becoming settled by the Saxons in the east, this border would be all the more significant to those in Britannia Prima.

There is, though, little evidence to show that the provinces survived much beyond the middle of the fifth century. Charts identifying the distribution of Saxon occupation by the late fifth century show them penetrating little further west than the line of Dere/Ermine Street, though with probable forays across the Midlands into eastern Powys which, at this time, stretched more into the centre of Britain. Barbara Yorke, writing in *The Blackwell Encyclopedia of Anglo-Saxon England*, stated: "There is a marked contrast in the archaeological record between the 'Celtic' culture of western Britain and the 'Anglo-Saxon' culture of the east, especially in the sixth century."*

The Dream of Rhonabwy, later included as part of *The Mabinogion*, talks of the battle of Badon as Caer Faddon, and places it near to Welshpool (*see* Chapter 8). Although the story dates from more than seven centuries after Arthur, it is clearly a memory of a major confrontation with the Saxons. It may not have been *the* battle of Badon, as recalled by Gildas, but it must have been a significant battle at a place with a name sufficiently similar to Badon to become identified with it.

The battle of Caer Faddon probably took place in the late sixth century, a hundred years after Badon and twenty years after Gildas's death, though we can't be certain of that. Even before Gildas died the Saxon war machine had stirred again. In 556 Cynric and Ceawlin fought the British at *Beranbyrg* (Barbury Castle), close to Liddington Castle in Wiltshire.

---

* Lapidge, Michael (ed.) (1999), p. 416. See also maps in Myres (1986), p. 88 and Oppenheimer (2006), p. 370.

The date may not be wholly accurate, because the next victory isn't recorded until 571, when the West Saxons captured four towns in the Thames Valley. Then came the major defeat of the British at Dyrham in 577 followed by another at *Fethanleag* in 584 and "great slaughter" at Woden's Barrow (possibly Wanborough) in 592. All this is recorded in the *ASC*. We know that at the same time the Angles under Creoda were advancing across the British Midlands, carving out what became the kingdom of Mercia. Creoda died in 593 and there must have been many skirmishes, if not wholesale battles, before then, and certainly under his successor Pybba. So whereas the 480s and 490s saw the British rise up and force back the invaders, the 580s and 590s saw the reverse with the British slaughtered under a massive Saxon onslaught.

Under those circumstances the western frontier as shown in Map 8 takes on a new reality, but a century after Badon. This is the time of Artúir of Dyfed, Meurig of Gwent, Cynan of Powys, and Cynfor Host-Protector of the North. Cynan of Powys spent his time harrying his neighbours rather than fighting the Saxons. That was left to Cyndrwyn, a rival ruler of Pengwern, an outcrop kingdom of Powys, around Shrewsbury. Thanks to Cyndrwyn and his sons, including the famous Cynddylan, the men of Pengwern fought bravely to protect their lands against the Mercians. Cynfor Host-Protector doubtless rallied the Men of the North, though nothing is now remembered of his battles. In Gwent, Meurig and his famous father Tewdrig, who came back from retirement to fight one last battle against the Saxons, are long remembered in song. Meurig's son Athrwys possibly fought alongside them.

Between them, Meurig, Cyndrwyn and Cynfor could doubtless have held that frontier line and fought at those battles in Nennius's list. Yet, none is associated with them in legend, unless it is via Athrwys ap Meurig. We know virtually nothing about him, not even whether he succeeded to the kingdom of Gwent. He signed no charters as king, and the records show that Meurig, who had a long life, was succeeded by his grandson Morgan. This would, of course, fit in with Nennius's description of Arthur as a *dux bellorum*, and not necessarily a king. Perhaps Athrwys was killed in battle, and perhaps he fought alongside Cyndrwyn and Cynfor in holding the western frontier. If he did, those are not the names he is associated with in legend. And though Athrwys could not have fought at the Badon remembered by Gildas, he could have fought at Caer Faddon.

The western frontier is thus more plausible a century after Badon.

Northern frontier

One ruler dominated the north in the late fifth century. In the territory between the Walls the main force was Dyfnwal Hen, Pendragon after the death of Brychan of Brycheiniog, and one of the most powerful warriors of his day. Table 5 suggests that he lived from about 455–525, so he would be in his late thirties during the battle campaign. His grandfather was Ceretic of Strathclyde, and his sons became rulers of the territories between the Walls. One of his daughters married Brychan of Manau, possibly a son of Brychan Brycheiniog. His descendants were notably wealthy and later owned part of the legendary "Thirteen Treasures of Britain" sought by Merlin, including the halter of Clydno Eityn and the magic sword of Rhydderch Hael. Dyfnwal appears in the Irish stories about Cú Chulainn, in which he is known as Domnal, the warlike ruler of Scotland.

Dyfnwal's main opponents, apart from the Picts and the Scots, would have been the British tribes south of Hadrian's Wall, including the Gododdin and descendants of Coel, the Coelings. In contrast to Dyfnwal's descendants, the Coelings of that generation were poor. There was Merchiaun (Mark the Lean), his son Cinmarc the Dismal, and Mark's cousin Sawyl (Samuel) the Humble. However, Sawyl's cousin Einion was the father of Rhun the Wealthy, suggesting at least some change of fortune. How much of that might have been due to another cousin, Eliffer of the Great Host, is open to speculation.

Eliffer and his sons ruled the eastern Pennines, and thus were on the front line facing the rising menace of the Angles who, under Soemil, had laid claim to Deira, the area between the Humber and the Tees around the middle of the fifth century. Eliffer's father, Arthwys, must also have been involved in these battles. There would be few reasons or opportunities for the Coelings to venture north of the Wall unless threatened by Dyfnwal's sons. They had enough to cope with facing the Angles and the Irish. The pattern of battles in Map 7 is too haphazard to reflect any consistent campaign between the Coelings and the Gododdin, and is far more suggestive of battles between the Gododdin and Strathclyde marking Dyfnwal's territorial gains.

The epicentre of these battles is around the Eildon Hills and the Roman fort of Trimontium. This had ceased to be occupied by the end of the second century, but the Celtic fort at the top of one of the Eildon Hills showed evidence of reoccupation by the end of the fourth century. In *Arthur and the Lost Kingdoms*, Alistair Moffat has speculated that a Romano-British cavalry unit under Arthur re-established itself in this area, perhaps first at Eildon but then further east at what became Roxburgh. This unit was primarily engaged against the advancing Angles. Moffat does not identify all of the sites from Nennius's list, suggesting sufficient in the area to presume that all belong there (though surprisingly he concedes that Badon probably was at Bath). There are certainly enough potential sites here to make this area a distinct possibility, whether it relates to Dyfnwal's expansionism or a cavalry unit holding back the Angles.

These sites mean that the battles were fought primarily on Gododdin soil, but if at this time the area was under the control of Dyfnwal and his sons, there is no room for anyone called Arthur. The only like-named individual in the region, the Coeling Arthwys, could not have managed a campaign this far north.

It is possible, though, to map out an alternative northern frontier. In *From Scythia to Camelot*, Linda Malcor and

C. Scott Littleton propose a sequence that could have been fought by Lucius Artorius Castus against the Picts, around the year 185. They suggest that the campaign could have started at the fort of Ribchester (Breguoin), then under Castus's command, and from there along the Ribble to its estuary (Tribruit). The pursuit then moved south to a sequence of battles along the Douglas, before the Caledonii headed across the Pennines to York. Castus drove the Picts north to Binchester (Guinnion) and from there back across Hadrian's Wall where they met again at Yeavering Bell (River Glein). The Picts were now in full retreat, but Castus engaged them again in the Forest of Celidon before pursuing them north to the final victory at Dumbarton (Badon).

Malcor and Littleton don't offer a site for Bassas, but a site near Stirling would certainly fit their scenario. There are two concerns, however. Firstly, would this campaign be remembered three centuries later, by then somehow attributed to another whose own battles may have echoed those of Castus? And secondly, how does Badon fit into the timetable when it happened in the year of Gildas's birth? Badon (as Dumbarton) is the one weak link in an otherwise feasible proposal, and it raises again the possibility that Badon was not part of the same campaign, but the culmination of a series of battles against the Saxons.

Malcor and Littleton's proposal might also fit an alternative northern campaign. A campaign against the Angles could have started at York, and moved south along the Humber to face them in their heartland near Barton at Glanford Bridge (Glein) and then headed north to Binchester (Guinnion) and up to the Wall at Corbridge (one or more of the Dubglas battles). It would not need much of a trespass beyond the Wall to engage the Angles again in the Forest of Celidon. This may have marked the end of one campaign and could have been led by Eliffer of the Great Host from York, perhaps assisted by his father Arthwys. The threat then shifted to the west coast with the Irish raiders. Battles could have taken place at Ribchester

(Bregouin), along the Ribble Valley (Tribruit) and the River Douglas (thus causing a mental link with the previous campaign). This covers all of the sites except Bassas and Badon. Bassas, which we have suggested means "shallows", might relate to any of the shoreline in Morecambe Bay which was once above sea level but was later engulfed. And if Badon was a separate battle, and not part of this campaign, it need not have been in the north. This second campaign may well have been led by Arthwys in conjunction with Mark of Rheged and other southern rulers.

There are later events that may have caused these battles to become embedded in the Arthurian legend. The battle of Arderydd, for instance, which happened eighty years after Badon, in 573, was between Arthwys's grandsons, Gwenddoleu, Peredur and Gwrgi. The reasons behind this battle are uncertain but it suggests some climactic vendetta between the two sets of families. The fact that it happened north of Hadrian's Wall, in the territory of Rhydderch Hael, suggests that Gwenddoleu may have betrayed the Coelings and was now in the pay of the sons of Dyfnwal. Gwenddoleu was known for his wealth as he also had one of the Thirteen Treasures of Britain, a gold and silver chessboard. There is another tradition that states that the battle was between Gwenddoleu and Rhydderch, and that the sons of Eliffer were not involved. This may make more sense, as it suggests that one of the Coelings, who had become wealthy, saw an opportunity to gain territory from a young and as yet untried Rhydderch, with fatal consequences. Gwenddoleu was killed and his bard, Myrddin, went insane after the battle and fled into the Forest of Celidon.

A brief aside is perhaps appropriate here about Myrddin. He was a bard at the court of Gwenddoleu which, according to the researches of W.F. Skene, was at what is now Carwinley (i.e. Caer Wenddoleu), just north of Longtown in Cumbria. This places it between the ancient kingdoms of Rheged and Strathclyde, a strategic locale which apparently came under pressure from the sons of Eliffer, Gwrgi and Peredur, resulting in the notorious battle at Arderydd. Myrddin lost not only his lord in that battle but also his brothers and his sister's children. Table 4 shows that Myrddin was an exact contemporary of Gwenddoleu and his life-span was probably around 520 to 590. He is thus far too late to have had any association with the Arthur of Badon, though he was contemporaneous with Artúir ap Aedan of Dál Riata, who lived from about 560 to 596. The two would certainly have known each other, and it was probably this that caused Geoffrey of Monmouth to make the erroneous connection between Merlin and Arthur. There is no doubt that Myrddin the Bard was a genuine historical figure (whose real name may have been Lailoken) but he will not help us identify Arthur of Badon.

Arderydd may have been remembered generations later rather like Camlann, and its closeness to Camboglanna on Hadrian's Wall may have compounded the error. What's more, Arderydd is situated in the Forest of Celidon and thus may be the same as Nennius's seventh battle. The connection with Myrddin/Merlin adds further confusion. Add to this the memory that Dyfnwal was the Pendragon, and the mix could certainly add fuel to a tradition of a northern Arthur.

Gwenddoleu's cousin was Urien of Rheged who fought against the Angles in Northumbria during the 570s and 580s, with his cousins Gwallawg of Elmet and Morcant of Lothian. This included a major siege at Lindisfarne where, due to betrayal by Morcant, Urien was murdered. The disaster at Catraeth soon followed, the beginning of the end for northern resistance against the Angles. Urien's battles are commemorated in Taliesin's battle poem *Arise, Reget*, and these may include at least one that coincides with Nennius's list, the eleventh battle of Breguoin, "the halls of Brewyn". Otherwise Urien's battles do not overlap with Arthur's and since the end result is Arthur's victory as opposed to Urien's defeat, it suggests that Urien's campaign is not the source for the battle list. It could still, though, have blurred in the memory, with one

sequence of battles ending in a betrayal becoming confused
with another battle campaign which also, if you include Camlann, ends in betrayal. Urien features in the later Arthurian
legends, but he stands sufficiently bold as a possible Arthur
himself.

Eastern frontier

In Chapter 5 I discussed Gildas's reference to "the unhappy
partition with the barbarians" in *De Excidio*, and suggested
that this boundary may have been delineated by the Roman
roads Dere Street and Ermine Street, the modern-day A1. If we
plot the battle sites against this road there is a surprising match.
It would need to include a few dubious sites, such as those
around Stirling, for Tribruit, and that at Stow for Guinnion,
but otherwise follows several very feasible locales.

This frontier has the advantage of following Gildas's partition and of linking together the boundaries of the original
Anglo-Saxon settlements in Bernicia, Deira, Lindsey and East
Anglia. Apart from the problem of identifying this boundary
around London, it is otherwise supported by archaeological
evidence which shows no extensive Saxon settlement west of
that frontier until the mid-sixth century.

The major problem is that this frontier runs the length of
Britain and thus crosses several British kingdoms. Unlike the
other frontiers, which are relatively self-contained and thus
could be held by one chieftain, perhaps with the help of
neighbouring kings, this one would require a significant consortium of kings. Yet this is exactly how Nennius describes it
when he says that "Arthur, with the kings of Britain" fought
the enemy. The individual best placed to work along this line
would have been Arthwys of the Pennines since his territory,
probably around the southern Pennines, was midway along
this route. We have established that the original battles, under
Vortimer, took place along the Humber estuary and this would
be the obvious place for the battles to start around Brigg and
York, locations also favoured by Geoffrey of Monmouth (*see*

Chapter 9). There would have been a series of battles in the north, where the Angles were most strongly established, before other battles, doubtless encouraged by Aelle, erupted further south. Arthwys would have been reinforced here by the British rulers of Calchvynydd and Rhydychen, the territories around Oxford and the Chilterns, and it's possible that other battle sites with names now lost ought to be placed in this vicinity.

Badon need not be part of this frontier. The final battle could have marked a last-ditch effort by the Saxons to force the British back. It could suggest a pincer movement by Aelle from the south plus the Saxons of Lindsey and East Anglia, perhaps under Octa (who Nennius tells us came south) who came down the Ridgeway or the Fosse Way into the British heartland. That defeat proved to the Saxons that they could not advance so far west and allowed the partition.

Southern frontier

This frontier could have been controlled by a commander based at any of several major forts, not only those we have already discussed, including Caerleon in Gwent, Solsbury Hill near Bath, or Liddington Castle, near Swindon, but other strengthened hill forts such as South Cadbury, Glastonbury, and Cadbury-Congresbury near Bristol, the first two with close Arthurian associations. To this we must add the Wansdyke and other defensive earthworks in the area which are the only firm signs of a genuine frontier. We can, to a degree, place the battle list along or close to this frontier and with connections to some of the known conflicts with the Saxons.

The first of the battles could have taken place at Glyndebourne, near Lewes (Glein), defeating Aelle before moving along the coast to face another Saxon advance (attributed to Cerdic, but probably one of the other eponymous adventurers, such as Port or Wihtgar) at Blackwater (Dubglas) near the Solent estuary. Several engagements could have happened here allowing for a series of Saxon landings. The British may then have retrenched at Old Basing (Bassas), which formed the start of a defence across the south as Saxons now advanced from the north. Another battle at White Hills (Guinnion), Swindon, held the Saxons at bay and this may have ended the first series of assaults.

The second campaign may have started with some daring Saxon or Irish raids up the Severn and into South Wales, leading to battles at Pontardulais, Gellideg (Celidon), Caerleon (City of the Legion) and the Trwc estuary (Tribruit), before pushing the Saxons back across the Severn to Catbrain (Bristol) and the final engagement at Badon (either Bath or Liddington Castle).

This campaign could have started under Ambrosius, being perhaps the end of a much longer campaign by Ambrosius based at Cadbury. A young Arthur may have been in his ranks. Arthur could have taken over as commander of the second campaign. If so, this might suggest we would find some mention of Ambrosius rewarding Arthur as he hands over command. Although Pascent received lands from Ambrosius, as they were probably of the same generation, Pascent is unlikely to have taken over as commander. But Pascent's son is another matter. This was Riocatus, whom we have encountered before as Faustus's nephew.

Riocatus's name, meaning "king of battles", might imply that he became Ambrosius's military successor. Riocatus need not have succeeded his father by then; indeed, that may not have happened until around the year 500, after Badon.

Riocatus was the cousin of Cadell of Powys, known as "Gleaming Hilt", a strange cognomen which seems to suggest some gloriously decked hilt or scabbard to his sword. This is reminiscent of Arthur's sword Excalibur, because it was the scabbard, rather than the sword, that had magical qualities and would protect Arthur.

One might expect Ambrosius to be succeeded by his own son rather than Cadell, but although we know from Gildas that he had grandchildren, these may have been via a daughter. Alternatively, if Ambrosius was Riothamus, then his children may have lived in Armorica and inherited lands there.

Cadell of the Bright Sword and Riocatus, King of Battles, as joint successors to Ambrosius ruling from the one city in Britain that had not fallen into ruin – Viriconium – might well have become conjoined in later years as a legendary Arthur. If either of these, fighting under the banner of Ambrosius, led an army to Badon, with the final defeat of the Saxons, that would be enough to imprint that memory indelibly into the folklore of the British.

This is all highly conjectural and based on the flimsiest of evidence, but in the Arthurian world there is little else. This suggestion does fit a pattern of battles, and does provide a locale for a possible Arthur-like figure.

There are, of course, many other interpretations of these battle sites, both in terms of new locations or how the battle sequence may have run across the country. In *King Arthur, a Military History*, Michael Holmes discusses the Anglo-British battles and where Arthur's campaigns might be located. He generally follows the more traditional locations (Glen in Lincolnshire, Bath for Badon and so on) and allows Arthur free rein across the whole of Britain but in a series of battles spread over several years. He accepts Arthur as the High King successor to Ambrosius, but does not otherwise identify him beyond recognizing him as a great military commander.

Conclusion

Having explored all of the battles and dozens of sites we have been able to make a potential link between some sites and some individuals. Only one of these, Arthwys of the Pennines, has a name which may be resonant with Arthur, but we are, after all, looking as much for the victor of the key battle of Badon, whose memory may have become attached to a later Arthur. This has helped us identify several individuals, especially Dyfnwal, Cadell and Riocatus, who must have been alive at the time of Badon and probably fought there.

Each of the suggested frontiers has its strengths and weaknesses, though the patterns in North Wales and North Britain are not best placed for sustained campaigns against the Saxons. Neither is the western frontier, for all that a campaign could have been masterminded from Wroxeter. My own belief is that only the southern or eastern frontiers provide a plausible explanation for a sustained battle campaign. The eastern frontier has the advantage of linking to a known subsequent "partition" and allows for the likely presence of Arthwys of the Pennines. The southern frontier presents a better explanation for the hill forts in the south and a focused campaign against Aelle as *Bretwalda*.

Before we take this further, though, we need to remember that the battle list does not cover all of Arthur's exploits. For a more complete picture we must turn to the Welsh tales.

8

THE WELSH TRADITION – THE OTHER ARTHURS

When we turn to the Welsh tradition, as distinct from the *Welsh Annals*, a different Arthur emerges. In this section we will explore the relevant stories in *The Mabinogion* and other Welsh texts.

1. *The Mabinogion*

It may seem strange to include discussion of *The Mabinogion* as a historical text, and it is true that the stories do cross the divide, being more legend than fact. But, as we shall see throughout these explorations, there are factual elements, and the divide could be drawn almost anywhere. It is worth reflecting upon a comment by Gwyn Jones and Thomas Jones in their translation of *The Mabinogion* (Dent, 1949):

> . . . when we recall that Arthur was not a French, German or English, but a British king, it is not unreasonable to emphasize

the significance of British material relating to him. British material, that is, uncontaminated by the Cycles of Romance, though necessarily affected by the vast complex of Celtic myth and legend.

The Celtic tales of Arthur incorporated into *The Mabinogion* are amongst the earliest to survive, certainly predating Geoffrey's *History*, though not all necessarily surviving in written form from an earlier date.

The Mabinogion is a collection of Celtic tales, edited by Lady Charlotte Guest, with the help of Ioan Tegis who helped transcribe them into English, in 1846. She incorporated twelve in her first edition, although technically only the first four belong to the "Mabinogi", the stories about the hero Pryderi. It was Lady Charlotte who concocted the phrase "mabinogion" on a misunderstanding of the text. "Mab" means son, and the phrase is generally taken to mean "tales of youth". It has become a convenient tag for a collection of early Celtic tales, and so it will remain.

The stories incorporated into *The Mabinogion* come from two ancient collections, *Llyfr Gwyn Rhydderch* (*The White Book of Rhydderch*) which was committed to parchment in the early 1300s, and *Llyfr Coch Hergest* (*The Red Book of Hergest*), which was written down around 1400. Other versions of these stories survive in manuscript form from at least a century earlier, and were clearly part of an oral tradition long before that. But, as with the sources for Nennius and Geoffrey, since we lack the earliest versions we have no way of knowing how much they have been corrupted in the seven centuries since Arthur's day.

The four branches of the Mabinogi proper do not feature Arthur, although some of the characters reappear in the later tales. Here, I intend to discuss only two stories, *Culhwch and Olwen* and *The Dream of Rhonabwy*, which are of historical import. The other three, *The Lady of the Fountain, Peredur, Son of Evrawc* and *Gereint, Son of Erbin*, although they all feature Arthur, are related to the later romances told by Chrétien de Troyes and are not relevant here.

2. *Culhwch and Olwen*

Culhwch and Olwen is the oldest of the texts used by Guest in her *Mabinogion*. Scholars believe it was written down in its final form around the year 1100, but the linguistic evidence suggests it reached a final oral form perhaps a century earlier. It thus predates Geoffrey's *History*, and is little more than a century later than Nennius. Yet, as we shall see, it bears no relationship to either.

The basic story can be summarized briefly, and illustrates how Arthur was perceived by the tenth and eleventh centuries. Culhwch, a cousin of Arthur, is born in a pigsty when his heavily pregnant mother Goleuddyd is frightened by the pigs. She gives birth but flees, and the baby is rescued by the swineherd and taken to the court of his father, Cilydd. After the death of Culhwch's mother, his father's new wife desires that her own daughter from a previous marriage should marry Culhwch. He refuses because he is still young, so his stepmother curses him and says that he will marry no one but Olwen, the daughter of the giant Ysbaddaden. Despite never meeting Olwen, Culhwch falls in love with her, and seeks the help of Arthur and his court to find her. The quest lasts a year and when at last Olwen is found, she agrees to marry Culhwch only if he carries out her father's wishes. She knows her father will refuse because when she marries, Ysbaddaden will die. Ysbaddaden sets Culhwch forty impossible tasks. These are achieved mostly by heroes from Arthur's court. Ysbaddaden dies, and Culhwch and Olwen are married.

It's a wonderful heroic tale full of adventure and larger-than-life characters. The supernatural elements no doubt grew in the telling, and more and more heroes were doubtless added, but there is no reason to suspect that the location of the story changed much because part of the story's strength lies in the knowledge of the locality. Let us therefore work through the

people and places in the story, and see how much can be related
to the historical elements we have already covered.

(a) Amlawdd Wledig

We learn at the outset that Culhwch is Arthur's first cousin.
Culhwch's mother Goleuddydd was the daughter of Amlawdd
Wledig, as was Arthur's mother Ygraine, and Rhieinwylydd,
the mother of St Illtud. Amlawdd has been accused of being a
genealogical convenience in order to provide family links
between individuals (*see* Table 17). If that were the case,
however, someone would have had to invent him first, and
why should later kings want descent from a fictional nobody?
Amlawdd's name may have been corrupted, but it must have
meant something at the time.

Table 17 Arthur's maternal family

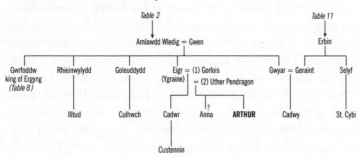

Peter Bartrum remarks that the name is unique in Welsh and
seems to have a Nordic root, *Amlói*, or *Amleth*, the same as
Shakespeare's Hamlet. There is a whole body of research,
going back at least as far as 1880, which proposes that Ham-
let/Amlethus was a variant of Anlaf, itself an anglicization of
Olaf and that all these characters are represented in legend by
Havelok the Dane. In this Anglo-Danish story, which became
popular at the same time as the Welsh Arthurian legends,
Havelok is a dispossessed Danish king (from the Danish
settlements in England), who is serving as a scullion under

the name of Cuaran in the court of King Godric of Lincoln/ Lindsey.

Cuaran was the nickname given to Olaf Sihtricson, who became king of Jorvik (York) in 941, and ruled Danish Mercia (including Lindsey) until expelled by King Edmund of Wessex in 942. Olaf had been the son of an earlier Danish king of York, Sihtric, but, being a child when his father died, was smuggled out of England to relative safety in Ireland by his uncle Gothfrith (Godric).

There are some remarkable connections here. In the multi-lingual world of tenth century Britain, Olaf>Anlaf> Amlethus>Amlawdd would have been regarded as a hero, especially by the non-Saxons, and in later years, when his precise *floruit* had become confused, there would have been those who wanted to claim descent from him. In all likelihood, therefore, the name *Amlawdd* did not exist in the fifth century.

That does not mean that all of Amlawdd's "legendary" descendants also belong to the ninth century. Clearly St Illtud does not. It simply means that Amlawdd might have been a ninth-century hero transposed back in time as a convenient ancestor to various British (or non-Saxon) heroes. But it may also mean that some of his legendary descendants are from the ninth century. This is especially interesting because Olaf/ Amlethus was the ancestor of the Norse kings of the Isle of Man. His great-great grandson was Godred Crovan ("White Hands"), who conquered Man in 1079 and established a dynasty that lasted for two hundred years. In later years Godred was remembered as King Gorry, and it's possible that his name passed into Arthurian legend as the name for the kingdom of Gorre, associated with Urien of Rheged.

There may, however, be another interpretation of the name Amlawdd. It is possible that it became confused with the name Emyr Llydaw. *Emyr* is not a personal name but a title, meaning "leader" (*amris*); thus Emyr Llydaw is "ruler of Llydaw". *Llydaw* was the Welsh name for Armorica (called Letavia in Latin), but it was also local to Wales. There is, for

instance, a Llyn Llydaw, a lake in Snowdonia near a possible
site for Camlann, close to Ambrosius's fort at Dinas Emrys.
There is also a territory in south-east Wales, around Ystrad Yw
between Brycheiniog and Ergyng, called Llydaw.

Llydaw may be derived from *Luyddog* ("host" or "army").
This probably goes back to the time of Magnus Maximus, who
withdrew many of the Roman forces from Britain to support his
campaign in Gaul for the imperial crown. The Welsh tale, *The
Dream of Macsen Wledig*, also included in *The Mabinogion*, tells
how Maximus married the daughter of Eudaf Hen, Elen Luyddog, or "Elen of the host". The name subsequently took on
religious significance, but I suspect it originally referred to the
army that was taken away from Britain. Magnus doubtless en-
treated Eudaf for his support, which was sealed by marriage to
Elen. Maximus granted these soldiers territory in Armorica, and
the name Llydaw followed. Whoever was commander of these
troops may have been known as the Emyr Llydaw. In fact, the
early king of Armorica, Budic, is called the son of Emyr Llydaw.

Does this help us identify Emyr Llydaw and Amlawdd?
Amlawdd could either be a contraction of Em[yr] Llyd[aw], or
a synonym. *Ymladdwr* is the Welsh for "fighter", or, more
specifically, soldier. Amlawdd Wledig could, therefore, be the
same title, "leader of soldiers", not unlike a *dux Britanniarum*.
Amlawdd or Emyr Llydaw would therefore not be one individual but several. It would explain why Amlawdd seems to
be the father of so many children.

The original Amlawdd may have returned to Wales at some
stage, perhaps in the service of Owain Finddu or Vortigern. If
he settled in northern Ergyng, the territory may have been
called Llydaw after him. Later in *Culhwch and Olwen* we learn
that the Men of Llydaw assembled at Ystrad Yw, near Crick-
howell, in Gwent, to help Arthur. These men could have been a
special force that had once been commanded by Amlawdd,
Arthur's grandfather, and were now at Arthur's command.

Amlawdd is usually regarded as the father of a host of
daughters, who, through marriages, became mothers of various

early British notables. However, *Culhwch and Olwen* refers to two of Arthur's mother's brothers, who must therefore be sons of Amlawdd. These are Llygadrudd Emys and Gwrfoddw Hen, both of whom are killed during the boar hunt at Ystrad Yw, towards the end of the story. There is no separate record of Llygadrudd Emys (the name means "the red-eyed stallion"), but Gwrfoddw Hen is known. He was the last recorded king of Ergyng, and lived around the year 600. This location certainly fits in with our speculation on Amlawdd and makes him a contemporary of both Athrwys of Gwent and Artúir of Dyfed.

(b) Arthur's warriors

When Culhwch arrives at Arthur's court, he is refused admittance and challenged by Arthur's head porter, Glewlwyd. The altercation of porter and visitor is evidently a set piece in Celtic folk history as it is also the basis for the poem *Pa Gur* (*Who is the gatekeeper?*), recounting the exploits of Arthur and his men, which we will return to later in this chapter.

Although Glewlwyd seems to have become forgotten in most Arthurian literature, he was clearly well known in Welsh tradition. He appears in several of the *Mabinogion* tales, where he is described as Glewlwyd Mighty Grasp, known for his size and strength. He is also remembered in the Welsh Triads as one of the "Three Unopposable Knights".

Culhwch is eventually admitted, and when he requests the aid of Arthur to find Olwen he recites the names of over 200 warriors and courtiers, and of twenty-one maidens. The list is an excuse to name the famous heroes of old and cannot be trusted as a true record of Arthur's men. It includes, for instance, heroes capable of super-human feats, such as Clust, son of Clustfeinad ("Ear, son of Hearer"), who could hear an ant stir from over fifty miles away even if it were buried seven fathoms deep, or Gwaddyn Oddeith ("Sole-blaze"), whose shoe soles could burn a swathe through any forest.

There are several names one would expect, such as Bedwyr, Cei and Gwalchmai, better known in the later tales as Sir Kay,

Sir Bedivere and Sir Gawain. These are the most ancient names
of Arthur's warriors. Other names reappear amongst Arthur's
knights, converted into Norman French by Chrétien de
Troyes. Arthur's bishop, Bedwini, for instance, becomes Sir
Baudwin, Caradog becomes Sir Carados, Cynwyl becomes
Sir Griflet, and Madog becomes Sir Mador.

Certain key names are missing. There's no Lancelot,
although there is the warrior Llwch Llawwynniog ("Llwch
of the Striking Hand"), who is believed by some to be the
original Lancelot. There is no Merlin, although there is an
enchanter called Menw, possibly Merlin's fictional prototype.

There are some unexpected names in the list, including
Gildas, along with all of his brothers. We know that Gildas
was a contemporary of Arthur, as he was born in the year of
Badon, but one would not expect him to be close to Arthur.
The list also includes Taliesin, "Chief of Bards". Taliesin is
associated with Arthur's court in other writings, including the
Triads, but his appearance causes a problem with dates.
Taliesin is more closely associated with the courts of Urien
of Rheged, who ruled in the 570s, and of his son Owein, to
whom Taliesin composed a eulogy. According to legend,
Taliesin was summoned as a child to the court of King
Maelgwyn. Maelgwyn died in 549, placing Taliesin's birth
perhaps around 530–535. Since he apparently died at a great
age, he may have lived as late as 610. This allows for him to
have been present at the court of Arthur of Dyfed, who ruled
in the 590s.

Returning to the list of warriors in *Culhwch and Olwen*,
there are several interesting asides about a few otherwise little-
known names. We learn, for instance, of Gwyn Hyfar, a name
which, on the surface, sounds compellingly like Gwenhwyfar
(Guinevere), but which apparently means Gwyn "the Iras-
cible" or "the Modest". According to Gwyn and Thomas
Jones's translation, Gwyn was "one of the nine who plotted
the battle of Camlann". Lady Charlotte Guest translated this
phrase as "the ninth man that rallied the battle of Camlann".

Both opposing interpretations agree that Gwyn Hyfar was an overseer of Cornwall and Devon.

Among the list of warriors are various sons of Iaen, collectively described as "men of Caer Dathyl, kindred to Arthur on his father's side". Caer Dathyl is in North Wales, in the Lleyn Peninsula, and is mentioned in *The Mabinogion* as the stronghold of the ensorcelled Lord of Gwynedd, Math. Amongst the old documents known as the *Hanesyn Hen*, there is a list of the children of Iaen, including a daughter, Eleirch, who is described as the "mother of Cydfan ab Arthur". She is not described as Arthur's wife. We cannot be certain this is meant to be the same Arthur, but the spelling and connection are cause enough for thought.

(c) Lost lands

One other name raises an interesting association with lost lands. There is a reference to Gwenwynwyn, called Arthur's "first fighter" or "champion", whose name appears in the Welsh Triads as one of the "Three Seafarers of Ynys Prydein". Though completely forgotten today, this hero has an interesting family history. Gwenwynwyn's grandfather was Seithennin, who is remembered as the man who allowed the Kingdom of Maes Gwyddno to be flooded by the sea. Seithennin was keeper of the sea-walls and flood-gates of Gwaelod, part of the territory of Gwyddno Garanhir of Ceredigion, but one night Seithennin was drunk and failed to keep watch, and the lands flooded.

There are many legends of lost lands around Britain's coast, such as Lyonesse, the land believed to be buried between Land's End and the Scilly Isles off the south-west tip of Cornwall. But various Welsh sources mention other similar inundations. One such is in Cardigan Bay, which may well be Maes Gwyddno. There are several princes called Gwyddno, causing confusion over the identity of Garanhir ("Long-Shanks"). There is a Gwyddno, Prince of Merionydd, who lived in the early seventh century, contemporary with Arthur of Gwent and Arthlwys of Ceredigion, but his link with the legend is a late assignment. Others suggest Gwyddno ap Cawrdaf, one of the Men of the North, who was thus a contemporary of Arthur of Dyfed.

Gwyddno's name is remembered in Porth Wyddno, listed in a Triad as one of the "Three Chief Ports" of Britain. This has been identified with Borth, north of Aberystwyth, on the borders of Dyfed and Ceredigion, which would connect Maes Gwyddno with lands believed lost in Cardigan Bay. However others suggest that it was a harbour on the River Conwy in North Wales or on the coast of Rheged which was buried when the waters of Morecambe Bay rose during the sixth century, perhaps as a consequence of the comet catastrophe of the 540s.

Gwenwynwyn must, therefore, have lived around 610–630, a century too late for Arthur of Badon, but not too late for Arthur of Dyfed. This great sailor would have earned his reputation because of the perils of the sea during the sixth century, not just the rising sea levels, but the constant battles with the Irish who remained a threat to the western coast of Wales, the very shores of Dyfed which the Irish had colonized in late Roman times when it was known as Demetia. Gwenwynwyn became the master of Arthur's fleet in Dyfed, a role that could easily see him classified as Arthur's champion.

The list includes one other member of Arthur's court, providing further evidence for the former existence of these flooded lands. This is Teithi the Old, "whose dominions the sea overran". One of the Welsh Triads places this kingdom, originally called Ynys Teithy, and later Kaerrihoc, in the west between Menevia and Ireland. *Menevia* is the old name for the town of St David's on the western coast of Dyfed, suggesting that Ynys Teithy was an island or peninsula further out into the Irish Sea that was destroyed by flooding. It is difficult to provide a date for Teithi. It seems that Ynys Teithy was still referred to during the tenure of Oudoceus, archbishop of Llandaff, who held the prelacy from about 580 to 615 and was thus a contemporary of Arthur of Dyfed. Presumably the inundation of Ynys Teithi happened during this period. The Irish also remember him as Tethra, king of the Fomorians (*fo* meaning "under", and *mor* meaning "sea").

We can imagine a folk memory of these refugees from deluged lands living at the court of Arthur, and this may be how such tales as Tristan of Lyonesse began.

(d) Camelot, Celliwic and the god Artaius

Arthur's fabled castle Camelot does not appear in these Welsh tales. The list of notables at Arthur's court includes Glwyddyn the Craftsman, who is credited with building Arthur's Hall, called *Ehangwen* (meaning "expansive white"), and implying a beautiful white building seemingly too large to take in at once. Later poems state that the hall shone with gold, so the image is of a bright shining palace, very similar to how Camelot is envisaged.

Arthur's Hall is placed in Celliwic, or Gelliwig, in Cernyw. The first of the Welsh Triads, "Three Tribal Thrones of Britain", lists Arthur's thrones as being at Mynyw, Celliwig and Pen Rhionydd. Because of Charlotte Guest's translation of Cernyw as Cornwall, people have been searching for Celliwic in the south-west, although no place by that name survives there. Various sites have been suggested, including Callington on the border of Devon and Cornwall, Castle Killibury, an ancient hill fort near Wadebridge, Callywith near Bodmin, and Willapark at Bossiney near Tintagel. Most of these are based solely on connections to ancient hill forts. Killibury is the most favoured, although none of these places has been adequately researched, and none has a logical Arthurian connection.

That there once was a Kelliwic in Cornwall is not disputed. There is a record of a Thomas de Kellewik in 1302, who lived at Gulval, north of Penzance. *Celli wig* means "the grove in the wood", and thus is a phrase that could have occurred in several places.

However, whilst there is no Celliwic in Cornwall, there are two in Wales. We have already established that Cernyw should not be translated as Kernow or Cornwall, but as Cernyw in South Wales, in Gwent, being the territory between Chepstow and Cardiff. In *Journey to Avalon*, Chris Barber and David Pykitt put forward the case that Gelliwig is the ancient hill fort now called Llanmelin, near Caerwent. The old name for Llanmelin was *Llan y Gelli* ("church of the grove"), but over time as the grove was forgotten and superseded by a mill, it became *Llanmelin* ("the church of the mill"). Barber and Pykett suggest that during that transition it would for a while have been known as Caer Melin, a name that Chrétien de Troyes corrupted into Caer-Malot, or Camelot. It is an intriguing argument, all the more so because nearby are the Bedwin Sands, named after Bedwini, bishop of Celliwic.

Barber and Pykett also suggest that Caerwent was Arthur's capital, not nearby Caerleon, and that Geoffrey of Monmouth mistook the two. Caerwent, the Roman town of Venta Silurum, was the former capital of the Silures, and thus more likely as the court for a post-Roman king of Gwent. The final link in the chain is that the Welsh Triads name Caradog Vreichfras as the chief elder of Celliwig, and Caradog was ruler of Ergyng in the sixth century.

The case for Llanmelin as Arthur's court sounds convincing on philological grounds. As yet, however, there is no archaeological evidence to support it. An excavation in the 1930s showed it to have originated as a hill fort in the third century BC, with a progressive series of occupations and growth, particularly around 50BC. But it seems to have been abandoned around 75AD, and there is no evidence of post-Roman occupation. This is perhaps not surprising as from 75AD onwards the people would have come under Roman control and settled within Caerwent. The name Gelliwig survived amongst the Silures, and doubtless the location became a revered place, and thus a more suitable name in the tales for Arthur's court.

The other Gelliwig is in North Wales, on the Lleyn Peninsula. The name still survives as Gelliwig, with no corruption or revision. Its case is made by Steve Blake and Scott Lloyd in *The*

Keys to Avalon. The name Gelliwig is still found in Gelliwig Farm, near Botwnnog, Pwllheli. There has long been a manor house on the site and it has never been excavated, so it is not known whether a Dark Age hall once stood there. The location seems remote for Arthur's main castle. We have already seen the Lleyn Peninsula associated with Vortigern, and his stronghold at Nant Gwrtheyrn was some ten miles north-east. We have also seen that Arthur had kindred at Caer Dathyl, which Guest connected to the village of Llanrwst, though it has also been linked to Caer Engan, near Penygroes, both of which are on the outskirts of Snowdonia.

Caer Dathyl was the stronghold of Math, son of Mathonwy, lord of Gwynedd, who is the eponymous protagonist in the fourth branch of *The Mabinogion*. This is a dark story of death, rape and rebirth. Central to it is Math's nephew Gwydion, whose brother Gilfaethwy lusts after Math's maidservant, Gowein. Gwydion contrives for Gilfaethwy to see Gowein, but the meeting ends in rape and Math punishes the brothers by turning them into different animals each year, in which guise they have to father young. In later mythology, the role of Gwydion was replaced by that of Artaius, a god of the air, who was worshipped in Gaul. Gwydion was a shape-changer and can be seen as a form of proto-Merlin. Artaius was originally a pastoral deity but, at the time of the great barbarian and Celtic post-Roman migrations, it seems that Artaius superseded Gwydion, coming to Britain possibly via Brittany. Between them Gwydion-Artaius became the god of rebirth, a Celtic sun-god who was worshipped at the time of the winter solstice.

Some have argued that the character of Arthur may have been a manifestation of Artaius. However, it is more likely that the original Arthur later became associated with Artaius, rather than the other way round. The association with Artaius doubtless also brought forth the shape-changing Gwydion aspect in the form of Merlin and his prototype Menw. There may have been a cult that worshipped Artaius on the Lleyn Peninsula, encouraging the association with King Arthur.

The Artaius connection may also have a link with the origin of
Arthur's name. Firstly, and most mundanely, he may have been
named after the god Artaius at birth. Secondly, his name may not
have been Arthur, but he may have been dubbed that after his
death by his followers because of the Artaius connection.
Thirdly, he may not have been Arthur by birth but assumed
the name during his lifetime in order to make the connection to
the idea of rebirth, effectively being born again and giving new
life to the British nation. This option gives significance to the idea
of the once and future king, who had not died but would return.
It also suggests a possible identity change. Perhaps Cadell or
Riocatus, or even Ambrosius, could have taken on that epithet as
symbolic of the change in fortune after Badon.

Since the name Gelliwig/Celliwic appears so prominently in
Culhwch and Olwen it is a little surprising that Geoffrey did
not use it in his *History*, preferring instead Caerleon. Surprising, because Geoffrey was aware of other items associated with
Arthur, which he lifted directly from the story. When Culhwch
first arrives at Arthur's Hall and before he invokes the roll call
of names for his boon, Arthur refers to:

> Caledvwlch, my sword; and Rhongomyant, my lance; and
> Wynebgwrthucher, my shield; and Carnwenhau, my dagger;
> and Gwenhwyvar, my wife.

We have become used to the name of Arthur's sword being
Excalibur, but in his *History* Geoffrey calls it Caliburn. The
Welsh *caledvwlch* means "hard cut", and was almost certainly
derived from the Irish sword *Caledbolg*, which belonged to
Fergus mac Roich and which means "hard lightning". *Caliburn* itself is believed to be derived from the Latin *chalbys* for
"steel". Geoffrey also calls Arthur's lance "Ron", describing it
as "fit for slaughter"; the Welsh *Rhongomyant* means "slaying
spear". Geoffrey did not pay too close attention, however,
because he calls Arthur's shield Pridwen, whereas originally it
was *Wynebgwrthucher*, meaning "face of evening". Pridwenn,

or Prytwenn, as revealed later in *Culhwch and Olwen*, was the name of Arthur's ship, meaning "white form" or "fair shape".

(e) The cauldron of Dwrnach

One of the impossible tasks set by Ysbaddaden involves the theft of the cauldron of Dwrnach. Like all cauldrons in Celtic folklore, it has special properties. In this case, the cauldron will not boil the food of cowards. A similar quest for a cauldron arises in the poem *The Spoils of Annwvyn*, and has many similarities to the episode in *Culhwch and Olwen*, suggesting that both came from the same source. These stories represent an early prototype for the story of the Quest for the Grail.

(f) The hunt of the giant boar

Another of the forty tasks that Ysbaddaden set Culhwch was the hunt for the wild boar, Twrch Trwyth (*twrch* meaning "hog", and *trwyth*, or *triath*, "chief"). I suspect there was a deliberate pun here, as Trwyth can also mean "urine", so that the boar was known colloquially as "pig's piss".

Legend makes Trwyth the son of a king, Taredd Wledig, but because of his wickedness he had been turned into a boar, along with seven of his men, who are referred to as his piglets. The imagery is clearly allegorical for a prince who had become a violent and vile outlaw. Unfortunately, the name Taredd is not known outside the legend, and we cannot identify either him or his son.

Trwyth begins by terrorizing Ireland, then crosses the sea to Dyfed and lays waste South Wales. Arthur and his heroes pursue the boar and drive him into the Severn estuary and eventually out into the open sea, but no more is heard of him. Thanks to Lady Charlotte Guest's original translation, the hunt seems to have taken place in Cornwall, but as discussed previously, Cernyw was along the southern shores of Gwent, west of Chepstow. That location makes far more sense than Cornwall, and provides a consistent route for the pursuit of Trwyth (*see* Map 9).

The pursuit falls into two distinct halves, the first confined to the territory of Dyfed, whilst the second takes place wholly in Gwent. Trwyth lands near St David's at Porth Clais, and is pursued around the coast to present-day Milford Haven,

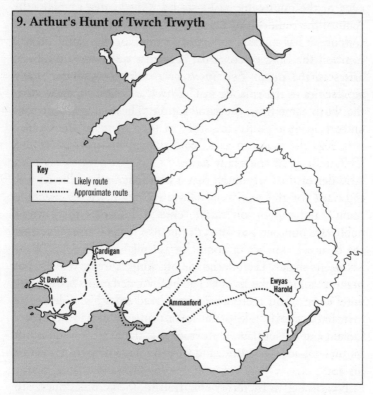

9. Arthur's Hunt of Twrch Trwyth

Key
----- Likely route
·········· Approximate route

Cardigan

St David's

Ewyas
Harold

Ammanford

before heading inland and up into the Preseli Mountains where, at Cwm Cerwyn, he slaughters many of Arthur's men, including Arthur's son Gwydre.

The pursuit of Trwyth then zig-zags out of the Preseli Mountains through Cardigan, and then the boar is lost to the east. Trwyth reappears in the Loughour Valley near Ammanford, where the hunt continues through the Black Mountains and Brecon Beacons, into the Vale of Ergyng and along the valleys of the Monnow and Wye, until the boar is driven into the Severn near Chepstow. Trwyth resurfaces along the Cernyw coast near Caerwent, but is soon driven out into the Severn estuary.

These two halves seem to represent two campaigns, perhaps even against different enemies and fought by two different Arthurs, the first by Arthur of Dyfed, the second by Arthur of Gwent. The first part of the hunt is very specific in its naming of sites and suggests a series of battles well known at the time. The second sequence is more vague, and, though it may have represented a separate campaign, by the time it was added to the whole story, its precise location was no longer so well known.

It begs the question as to who the real villain was behind Trwyth. The battles in Dyfed may relate to Irish raiders who were defeated but at a high cost, including the death of Arthur of Dyfed's son. The Gwent battles probably relate to another enemy. The implication is that it was a prince who was once of noble Welsh blood but turned renegade. This once again raises the name of Cerdic, who was British, yet founded the West Saxon dynasty. In *Journey to Avalon*, Barber and Pykitt suggest that the pursuit of the boar Trwyth was a battle against the Gewisse, and that Cerdic was their leader.

If Barber and Pykitt are correct, then whoever expelled Cerdic cannot have been Arthur of Gwent, who lived a full century after Cerdic. If we accept that Cerdic rose to power in the 530s, then his contemporary in Gwent was Nynnio, whilst Ergyng was ruled by Nynnio's brother Peibio. Both rulers are referred to in *Culhwch and Olwen* as the Ychen Bannawc, the "Horned Oxen", because God transformed them into oxen for their wickedness. Evidently they are not the heroes most likely to have expelled Cerdic. Those would have been Riocatus or Cadell, who ruled the lands just to the north.

There is a temptation to wonder whether the battles fought against the Giant Boar might relate to Nennius's battle list which would neatly link two traditions. Yet this seems unlikely because the culmination of Nennius's list is Badon whereas the

boar hunt clearly ends at the Severn, near Caldicot. The only
likely Badon site in South Wales, at Mynydd Baidan, is not
sufficiently close to the hunt trail. The only sites which are
close, such as Dulais Court at Ewyas Harold and the River
Troggy at Caldicot are themselves almost too contrived to fit.
Tempting though it is, I can see no correlation between the two
sets of battle sites.

There is, in fact, a third boar hunt in the story. Culhwch is set
the task of obtaining the tusks of the Chief Boar, Ysgithyrwyn.
Ysgithyr means "tusk", so the name is really only an exaggeration for the Mighty Tusked Boar. Although at the start Arthur
goes to the "west of Ireland" to seek the huntsman, Gwrgi
Seferi, we are next told that Arthur "went into the North" to
find Cyledyr the Wild, recorded as the son of Nwython (or
Neithon, a Pictish name). The hunt for Ysgithyrwyn is conducted mainly by Caw, the father of Gildas, identified in the
tale as being from Pictland. The records show a Caw ruling in
the north at the time of Arthur of Badon, though he is usually
associated with Strathclyde or Galloway. Galloway takes its
name from the Gaels, or Irish, and thus Arthur's venture to the
"west of Ireland" may not have been to Ireland at all, but to
the islands off the west coast of Scotland which were then
occupied primarily by Irish. Thus this hunt probably took
place in Galloway, and may once have been an adventure
relating to Caw and nothing to do with Arthur at all. In
The Figure of Arthur, Richard Barber suggests that this boar
hunt may have once been attributed to Arthur of Dál Riata,
even though he lived a century later.

The likelihood is that by the time *Culhwch and Olwen* came
to be written down, it had become a compendium, a grand epic
tale of the adventures of all past heroes about whom the bards
knew, linked together by the might and authority of Arthur.
One example is the quest to obtain the blood of the Black
Witch Orddu, at Pennant Gofud (the Valley of Grief) in the
Uplands of Uffern ("Hell"). The brothers Cacamwri and

Hygwydd at first try to seize Orddu, but are cast to the ground. Two more, Amren and Eiddyl, venture into her cave, but they suffer even worse. Now Arthur takes control, casting his knife into the cave and cutting Orddu in two. But it is Caw who takes the witch's blood, and thus probably Caw who was the original hero. In fact, during the course of this adventure Arthur is advised by his warriors that it is "unseemly" for them to see him fighting with the hag, as if this was an excuse for having Arthur present but not directly involved. Arthur has clearly been incorporated into this tale at a later stage and, in all likelihood, has been written into many of the other ones.

Culhwch and Olwen has raised a number of issues. The story seems to be set mid-way through Arthur's reign, in the 510s, and some of the characters do fit into that time scale. However, others, such as Taliesin, belong to the late sixth century, and their lives fit more comfortably with either Arthur of Dyfed or Arthur of Gwent. Arthur of Dyfed seems connected to legends about flooded lands, but Arthur of Gwent is more suited to one of the likely locations for King Arthur's fortress, Gelliwig or Caerwent. It has also opened up the possibility that Arthur's name may be related to Artaius, the Gaulish pastoral god. Finally, it may be that Arthur's name became a catch-all for the exploits of other heroes who preceded him, in particular Caw of Pictland and Cadell of Powys.

3. *The Dream of Rhonabwy*

The Dream of Rhonabwy is exactly what it says it is – an account of a dream. As such it has a strange, disconnected quality that can have little bearing on true history, and yet it raises some intriguing points. It probably wasn't composed until the late thirteenth century, its author looking back to what he clearly regards as a Golden Age that is threatening to fall apart.

The story starts with Madog, son of Mareddud, who "held Powys from end to end". This places the story at the start of

Madog's reign, in 1132, for by the 1140s Powys was under threat from the expansionist regime of Owain Gwynedd. This makes the story contemporary with Geoffrey of Monmouth, and Geoffrey could well have known Madog, who was on friendly terms with the court of Henry I. It means that even if the story drew upon earlier tradition, it was composed some six centuries after Arthur and thus has no direct historical value. Yet because it describes the battle of Badon, it cannot be wholly ignored.

At the outset, Madog's brother Iorweth is jealous of his brother's power and goes on a rampage through Powys. Madog sends bands of warriors to track him down, one of whom is Rhonabwy. He and his companions spend the night in a dirty hovel, and Rhonabwy has a dream of the Arthurian age. The rest of the story describes that dream, a succession of unconnected visions of Arthur's warriors questing or in battle, while Arthur and Owain play a game similar to chess.

Rhonabwy finds himself and his companions travelling across the Plain of Argyngroeg, known today as Cyngrog, or Gungrog, just north of modern-day Welshpool, along the floodplain of the River Severn. One of the tributaries of the Severn here is called the River Camlad.

They are met by a knight who announces himself as Iddog ap Mynio, known as "Cordd Prydain", or "the Embroiler of Britain". While serving as messenger for Arthur the Emperor, he earned the name stirring up strife between Arthur and his nephew Medrawd, thus causing the battle of Camlann. Although Arthur's messages to Medrawd were sincere, Iddog distorted them. He repented of his deeds and did seven years' penance. While they talk, Rhonabwy and Iddog are joined by Rhufon Befr (the "radiant"). He is also listed amongst Arthur's warriors in *Culhwch and Olwen*, and in one of the Welsh Triads as one of the "Three Fair Princes".

Continuing his dream-journey, Rhonabwy and his companions reach the ford of Rhyd y Groes and find a large encampment. There they see Arthur sitting with Gwarthegyd, son of Caw, and Bishop Bedwini. Various armies are arriving. Addaon ap Taliesin rides through the ford and splashes Arthur, causing Elffin ap Gwyddno to strike Addaon's horse with his sheathed sword. Both Elffin and Addaon appear in the genealogies, a generation apart. Their lives would have overlapped in the early 600s, and neither would be contemporary with Badon.

Then a tall and stately individual, identified as Caradog Vreichfras ("Stout-arm"), Arthur's chief counsellor and cousin, remarks that it is surprising that so great a host should be assembled in such a confined space, and that they should be here when they had promised to fight Osla Gyllellvawr ("Big Knife") at Badon that day. Arthur agrees that they must move on. They cross the ford, heading towards Cefyn Digoll, whilst Rhonabwy is told that the other troops he sees are the men of Norway under the command of March, son of Meirchion, and the men of Denmark under the command of Edeyrn, son of Nudd. Soon after crossing the ford, they arrive below Caer Faddon, the site for the battle of Badon.

This site cannot be far from Rhyd-y-Groes, perhaps an hour or two's march. Rhyd-y-Groes is still marked on the Ordnance Survey map, though it is now the name of a farm. There was a ford here, over the Camlad, near Forden, where the river joins the Severn. Between Forden and Garthmyl was a fort called The Gaer, probably the old Roman fort of Levobrinta. A Roman road runs almost north–south along the Severn at this point, leading to Viriconium/Wroxeter. Arthur and his men almost certainly turned north along this road as it passes directly by Caer Digoll, now the Beacon Ring hill fort, as the story describes.

The army cannot have travelled much beyond Caer Digoll. Many years ago, Egerton Phillimore deduced that Caer Faddon was the name for the Black Bank spur of Long Mountain, just over two kilometres south-east of Buttington, near Welshpool. There are several hill forts and ancient settlements in this area, all possible candidates. Steve Blake and Scott Lloyd have suggested the likely-sounding Breidden Hill, north-west of Middletown.

This territory is in Powys, not usually associated with Arthur, but which we have repeatedly encountered in relation to Cadell. Clearly the author of *The Dream of Rhonabwy* is remembering a famous battle in that area with which he has associated the name Badon, or Caer Faddon. But whether this is Arthur's Badon is another matter. The area has been the site of several battles; perhaps the most notable was that between the combined forces of Cadwallon of Gwynedd and Penda of Mercia, against Edwin of Northumbria, at Cefyn Digoll around the year 630. Cadwallon fought a further dozen battles across the north, leading to the defeat and death of Edwin. His victories were the last glory days of the British, and could easily have been remembered five hundred years later as an Arthurian conquest. In 893, a combined force of Welsh and Saxons under Alfred the Great defeated the Danes at Buttington. Gruffydd ap Llywelyn, in 1039, defeated Leofric of Mercia at Rhyd-y-Groes. This last battle would be within three generations of the composition of *The Dream of Rhonabwy*, and would still be remembered. The author may have chosen that site in order to compare it with an Arthurian golden age, in a location known to have seen many decisive battles.

The *Welsh Annals* refer to a second battle of Badon in 665. The exact date can be confirmed by a reference to the Saxon celebration of Easter, which arose following the Synod of Whitby, called by Oswy, king of Northumbria in 664. As ever, the entry provides little information, not even who the combatants were. It refers to the death of Morgan, but does not say who he was or whether he died in the battle. He could be Morgan ap Athrwys, the ruler of Gwent and successor to Athrwys ap Meurig. Morgan was known as a warrior king, as much for his fighting within his borders as with the Saxons, although 665 is early for his death.

The *ASC* makes no reference to a second Badon any more than it did to the first, so it was probably an all-Welsh affair. The site in

The Dream of Rhonabwy cannot be ruled out. Bards writing a century or two later could easily have linked the site of one battle with another, for although it is described as "the second battle of Badon", we should not automatically assume the two battles are in the same place. The possibility that Morgan ap Athrwys was killed at this second Badon makes it yet another tantalizing link with the Arthur of legend. Moreover, the possibility that the two Badons were at the same site and in Powys is another, equally tantalizing, link to Cadell.

The bizarre dream-like quality of the story is most evident when the battle is described by characters who appear while Arthur and Owain play chess. Eventually a truce is granted for a period of a month and a fortnight. The description of the battle, such as it is, does not match that recalled by Nennius, in which Arthur's men seemed to wipe out the enemy over a period of three days. That suggests these are not the same battles, and that the author of the tale chose it because it was associated with past victories.

When considering the truce, Arthur summons his counsellors, and there follows a list of over forty names. Also present, though not listed as one of the counsellors, is Rhun, son of Maelgwyn. Rhun was the powerful king of Gwynedd who ruled from around 549 until the 580s, and therefore a contemporary of Arthur of Dyfed (rather than Arthur of Gwent). The counsellors include Bishop Bedwini and Caradog Vreichfras, both linked with Arthur of Gelliwig in the Welsh Triads, Cador of Cornwall, Gwalchmei, Gwenwynwyn and Peredur Longspear. Cei is mentioned elsewhere, but not amongst the counsellors, and Bedwyr makes no appearance. Also mentioned are Dyrstan ap Tallwch, one of the earliest appearances of Tristan, although he otherwise plays no part in this story, and Llacheu, son of Arthur, remembered as Loholt in the romances.

4. Caradog Vreichfras

This is an appropriate moment to give further thought to Arthur's adviser Caradog Vreichfras, who has a significant role in this story, and appears in other Arthurian tales.

Caradog is described as Arthur's most senior counsellor, a position which allows him to speak his mind bluntly. He is portrayed as an acerbic character, not unlike that ascribed to Cei in the romances. His epithet, *Vreichfras*, means "strong-arm". Apparently Caradog's arm was broken in battle but mended more powerful than before. In the later French romances this became *Briefbras*, derived from *Brise-bras*, for "broken arm", but thereafter translated as "short arm" or "withered arm".

Caradog is associated with both Brycheiniog and Ergyng, plus the region known as Llydaw. He is infuriatingly difficult to date, because his name is so common and his ancestry confusing. In legend, he is made the son of Llyr Marini, who has no historical basis. The name seems to be a later fabrication to link Caradog with the god Llyr. The same legend makes his mother a fairy.

There are several pedigrees for Caradog Vreichfras. Two of these are late and may be treated as fanciful. One of them, reported by T. Wright in "Carnarvonshire Antiquities" in *Archeologia Cambrensis* (January 1861), identifies him as Earl of Hereford and the great-grandson of Cunedda, through Einion. This would make him a contemporary of Maelgwyn, living in the early sixth century. Ergyng, with which Caradog is most closely associated, became Archenfield, which is in south-west Hereford. Of the older pedigrees, there are four to whom the epithet *Vreichfras* has become attached.

1. Caradog, father of Eudaf Hen, *fl.* 320s. Eudaf was Duke of the Gewisse in Ergyng and we may deduce that this Caradog was also a "ruler" (that is Roman magistrate) of Ergyng.
2. Caradog, father of Ynyr, *fl.* 420s, a possible king of Gwent. The pedigree of Ynyr is confusing and Caradog may have been his father or his son. Hence:
3. Caradog ap Ynyr, *fl.* 470s, a king of Gwent.
4. Caradog ap Gwrgan, *fl.* 590s, ruler of Ergyng.

The latter three seem to belong to the royal family of Gwent, so may all be descended from Eudaf and the first Caradog. We cannot dismiss the possibility that because one Caradog was known to be a ruler of Ergyng, tradition has linked all the others to that territory. But Caradog was such a popular name that it may well have passed down through a family, particularly one as noted as Eudaf's, which claimed descent from the original Ceretic, or Caratacus, ruler of the Catuvellauni at the time of the Roman invasion. Caratacus fled to the Silures in Gwent to mount a defensive campaign against the Romans, before being exiled to Rome with his brother Arviragus, who returned to Britain and settled among the Silures. There is thus a case to be made that Caradog became a family name of the rulers of the Gwentian Silures throughout the period of Roman occupation.

Of particular interest are (3) and (4), as one is contemporary with Arthur of Badon, and the other was probably alive, as a senior official, during the life of Arthur of Gwent. Most legends about Vreichfras have become too wrapped up in myth to be of value as history, but there is enough in *Culhwch and Olwen* and *The Dream of Rhonabwy* to suggest that a once great warrior was now a highly respected counsellor at Arthur's court.

The idea that Caradog and Arthur became enemies has no basis in these stories, and may have arisen from two factors. Firstly, the idea that Caradog may be the same person as Cerdic of the West Saxons. This is a very tempting idea and, if we accept the *ASC*'s original dates of Cerdic arriving in 495 and succeeding to the West Saxon kingdom in 501, it would make him a contemporary of Caradog ap Ynyr. However, we have determined that Cerdic lived at least a generation later. Perhaps Cerdic was related to Caradog, possibly as a nephew. That alone may make it sufficient for Caradog to be regarded as a traitor to Arthur. We might even go so far as to propose that Caradog is just old enough to have been Hengist's interpreter, but that is pure conjecture.

The other reason is because Caradog has also been called a ruler of Armorica, and may have deserted Arthur to establish a new kingdom over the sea (possibly explaining the Llyr Marini patronym, as both names mean "of the sea"). However, as we established earlier, Caradog conquered the territory of Llydaw between Ergyng and Brycheiniog, which is also the Welsh name for Armorica, and the two have become confused.

This may provide another connection with Cerdic. Cerdic is always called the leader of the Gewisse, whilst Eudaf Hen, son of the first Caradog listed above, was also called a duke, or *dux*, of the Gewisse. Could Caradog Vreichfras have inherited the title of duke of the Gewisse and, if so, what connection does this have to Cerdic?

There may be none. The simple answer may be confusion between the words Gewisse and Guuennessi. The first means "confederates" or "allies", and is usually taken to mean an army of mixed Romano-British and Germanic warriors, who were the band of mercenaries with which Cerdic carved out his kingdom. Cerdic's grandfather (or great-grandfather) was called Gewis, and his descendants became the Gewisse, or, more accurately, the Gewissingas. *Guuennessi* means "people of Gwent", of whom Eudaf was the *dux*, or more probably governor.

The confusion arises because Geoffrey of Monmouth called Vortigern a leader of the Gewisse. We know that Vortigern was descended from the men of Gloucester and established a dynasty in Powys, but was not himself from Gwent. He could, of course, have usurped the title, which would not have been out of character, or Geoffrey could simply have been mistaken.

However, we have seen that the first Saxon *adventus*, perhaps at Vortigern's request, was around the year 428. Their leader was more likely to have been someone like Gewis than Hengist who, as we explore in the next chapter, comes later. If the Saxons became Vortigern's personal army they may have been known as the Gewisse, and Vortigern as their *dux*. The question arises as to whether there is a link between the Gewisse and the Men of Llydaw, the "host" once commanded by Eudaf Hen. If there was confusion over Eudaf as both leader of the Gewisse and the Men of Llydaw might there not have been later confusion between Caradog and Cerdic in the same roles? Perhaps the Men of Llydaw and the Gewisse combined.

Either way at some stage Cerdic took command of the Gewisse, possibly the result of a conflict between Cerdic and his "uncle" Caradog, a conflict which would have been at about the time of the battle of Camlann. Could it be that Camlann, which was an internal squabble, was really a battle for the control of an elite army (an early concept of the Round Table) which Cerdic was able to wrest away from Arthur and Caradog, and out of which he created the kingdom of Wessex?

It is a shame to let facts get in the way of a good story, and all of this is entirely speculation based on nothing more than loose connections between names. However, let me throw in another thought to allow speculation to ferment further.

If the *ASC* story of Cerdic is correct, then his early conquests in the 530s were in Hampshire and Wiltshire, north of Southampton. However, such archaeological evidence as there is for the early settlements of the West Saxon Gewisse places them in the upper Thames valley, between Dorchester and Swindon (close to two of the suggested sites for Badon). As the Gewisse became established, their name evolved into the Hwicce, the name of the province mentioned by Nennius as the location for Badon. This territory was later lost to the Mercians, who continued to hold Hwicce in high regard. Penda made Hwicce into a sub-kingdom, a bishopric was later established here, and Offa chose it as a site for one of his palaces. There was something special to the Saxons about the Hwicce, something now forgotten, but which may have had its roots in the Gewisse, Caradog and Cerdic.

Arthur's opponent at Badon in *The Dream of Rhonabwy* is given as Osla Gyllellvawr ("Big Knife"), usually interpreted as being Hengist's son Oisc, or Oisc's son Octha. In fact, *Osla* is remarkably similar to *Esla*, the son of Gewis, and therefore Cerdic's father or grandfather. If Esla and Osla were the same man, then Arthur's battle at Badon was against Cerdic's father. It has puzzled many authorities why, if Osla was Arthur's enemy at Badon, his name occurs in the long list of Arthur's warriors in the story of *Culhwch and Olwen*. But this might be so if Osla was really Esla, commander of the Gewisse for Llydaw, turned rebel. It would explain why Cerdic was believed to come from Llydaw (Armorica), when in fact he came from Llydaw (Ergyng), and how Eudaf, Vortigern and Cerdic could all be leaders of the Gewisse. And it might also explain the obvious reverence the Mercians had for the Hwicce, the "spiritual" descendants of the original Gewisse.

Tenuous though all these connections may be, they provide food for thought both as to the location of Badon and about its participants. The Arthur portrayed in *The Dream of Rhonabwy* does not seem to be either Arthur of Dyfed or Arthur of Gwent, despite the recurrence of several familiar names. The story has taken us into new territory, Powys, and thus made connections with its rulers and history.

Let us now turn to other Welsh texts to see what they say about Arthur.

5. Llongborth

This poem appears in the *Black Book of Carmarthen* and is a long elegy to another hero, Geraint, titled (possibly years later) *Geraint fil Erbin*.

> In Llongborth, I saw the clash of swords,
> Men in terror, bloody heads,
> Before Geraint the Great, his father's son.
> In Llongborth I saw spurs,
> And men who did not flinch from the dread of the spears,
> Who drank their wine from the bright glass.
> In Llongborth I saw the weapons
> Of men, and blood fast dropping,
> After the war cry, a fearful return.
> In Llongborth I saw Arthur's
> Heroes who cut with steel.
> The Emperor, ruler of our labour.

> In Llongborth Geraint was slain,
> Brave men from the region of Dyvnaint,
> And before they were slain, they slew.

Because the poem mentions "Arthur's Heroes", many have assumed that he or his men were present at the battle. However, other translations interpret the key verse as follows:

> In Llongborth I saw Arthur,
> brave men hewed with steel.
> Emperor, ruler of battle.

The reference to Arthur may simply be an allusion, though it has caused many authorities to presume it is contemporary with the Arthurian period, and must therefore relate to Geraint ab Erbin who not only appears in *Culhwch and Olwen* and *The Dream of Rhonabwy*, but also has his own *Mabinogion* story, *Geraint and Enid*.

Although the poem has been attributed variously to Taliesin and Llywarch Hen, there is no evidence as to its author and consequently we do not know when it was composed. Therefore, we do not know which Geraint the poem refers to. The genealogies of Dumnonia list two Geraints, both sons of Erbin, although in the second case the Erbin connection may be an error on the part of a copyist (*see* Table 11). The second Geraint lived at the end of the seventh century, and the *ASC* records that in 710 the king of Wessex, Ine, fought against Geraint, "king of the Welsh". The Saxons referred to the British of Dumnonia as the "West Welsh", and this Geraint was probably the last independent king of Dumnonia.

The first Geraint is known as one of the "Three Seafarers of Ynys Prydein" in the Welsh Triads. He was the uncle of St Cybi who was born around the year 485 (according to Bartrum), so Geraint may have been born in the 460s, and therefore have been a contemporary of Arthur of Badon.

The word *Llongborth* means "port of the warships", rather

pertinent if Geraint was one of the three seafarers. John Morris has suggested Portsmouth as a likely candidate for Llongborth, with the battle taking place at Portchester, just at the head of the natural harbour. This in turn has caused some to leap at the *ASC* entry for 501, which states:

> Here Port and his two sons, Bieda and Mægla, came with two ships to Britain at the place which is called Portsmouth and killed a certain young British man – very noble.

Could Geraint be this young nobleman? Unlikely, since as a major seafarer Geraint was not likely to be young, and he could well have been in his forties by 501. We cannot be sure that the *ASC* entry is genuine. The name Port is probably a back formation from Portsmouth (called *Portus* by the Romans). This does not preclude a Saxon and two sons landing there in 501 and doing battle or, indeed, a later scribe mistaking Llongborth for Portsmouth, so the date may be correct. However, there is no philological connection between Portsmouth and Llongborth. Also, if Geraint is more closely associated with Devon or Somerset, then Portsmouth, in Hampshire, is some way out of his territory.

As an alternative, W.F. Skene suggested Langport, in Somerset. In Saxon times it was called Longport, meaning "long market"; the word *portus* meaning both a naval port and a market place. Although now many miles inland, the river valleys of the Parrett and Cary were more navigable in Saxon times. Though it remains a credible site for a battle, as it is on the western limit of Saxon expansion in the sixth century, there is no evidence of any settlement at Langport before the year 880, nor is there evidence of any port or market there in the early sixth century.

Of more interest is Llamporth, in Wales. It is on the south side of Cardigan Bay near the village of Penbryn, where, even more strikingly, are sites called *Beddgeraint* ("the grave of Geraint"), and Maesglas, formerly *Maes Galanas* ("the field of the killing"). These sites have been identified both by Baram Blackett and Alan Wilson in *Artorius Rex Discovered*, and by Steven Blake and Scott Lloyd in *Pendragon*. The site, promising because of the Geraint connection, is also a wonderful natural harbour at what is now Tresaith, and it is in Dyfed, which ties in with the many previous Dyfed seafaring connections already explored in this chapter.

The major problem is that in referring to the death of Geraint, the poem says "Brave men from the region of Dyvnaint." *Dyvnaint*, meaning "dwellers in deep valleys", was the Celtic name for *Dumnonia*, which also means "deep ones", possibly linked to tin mining. Geraint seems inextricably linked to the West Country, even to the point that his son, Cado, is recorded in the *Life* of St Carannog as ruling in Devon (see Cadwr, Table 11).

The answer is almost certainly that although Geraint was a man of Dumnonia, he served at Arthur's court in Wales, probably in Dyfed. As a naval commander, he would have had no problem sailing between Dyfed and Devon, and Geraint probably retained close links with his home. But his main service to Arthur was in Wales, and it was there that he met his death.

It still begs the question as to whether the poem relates to Geraint the seafarer or the Dumnonian Geraint of 710. There are two factors. Firstly, the *ASC* does not record Ine as killing Geraint at that battle, and the *ASC* has never shied away from declaring such outcomes. Secondly, the battle of 710 was between Geraint and the Saxons, and if the site was Llamporth in Dyfed, as the evidence suggests, then the Saxons would not have been involved. A battle at Llamporth would have to have involved Geraint the Seafarer.

Dating the battle is more problematic. For Arthur and his men to have earned a sufficient reputation, it would need to have followed on from Arthur's campaign of the 480s and 490s, and is therefore probably post-Badon. If the battle was not against the Saxons, then the *ASC* entry is no longer relevant.

Rather tellingly, towards the start of the poem, Geraint is referred to as the "enemy of tyranny", suggesting that the battle may have been against a local "tyrant" – the same word used by Gildas to describe his usurper kings. One of these, Vortipor, was the ruler of Dyfed and reigned from about 515 to 540. Geraint may have fought against Vortipor early in his reign, and lost. He would have been about fifty when Vortipor became king, and about fifty-five at the time of the battle of Camlann. Llongborth could have happened during those five years, with Geraint supporting Arthur against the rising tyrant kings.

On this basis, conjectural though it is, the Llongborth poem does seem to support a historical Arthur of Badon.

6. What man?

There is a poem, which survives in an incomplete form, which is usually called *Pa Gur*, after the first two words of the first line. They translate as "What man is the gatekeeper?" The question seems to be asked by Arthur himself, because the gatekeeper, Glewlwyd Mighty Grasp, responds by saying "What man asks it?" and the response is "Arthur and worthy Cei."

We might at first seem to be back in *Culhwch and Olwen*, in which Culhwch also has an altercation with Arthur's gatekeeper Glewlwyd, but in fact we are in more chilling realms. Although it is not overtly stated, Arthur seems to be knocking on the door of the Other World, seeking admittance. Along with Arthur and Cei are "the best men in the world". Glewlwyd will not admit them unless Arthur states who they are, giving Arthur the opportunity to catalogue the names of his warriors and some of their heroic deeds.

The list has some telling names and even more revealing comments. The first name listed is Mabon ap Modron. Mabon appears in both *Culhwch and Olwen* and *The Dream of Rhonabwy*, renowned as a great hunter. Here he is described as "Uther Pendragon's servant". This is one of the few Welsh texts to refer to Uther Pendragon, who is otherwise believed to be an invention of Geoffrey of Monmouth's. The name invites us to ask when *Pa Gur* was written. It appears in the thirteenth century *Black Book of Carmarthen*, but Patrick Sims-Williams believes that the poem may date from around 1100 in its final form, possibly (but only just) predating Geoffrey's *History*. The reference to Uther Pendragon may have been added later, but if so, why? It is a passing mention, of little relevance. Why associate Mabon with Uther?

It's just possible that the line "Mabon, son of Modron, Uther Pendragon's servant", is suggesting that it was Modron who was the servant. Modron was Mabon's mother, not his father, and is regarded as the original of Morgan le Fay. Mabon's father is never named, and in *Culhwch and Olwen*, Mabon is taken from his mother as a baby and spirited away. This sounds remarkably like the legend of Arthur's birth. We could consider that Uther was really Mabon's father, making Mabon a counterpart of Arthur.

Later the poem refers to Manawydan, son of Llyr: "Manawyd brought home a shattered shield from Tryfrwyd." *Tryfrwyd* is the Welsh for Tribruit, a name given in Nennius's list of Arthur's battles. The poem continues:

> On the heights of Eidyn
> He fought with champions.
> By the hundreds they fell
> To Bedwyr's four-pronged spear
> On the shores of Tryfrwyd,
> Fighting with Garwlwyd.

This seems to place Tryfrwyd in the north, near Edinburgh (*Eidyn*). This is confirmed by the following stanza, which also makes a further reference to Arthur.

> And Llwych of the Striking Hand,
> Who defended Eidyn on the borders,
> Its lord sheltered them,
> My nephew destroyed them,

Cei pleaded with them,
While he slew them three by three.
When Celli was lost
Savagery was experienced.
Cei pleaded with them,
While he hewed them down.
Though Arthur was but laughing,
Blood was flowing
In the hall of Awrnach
Fighting with the hag.

Since Arthur has been narrating this poem until now, it seems strange that his name appears in the third person. Patrick Sims-Williams has suggested that the original wording was *aruthur* meaning "terrible" or "strange", and that the poem is saying how frighteningly Cei was laughing as he hewed them down. There is a similar scene in *Culwch and Olwen*, in which Cei fights ferociously in the halls of Awrnach. Awrnach, or Wrnach, may be modern Cardurnock in the northernmost tip of Cumbria, about sixteen kilometres west of Carlisle. It was the site of an old Roman fort, and may have remained fortified under Coel and his descendants as a defence against the Irish.

If this is Arthur narrating first hand, then the reference to his nephew suggests Mordred, who was both Arthur's nephew and his incestuous son in the legends. In this part of the poem, the nephew's actions are linked with the loss of Celli, possibly Arthur's hall at Gelliwig, and thus may well relate to Mordred's treachery – or at least that of one of Arthur's nephews.

The poem also links Cei (Kay) with Arthur's son Llacheu, saying they "used to fight battles, before the pang of livid spears". One of the later stories says that Kay murdered Loholt (Llacheu), and the line in this poem is ambiguous since it is not clear if Cei and Llacheu are fighting against a common foe, or against each other.

What we have in *Pa Gur* are tantalizing comments about the Arthur of legend that suggest that something of the historical

Arthur is not far beneath the surface. Its relationship with the characters and events in *Culhwch and Olwen* may suggest that the two texts had a common origin, but the degree of factual evidence behind either is difficult to confirm. Whilst *Culhwch and Olwen* seems to relate more to the Arthurs of Gwent or Dyfed, *Pa Gur*'s northern references may hint at some memory of Arthur of the Pennines or Artúir of Dál Riata.

This leads us to one of the major poems of Celtic literature.

7. Catraeth

The earliest known reference to Arthur is usually cited as appearing in a series of elegies to dead warriors, *Y Gododdin*** ("The Gododdin"), which celebrates the valour and bravery of those soldiers in their ill-fated battle at Catraeth. The poem credits itself to Aneirin, a contemporary of Taliesin who lived during the late sixth century, and who is described in one of the triads as the "prince of bards".

The original oral version was probably composed soon after the battle, with a written version existing by the 630s. The oldest surviving copy is included in a collection of poetry held in the Cardiff Public Library known as *Llyfr Aneirin* (*The Book of Aneirin*), dating from around 1250. In fact, *Y Gododdin* survives in two forms, usually referred to as the A and B texts. The A text is longer and more complete, but the B text could well be an older, more contemporary version.

Ifor Williams, writing in 1938, suggested that Catraeth is the modern-day Catterick in Yorkshire, still the generally accepted view. Once the mighty Roman fort of Cataractonium, which covered a site of eighteen acres, it would still have been impressive in the sixth century.

The Gododdin, previously known as the Votadini, once occupied the territory stretching from Edinburgh and the Lothians down to Newcastle. By the end of the sixth century,

---

*   The most complete translation of the poem and its variants is *The Gododdin of Aneirin* edited by John T. Koch (University of Wales Press, 1997).

their territory was being taken over by the Angles, who had established their own kingdoms of Bernicia and Deira in the former British territories of the Southern Gododdin and York. The battle of Catraeth is usually seen as a last-ditch effort to recover lost territory after the death of Urien. Urien, king of Rheged, is sometimes called the Lord of Catraeth, and presumably had at some time taken hold of territory east of the Pennines, perhaps in the domain of one of his rivals, Morcant of the Gododdin.

The raid, which is how the battle began, was a disaster for the Gododdin. According to Aneirin, who was not only an eyewitness but was captured at Catraeth (Version A, §46; B §48), only one Briton survived the battle (though elsewhere it appears that three survived). The rest were slaughtered, though they fought valiantly. In true heroic style, the Gododdin were wildly outnumbered. One translation gives their number as 300, whilst their enemy numbered 100,000 (A §10). Both numbers are probably poetic licence, but the Angles probably still outnumbered the Gododdin by ten to one.

The reference to Arthur comes at the end of version B, when describing the heroic death of one of the warriors. Translations of this verse vary: this version is by Joseph Clancy, in *Earliest Welsh Poetry*:

> He thrust beyond three hundred, most bold, he cut down
>   the centre and far wing.
> He proved worthy, leading noble men; he gave from his
>   herd steeds for winter.
> He brought black crows to a fort's wall, though he was not
>   Arthur.
> He made his strength a refuge, the front line's bulwark,
>   Gwawrddur.

This reference to Arthur is usually seized on as proof that Arthur existed, and that he was probably of the Gododdin. But the poem says no such thing. Clearly, the warrior Gwawrddur is being compared to Arthur, as some great standard of heroism but, despite his valour, "he was not Arthur". This does suggest that by the 590s Arthur was already a synonym for heroism. It is not clear if Arthur is dead or still alive. Arthur could have been remembered of old, and need not have been of the Gododdin himself. The warriors had been invited from all over Britain, and Aneirin's poem would have been heard throughout the surviving British kingdoms.

Some authorities have suggested that the Arthur referred to was Artúir mac Aedan, of Dál Riata. Artúir was killed in a battle with the Mæatae, possibly in 596. There is some dispute over the precise year. John Bannerman, in *Studies in the History of Dalriada*, believes it may have been as early as 590. If Artúir mac Aedan was dead by 590, and if it is to him that the poem refers, then it would be celebrating a past and glorious hero. If Artúir were still alive, however, the poem would enhance his status, as a British poet is commemorating British heroes in a tragic defeat, and comparing their heroism with that of a living warrior. One of the main arguments against Artúir mac Aedan being the Arthur of *Y Gododdin* is that it seems unlikely that the British would want to compare one of their own heroes, Gwawrddur, with an Irish/Gaelic warrior when the Irish had been their enemy for the last two centuries. However, the pedigrees suggest that Artúir's mother, one of Aedan's three wives, was the sister of a British king. Likewise, Aedan's own mother was purportedly Luan, daughter of Brychan of Manau. If these genealogies are correct, then Artúir was three-quarters British and therefore perhaps an acceptable "British" hero.

It has been suggested that the word "Arthur" may itself be a copyist's error, and that a scribe, coming across *aruthur*, copied it, either by accident or enthusiasm, as Arthur.* If this were

* See E.V. Gordon, "Middle English", in *The Year's Work in English Studies 1924*, 5(1): 78–98 and Barber (1993), p. 15.

true, then the line would mean that despite his valour and heroic deeds, Gwawrddur was not terrible. But surely his battle fury must have been terrifying to behold. Whilst there may be instances when *aruthur* mutated to Arthur, this does not seem to be one of them.

Elsewhere the poem contains a more telling Arthurian reference, not usually cited. Verse 19 in Version A describes the heroics of Cadwal ap Sywno:

> When Cadwal charged in the green of dawn a cry went up
>   wherever he came.
> He would leave shields shattered, in splinters.
> Stiff spears this splitter would slash in battle, ripping the
>   front rank.
> Sywno's son, a wizard foresaw it, sold his life to purchase a
>   high reputation.
> He cut with a keen-edged blade, he slaughtered both
>   Athrwys and Affrei.
> As agreed on, he aimed to attack: he fashioned carcasses of
>   men brave in battle,
> Charged in Gwynedd's front line.

It is tempting to think that Athrwys might be either Arthwys of the Pennines or Athrwys of Gwent. However, if this battle dates to the 590s, by then Arthur of the Pennines was long dead and Arthur of Gwent had not yet been born.

Could it be that this verse recalls an earlier battle? A study of the poem suggests that it is an amalgam of eulogies, and not necessarily solely about the heroes of Catraeth. Cadwal would seem to be a man of Gwynedd, but he is not otherwise known. Even so, the episode may refer back to some ancient conflict between the descendants of Cunedda, once settled in Gwynedd, and their continued rivalry with the sons of Coel. Urien of Rheged was also a Coeling, and there are several references in *Y Gododdin* which suggest that the Coelings had sided with the Angles in a battle against the Gododdin.

The date of the battle is uncertain, with estimates varying

from the 570s to the 590s. It would seem likely, though not absolutely certain, that it happened after the death of Urien (*fl.* 530–570). We know from Nennius that he was murdered during the siege of Lindisfarne at the instigation of Morcant (§63). The Bernician king at that time was probably Theodoric, who, if we take Nennius's account at face value, ruled from 571–578. However, an ambiguity in the text suggests that Urien may have been besieging Hussa, who reigned from 584–591. Therefore, Urien was either murdered in 591 when he was in his sixties, or in 578 when he was in his fifties.

Since the battle of Catraeth happened soon after then it may have been in either 579/80 or 592/3 (the poem tells us the Catraeth raid was planned for a whole year). It is usually believed that the British defeat at Catraeth allowed Hussa's successor, Athelfrith, free rein in the North, and to start his invincible campaign to massacre the British and establish what became the Northumbrian kingdom. If so, then the battle happened in about 593 and the Arthur mentioned could well have been Artúir mac Aedan, who would have been too young in the late 570s.

If Catraeth had been such a victory for the Bernician kings, it is perhaps curious that there is no record of it in the *ASC*. The entry for 593AD records that Athelfrith succeeded to the kingdom, but there is no mention of a resounding slaughter of the Gododdin. Indeed, apart from a few not entirely accurate references to Ida, Aelle, and Athelfrith's father Athelric, there is no mention of the Northumbrians at all prior to 603. It is as if nothing much happened in the north until Athelfrith, who established the English in Britain.

Bede, however, noted that "no ruler or king had subjected more land to the English race or settled it, having first ex-terminated or conquered the natives". Evidently Bede knew of Athelfrith's near-genocide of the British, probably including the battle of Catraeth, but the fact that he doesn't mention it causes some authorities to suspect that Catraeth is not the same as Catterick, and was not even in northern Britain. Steve Blake and Scott Lloyd, in *The Keys to Avalon*, make the case – or rather reiterate one put forward by Dr John Gwenogfryn Evans in the early 1900s – that Catraeth was on the island of Anglesey, along the shores of the Menai Straits. They base this theory on a twelfth-century poem about the wars of Rhodri ap Owain Gwynedd, which refers to the "lands of Catraeth" in connection with Rhodri's battles in western Gwynedd. Yet it seems unlikely that the Gododdin, clearly established as from Din Eidyn (Edinburgh), would travel all the way down to Anglesey to fight at Catraeth. It is far more plausible that men from Gwynedd would travel north to meet the Gododdin at Catraeth.

As far back as 1869, John Stuart Glennie suggested that Catraeth may be the same as the old name Calathros (*Calatria* in Latin and *Galtraeth* in British). The Irish Annals refer to Calathros as adjoining Cairpre (Carriber) on the Avon, just south of Linlithgow. *Gal-traeth* means "shore of sorrow", a suitable name for a memory of slaughter. To be on the shore and adjoining Carriber, it has to be north of Linlithgow on the shores of the Forth, possibly at Carriden. This is certainly a more logical location for warriors from Din Eidyn to venture into battle, as it is only some 25km (16m) west of Edinburgh. The site suggests it is more likely to have been a battle against either the Picts or the Scots, rather than the Angles, although the Angles had themselves sometimes combined forces with the Picts in fighting a common enemy. It is difficult to understand, however, how Urien could be lord of Catraeth at somewhere so evidently part (or once part) of Gododdin territory. Nevertheless, this area has possible Arthurian connections because Bouden (or Bowden) Hill, one of the suggested sites for Badon, is just south of Linlithgow, near Torphichen. If Badon had been fought within a few miles of Catraeth, then the comparison of a warrior with Arthur becomes all the more potent. Arthur's tenth battle, Tribruit, could also have been fought in this vicinity.

Like so much else, *Y Gododdin* presents an enigma. The weight of evidence suggests a battle in the north and that the

Arthurian reference is to a northern hero. If Arthur of Badon was already entering legendary status a century after Badon, he would have been remembered right across the British king-doms. Even so, it seems hard to imagine that the Arthurs of Llongborth and of Catraeth are one and the same, and neither would seem to be Arthur of Dyfed or Arthur of Gwent. Perhaps Arthur of the Pennines is at last showing his hand.

8. The triads

The *Trioedd Ynys Prydein* ("The Triads of the Isle of Britain") are a series of records that function as mnemonics, to assist in remembering key names or events. They are always grouped in threes, such as the "Three Fair Princes" or the "Three Frivo-lous Bards", and sometimes a fourth name might be added as better (or worse) than all three. Triad No. 2, for instance, lists the "Three Generous Men" of Britain – Nudd, Mordaf and Rhydderch – and then says, "And Arthur himself was more generous than the three." This reads too much like a later addition to rectify the omission of Arthur, and references such as this are of no value at all. Only those triads that incorporate Arthur within the list and say something meaningful are worthy of consideration.

The triads turn up in various sources, primarily the *Red Book of Hergest* and the *White Book of Rhydderch*, but are part of a rigid oral bardic tradition, and some may date back to the sixth century. Tradition ascribes them to various bards such as Taliesin and Myrddin, but we now have no way of knowing who first wrote what, or when. Like all oral records they are subject to change over time, with new names substituted to reflect current thinking. Their reliability, six centuries after Arthur, is suspect, but just occasionally there may be some information, as much in what they don't say as what they do.

The translation and ordering of the triads has been ration-alized by the work of Dr Rachel Bromwich in *Trioedd Ynys Prydein* (1978), and most quotes from triads now follow her numbering. She lists ninety-six triads, but other incomplete lists exist in different sequences suggesting that there are more. Nevertheless, for consistency I shall follow Dr Bromwich's numbering. Of those ninety-six, about twenty-six actually mention Arthur. However, some of these, such as the "Three Knights of Arthur's Court who won the Graal", are clearly late compositions. I've selected those few which do raise points of interest.

1. Three Tribal Thrones of Britain
   - Arthur as Chief Prince in Mynyw, and Dewi as Chief Bishop and Maelgwyn Gwynedd as Chief Elder.
   - Arthur as Chief Prince in Celliwig in Cornwall, and Bishop Bytwini as Chief Bishop and Caradawg Strong-Arm as Chief Elder.
   - Arthur as Chief Prince in Pen Rhionydd in the North and Gyrthmwl Wledig as Chief Elder and Cyndyrn Garthwys as Chief Bishop.

This tells us the three principal courts of Arthur: Mynyw (St David's), Celliwig (here sited in Cornwall because of the translation of Cernyw), and Pen Rhionydd. This last court has caused much conjecture. Its bishop, Cyndyrn Garthwys, is St Kentigern, and the reference to the North has caused most to suppose it is near Kentigern's bishopric in Glasgow. Since his parish covered most of Strathclyde and Rheged (Kentigern was the grandson of Urien of Rheged), Pen Rhionydd could have been anywhere in what is now Cumbria and Galloway. Bromwich, in her interpretation of the triads, has suggested it is the Rhinns of Galloway.

Depending on the location of Pen Rhionydd, this triad could be an accurate record of the three Arthurs. The Chief Prince of Mynyw was Arthur of Dyfed (though it is odd to see Maelgwyn of Gwynedd there). Arthur of Gwent ruled from Celliwig, and the third could relate to Arthur of the Pennines or Artúir of Dál Riata. The clue lies in identifying Gyrthmwl Wledig.

Although he appears in *The Dream of Rhonabwy* as one of Arthur's counsellors, he is seldom referred to. He is mentioned in the "Stanzas of the Graves", described as being "a chieftain of the North" but buried at Celli Frifael, which is in the Gower Peninsula in South Wales. His name appears in another triad as one of the "Three Bull Spectres" of Britain, suggesting that he had already passed into legend, and that there was some otherworld adventure involving his ghost. The mystery is not helped by his name, which was probably a melding of *Gwyrth-Mael*, or "Miracle Prince".

Curiously, the name *Gyrthmwl* appears in a poem composed by Heledd, the sister of Cynddylan, written sometime in the mid-seventh century.

> If Gyrthmwl were a woman, she would be weak today,
> her wail would be loud:
> she is whole, but her warriors are destroyed.

Ifor Williams has interpreted *Gyrthmwl* as a place name, and in fact it's one we've already encountered as Garthmyl, in Powys, close by the Roman fort of The Gaer, near Welshpool. It is from near here that Arthur leads his army to the battle of Caer Faddon in *The Dream of Rhonabwy*. Could it be that the composer of the triad confused the name of one of Arthur's strongholds with an individual? Or, more likely, was Garthmyl named after its lord? He may have been related to the Cadellings of Powys and commanded The Gaer on behalf of Arthur.

But how does this relate to "the North" and the parish of Kentigern? In his middle years, Kentigern allegedly moved to North Wales and founded a monastery at Llanelwy, now St Asaph, in Gwynedd. This has since been rejected as a Norman fabrication, but the triad may have been repeating that fabrication, so that even though based on a false premise, the location may still be accurate. Twenty-five kilometres to the west of St Asaph is Penrhyn. In *The Keys to Avalon*, Steve Blake and Scott Lloyd suggest that Pen Rhionydd ("Headland of the

Maidens") is related to another locale, Morfa Rhianedd ("Sea-strand of the Maidens"), which runs between Llandudno and Conwy. Located here is Deganwy, one of the courts of Maelgwyn Gwynedd.

The "North" would then seem to mean North Wales. Since Deganwy was Maelgwyn's stronghold, it seems odd to place him at Mynyw and Gyrthmwl at Deganwy. However, if we think back to Gildas's commentary upon Maelgwyn, we know that he first came to the throne by murdering an uncle, repented and went into a monastery, and then returned to his murdering ways. He probably usurped Deganwy in his later years, in the 530s or 540s, after Arthur's death. Near Borth is a stretch of shore called Traeth Maelgwyn where legend has it that Maelgwyn won his kingship.

This triad may be remembering, albeit awkwardly, a period when Arthur, as High King of Wales, appointed three sub-kings to govern Wales on his behalf. Maelgwyn took the west, Caradog the south and Gyrthmwl the east and north. This arrangement may not have lasted long because another triad, about the "Three Horse Burdens" of Britain, tells how Gyrthmwl's sons avenged his death when they attacked Dinas Maelawr, in Ceredigion. This has been idenitified as the fort of Pendinas, in Aberystwyth, suggesting conflict between Maelg-wyn and Gyrthmwl.

9. Three Chieftains of Arthur's Court
   - Gobrwy son of Echel Mighty-thigh
   - Cadrieth Fine-Speech son of Porthawr Gadw
   - And Fleudur Fflam.

If ever there were three forgotten Arthurian names it must be these three. No legends have grown up around them, but they also appear in *Culhwch and Olwen* and *The Dream of Rhonabwy* as counsellors at Arthur's court. Since they are otherwise unknown, in all likelihood this triad has remained true and they probably were amongst Arthur's advisers.

Cadrieth was also the name of one of the survivors of Catraeth, but there is no way to tell if they are the same person.

54. Three Unrestrained Ravagings of Britain
- When Medrawd came to Arthur's court at Celliwig in Cornwall.
- When Arthur came to Medrawd's court.
- When Aeddan the Wily came to the court of Rhydderch the Generous at Alclud.

It is unfortunate that the name of Medrawd's court is not given but, in any case, the triad does no more than emphasize the rivalry between Arthur and Medrawd. We know from Table 8 that Medrawd was ruler of Ergyng at the same time as Athrwys of Gwent. The third line repeats a tradition that Aedan mac Gabhran, the future king of Dál Riata, took advantage of Rhydderch of Strathclyde. The legend recounts that Aedan incited a rebellion against Rhydderch, who was forced to flee to Ireland. Rhydderch returned, however, leading to the bloody battle of Arderydd in 574 (listed in the *Welsh Annals* under 575). The battle was between Rhydderch and Gwenddoleu, a renegade chieftain operating throughout Galloway and Rheged. Aedan allied himself with Gwenddoleu, whilst Rhydderch's men formed part of a confederate army organized by Peredur of York and his brother Gwrgi. Arderydd, also known as Arthuret, was evidently one of the great showdowns in British history. Gwenddoleu was killed and, so legend has it, his bard Myrddin went mad with grief and ran wild in the Caledonian forest. Aedan fled back to Dál Riata, whilst Rhydderch regained Strathclyde and became one of the great kings of the North.

59. Three Unfortunate Counsels of Britain
- To give place for their horses' fore-feet on the land to Julius Caesar and the men of Rome.
- To allow Horsa and Hengist and Rhonwen into this Island.

- The three-fold dividing by Arthur of his men with Medrawd at Camlan.

Here there may be a hint of memory of Arthur's fatal battle at Camlann, where, perhaps, his battle tactics were flawed. There have been few references to Camlann in our trawl through fabled history, but its memory permeates the triads, which dwell on the futility of the battle. One such reference is in Triad 53, the "Three Harmful Blows" of Britain, where it says: "The blow Gwenhwyfach struck upon Gwenhwyfar: and for that cause there took place afterwards the action of the Battle of Camlan." Gwenhwyfach, wife of Mordred, and her sister Gwenhwyfar/Guenevere quarrelled while collecting nuts. One sister struck the other and, from that, enmity arose between Mordred and Arthur, leading Mordred to abduct Guenevere and claim the kingdom, and to the final battle.

65. Three Unrestricted Guests of Arthur's Court, and Three Wanderers
   - Llywarch the Old
   - Llemenig
   - Heledd

Llywarch was cousin to Urien of Rheged. The Men of the North fought amongst themselves and Llywarch found himself hounded out of Rheged and reduced to poverty with most of his sons killed. He eventually settled in Powys in the late sixth century, where he died at an advanced age, a sad and somewhat lonely man. In one of his poems, he confirms that, "They welcomed me in the taverns of Powys, paradise of Welshmen." Llemenig is a shadowy character but one who might be a prototype of Lancelot. Heledd was the sister of Cynddylan, king of Powys in the mid-seventh century. This seems to suggest that Arthur's court was in Powys. By the time of Llywarch, the ruler of Powys was either Brochwel of the Tusks or Cynan the Cruel. Nevertheless, the court may still have been remembered as Arthur's.

73. Three Peers of Arthur's Court
- Rahawd son of Morgant
- Dalldaf son of Cunyn Cof
- Drystan son of March

Here are two more names that have faded into obscurity. Rahawd appears in Triad 12 as one of the "Three Frivolous Bards" at Arthur's court, along with Arthur himself! He also appears as one of Arthur's counsellors in *The Dream of Rhonabwy*, but otherwise his name is not known, and may be a late Norman addition. Dalldaf is another of Arthur's courtiers who appears in *Culhwch and Olwen*. Bartrum has suggested he may be the same as Doldavius, king of Gotland, whom we shall meet in Geoffrey's *History*. Drystan is another matter, as he is the well-known figure of Tristan.

The majority of the triads which mention Arthur are amongst the most fanciful and least historic, suggesting that they were added later as Arthur's legend grew. Elsewhere, triads in which one might expect to find Arthur in his role as High King do not mention him.

5. Three Pillars of Battle of Britain:
- Dunawd son of Pabo, Pillar of Britain
- Gwallawg son of Lleenawg
- Cynfelyn the Leprous

We have encountered the first two in the battles in the North – indeed, Gwallawg is the nephew of Arthur of the Pennines who, had he really been a major force in the North, ought to feature in at least one triad. Cynfelyn the Leprous was also related, being a distant cousin, and may have earned the honour because of an unrecorded role at Arderydd. The following triad is similar.

6. Three Bull-Protectors of Britain
  - Cynfawr Host-Protector
  - Gwenddolau son of Ceidiaw
  - And Urien son of Cynfarch

These are also all Men of the North. Urien and Gwenddolau
we have met. Cynfawr was the brother of Cynfelyn the
Leprous, and although he is otherwise all but unknown, his
epithet of "Host Protector", as identified by Bartrum, is similar
to the Irish title "of the hundred battles", applied to the near
legendary High King Conn. This suggests that Cynfawr, and
no doubt Cynfelyn, were survivors of many battles in the
North.

Yet Arthur is not amongst them, and if he had been such a
Protector of the North, surely he would feature somewhere.
Neither does he appear in the "Three Chief Officers" of Britain
(Triad 13), who are Caradawg, Cawrdaf and Owain. He is not
one of the "Three Battle Horsemen" (Triad 18), who include
Caradog Vreichfras, or the "Three Enemy Subduers" (Triad
19), of whom one is Drystan/Tristan. Arthur is not even one of
the "Three Battle Leaders" of Britain (Triad 25), who are Selyf
ap Cynan, Urien of Rheged and, surprisingly, Addaon, the son
of Taliesin, whom we met in *The Dream of Rhonabwy*.

Whenever you expect to find Arthur in a triad, he isn't there,
and when he does appear, it is usually as an echo of some aspect
of his legend. Rather than the triads supporting the existence of
Arthur, they tend to underscore the development of the legend
in later years. Only three of them tell us anything pertinent
about Arthur. Triad 1 shows how his administration was
divided and where his three main courts were, Triad 65
suggests that he had a court in Powys, and Triad 59 reveals
how he mismanaged his tactics at Camlann.

9. The Irish Annals

The Irish Annals are considerably more extensive than the
Welsh, and it is strongly suspected that some of the *Welsh*

Annals were rebuilt from the Irish ones many years later. The Irish Annals have little bearing on Arthurian history. They deal primarily with Irish history, and, although they do make occasional references to significant events in Britain, they are of little help in our deliberations.

Except, that is, for the following. There are six primary Irish Annals, starting with the *Annals of Inisfallen*, which survives from the eleventh century. The others are the *Annals of Ulster*, the *Annals of Clonmacnoise*, the *Annals of Tigernach*, the *Chronicum Scotorum* and the wonderfully named *Annals of the Four Masters*. Four of these have the following entry variously dated from the year 620AD (*Four Masters*), to 625/6 (*Scotorum* and *Inisfallen*). The most complete version is that in the *Annals of Clonmacnoise* (624):

> Mongan mac Fiaghna, a well-spoken man and much given to the wooing of women, was killed by Artúir ap Bicor, a Briton, with a stone.

A brief entry, but an intriguing one, which makes the point that Artúir was a Briton (sometimes translated as a Welshman), and therefore not Irish. Mongan is a historically recognized king, so there is no reason to presume his death from Arthur's missile is fabricated. That makes this Arthur very real, but we are in the period 620–626, a hundred years later than the events of Badon and Camlann.

The tale behind this Arthur takes us to one of the more famous legendary exploits of the Irish. Perhaps the best-known of all of the Irish seafarers was Brendan, also known as Bran, the founding abbot of Clonfert. Brendan lived throughout the Arthurian period, around 486–575, and became immortalized through his travels, particularly the one recorded in the ninth-century poem, *The Voyage of Bran*. This includes an episode in which Bran meets Manannan mac Lir. Manannan tells Bran that his destiny is taking him to Ireland, where he will father a son, the future hero Mongan, with the wife of the king,

Fiachna. The poem includes some predictions about Mongan, including the following quatrain:

> He will be – his time will be short –
> Fifty years in this world:
> A dragonstone from the sea will kill him
> In the fight at Senlabor.

This prophecy was, of course, compiled by the bards many years after Mongan's death, but one wonders how significant the word "dragonstone" is. Did they mean a stone of the Pendragon?
The Voyage of Bran continues:

> He will be throughout long ages
> An hundred years in fair kingship,
> He will cut down battalions, a lasting grave –
> He will redden fields, a wheel around the track.
> It will be about kings with a champion
> That he will be known as a valiant hero,
> Into the strongholds of a land on a height
> I shall send an appointed end from Islay.
> High shall I place him with princes,
> He will be overcome by a son of error;
> Moninnan, the son of Ler,
> Will be his father, his tutor.

Does the "son of error" mean that Artúir ap Bicor was illegitimate? The poem also suggests that Mongan's killer would come from Islay. A later lament on the death of Mongan, attributed to the Ulster king Becc Boirche, also says:

> Cold is the wind across Islay,
> Warriors of Cantire are coming,
> They will commit a ruthless deed,
> They will kill Mongan son of Fiachna.

Islay was part of the kingdom of Dál Riata, carved out in Argyll and Kintyre ("Cantire") by the Irish from their own kingdom of Dál Riata, in Ulster. At the time of Mongan's death in 620–626, the king of the Kintyre Dál Riata was Eochaid Buide ("the Fair"), the youngest son of Aedan mac Gabhran. Eochaid's inheritance of the kingship was foretold by St Columba, when Aedan asked the missionary which of his four sons would succeed him. Columba declared that three of them, Artúir, Eochaid Find and Domangart, would pre-decease Aedan. It was the youngest, Eochaid Buide, who would succeed.

Artúir mac Aedan's name appears in the genealogies of the *History of the Men of Scotland* and, more significantly, his death is recorded in the *Annals of Tigernach*. Tigernach was the Abbot of Clonmacnoise in Ireland who died in 1088, but it is believed that he continued a set of annals maintained at the abbey since the year 544, when it was founded. They record the deaths of Artúir and Eochaid Find in 596 in a battle against the Mæatae north of the Antonine Wall, and therefore close to the territory of the Manau Gododdin. Their main fortress was at Dunmyat, in what became Clackmannanshire. Aedan of Dál Riata was expanding his regime and encountering conflicts on all sides. Although he was victorious over the Mæatae, it was at the cost of his sons Artúir and Eochaid Find.

The campaigns of Aedan hold some other tempting morsels. Though he was king of Dál Riata in Britain, Aedan was still subject to his Irish overlord in Ulster, Baetan mac Cairill, the most powerful king in Ireland at that time, who came to power in 572 and rapidly exerted his authority over the Dál Riatan settlement in Britain. Aedan was determined to keep his independence and, in 575, met Baetan in battle at Dun Baetan in Ulster. Aedan was defeated, and forced to pay homage to Baetan at Islandmagee, near Carrickfergus. Aedan's young son Artúir was present at Dun Baetan. Laurence Gardner, in *Bloodline of the Holy Grail*, tells us that this was the second battle at Dun Baetan (*see* Chapter 7). The first, in 516, had been between Aedan's father Gabhran, who augmented his troops with those of Ambrosius Aurelianus, and Baetan's father Cairill. The result was a remarkable victory for the Scots.

Gardner believes it was this battle that Gildas recalls in *De Excidio*. The 574 battle is the one recalled by Nennius, but over time memories of the two have merged.

Aedan continued to do battle against the Ulster overlord. In 577, Baetan captured the Isle of Man, but was forced to retreat the following year. Baetan died, somewhat mysteriously, in 581, and in 582 Aedan, and presumably Artúir who would now have been aged about twenty-three, succeeded in driving the remaining Irish out of Man and taking control of the island. Aedan remained a powerful ruler in the north throughout the rest of the sixth century, but met his match in 603 when he set out to teach Athelfrith of Northumbria a lesson. He was soundly defeated at Degsastan (probably Dawston, in Liddesdale). Bede records that he "took to flight with a few survivors while almost his entire army was cut down".

If Artúir mac Aedan died in battle in the year 596, he cannot be the Artúir who killed Mongan in 620. It would, in any case, be difficult to equate Artúir's father Aedan with Bicor. The implication of the reference to Islay and Kintyre is that Artúir ap Bicor was one of the Scottish Dál Riata, but would an Irish annalist refer to him as British? By this time we are four generations removed from Fergus, whose son Domangart was also born in Ireland, so we are at best only talking of grandchildren of settlers.

However, there had been Irish settlers in Kintyre for over a hundred years before Fergus established his separate kingdom, and these settlers would have interbred, and may well have been regarded as British by the Irish. If so, then we can go no further in our quest for Artúir ap Bicor. In all probability, he was a warrior in the army of Eochaid the Fair, who had been given his name in honour of Aedan's heroic son, and who in turn had his five minutes of fame.

Is there a case for looking further? Looking back to our pedigrees, we see that the only other contemporary Artúir was Artúir ap Pedr, who lived perhaps a little too early for this event. Like a Kintyre Arthur, this Artúir was also descended from Irish settlers, but by now over eight generations, so may well have been regarded as a Briton by the Irish.

In consulting this Arthur's pedigree in *The Expulsion of the Déisi*, we find that his father's name is given as *Retheoir*, which may mean "lance-man" or "lance wielder". This form of name may also equate with Bicor, which means "good throw" or "lucky throw". Thus the apparent patronymic *Bicor* may simply have been a nickname for Arthur, who after his success in killing Mongan became known as "Arthur of the lucky shot".

We can, perhaps, play this game a little further. At the same time that Artúir ruled Dyfed, his neighbour in Ceredigion was Arthfoddw ap Boddw, whose name may also incorporate a nickname, "Arth the lucky". Could "Arth the lucky" and "Arthur the lucky shot" be the same person?

We do not know enough about either Artúir of Dyfed or Arthfoddw ap Boddw to know why either might be fighting against Mongan in Ireland, or why they should be linked with Kintyre. The coasts of both territories were subject to attacks by Irish raiders and this may have been a retaliation, but it seems unlikely. I strongly suspect that Artúir ap Bicor is a red herring, though a useful one, because it does show that the name Artúir was perhaps becoming more prevalent by the seventh century.

We have now explored the vast majority of the Welsh Arthurian tradition. There are further minor references in other poems, but they tell us no more about a historical Arthur.

What is most obvious about the Welsh tales is that they provide none of that background supplied by Nennius, and later by Geoffrey. The Welsh stories tell us nothing of the background of Vortigern and Ambrosius, and nothing significant about Arthur's campaign against the Saxons. If anything, Arthur's battles seem to be against other British or Welsh warbands. Badon is mentioned in *The Dream of Rhonabwy*, but not in the Triads, although Camlann does feature.

Furthermore, most of the dates relating to the Welsh Arthur are in the mid- to late sixth century, and only a few, such as Geraint's, relate to the time of Badon.

Almost all of the references to Arthur in the Welsh tales relate to either Arthur of Dyfed or Arthur of Gwent, with perhaps a hint of Arthur of the Pennines. Only the elegies of Llongborth and Catraeth possibly contain a distant memory of the hero of Badon. The triads add little of merit, but we may again get a hint of Arthur's courts and of his battle tactics.

Despite the wealth of material, Arthur of Badon still eludes us. But now we turn to the man who will reveal all: Geoffrey of Monmouth.

9

THE CREATION OF ARTHUR – GEOFFREY'S VERSION

1. Geoffrey of Monmouth

Geoffrey of Monmouth's *Historia Regum Britanniae* (*History of the Kings of Britain*), completed around 1138 (thus more than six centuries after Arthur's time), was the work that really created the legend, taking a character known from folktales and turning him into Britain's greatest hero. Even now, almost nine centuries after Geoffrey's work took the Norman world by storm, questions are still asked about its authenticity. Virtually every scholar treats Geoffrey's story as a fabrication, but it is peppered with enough tantalizing facts to lure the reader into believing the rest.

Over three hundred years have passed since Nennius compiled his *Historia Brittonum*, and in that time Britain had changed radically. The Saxon conquerors had themselves been conquered by the Normans seventy years earlier in 1066, many becoming serfs within the growing Norman empire. The Welsh remained independent, but although not conquered by the Normans were regarded as a vassal state. The Welsh nevertheless retained a fierce national pride, particularly strong under Gruffydd ap Cynan, king of Gwynedd, the most powerful ruler in Wales. Despite being held prisoner by the Normans at Chester for over ten years, Gruffydd continued to fight, although he was soundly defeated by forces under William II in 1098, and again by Henry I in 1114. For the rest of his life, which was long, Gruffydd ap Cynan strove to establish a national Welsh identity and heritage, becoming a patron of music and the arts, and bringing order to the bardic tradition. Gruffydd had a passion for bardic stories, and there is no doubt that during these years, especially the 1120s, his court was a crucible for the formation of the Arthurian legend.

We know little about Geoffrey's early years. He calls himself Galfridus *Monumotensis*, or "of Monmouth", which probably means he was born there. Monmouth over the centuries has been claimed by both Wales and England. It was in the old kingdom of Gwent, or more accurately Ergyng, which places Geoffrey's childhood in the area where we know from Nennius that both Vortigern and Ambrosius, and therefore possibly Arthur, lived. Geoffrey doubtless grew up with the legends as part of his childhood, and apparently sometimes called himself Arthur, which may also have been his father's name. It is probable that his parents, or at least one of them, came from Brittany and that Geoffrey may have lived there for some years. We do not know when he was born, but it was probably in the 1080s, and he and his family may have returned to England from Brittany during the reign of Henry I, who became king in 1100.

We first learn of Geoffrey as a teacher and secular canon at St George's College, Oxford, in 1129. The university did not yet exist, but Oxford was already becoming established as a seat of learning. Geoffrey was by then of sufficient status to be a witness to a charter, so he may have been there for most of the 1120s. He remained in Oxford until 1151 when he became bishop-elect of St Asaph's in North Wales. He was ordained at Westminster

Abbey in February 1152, but probably never visited St Asaph's due to the renewed conflict between the English and Welsh under Owain Gwynedd. Owain had taken advantage of an England weakened by civil war during the reign of Stephen to establish himself as the most powerful ruler in Wales. This conflict makes it clear that Geoffrey must have been regarded as a Breton rather than Welsh by his Norman peers, who would never have put a Welshman in charge of a bishopric. Nevertheless, Geoffrey's loyalties must have been divided, and this has to be borne in mind when studying his *Historia*.

Geoffrey probably worked for much of the 1120s and into the 1130s on the *Historia*, almost a fifth of which concentrates on the life and glory of King Arthur. He published separately, in 1134 or thereabouts, the *Prophetiae Merlini* (*The Prophecies of Merlin*), later incorporated into the *Historia*, and the *Vita Merlini* (*Life of Merlin*) in about 1150.

It seems strange that a book that glorifies a hero of the British – the descendants of whom were now the Welsh – should prove so popular with the Normans. Geoffrey's work could be seen as a rallying cry to the Welsh to show that they had once had a hero capable of defeating the enemy. What they did once they could do again. The need to write his *Historia* could have been spurred by Gruffydd ap Cynan's desire to develop the bardic tales. Yet the book also had a strong message for the Normans, now settled in England for nearly a century. The Norman kings were still dukes of Normandy and, in a strange parallel with Arthur, William the Conqueror had been the duke (*dux*) who had become a king. More significantly, Britain had been treated as a rich but rather backward country by the French, who had a powerful heroic history in their own tales of Charlemagne, founder of the French Empire. In giving Britain Arthur, Geoffrey created a national hero who could rank alongside Charlemagne, and in whom the Normans, as conquerors of Britain, could take equal pride. Geoffrey's book was, therefore, as much propaganda as it was history, and it is as propaganda that it must be read.

Equally, while teasing the facts out of the fancy is not easy, we should not dismiss it entirely as fiction. There is a confused but genuine history hidden amidst the myth.

Geoffrey's problem lay in organizing that myth into a sequential history. In effect, what he did was to take all the facts and, like pieces of a jigsaw, try to force them together into a story. Whilst forming a continuous narrative, the historical thread became jumbled, and the events or persons contemporary with Arthur are cast back in time and disconnected from him.

But where did Geoffrey get this information? So far, we have trawled through the surviving texts and none of them provides the degree of detail that Geoffrey does, particularly about Arthur. In both Nennius and the *Welsh Annals*, the Arthurian elements seem to be tucked in as extras, and not part of the natural flow. This is one reason why Geoffrey, even during his lifetime, has been accused of inventing most of his history. William of Newburgh, a far more fastidious historian than Geoffrey, who was writing his own history of Britain in the 1190s, accused Geoffrey with typical Yorkshire bluntness of having made it all up, "either from an inordinate love of lying or for the sake of pleasing the British".

There is a wonderful fourteenth-century document called the *Polychronicon*, by Ranulf Higden, which says:

> Many men wonder about this Arthur, whom Geoffrey extols so much singly, how the things that are said of him could be true, for, as Geoffrey repeats, he conquered thirty realms. If he subdued the king of France to him, and did slay Lucius the Procurator of Rome, Italy, then it is astonishing that the chronicles of Rome, of France, and of the Saxons should not have spoken of so noble a prince in their stories, which mentioned little things about men of low degree. Geoffrey says that Arthur overcame Frollo, King of France, but there is no record of such a name among men of France. Also, he says that Arthur slew Lucius Hiberius, Procurator of the city of Rome in the time of Leo the Emperor, yet according to all the stories of the

Romans Lucius did not govern in that time – nor was Arthur born, nor did he live then, but in the time of Justinian, who was the fifth emperor after Leo. Geoffrey says that he has marvelled that Gildas and Bede make no mention of Arthur in their writings; however, I suppose it is rather to be marvelled that Geoffrey praises him so much, whom old authors, true and famous writers of stories, leave untouched.

Did Geoffrey make it all up?

2. Geoffrey's ancient book

It is evident from the start that Geoffrey drew upon the works of Nennius and Gildas and upon other, more traditional, sources. In his lengthy dedication to Robert, Earl of Gloucester, the illegitimate son of Henry I and a supporter of Matilda during the civil war, Geoffrey states, with regard to his research:

At a time when I was giving a good deal of attention to such matters, Walter, Archdeacon of Oxford, a man skilled in the art of public speaking and well-informed about the history of foreign countries, presented me with a certain very ancient book written in the British language. This book, attractively composed to form a consecutive and orderly narrative, set out all the deeds of these men, from Brutus, the first King of the Britons, down to Cadwallader, the son of Cadwallo. At Walter's request I have taken the trouble to translate the book into Latin, although, indeed, I have been content with my own expressions and my own homely style and I have gathered no gaudy flowers of speech in other men's gardens.

In other words, Geoffrey freely adapted this book into his own style. But what book was it? He doesn't name it, and evidently William of Newburgh did not know of it. Some have conjectured that it was Geoffrey's own invention, presenting the story as if derived from some long-lost factual source. However, he states that the book was given to him by Walter,

Archdeacon of Oxford, and Walter, who died in 1151, was still alive at the time the *Historia* was issued. If there was no such book, then Walter was in on the hoax, and we are once again dangerously close to the territory of conspiracy.

It is possible that Geoffrey's book was the *Ystoria Britanica*, which was consulted by the Breton monk William in 1019 for his *Legenda Sancti Goeznovii* (see page 133), which introduced the character of Riothamus. Whilst Geoffrey may well have consulted it, it is unlikely to have been his "very ancient book", as it was written in Latin and there was no need to translate it. Others claim that Geoffrey drew upon the *Brut y Brenhined* (*Chronicle of Kings*), though all known versions of this appear to be translations of Geoffrey's own *Historia* into Welsh. In some cases the translators added their own details to the text, thus providing variants, but there is no evidence that the *Brut y Brenhined* existed before Geoffrey's *Historia*.

Another possibility is the ancient text known as the *Brut Tysilio* (*Chronicles of Tysilio*). There has been much dispute as to when these chronicles were first written. Tysilio was a sixth-century prince of Powys, son of Brochwel of the Tusks and great-grandson of Cadell. Legend has it that Tysilio yearned for the religious life, eventually fleeing to Brittany where he established a monastery. It is possible that this story represents two different Tysilios. In any case, neither Tysilio lived into the reign of Cadwaladr whose exploits conclude the *Brut Tysilio*, causing some to conjecture that the chronicle was continued by others. The copy in Jesus College, Oxford, is from the early 1500s, and thus post-dates Geoffrey's work. Intriguingly, copies of the *Brut* – including the one at Jesus – have a colophon which says:

> I, Walter, archdeacon of Oxford, translated this book from the Welsh into Latin and, in my old age, have again translated it from the Latin into Welsh.

One might puzzle as to why Walter should do that. Perhaps he had lost the original Welsh edition; and it is possible too that the Latin version from which he translated the book back into Welsh may not have been his own, but that undertaken by Geoffrey. If this is the case, it means – unfortunately – that the *Tysilio* translated back into Welsh would be derived from Geoffrey's work rather than from the original, which has us chasing our own tails!

There are many differences between the *Brut Tysilio* and Geoffrey's *Historia*, sufficient to suggest that they may both be translations of the same earlier text, but that the *Tysilio* is more faithful to the original. The noted archaeologist Flinders Petrie satisfied himself that the *Tysilio* was authentic and not a revision or contraction of Geoffrey's *Historia*. He argued that on a few occasions Geoffrey confirms that he is adding items, but that those elements are missing from *Tysilio*, whereas one would expect some reference to them if it were a direct translation. Others have noted that the versions of names used in the *Tysilio* show a closer relationship to the Celtic original, whereas some of those in the *Historia* could easily be scribal errors. An example appears in book *iii.17*, where Geoffrey refers to "Archgallo, the brother of Gorbonianus". In *Tysilio* this name appears as "Arthal". *Archgallo* is not a Latinization of *Arthal*, but a misreading of the script, in which the *t* would have appeared as a Celtic ᚈ, and easily misread for the letter *c*. Such an error is unlikely to arise in reverse.

Until an earlier version of *Tysilio* is discovered we will not know. Certainly the surviving text is sufficiently close to Geoffrey's, including many of his errors, asides and comments, that it would seem to be a direct translation, augmented and corrected in the light of their own knowledge and beliefs by later scribes.

My own belief is that Geoffrey did have an ancient text to work from, but that this was a miscellany rather like Nennius's, a hotchpotch of dates and legends and anecdotes which he endeavoured to rework into a single narrative. Clearly Geoffrey had no idea who Arthur was or when his period in history fell, but that did not stop him creating both an exciting story and a wonderful piece of propaganda.

3. Geoffrey's Vortigern and Ambrosius

Geoffrey's *Historia* is too long to consider every element in detail. For the present I shall concentrate on the period involving Vortigern and Arthur, which is almost half the book.

Geoffrey tells the story of Britain separating from the Roman Empire and being attacked by Picts and Saxons, in much the same way as Gildas and Nennius do. After the abortive appeal to Agicus (Aëtius), Guthelinus (Vitalinus), Archbishop of London, turns to Aldroenus (*Aldwr* in British), ruler of Armorica/Brittany, and offers him the kingdom of Britain. Aldroenus admits that, although he once would have been interested, the present state of Britain offers no allure. However, Aldroenus suggests that his brother Constantine should return to Britain with two thousand soldiers on the understanding that if he frees Britain of its enemies, then he should inherit the crown.

Constantine is duly made king, marries a noblewoman whom Guthelinus himself had raised, and has three sons. The oldest, Constans, is promised to the church, and Aurelius Ambrosius and Uther are handed to Guthelinus to raise. Ten years pass, presumably in peace, until Constantine is killed by a Pict. A dispute arises over who should inherit the crown because Constans is now a monk and the other two are still children "in their cradles" (*vi.7*). Vortigern, whom Geoffrey calls "leader of the Gewissei", now appears on the scene (*vi.6*). He tells Constans that he will help him become king, crowns him, and becomes his adviser. With Constans a puppet ruler, Vortigern plots to become king himself. Other contenders for the throne – the "older leaders of the kingdom", as Geoffrey calls them – were all dead, and Constans was Vortigern's only hurdle.

Vortigern assumes control of the treasury and places his own men in the major towns, telling them that there is fear of further attack from the Danes and Saxons. He also convinces Constans that he needs a bodyguard of select Pict soldiers. Vortigern, knowing that the Picts are untrustworthy, pays them handsomely, and then states that he plans to leave Britain. The Picts don't want him to go, and to keep him they murder Constans, presenting his head to Vortigern. Vortigern feigns anguish and has the Picts executed. Amidst suspicion that he planned it all, Vortigern crowns himself king.

Let's pause there a moment and consider how all this fits together. We should have one firm starting point, the letter to Aëtius, which we have dated to between 446 and 452, probably 451. Then follows Constantine's victory over the Picts, his coronation, marriage and raising children. Geoffrey says that ten years pass, but Constans is clearly older than ten, and old enough to be a monk. If Constans is about eighteen when Vortigern insinuates his way into the royal household and brings him (briefly) to the throne, that moves us on to 469. Ambrosius is still a baby, yet the chronology derived from Gildas and Nennius has him in the prime of manhood by now. Clearly Geoffrey is in error.

In all likelihood, Geoffrey confused Guthelinus's letter to Aëtius with the original plea to the Romans in 410, when Honorius abandoned Britain to its fate. Eighteen years added to 410 is 428, quite close to Nennius's date of 425 for Vortigern's rise to power. This is more satisfactory, because it allows Guthelinus, who is regarded as Vortigern's father or grandfather (according to Nennius's genealogy), to be archbishop during these years and dead by 428.

However, we have to fit another sequence into this. In 410 Guthelinus had appealed to Aldroenus, whom he describes as the fourth ruler in line from Cynan who had been granted territory in Armorica by Magnus Maximus in 383. The four kings would be Cynan, Gadeon, Saloman, and then Aldroenus. Do we know enough about these semi-legendary rulers to date their reigns? The brothers Cynan and Gadeon, sons of Eudaf, may have ruled together, and would have been in their sixties and possibly older by the early 400s. Although Alain Bouchart and Bertran d'Argentré have assigned the dates 405–412 to Saloman's reign, these dates are highly dubious. The

chronology of the various rulers of Armorica is almost impossible to piece together, and the details in Table 11 should be
regarded with some circumspection.

We do not know the ancestry of Saloman, but we do know
that of Aldroenus, called Aldwr by the British. Aldwr and his
brother Constantine (Custennin) were the sons of Cynfor ap
Tudwal, a chieftain in southern Cornwall who lived in the early
to mid fifth century, a generation adrift from Geoffrey's time
scale. Cynfor has been identified with Cunomorus, whose
name is inscribed on a stone at Castle Dore near Fowey. He
is also associated with the Tristram legend, and is sometimes
identified as King Mark. However, this Cunomorus lived later,
in the early sixth century. Although Cynfor himself is unlikely
to have migrated to Brittany, it is possible for Aldwr to have
done so. His brother has been called Custennin *Fendigaid* (the
"Blessed") and *Waredwr* (the "Deliverer"), and is included in
the list of "The Twenty-Four Mightiest Kings".* Evidently
this much-praised prince succeeded his father as king in the
West Country, but must have spread further afield, as his name
is associated with the founding of Chepstow, Warwick and
Worcester. He was probably contemporary with Arthur of
Badon but because the dates in Table 11 are suspect he could
just fit into Geoffrey's time scale.

Geoffrey probably latched on to the name Constantine because of the usurper emperor who ruled from 408–411, whose
son Constans was indeed murdered, by his general Gerontius. So
Geoffrey took the real history of Constantine III and trans-
planted it onto the Dumnonian prince Custennin, with the evil
Vortigern taking on the role of the commander Gerontius.

If we cannot place much credence in Geoffrey's Constantine
and Constans, is it any more likely that Constantine was the
father of Ambrosius and Uther? We have already seen the
plausibility of an Ambrosius the Elder, of whom Vortigern was
afraid, and since the younger Ambrosius was, according to

* Detailed in *Études celtiques XII* (1970), pp. 172–3.

Geoffrey, still a baby in 428, he is clearly not the antagonist at the battle of Guoloph in 437. Therefore, in Geoffrey's world, Ambrosius the Elder would be equal to Custennin/Constantine. The association of Custennin with Chepstow and Worcester is interesting as both these towns are in the Severn Valley, in the area of Gwent and the Gewisse, and would be associated with both Ambrosius and Vortigern. Though it is almost certainly oral tradition, it places Custennin in the right location. However, this would mean that either Custennin or his father Cynfor "wore the purple", to tally with Gildas's description. Clearly Constantine III, on whom Geoffrey's Constantine is based, did wear the purple, but Gildas would have regarded him as a usurper and a tyrant, and would not have heaped praise on him as he did on Ambrosius and his father. So we cannot accuse Gildas of confusing the Constantines as Geoffrey did. Custennin/Constantine does not fall neatly into the pattern of the Ambrosii, and Geoffrey's jigsaw is simply forcing the wrong pieces together.

So far, little that Geoffrey has written holds much water, yet his date for the birth of Ambrosius, around 427/428, is ideal for the chronology that has been developing. It would make him in his thirties and forties at the height of his glories in the 460s and 470s, and he could still, although elderly, have witnessed Badon. Unfortunately, there is nothing in the way of concrete evidence to support Ambrosius's birth at that date, so we remain in the realms of conjecture.

Returning to Geoffrey's narrative – with Vortigern's rise to power the young Ambrosius and Uther are taken to Armorica where they are welcomed by King Budicius (Budic), who ensures that they are properly cared for and educated. Meanwhile, in Britain, Vortigern's treachery is discovered, and he now lives in fear, knowing that Ambrosius and Uther are alive and may yet take their revenge.

There were several rulers of Armorica called Budic, but none at this time. The earliest, the grandson of Iahann Reeth (the possible Riothamus), did not reign until around 510. The *Brut*

Tysilio, however, calls the ruler Emyr Llydaw. Emyr Llydaw, was not a name but a title – Leader of the Men of Llydaw (a territory in northern Ergyng – *see* Chapter 8).

The Celtic *Stanzas of the Graves* credit this Emyr with a son, Beidawg Rhudd, a name that could easily be construed as Budic. The original story may have meant that Ambrosius and Uther were kept safe in Llydaw in Ergyng, not in Armorica. This would tie in with Nennius's claim that the young Ambrosius was found in Gwent.

Geoffrey next announces the arrival of Hengist and Horsa with a boatload of warriors. Vortigern, who is in Canterbury, agrees to meet them. Hengist explains that it is their country's tradition to draw lots now and again, sending the surplus population to look for new lands. So they set sail, and their gods have brought them to Britain. Vortigern is disappointed that they are pagan, but is willing to negotiate. He suggests that if Hengist and his men offer to help him fight the Picts, he will consider their request. Soon afterwards the Picts cross the Wall into the North Country, and the Saxons join a British army to do battle. The Saxons are so powerful that the British hardly have to fight, and the Picts are soon defeated. Impressed, Vortigern grants Hengist and his men land in Lindsey.

Hengist reminds Vortigern that there is a faction keen to make Ambrosius king, and suggests bringing reinforcements from Saxony. In return, Hengist asks for a title. Vortigern refuses, but does grant him enough land to build a settlement. In due course Hengist builds his castle at Thanceastre (*Kaer-carrei* in British). The name means Castle of the Thong, because Hengist measured out the land by a long leather thong, cut from the hide of a bull. There are places called Thong in Kent and Thwing in North Yorkshire, but Hengist's settlement is unlikely to be either of these. The most likely place is Caistor near Grimsby, for which the old Saxon name was Tunne-Caistor, and which was known to be an earlier British settlement called Caeregarry. Bede refers to the town, and notes that the town's name came from the monk

Tunna, who lived in the late seventh century. Near to Caistor is Horncastle (previously *Hornecaestre*), which could equally have been Geoffrey's original source. Both towns are on the edge of the Lincolnshire Wolds in the territory of Lindsey, thus supporting the idea that this was the Saxons' first settlement, and not Thanet in Kent. Lindsey, like Thanet, was an island in those days, cut off from the surrounding land by marshy fens. Several village names in Lindsey, such as Firsby, Freiston and Friesthorpe, attest to early settlement by Friesians, Hengist's kinfolk.

Lindsey as the likeliest place for the settlement of the Saxons and Angles is supported by genetic research. Stephen Oppenheimer reveals that in areas of eastern England, most notably around the Fens, Lindsey and Norfolk, there was a modest but significantly detectable intrusion of Angles and Saxons – a figure of 15 per cent compared to 5.5 per cent in the rest of England. Archaeological research has shown the presence of Germanic artifacts from the early fifth century.*

Geoffrey's narrative continues, telling of the arrival of reinforcements in Britain, including Hengist's daughter whom he calls Renwein. The story continues as per Nennius, with a drunken Vortigern besotted by Renwein and desiring her as a wife even though he is already married. Hengist agrees, exchanging his daughter for the territory of Thanet, allowing for a more plausible second settlement in Thanet.

Geoffrey now recounts the visit of Germanus and Lupus to Britain (*vi.13*). We know this to have happened in 429, and it seems scarcely credible that all that Geoffrey has recounted since Vortigern seized the throne could have happened in one year. Geoffrey gives no clue as to a time span, but the implication is that Ambrosius is old enough to have become a threat, and that we must have moved on perhaps twenty to twenty-five years, taking us to 448–453. Interestingly, this is the period often attributed to Germanus's second visit to

* *See* Oppenheimer (2006), pp. 435–9; and Bassett (1989), pp. 208–10.

Britain, although, as we established earlier, 436 is a more likely date. This passage appears in the *Brut Tysilio* as an interpolation, which suggests its compiler did not know where to place it and just guessed, so that if Geoffrey was drawing upon *Tysilio* he perpetuated the error.

Geoffrey's narrative follows closely the story in Nennius. Under the spell of Renwein, Vortigern gives in to Hengist's demands, and Hengist is allowed to bring in further reinforcements, including his sons Octa and Ebissa, and a man called Cherdic (spelled Chledric in *Tysilio*). This sounds suspiciously like Cerdic, and it is strange that Geoffrey, Tysilio and Nennius all mention him, as he does not reappear. Later, when referring to Cerdic of Wessex, Geoffrey calls him Cheldric. It is as if Cherdic had been introduced for a future story and then forgotten about, so that when Geoffrey picks up the thread again the name has changed. It is rather too late for him to be the same Ceretic as Hengist's interpreter, since Hengist seems to have coped well enough without him for the last decade or more. The *Tysilio* refers to Octa and Ebissa as Octa (or Offa), Hengist's son, and his uncle Ossa. *Ossa* may be a confusion for Horsa, although Ossa (or *Oisc/Aesc*) was also the name of Octa's son. It is also worth noting that the Offa who was the ancestor of the East Anglian kings was a contemporary of Octa (*see* Table 12), and, since the area around Lindsey was where Octa first settled, they could well have been related.

The growing Saxon forces unsettle the British and Vortigern's son Vortimer rebels. Commanding the British, he succeeds in defeating the Saxons and driving them back to the coast. Geoffrey notes the same battles as listed by Nennius, on the River Derwent, at Episford and on the sea-coast, from where they took refuge on Thanet.

The Saxons eventually sail away, but leave their women and children behind. Renwein, a folkloristic image of the evil stepmother, poisons Vortimer. Vortigern is restored to the throne, and Hengist returns to Britain, now supported by 300,000 troops. Although this figure is an obvious exaggeration, it is probably indicative of an overwhelming force. Vortigern convinces his fellow earls and counts to join him in a celebration of peace with the Saxons. What follows is the account of the "Night of the Long Knives", in which Hengist's men treacherously slay the British nobility (a figure is given later of 480 leaders [*viii.5*]). Only one man apart from Vortigern survives – Eldol (or Eidiol), Count of Gloucester, who, armed only with a stake, kills seventy men and escapes to tell the tale.

This section gives us two options. On the one hand, we can presume that Hengist arrived soon after Vortigern's accession, around 428/9, the date given by Nennius. The alternative is that the first wave of Saxons was pushed back, to return in a second wave during the 440s, and that this was when Hengist arrived. For many years, this has been most historians' standard interpretation. To resolve these two theories, we need to know more about Hengist.

4. Hengist

The name Hengist appears in both the epic poem *Beowulf* and the related fragment, *The Fight at Finnesburg*. In both tales Hengist is a prince of northern Frisia, driven into exile by interdynastic rivalries, who joins an army of Half-Danes, a mercenary warband led by Hnaef. While visiting Finn, king of the East Frisians, at Finnesburg, Hnaef is killed when a fight breaks out. The rest of the *Finnesburg* poem is lost, but an aside in *Beowulf* tells us more. After Hnaef's death Hengist became leader of the Half-Danes. They were forced to winter at Finnesburg, but the following spring, fighting resumed. This time, Hengist's men were victorious and Finn was killed. We do not know for certain that Geoffrey's Hengist and the Hengist of *Beowulf* are the same, but the respective descriptions of him as "banished" and an "exile" are suggestive, and it seems somewhat beyond coincidence that there would be two princes called Hengist exiled from Frisia at the same time.

Of course, this assumes that we are speaking of a real individual recorded in contemporary documents. Since we know no more about when any of these documents was composed, other than that it would have been at least three centuries later, then Hengist could simply have been a standardized hero dropped into any story as a recognizable character. The main argument against this is that Hengist is not central to *Beowulf*, but is mentioned as an aside, giving the story the feeling of authenticity. The legend of Hengist was so well known that it is almost certainly based on fact, and there is no reason to presume that the tales relate to more than one individual.

Unfortunately, neither *Beowulf* nor the *Finnesburg* fragment provides a date for these events, and testing the chronology of the genealogies also causes a dilemma. Hengist is regarded as the ancestor of the kings not only of Kent, but also of Swabia through another son, Harthwig (or Hartwake). Dates for the Swabian rulers are as uncertain as for the early Kentish kings, but a later king of Swabia, Bertold, is assigned the dates 568–633 with some degree of certainty. He was fifth in descent from Hengist, and allowing the usual average of twenty-five to thirty years per generation gives a mid-life date for Hengist of about 460.

We can compare this to the ancestors of the Icelingas, the tribe of Angles who settled in Britain under Icel. Icel's great-great-grandfather, Wermund, and Wermund's son Offa, are remembered in the heroic poem *Widsith* and in the Danish history by Saxo Grammaticus. Describing conflict between the Angles and the Saxons, these two works place Wermund's long reign towards the end of the fourth century. This would place Icel's mid-life at about 485. The genealogies make Icel contemporary with Hengist (*see* Table 12), which would give Hengist a prime-of-life of around 470–500, which overlaps with the previous calculation though could place him as much as a generation later.

We can also test it against Cerdic's ancestry. Amongst Cerdic's ancestors are Freawine and his son Wig, and both also feature in the life of Wermund as told by Saxo Grammaticus. From this we may calculate Wig's mid-life at around 400.

Cerdic is four generations descended from Wig, making his mid-life around 510. We know that Cerdic is at least a generation later than Hengist, giving a mid-life for Hengist of around 480.

All of these calculations, no matter how vague the data they are based on, bring us to a mid-life date for Hengist of 460–490. According to the *ASC*, he was dead by 488. It is difficult to push his life back earlier.

If this is true, then it is impossible for Hengist to be the individual whom Vortigern welcomed to Britain in 428, and more plausible for him to belong to the second *adventus* in 449. It means we do not know who met Vortigern in 428 – if that date is correct – although Table 12 suggests it may have been any of a half-dozen names, including Soemil (who we know from Nennius was in Britain by 450) and, more intriguingly, Cerdic's great-grandfather Gewis (*see* page 230).

We could conjecture that although Saxons had been arriving and settling throughout the first half of the fifth century, the significance of the *adventus* under Gewis was that he became integrated into the British administration under Vortigern, most likely as some sort of personal bodyguard. This could have been in 428, and would have allowed for a generation to become established by the time of the second *adventus* in the 440s. Gewis and his army may subsequently have settled in Lindsey, but it is more likely that if they did serve as Vortigern's personal army their land would initially have been near Vortigern's court, possibly in or around London or, more likely, near Powys. Intriguingly, flowing down from the Berwyn Mountains in North Powys, and joining the River Vyrnwy just a few kilometres north of the Gaer Fawr hill fort at Guilsfield, is the River Tanat. It is possible that Gewis and his family were granted land in the Valley of the Tanat, a name which became confused with Thanet when Hengist and his followers claimed land there a generation later.

Before we set the above in stone, however, we need to follow the rest of Geoffrey's narrative. After the massacre of the

British nobility, the Saxons release Vortigern, but only after his total capitulation and handing over of his townships. They capture London, York, Lincoln and Winchester, ravaging the countryside as they go. Vortigern flees to Wales and summons his magicians. Calling them "magicians" suggests that Geoffrey's narrative has now turned to fantasy, and that he is in fact paving the way for the introduction of Merlin. Geoffrey is recounting the same story as told by Nennius, except that Nennius uses the phrase "wise men", sometimes translated as "wizards". This is also the point at which Nennius introduces Ambrosius Aurelianus. Since Geoffrey had already introduced Ambrosius by this point, he adapted this section to introduce Merlin.

Merlin warns Vortigern that Constantine's sons, Aurelius Ambrosius (as Geoffrey calls him) and Uther, are sailing for Britain and will land the next day. Vortigern seeks safety in his castle at Genoreu, in Ergyng, usually identified as the hill fort at Little Doward, north-east of Monmouth, and near Symonds Yat, where the tiny village of Ganarew survives today.

Ambrosius and Uther arrive, and Ambrosius is crowned king. He demands the immediate death of Vortigern, marches on Genoreu and burns down the castle. Ambrosius then turns his attention to the Saxons. Having heard tales of his bravery and prowess, the Saxons retreat beyond the Humber. Hengist is encouraged when he discovers that Ambrosius's army is only some 10,000 men compared to his 200,000. Overconfident, Hengist advances south. The first engagement, at Maisbeli, goes in favour of the British. Hengist then flees to Cunungeburg (almost certainly Conisbrough, near Doncaster) for the showdown. *Maisbeli*, which has not been satisfactorily identified, means "the field of Beli", which could indicate a site of pre-Christian worship sacred to the earlier British king Beli, or it may be a field where the Beltane festival was celebrated. A possibility is Hatfield, the old name of which was Meicen, which had been a small Celtic territory in the locality of Doncaster.

After re-establishing his base at Gloucester, Ambrosius would have led his army along Ryknild Street, the main Roman road from Gloucester towards the Humber. Following this he would have passed through Conisbrough and Hatfield, all only a few kilometres inland from the original Anglo-Saxon settlements in Lindsey.

The battle of Cunungeburg is more evenly fought, and the Saxons might have won had not a further detachment of Bretons arrived. Eldol, the survivor of the massacre of the nobles, who has been looking for an opportunity to kill Hengist, is able to capture and subsequently behead him. A tumulus at Conisbrough has long been believed to mark Hengist's grave.

Geoffrey tells us that Hengist's son Octa flees to York, where he is besieged. Realizing that resistance is futile, Octa submits. Amazingly, he is pardoned, as is his kinsman Eosa, who has fled to Alclud (Dumbarton). Ambrosius grants them "the region near Scotland" (*viii.8*), which may be intended to mean Bryneich (Bernicia).

The most interesting thing about this section is how soon Hengist is killed after the death of Vortigern. Geoffrey's narrative can often take no cognisance of passing time, but here he makes it clear that events follow rapidly one after the other. If Geoffrey's source is accurate then we have to accept either that Vortigern lived longer than previously thought, or that Hengist died earlier, and not as late as 488. I mentioned earlier that the entries between 457 and 473 seem stretched out as if trying to fill a gap, and it does seem unlikely that Hengist's campaign really lasted for twenty-five years or more. However, these entries may also be subject to the nineteen-year discrepancy described elsewhere, in which case the *ASC* entry for 473 – which may mark Hengist's last victory – should be 454. This could mean that Hengist was killed in battle some time between 455 and 460. If this is true, then we have driven a wedge between Hengist and Aesc/Octa. The entry for 488, identifying Aesc as succeeding to the kingdom of Kent, makes no reference to him succeeding Hengist, and it would explain why the subsequent ruling family of Kent were called the Oiscingas and not the Hengistingas. In effect, Hengist may not have been Aesc/Octa's father, or even related to him at all.

The next few sections we can skim. They tell of Ambrosius travelling to the destroyed cities and initiating a programme of rebuilding. He organizes the burial of the massacred nobles at Kaercaradduc, which Geoffrey tells us is Salisbury. Ambrosius wants a permanent memorial to these noblemen, and consults Merlin. The result may be Stonehenge, although Geoffrey does not actually call it this, referring to it instead as the Giant's Ring. He may have confused Stonehenge with the ring of Avebury, and likewise be confusing Avebury with Amesbury. He refers to the ring being built at the site of Mount Ambrius, where the nobles had been massacred. The origin of the name for Amesbury has long been associated with Ambrosius or, according to Geoffrey, with the monk St Ambrius. It has been suggested that Ambrosius's coronation, which Geoffrey has take place at the stone circle at Mount Ambrius, may have been at Avebury, and that this originated the legend of the Round Table.

After the ceremony, Ambrosius appoints as his bishops Samson to the see of York and Dubricius to the City of the Legions. Establishing dates for Dubricius (*Dyfrig* in British) is difficult but important, because he is closely associated with Arthur. Samson's death is recorded – surprisingly specifically, but not necessarily accurately – as 28 July 565. We know that he was a contemporary of Gildas, who died around 572, and that both Samson and Gildas were pupils of Illtud, probably in the early 500s. Illtud was also the "instructor" of King Maelgwyn whom we have dated to the same period. Dubricius, a contemporary of Illtud's, ordained Samson as bishop. Thus Dubricius has to be alive around the year 500, and could not have died in 612 as noted in the *Welsh Annals*. He is closely associated with the territory of Ergyng, and, according to the scattered facts of his life recorded in the *Book of Llandaff*, was born at Chilstone ("Child's Stone") and raised in nearby

Madley, Hereford. There was once a St Dubricius's chapel at Lower Buckenhill, near Woolhope. Five charters in the *Book of Llandaf* were purportedly witnessed by Dubricius, although these span over a century. The earliest of them, a grant of land by King Erb of Gwent at Cil Hal near Harewood End, may be accurate (if a little doctored, as Dubricius is described as an archbishop). This could well date to around 500. Bartrum suggests that Dubricius lived from around 465 to 521, whilst Nikolai Tolstoy dates his death to 532.

These dates for Samson and Dubricius are too late for them to have been appointed archbishops by Ambrosius in around 460, which is where we currently find ourselves in Geoffrey's chronology. If there is any truth in Geoffrey's claim that Ambrosius himself appointed them, the date would have to be closer to 500. Nothing in our analysis so far allows us to accept Ambrosius as ruling as late as 500, and he may well have been dead by then. Either Dubricius or Samson lived earlier (despite most other records suggesting they lived later), or Geoffrey has slipped a cog and jumped forward in time. As we shall see in Geoffrey's next section, he has almost certainly conflated two stories from different periods, and somehow Dubricius and Samson have been pasted on to Ambrosius, though they belong to a later time.

From this point on, Geoffrey's story lapses more into legend, suggesting that he switched his research from one set of old documents to another. It is now that he sows the seeds for the creation of Arthur.

5. Uther Pendragon

According to Geoffrey, Ambrosius's kingship is short-lived. Pascent, son of Vortigern, rises up against Ambrosius, first in league with an army of Saxons and then, following his defeat, with Gillomanius, or Gillomaurius, king of Ireland. Pascent offers a fortune to anyone who will rid him of Ambrosius, and a Saxon called Eopa (or Eppa), takes on the task. Disguised as a doctor, he succeeds in gaining access to Ambrosius, who is lying ill at Winchester, and poisons him.

This version is totally adrift from that told in Nennius (§48) which states that Ambrosius was beneficent towards Pascent and made him king of Vortigern's old territory. Nor is there any indication that Ambrosius was poisoned – Gildas would certainly have known if that were true, and used it as a further argument in his attack on his contemporaries.

What's probably happened here is that Geoffrey (or Tysilio before him) has confused two Pascents. Pascent was also the name of the son of Urien of Rheged who, unlike Vortigern's son, was a surly belligerent individual, remembered in the Welsh Triads as one of the "Three Arrogant Men" of Britain. Pascent ap Urien lived at the end of the sixth century, a hundred years after Vortigern. This explains not only the sudden shift in dates, and thus in the individuals, but in the locale of Geoffrey's next chapter. Pascent almost certainly raised a mercenary army, which quite probably included Irish and Saxon troops, but whether or not he sponsored a plot to poison someone whom Geoffrey regarded as Ambrosius, we cannot say. It has all the trappings of folklore, as well as Geoffrey's evident fondness for kings being poisoned.

It is always intriguing when Geoffrey drops real names into a story, as it implies a basis of truth. The name *Eopa* (variously spelled *Eoppa*, or *Eobba*) is known in historical documents as the father of Ida, the first Angle ruler of Bernicia, and thus ties in with our shift to the north. Since Ida's reign began around 547 or later, Eopa's heyday would have been in the 520s, again too late to have killed Ambrosius, but certainly contemporary with Dubricius and Samson. We can well believe that in the days of the Angle settlement of the north, a generation or two after Octa, Ida and his father would have been involved in many battles and dark deeds, possibly even in the murder (poison or otherwise) of one of the Men of the North.

Geoffrey tells us that Ambrosius's death is marked by a comet called the "dragon star", which is interpreted by Merlin as a good omen. Ambrosius's brother Uther defeats and kills Pascent and Gillomanius. Returning to Winchester, he is appointed as successor to Ambrosius. He adopts as his emblem the sign of the dragon, fashioned in the style of the comet, and from then on is known as Uther Pendragon.

Comets were not unusual in the fifth and sixth centuries. Gary Kronk, in *Cometography* (1999), lists fifty known observations during that time, mostly by Chinese astronomers, and it is not certain how many of these were evident to observers in Britain. Those of 467 and 520 may have been. One in 530 was so bright it was called "the Firebrand" by Byzantine astronomers, and is believed to have been a visitation by what we know as Halley's Comet. Another, in 539, was so long and pointed it was nicknamed "the Swordfish". A third, in 563, appeared during a total eclipse of the sun, and thus was visible during the day. Any of these may be Geoffrey's "dragon star", though there seem to be no records of any during the 470s and 480s, which is where we should be in Geoffrey's timeline.

Following Ambrosius's death, Octa believes he is now freed from his agreement. He raises an army, including the followers of Pascent and, with Eosa, lays waste to the north of Britain. Uther catches up with him at York, but the Saxon numbers are superior and the British are driven back to seek refuge in the foothills of Mount Damen, or Dannet. The likeliest survival of that name today is Damems, part of Keighley in Airedale. Damems is about forty miles from York, and so could be a day's hard riding. However, a later variant version of the *Historia*, compiled by the Welsh monk Madoc around the year 1300, states that Mount Damen "is Wingates, above the head of Chochem", presumably Windygates Hill in Northumberland, at the headwaters of the Coquet River. This is just north of the Roman fort of Bremenium at High Rochester, a very long way from York.

Advised by Gorlois, Duke of Cornwall, Uther attacks the Saxons at night. Surprised, they are defeated, and Octa and Eosa are taken as prisoners to London. Uther then tours Scotland, inspecting the damage caused by the Saxons. It is clear that Geoffrey has slipped ahead a century, and the story he is telling has nothing to do with Ambrosius or with Octa and Eosa. He has confused Octa's and Eosa's expedition with a much later battle for the north between the British and the Saxons, during the latter half of the sixth century.

Geoffrey is usually credited with "inventing" Uther. Certainly he made a major figure out of him, just as he did of Ambrosius, The name *Uthr*, or *Uthyr Pendragon*, does appear in other sources, albeit briefly. We've encountered one in the poem *Pa Gur*, which speaks of Mabon as the "servant of Uthr Pendragon". Uther is also mentioned in one of the Welsh Triads, the "Three Great Enchantments", which he is supposed to have taught to Menw ap Teirgwaedd. Menw, who appears as a shapechanger and magician in both *Culhwch and Olwen* and *The Dream of Rhonabwy*, is one of the "Three Enchanters" of Britain (Triad 27), and is arguably the prototype for Merlin. But for Menw to have learned an enchantment from Uther (rather than the other way round), suggests that Uther was of an older generation and very possibly regarded as something of a mage in his own right. Taliesin refers to Uther's son Madog, noting that before his death Madog's fortress was one of "abundance, exploits and jests", almost like Arthur's Camelot. Madog was in turn the father of the "golden-tongued knight" Eliwlod, who in another ancient poem speaks to Arthur from the grave in the form of an eagle.

Unfortunately, no surviving pedigree links Madog or Eliwlod with Arthur, even though they were his brother and nephew respectively. It suggests that Uther > Madog > Eliwlod existed independently as part of a much older tradition, and that Arthur was later grafted onto their stories, as he was onto so many hero tales.

Madog is a common Welsh name, and several Madogs appear in legend. According to one of the pedigrees Merlin, or more properly Myrddin, was the son of Madog Morfryn, himself the son of Morydd, a brother of Arthwys of the Pennines. Madog's cousin was Eliffer of the Great Host, and the Latin for Eliffer is Ele*uther*ius. It would be easy for these early pedigrees to have become confused, and for Madog to be treated as a son of Eleutherius. Madog's position in the pedigrees is far from clear, and it's entirely possible that he was one of Eliffer's sons. Another, later pedigree of the princes of Powys (*see* Table 10) shows a Merin, son of Madog, who lived in the early seventh century. Geoffrey could have mis-copied *Merin* as *Merlin*.

Geoffrey may originally have got the name Uther from Maximus's son Victor. *Victor*, in the sense of "victorious", may be rendered as *uabhar*, which means "proud" in Gaelic and is related to *aruthr*, the Brythonic for "terrible", as in a conqueror or tyrant. Geoffrey may also have made the leap to *Eleutherius*, which also means "famed" or "honoured", as in victor.

Eliffer was credited in the *Black Book of Carmarthen* with having had seven sons. One of the Welsh Triads, "Three Fair Womb-Burdens", refers to the triplets born to Eliffer's wife: Gwrgi, Peredur and Arddun. Arddun (pronounced *Arth-oon*) was a girl, but a later translation of this triad, now held at Jesus College, Oxford, and quite possibly once accessible to Geoffrey, corrupts *Arddun* to Arthur. Geoffrey, ever able to make two and two equal five, might well have discovered this identification of [Ele]Uther[ius] as the father of Arthur, and that was all he needed. In reality, Arddun (some records call her Ceindrech) was not the daughter of Eliffer but of Pabo, Eliffer's uncle.

Eliffer was justly famous in his day, as were his sons Gwrgi and Peredur, whose deaths in 581 were noted in the *Welsh Annals*. Eliffer is exactly contemporary with Dubricius and Samson, although it is unlikely their paths crossed as his domain was in York, the setting for so much of Geoffrey's narrative. Eliffer's reign, from the 530s to the 550s, would have been one constant battle against the Angles, under Eopa, and doubtless against his fellow British as each ruler sought to protect his own territory. Eliffer was, for a while, the most powerful ruler in Britain, and there is no doubt that there would have been a period during his reign when he worked through the north, quelling his rivals. He might also have become king in either 530 or 539 at the time of a comet perihelion.

Returning to Geoffrey's narrative, we now enter familiar territory. After his tour of the north, Uther returns to London, and the following year holds a celebration of his victory, inviting all his nobles. These include Gorlois of Cornwall and his beautiful wife Ygerna, or Ygraine. Uther lusts after Ygerna and, affronted, Gorlois storms away from the festivities. Uther demands an apology, and when none is forthcoming, raises an army and ravages Cornwall. Gorlois's army is too small to face Uther's. He places Ygerna in safekeeping at Tintagel Castle and seeks refuge, with his army, at the hill fort of Dimilioc. There still is a hill fort and territory known as Domellic to the north of St Dennis in the middle of Cornwall. Another contender is the Tregeare Rounds, formerly called Castle Dameliock, an impressive earthwork near the hamlet of Pendoggett, just six miles south-west of Tintagel.

The siege of Dimilioc is deadlocked and Uther, pining for Ygerna, seeks the aid of Merlin. Merlin agrees to change the appearance of Uther into that of Gorlois so that he can gain access to Tintagel Castle. Uther/Gorlois is welcomed by Ygerna and taken to her bed, and that night Arthur is conceived. In the meantime, Uther's men attack Dimilioc and manage to take the fort, killing Gorlois. They are perplexed when they travel to Tintagel and find a man whom they believe to be Gorlois there. Uther changes back to his own self, and returns to capture Tintagel and Ygerna. They marry and have two children, Arthur and Anna.

This whole episode appears as an aside in Geoffrey's narrative, after which he returns to the story of Octa and Eosa. It was clearly drawn from a popular folk tale about Arthur rather than from any historical source. Geoffrey's story now leaps ahead fifteen years. Anna is married to King Loth of Lodonesia, though she cannot have been more than fourteen. During these years, the soldiers who guarded Octa and Eosa set their captives free, fleeing with them to Germany. They raise an army and once more return to plunder and ravage the North. Loth is put in charge of the British forces. The war is long and protracted with no victory to either side. Uther is furious and, though now old and "half dead", reprimands his nobles and leads his forces against the Saxons who are laying waste to St Albans. In the ensuing battle, the British win and Octa and Eosa are killed. The Saxons retreat to the North and continue to harry the land. They send spies to watch Uther and, discovering his water supply, they poison it, thereby killing the king and hundreds of others.

6. Enter Arthur

Geoffrey places the showdown between Uther and the Saxons at St Albans. There is no specific historical reference to a battle here in the fifth century, but as we considered earlier with Gildas's *De Excidio*, St Albans, which remained a British enclave throughout the fifth century, was right on the edge of the division created post-Badon between the British and the Saxons, so would have been subject to periodic assaults from the Saxons. According to the *ASC*, Aesc/Octa died in 512, so in theory Geoffrey's narrative has now reached this year although many of the British characters he refers to lived half a century or more later.

However, if we try to follow a timeline for Geoffrey's narrative we find we are much earlier, around the year 485. Our last "fixed" point was the death of Hengist around 457/ 460, the year of Ambrosius's coronation. Ambrosius's reign must have been long enough to see the start of a rebuilding programme, but unless Geoffrey has left out other detail, it cannot be much more than a decade, and we must presume in Geoffrey's timeline that Ambrosius's reign was over by the late 460s. Uther then quells the North, captures Octa and Eosa, and seduces Ygerna, suggesting that Arthur's birth would be around 470. The deaths of Uther and Octa, fifteen years later, must be around 485. To push them as far as 512 would mean that Ambrosius's reign lasted nearly forty years, and since Geoffrey places his birth at around 426, he would by then have been eighty-four. Uther, who was Ambrosius's younger brother and thus probably born around 428, would be nearly sixty in 485, which fits in with the narrative. However, this date is far too early for the death of Octa, which cannot be earlier than 512, and was most probably later. It is evident that Geoffrey's narrative has now split into two overlapping time-lines as he seeks to fit later events into his earlier chronology.

It is at this point (Book 9), that Geoffrey commences the story of King Arthur. This is the original story, not the legend we know from the French romances and Malory.

Geoffrey relates that with the death of Uther, the Saxons become more invasive. A new leader is appointed, Colgrin (or Colgrim), who, with his brother Baldulf, has brought more forces from Germany and is laying waste to the far North. An urgent response is required, and the nobles wish to appoint Uther's son Arthur as their new king, even though he is only fifteen. He is crowned by Archbishop Dubricius at Silchester. Arthur promptly gathers together an army and marches on the Saxons at York, where Colgrim meets him with "a vast multi-tude", a combined army of Saxons, Scots and Picts. Their first battle is "beside the River Douglas", and the British are victorious. Colgrim flees, and Arthur pursues him to York and lays siege to the city. We have already discussed possible sites for these battles, derived from Nennius's list. It is evident that Geoffrey believed the River Douglas was near York.

Colgrim's brother is awaiting further reinforcements from Germany under the leadership of Cheldric, but learning of Colgrim's predicament he leads his troops overnight to York. He is attacked by Cador, Duke of Cornwall, in a vicious battle in which many are killed. Baldulf disguises himself as a minstrel and manages to get into York and be reunited with his brother. Arthur learns of the arrival of Cheldric's forces, and rather than face so large an army retreats to London.

Arthur calls upon Hoel, king of Brittany, who brings an army of 15,000 warriors to Britain. Geoffrey calls Hoel the son of Arthur's sister, but he had already stated that Anna, who was younger than Arthur, was married to Loth, and certainly could not have been married previously. According to Geoffrey, Hoel's father was Budic, the king who reared Ambrosius and Uther, and no direct relation to Arthur.

The Saxons Colgrim and Baldulf do not appear in other documents, which makes one wonder where Geoffrey found the names. I am convinced that he found most of his sources from old records, and though he may have elaborated some aspects of his stories the names are almost certainly based on genuine people. The name *Colgrim*, for instance, while it does not feature in the Anglo-Saxon histories, appears on some of the coins of Athelred the Unready and Canute in the early eleventh century, and was the name of the moneyer working at the Lincoln mint. The connection with Lincoln is interesting, because of the suggested site of Arthur's battles with Colgrim. *Colgrim* is actually a Norse name and so, once again, it seems likely that Geoffrey had found the name of a Scandinavian chieftain from a later vintage, who had nothing to do with the original Angle and Saxon settlement.

There are also some parallels between Baldulf and the Norse demi-god Balder, especially in the tale from Saxo Grammaticus's *History of the Danes* about the battle between Balder and the Danish king Høther (*III.69*). One night, during a pause in a violent battle, Høther disguises himself as a minstrel to infiltrate Balder's camp, and accidentally stumbles across Balder and kills him. In Geoffrey's story, it is Baldulf who disguises himself, but Geoffrey may have drawn his tale from the same source. The name *Høther* could have been treated by Geoffrey as Arthur.

The Norwegian philologist Sophus Bugge (1833–1907) believed that some of the sources for the early Scandinavian sagas were founded on Christian and Latin tradition imported to Scandinavia from England. Therefore, it is possible that some of the sources for Saxo's *History*, though told as Danish history, could owe their sources to earlier British events. Bugge suggested that Høther, in its original spelling *Höur*, could have been corrupted into Cador, and that Cheldric, or Cheldricus, may be a corruption of the Saxon king Gelderus, who was also defeated by Høther. As we shall see, there are various episodes from the early history of the Danes that have parallels, albeit slight, with Geoffrey's account.

Arthur and Hoel advance on Kaerluideoit (*Kaer-lwyd-coed* in *Tysilio*), which was being besieged by the Saxons. Geoffrey translates this as Lincoln, but it should be read as Lichfield (*Letocetum*). Though the town's name is supposed to mean "grey wood" (*llywd coed*), it was long believed to mean "field of corpses" (*lic feld*), referring to an ancient battle. It was called *Licitfelda* as early as 710. In his *Natural History of Staffordshire* (1686), Robert Plot relates the name to the martyrdom of a thousand Christians here following the death of St Alban. But the arms of Lichfield represent three slain kings on a field, and seem more appropriate to some long forgotten battle, possibly Arthur's. Making such an error shows that Geoffrey must have been working from an old document. Arthur lifted the siege and won a resounding victory, killing over six thousand Saxons.

The survivors flee, pursued by Arthur. The armies meet again at Caledon Wood where Arthur is able to lay siege to the Saxons. Eventually he starves them out, and agrees to grant the Saxons their lives if they return to Germany and pay tribute. The Saxons sail away but soon change their minds, sail round Britain and land at Totnes in Devon, ravaging the countryside of the south-west as far as the Severn estuary. Then they lay siege to Bath. Arthur, furious at their duplicity and swearing revenge, rushes south, leaving Hoel, who had fallen ill, at Alclud.

Geoffrey describes Arthur's preparation for the battle. Arthur dons his golden helmet with a dragon's crest, and across his shoulders is his shield Pridwen, on which is painted a likeness of the Virgin Mary. His sword is Caliburn and his lance is Ron. Dubricius says a prayer, and the battle commences. The first day is deadlocked and the Saxons retreat to a nearby hill, still confident they will win by sheer weight of numbers. The next day Arthur and his men valiantly fight their way up the hill. Again, the battle seems deadlocked until Arthur, as Geoffrey describes it, goes berserk. Drawing his sword, Arthur rushes into the thick of battle, killing men with every blow – 470 in total, Geoffrey reports. Both Colgrim and Baldulf fall in the battle. Cheldric admits defeat and retreats, pursued by Cador who captures the Saxons' ships and hunts the men down relentlessly. Although the Saxons seek safety in the Isle of Thanet, still Cador pursues them and succeeds in killing Cheldric, whereupon the remainder surrender.

Arthur, in the meantime, has hurried back to Alclud, where Hoel is being besieged by Picts and Scots. His battles rage across Scotland, even up to Moray and Loch Lomond. Gilmaurius, the king of Ireland, arrives with reinforcements for his fellow Scots, but Arthur defeats him as well. Eventually the Scots are driven to famine by Arthur's tactics and, taking pity upon them, Arthur relents and grants a pardon.

Clearly in this section, Geoffrey's description of the battle of Bath is the same as Nennius's of Badon, complete with the description of Arthur's shield with the image of the Virgin Mary. In a way that is almost convincing, Geoffrey paints a picture of Arthur defending his realm at two extremes, in the far north and in the south-west, not dissimilar to the valiant efforts of King Harold in 1066, who after defeating the Norse at Stamford Bridge, then marched south to fight the Normans at Senlac Hill.

However, it is only two days' ride from Lichfield to Wroxeter (Viriconium) and on to Welshpool, where *The Dream of Rhonabwy* places Badon at Caer Faddon. The retreat by the Saxons to "Thanet" could be to the River Tanat, just west of Breidden. It would also tie in with Clun, just south of Wroxeter and east of the River Tanat, being the Forest of Caledon.

On the Map 10 on page 291 I have plotted the campaigns of

Ambrosius, Uther and Arthur. With Arthur, I have taken the
liberty of showing his campaign where I believe Geoffrey's
"ancient book" meant. If we were to believe that he went from
York to Lincoln to Caledon in Scotland, and then down to
Bath, it would be nonsense. But if we accept a route from the
Douglas in Lancashire, on to York, down to Lichfield, then
over to the Clun Forest and Caer Faddon, then there is a clear
and straightforward pattern. This theory would support an
Arthur based at Wroxeter, Chester or York.

Having subjugated his enemies, Arthur returns to York to
restore law and order in the city. He appoints a new archbishop,
as Samson has been driven out. Geoffrey notes that there were
three brothers in York descended from the royal line, Loth,
Urien and Auguselus. To each of these, Arthur restores his
kingdom: Auguselus (whom Tysilio calls Arawn) receives Scotland; Urien receives Murray (Tysilio says Rheged); and Loth
(Llew) receives Lothian (Tysilio says Lindsey). Geoffrey also
says that Loth, "in the days of Aurelius Ambrosius had married
that King's own sister". This makes more sense than Loth
marrying Arthur's young sister Anna. We know nothing of
Ambrosius's sister, but it is here that Geoffrey says that she was
the mother of Gawain and Mordred.

There is much to ponder in this passage. If the kings
Geoffrey named were historical then we ought to have a record
of them. The best known is Urien of Rheged, who reigned
from about 570–590. Loth we have already mentioned, but it is
interesting here that Tysilio makes him a ruler of Lindsey,
rather than Lothian. Lindsey had been a separate kingdom but
was taken over by the Saxons at an early stage, and its earliest
attested ruler (if the genealogies are correct) was Crida (or
Critta), in the 580s. His successors included a king with the
British name Caedbaed, suggesting that the territory changed
hands at some stage. The third brother, Auguselus, is probably
Geoffrey's version of Angus, brother of Fergus of Dál Riata,
who had established himself as ruler in Argyll in 498. Angus
became chief of Islay and the surrounding islands. He was not

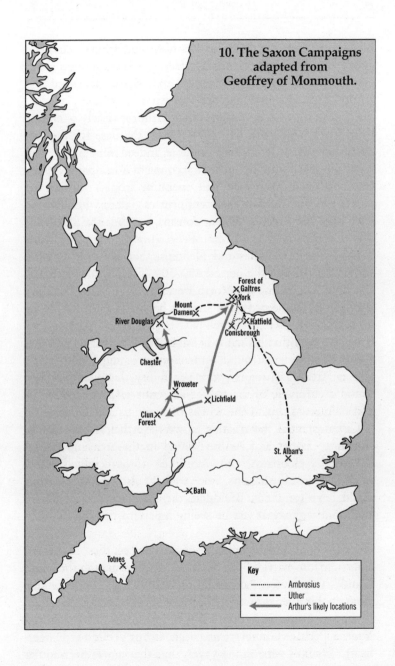

10. The Saxon Campaigns adapted from Geoffrey of Monmouth.

Forest of
Galtres
York
Mount
Damen
River Douglas
Hatfield
Conisbrough
Chester
Wroxeter
Lichfield
Clun
Forest
St. Alban's
Bath
Totnes

Key

.... Ambrosius
– – – – – Uther
⬅ Arthur's likely locations

related to Urien – indeed, he was not even British – and is a good example of how Geoffrey's *Historia*, like a sponge, soaks up individuals regardless of when and where they lived and works them into an apparently cohesive story.

Of most interest, however, is that Arthur is clearly operating from York, and York had always been the base for the *dux Britanniarum*. It is entirely possible, indeed very likely, that Geoffrey had found an ancient account of a campaign waged by a sixth-century prince, still operating from York like the *dux* of old, and rallying the other princes – all of whom would have been his direct or distant cousins – against the Saxons. If this was the Arthur of the *Welsh Annals*, with the dates corrected as per Gildas and Nennius, then we need to look for such a ruler in the period 480–500. Table 4 shows that at this time dominating the North were Arthwys of the Pennines and his son (some pedigrees suggest his brother) Eliffer of the Great Host. Eliffer could well have been based at York and we have also seen that his name is Latin was Eleutherius and that Geoffrey may have found a manuscript listing Eleutherius's son as Arthur. There is every possibility that Geoffrey had found a chronicle of the battles of Arthwys and Eleutherius and connected this to the works of Nennius and Gildas.

Circumstantial though this is, we nevertheless have names similar to Uther and Arthur, based in the area and period covered by Geoffrey, who were likely to have rallied fellow princes against the Saxons. Since we have also seen that Arthur could have fought at Breidden, the Caer Faddon of Welsh tradition, we may at last be seeing a pattern emerge.

Geoffrey continues by telling us that having set these matters to rights Arthur marries "the most beautiful woman in the entire island", Guenevere. According to Geoffrey, she is descended from a noble Roman family, and has been raised in the household of Cador. Cador is Arthur's half brother, son of Gorlois and Ygerna. Perhaps Guinevere had been Arthur's childhood sweetheart. Tysilio's version, however, says that it was her mother who was descended from the Roman nobility, and that her father was the hero Gogfran. Despite his hero status, we don't know much about Gogfran, or Ogrfan as he's often called. His home is variously placed at Aberysgyr (now Aberyscir), just west of Brecon or Caer Ogyrfan, the old name for Oswestry.

After his marriage, Arthur rebuilds his fleet and, with the coming of summer, sets off to take revenge against the Irish king Gilmaurius. Although Gilmaurius faces Arthur with a huge army, Arthur defeats him without any trouble.

Having subjugated Ireland, Arthur sails to Iceland, where he subdues the island, bringing immediate submission from the kings of "Gotland" and the Orkneys. Even assuming that Iceland was known to Irish navigators at this time, which has not been proven, it is not somewhere that Arthur or any other British ruler would be concerned with. In *Tysilio* this name is rendered as *Islont*, and it has been suggested by Peter Roberts, in his translation of Tysilio's *Chronicle*, that this means Islay, the island in the southern Hebrides ruled by the descendants of Fergus's brother Angus. It is far more likely that a sixth-century prince would be fighting the Irish Scotii in the Hebrides, and that Geoffrey is here recalling a campaign by a British warrior in the western and northern isles. It is also likely that this is where Geoffrey's "Irish" kings lived, amongst the Scotii of Kintyre.

However, it is worth noting that later, when Geoffrey lists all the notables attending Arthur's court, he refers to Malvasius, king of Iceland. *Malvasius* is Geoffrey's Latinization of Melwas, the king notorious in the Arthurian legends for the abduction of Guenevere. Melwas is usually described as the king of the Summer Country, or Somerset, but in Breton tales he was called the Lord of the Isle of Glass (Isle de Voirre), usually interpreted as Glastonbury, then an island in the Somerset marshes. Geoffrey may well have mistaken "glass" for "ice", and is really referring to Arthur's subjugation of Melwas. The story of Guenevere's abduction is not otherwise told by Geoffrey, but does appear in the *Life of Gildas*.

The use of the word *Gotland* by Geoffrey may seem strange at first. Tysilio uses Gothland, which normally means Sweden, when referring to that part of Scotland restored to Auguselus. By Geoffrey's day there had been considerable dispute between Scotland and Sweden/Norway (then one country) over ownership of the Hebrides and Orkneys. Most telling here is the story in one of the Icelandic sagas, of the ninth-century adventurer Ketil Flatnose, a Viking who had settled in the Norse kingdom of Dublin. King Olaf of Dublin, who had married Ketil's daughter, sent Ketil on a mission to rid the Hebrides of Danish pirates. Ketil was successful and set himself up as king of the Hebrides. After his death in about 870, his family left Britain and settled in Iceland. Ketil's grandson Thorstein later returned and established himself as a power in Caithness and Orkney.

However, Gotland is more likely a corruption of Geatland. The Geats were a people of south Sweden, and were amongst those who settled in eastern England between the sixth and tenth centuries. Beowulf was king of the Geats, and it has been suggested that there may be a connection between the Geats and the later ninth-century kings of Mercia, starting with King Wiglaf in 827. Wiglaf does not fit comfortably into the genealogy of the Mercian kings, and it is possible that he was related by marriage and came from the vassal rulers of the sub-kingdom of Lindsey. In which case, Geoffrey's reference to Geatland may be to the name by which Lindsey was known in the ninth and tenth centuries.

However, there was an earlier warlord whose battles followed this sequence. Aedan mac Gabhran, king of the Dál Riatan Scots, came to power in 574. In confirming his authority Aedan was in conflict with his Irish overlord Baetan map Cairill who defeated Aedan at Dun Baetan in that year. In 580, Aedan led a campaign to the Orkneys whose inhabitants were doubtless causing havoc around the Scottish Isles and, in 582, after Baetan's death, he conquered the Isle of Man. If we allow for Geoffrey to have confused Islay with the Isle of Man, we have both Arthur and Aedan in battle in Ireland, Man and the Orkneys. And accompanying Aedan on these campaigns would have been his son Artúir!

This northern theme continues in Geoffrey's next section. Apparently, after subjugating all the rebellious parts of Britain and Ireland, Arthur settles down to a reign of peace and harmony, a Pax Arthuriana. It is now that a code of courtliness and chivalry arises, and that Arthur's knights travel abroad, undertaking deeds of bravery. The other nations of Europe are so in awe of Arthur that they build major defences in case he should invade. Arthur reacts to this in what seems a sudden change of character. He becomes arrogant, and believes he can conquer Europe.

His first assault is on Norway. Geoffrey reveals that Loth, who is once again described as Arthur's brother-in-law, was the nephew of Sichelm, king of Norway. Sichelm had bequeathed Loth the kingdom but after Sichelm's death the Norwegians raised Riculf to the throne. Arthur invades Norway and in his usual manner sheds much blood, quells the country and is victorious. Both Norway and Denmark become subject to Arthur's growing imperial rule. Riculf is killed, and Loth becomes king.

The origins for this section of Geoffrey's narrative are not straightforward. Neither Norway nor Denmark existed as separate nations until a century or two after Arthur's day. It is possible that Geoffrey misunderstood Norway for *Norgales*, a common word in the Norman period for North Wales. But in any case, by Geoffrey's time both Norway and Denmark had proved themselves to be amongst the most powerful nations in Europe, through the domination of the Vikings. Both nations had ruled in Britain, most famously under Canute. Earlier, Alfred the Great had held on to Wessex by his fingernails when the Danes overran England, and his fight to defeat the Danes and recover his kingdom has some resonance with Arthur's story. After Alfred, England was divided for over a century with the Danes ruling half the country, and the Norse ruling, for a while, in York. Geoffrey probably knew this as history, and could have been influenced by Alfred's actions in present-ing his own narrative.

There may be two other sources for this story, which Geoffrey wove together. At the time Geoffrey was writing, the Orkney Isles were still owned by Norway. In the early 980s, the earl of Orkney was Ljot, and his claim to the throne was disputed by his brother Skuli, who succeeded in raising the support of Kenneth II of Scotland. Ljot, however, won so convincingly that he laid claim to much of northern Scotland. Soon afterwards, he was killed in battle by Maelbrigte, uncle of Macbeth. Ljot's authority in northern Britain may well have echoed down the years, and Geoffrey might have linked the name with the following episode which took place in Gaul, at a time contemporary with Geoffrey's other stories of Arthur. Gregory of Tours tells the story in his *History of the Franks*, and, as he was directly involved, the story is wholly reliable. In the 570s, the Count of Tours was Leudast, the son of a slave who had risen to prominence under the patronage of the wife of Charibert, king of Paris. Leudast was a schemer, working one faction against another, but after Charibert's death he fell foul of Chilperic, king of Soissons, and was removed from office. Leudast then told Chilperic that Bishop Gregory was scheming to have the son of the late King Sigebert elevated to his former post. Chilperic saw through Leudast and had him cast into prison, but Leudast contrived with a priest called Riculf to spread stories to discredit Bishop Gregory. Leudast promised Riculf that he would make the priest bishop in Gregory's place, but their plot was eventually uncovered after Riculf was tortured to within an inch of his life. Leudast fled, but later met his just deserts.

It is a remarkable coincidence to have both a Ljot and a Leudast (for which Geoffrey may have read Leodonus, or Loth) deprived of their titles and, in the latter story, a Riculf being promised the post of bishop. Further evidence that Geoffrey was drawing upon sources from the Frankish king-doms comes with Arthur's next exploit.

After conquering Norway and Denmark, Arthur invades Gaul. The tribune of Gaul is Frollo, who after his defeat retreats to Paris, where Arthur lays siege. After a month, with the inhabitants starving, Frollo suggests that the outcome be decided by single combat. Frollo, a giant of a man, almost defeats Arthur, but in a final rally Arthur cleaves Frollo's skull in two.

Some have suggested that Frollo is Geoffrey's version of Rollo, the Viking adventurer who became first Duke of Normandy in 911. Rollo, or Hrólfur, was the great-great-great-grandfather of William the Conqueror. Geoffrey's picture of Gaul suggests that the territory, although technically under the sovereignty of the king of France, belonged to England by right of prior conquest. In portraying Gaul in such a way, it would be rather foolish of Geoffrey to suggest that it was conquered by defeating the same Rollo who was the ancestor of Henry I. It is also hard to believe that Geoffrey did not know that Rollo was Henry's ancestor, and he's unlikely to have adopted the name by choice.

In all likelihood, Geoffrey used the name from another source. There was a Roman family by the name of Ferreolus, who played an important role in the final days of the empire and the development of the Frankish states. A member of this family was a tribune of Gaul in the 450s, and his son was occasionally referred to as Frolle. Frolle's son, Tonantius Ferreolus, was a patrician and three times Prefect of Gaul. Tonantius, a gifted diplomat, succeeded in gaining the support of the Visigoths in Rome's battle against the Huns. He also negotiated with the new Visigoth king, Thorismond, and saved the town of Arles from being sacked. Tonantius died in about 490, and thus was a contemporary of Clovis. Geoffrey may have chosen almost any of the Ferreoli, but the likeliest is Tonantius who, although he did not fight Thorismund in single combat, did negotiate with him one to one over a banquet, and thus lifted the siege of Arles. Geoffrey's imagination could make much of such material.

Geoffrey's narrative continues with Arthur's complete conquest of Gaul. He sends Hoel to take Poitou. Hoel is so successful that he also conquers Aquitaine and Gascony. Arthur's campaign takes nine years. He gives Neustria (Normandy) to his cupbearer Bedevere, and Anjou to his Seneschal Kay, as well as other provinces to other nobles. Satisfied, Arthur returns to Britain and decides to hold an imperial coronation at Caerleon.

The nine-year span is the first time-sensitive information Geoffrey has given since Arthur came to power. We have no clues to the time span of his original military campaign throughout Britain, or for the period when Arthur's reputation grows and the codes of chivalry are established. Logic would suggest that these must cover at least a decade, and probably two. To this we must add the nine-year Gallic campaign; thus, since Arthur was fifteen when he came to the throne, he must now be around forty-five, which would place us in about 515AD, according to Geoffrey's timeline.

All the great and the good attend Arthur's coronation. A few are worth mentioning here for the benefit of dating. Geoffrey lists four kings, all of whom we can date approximately. "Urian, king of Moray" is Urien of Rheged who ruled in the 570s. "Cadwallo Laurh, king of the Venedoti" is Cadwallon (Lawhir) "Long Hand" of Gwynedd, father of Maelgwyn, who ruled from about 500–534. "Stater, king of the Demetae" was more likely a title than a name. In Latin, *stator* is a magistrate's marshal. The name appears in the ancestry of Vortipor as a great-grandson of Constantine the Great, and although this pedigree is clearly confused, it would place Stater in the mid-fourth century. In *Tysilio* the name is given as Meurig, king of Dyfed, but this is clearly a late addition referring to an eleventh-century chieftain. Finally, there is "Cador, king of Cornwall" who lived in the early sixth century. Only Cador and Cadwallo are contemporaries, and fit within the time scale for Arthur that has been emerging. Also listed is Donaut map Papo (Dunod the Fat), who ruled a territory west of the Pennines in Yorkshire/Cumbria, which is

now named Dent after him. He was present at the battle of
Arderydd in 573, making him a contemporary of Urien, and
his death is given in the *Welsh Annals* in 595. Also named is
Rhun ap Neithon, who was a prince of the Isle of Man, and
lived around the 560s. Almost all of the names are of princes
and nobles alive in the mid-to-late sixth century.

The celebrations last four days, and at the end Arthur
receives an envoy from Lucius Hiberius, Procurator of the
Republic, bearing a letter admonishing Arthur for not paying
his tribute to Rome, and for attacking and claiming Roman
territory in Gaul and the islands. Arthur is summoned to Rome
to face a trial and due punishment. Failure to attend will lead to
the invasion of his territories. Arthur refutes the demands,
claiming that by the same token Rome should pay tribute to
him because his forebears Constantine and Maximus had both
once ruled Rome – another piece of Geoffrey's propaganda.
Arthur believes it is time to teach Rome a lesson and plans to
invade, amassing an army of over 180,000 troops.

When Lucius receives the answer to his letter, he determines
to invade Britain and raises an army of over 400,000 troops,
drawn from across the empire.

Arthur sets off from Southampton, leaving behind Guenevere as regent and his nephew Mordred in charge of the island's
defences. Upon landing in Gaul, Arthur undertakes a detour to
fight a giant who is occupying the island of Mont-St-Michel
and abducting maidens. Arthur soon despatches the giant and
returns to the matter in hand. He encamps at Autun on the
River Aube in Burgundy, and awaits Lucius's army. Arthur
sends three envoys to parley with Lucius, including his nephew
Gawain. Lucius's nephew Quintillanus taunts Gawain, who
reacts by decapitating him. Gawain and the envoys are chased
back to their army, though not before they have killed many of
the Romans. A battle ensues and is described in immense detail,
running to over twenty pages. Arthur is of course victorious,
but at a cost. Amongst the casualties are Bedivere and Kay.
Lucius Hiberius is also killed.

Who was Lucius? Although introduced as the Procurator of Rome, he is later identified as both the Emperor (*x.4*), and also simply as a general. Elsewhere, Lucius considers whether to wait for reinforcements from "the Emperor Leo" (*x.6*). As Geoffrey Ashe has analysed in *The Discovery of King Arthur*, only one Emperor Leo adequately fits this role, and this was Leo I, who was Emperor of the East in Constantinople, from 457 to 474. At that time the Empire in the West was in turmoil, with a succession of puppet emperors. One of these was Glycerius, who Ashe suspects may be Geoffrey's Lucius. He was emperor for little more than a year in 473/4.

Another suggestion is that Lucius is the Frankish king Clovis.* Clovis succeeded his father as chief of the Salian Franks in 481, when he was only fifteen (the age that Arthur was). His rise to fame came in 486 when he defeated Syagrius, the Roman ruler of Northern Gaul and son of Aegidius. Over the next nine years (the same period as Arthur's campaign), Clovis pushed his authority south. His campaign to the west in Armorica was far more difficult, but he steadily extended his empire. In 507, the Eastern Emperor Anastasius elevated Clovis to the rank of consul, and in 509 he was declared sole ruler of the Franks. But his efforts had exhausted him and he died in 511, aged only forty-five. Clovis seems an ideal candidate for the source of Geoffrey's writings about Arthur. Much of what Arthur achieved seems to be modelled on Clovis's own campaigns, and his dates are almost identical to those that we have identified for Arthur. It is surprising, too, that Geoffrey should have Arthur fighting in Gaul and yet not encounter Clovis. One could argue that the name *Clovis*, an early form of *Louis*, could be mutated into *Lucius*, and that Arthur was fighting Clovis in his role as consul (*read* procurator) of Gaul.

This whole episode of Arthur's venture into France has to be seen in the light of events in Geoffrey's own lifetime. Henry I, youngest son of William the Conqueror, had grabbed the

---

* See White, William, "Questions and Answers", in *Notes and Queries* vol. 98 (1898), p. 226.

crown of England in 1100 while his brother Robert, the rightful heir, was involved in the Crusades. On his return in 1101, Robert invaded England, but Henry bought him off. Robert retained the duchy of Normandy, but Henry kept the kingship. Five years later, Henry invaded Normandy, captured and imprisoned Robert, and regained control of his father's lands. At the same time, Henry was in conflict with the Pope. Henry had appointed as Archbishop of Canterbury the strong-willed Anselm, and Anselm was determined that only he, through papal authority, should be allowed to appoint bishops and other clergy. Henry disagreed. In 1103 Anselm went into self-imposed exile, and Pope Paschal II wrote to threaten Henry with excommunication. This communication from the Pope was similar to the letter received from Rome by Arthur. Henry eventually recalled Anselm, and reached a compromise whereby Anselm could appoint the bishops, but Henry retained authority over church lands. Meanwhile, Henry's campaign in France continued for over ten years, a combination of diplomacy and warfare culminating in the defeat of Louis VI (another suitable Lucius) in 1119. Through various marriages and alliances, Henry succeeded in controlling not only Normandy, but also Anjou and Maine.

In telling of Arthur's conquest of France, Geoffrey was finding precedents for Henry's position, and comparing Henry's achievements with those of Britain's greatest hero. There are even some parallels with Henry's final years and the breakdown of the world he had fought so hard to establish, but clearly this was an area in which Geoffrey would tread cautiously. It is perhaps pertinent that Geoffrey's work was not issued until after Henry's death, thus he was able to glorify Henry's reign whilst recognizing the perils of kingship. Remember that the book was dedicated to Henry's eldest illegitimate son, Robert, Earl of Gloucester, and appeared in an England once again riven by civil war.

After defeating Lucius, Geoffrey tells us, Arthur winters in Gaul, preparing to march across the Alps into Rome the

following summer. At this point, however, he receives news
that Mordred has seized the crown and is living adulterously
with Guenevere. Arthur entrusts Hoel with continuing his
campaign against Rome, and returns to Britain, landing at
Richborough. Mordred has entered into an alliance with the
Saxon Chelric, promising him all the land between the Humber
and Scotland, as well as Kent. He has also joined forces with the
Picts and the Scots, and a confederate army of 80,000 troops
advances to meet Arthur. It is a bloody battle and Gawain and
Auguselus die, but Arthur's army is able to push back Mordred
– or the "Perjurer", as Geoffrey calls him. Mordred retreats to
Winchester. Guenevere, fearing the worst, flees from York to
the City of the Legions (the *Tysilio* specifically says Caerleon),
and withdraws to a nunnery.

Arthur marches to Winchester, and a second bloody battle
ensues. Mordred loses the most men, and flees by ship to
Cornwall. Arthur follows, and a third and final battle takes
place at the "River Camblam" (*Camlan* in the *Tysilio*). Mordred is killed in the first onslaught, but the battle continues.
Arthur, we are told, is mortally wounded and taken to the Isle
of Avalon. He hands the crown over to Constantine, son of
Cador.

Many places have been associated with Avalon including
Avallon in France, which may have helped cement the name, or
the old Roman fort of Aballava at Burgh on Sands. Neither of
these is an island, although Robert de Boron in *Joseph
d'Aramathie* referred to the "Vales of Avalon", suggesting
Somerset as by his day it had become associated with Glastonbury. Other islands suggested are Anglesey, Arran, Bardsey,
Lundy, Isle of Man and Iona, plus two islands off the Breton
coast, Sein and Ile Aval. My own preference is for Lydney in
Gloucestershire, where there was a major healing sanctuary
dedicated to the Romano-British god Nodens. It was in use
into the early fourth century and although of pagan origin may
have continued to provide healing facilities to Christians.
Although it no longer appears a physical island, as the name

shows (Lydney, *Lida's Island*) it was once an island separated by two streams, and would have been seen as an isolated haven in the woods tucked away from the real world. The Lydney complex was originally surrounded by lakes, and would be the obvious sanctuary for the Lady of the Lake.

The final days of Arthur have their parallel in Henry I's last days. Henry had lost all male heirs to the throne. His second marriage was childless and he pinned his hopes on his daughter Matilda, but conflict erupted between Henry and Matilda's estranged husband Geoffrey of Anjou – a suitable Mordred in the eyes of the English nobles. Henry died before the war began, and the scene was set for civil war.

Mordred has since passed into legend as Arthur's nemesis. The Welsh form of Mordred is *Medrod*, and intriguingly only one person by that name appears in the pedigrees accumulated by P. C. Bartrum in *Early Welsh Genealogical Tracts*. This is Medrawt ap Cawrdaf, grandson of Arthur's counsellor Caradog Vreichfras, and a contemporary of Athrwys of Gwent (*see* Table 8). We do not know whether Athrwys inherited the Gwentian throne, since he does not seem to have survived his father. It is possible that he was made a sub-king of Ergyng during his father's long reign, perhaps because Medrawt was too young to inherit, or perhaps because of a military necessity during the growing campaigns of the Saxons after their success at Dyrham in 577. If so, it is possible that once Medrawt reached maturity he might have sought to claim his patrimony, or, as implied in the Triads, a minor quarrel became a battle. Medrawt may well have killed Athrwys, which is why he did not become king.

Remarkably, Geoffrey provides a date for Arthur's passing: "This in the year 542 after our Lord's incarnation." Geoffrey can only have calculated that date from the *Welsh Annals*, in which the battle of Camlann is given as year *xciii* (93), and which we have refined to 539. However, we now believe that date to be at least nineteen years out, and that it should be closer to 520. Earlier, we established that Arthur's coronation took place around 515, according to Geoffrey's timeline, and the Gallic/Roman campaign took at least two years, which brings us surprisingly close to 520. For all its vagueness and unlikelihood, there is a bizarre internal logic to Geoffrey's timeline that has taken us from the departure of the Romans in 410 to the fall of Arthur in 520. This suggests that Geoffrey must have been following a set or sets, of annals, perhaps a more complete version of the *Annales Cambriae*, which was subsequently lost.

Geoffrey tells us that Constantine continued in conflict with the sons of Mordred, who still headed a Saxon army. After a "long series of battles" the sons fled, one to London and one to Winchester, taking over those cities. Constantine regained the cities and killed Mordred's sons, both within churches. This was the sacrilege that Gildas recorded. Geoffrey cites this as happening around the time of the death of the saintly Daniel, bishop of Bangor, but his death is recorded in the *Annals* as *cxl*, or 586. Either Geoffrey misread the *Annals*, or he is referring to a possible later translation of Daniel's bones, though no other source refers to this.

Geoffrey states that Constantine died four years later, "struck down by the vengeance of God". The *Brut Tysilio* is far more specific and says that "in the third year of his reign Constantine himself was killed by Cynan Wledig". Geoffrey identifies this Cynan as Aurelius Conanus, another of the "whelps" whom Gildas decries. Geoffrey calls him Constantine's nephew, and states that Cynan killed another uncle who should have succeeded Constantine. The *Tysilio*, on the other hand, does not state that Constantine and Cynan are related, but agrees that Cynan/Conanus did kill an uncle and his two sons, who had a prior claim to the throne. Gildas called Conanus a parricide, so it is possible that he wiped out his father, his uncle(s) and his cousins. The *Tysilio* calls him "a young man, whose abilities were equal to the station, for he was prompt and spirited in war". However, his reign was brief and according to Geoffrey he died in the third year of his reign, or the second year, according to the *Tysilio*.

The next ruler was Vortiporius. He faced another onslaught of Saxons, whom he was able to defeat, and took control "of the entire kingdom". Geoffrey gives no length for his reign, but the *Tysilio* states four years.

Then came Malgo, or Maelgwyn Gwynedd. Geoffrey is generally full of praise for Maelgwyn, calling him "most handsome of all the leaders of Britain", who "strove hard to do away with those who ruled the people harshly". He was brave, generous and courageous, and became ruler of not only all of Britain, but also Ireland, Iceland, Gotland, Orkney, Norway and Denmark. However, he was "given to the vice of homosexuality". Geoffrey does not record Maelgwyn's fate, although the *Tysilio* does refer to him having died in a convent after seeing "the yellow spectre", or the plague. Unfortunately, neither source records the length of Maelgwyn's reign. After Maelgwyn, Geoffrey follows a catalogue of kings who sink into submission to the Saxons up to the death of Cadwaladr in the year 689, well beyond our period of interest.

We saw earlier that the end of Maelgwyn's reign is usually equated to the plague recorded in the *Welsh Annals* as occurring in the year 549. The length of his reign is uncertain, but it is commonly given as about fifteen years, starting in 534. Combining the data from Geoffrey and the *Tysilio*, the total span for the reigns of Constantine, Cynan and Vortiporius is about ten years, possibly more as Geoffrey does not state how long the battles with the sons of Mordred lasted. But ten to twelve years would seem about right overall. Previously we had reached the year 519/520 in Geoffrey's timeline, and the addition of ten to twelve years brings us to 529/532, certainly close enough to an uncertain 534 to link in with Maelgwyn's accession.

It is possible to re-create Geoffrey's internal chronology, adjusting his year of 542 by the nineteen-year discrepancy in the *Annals*. The result, like the ones extracted from Nennius, Gildas and the *ASC*, is not necessarily any more accurate, but it is one worth reviewing.

Table 18 An Arthurian chronology according to Geoffrey

410	End of Roman authority; appeal to Aldroenus; Constantine heads army; defeats Picts; made king.
410–426	Reign of Constantine. He marries and has three children: Constans (410), Ambrosius (425) and Uther (426).
426	Constantine dies; Constans made king under Vortigern's control.
428	Constans murdered; Vortigern king. Ambrosius and Uther smuggled to Brittany [Llydaw]. Arrival of Saxons [Gewis?].
428–440	Build-up of Saxons, including arrival of Reinwen who marries Vortigern. Visit of Germanus and Lupus.
440s	Saxon wars. Vortimer deposes Vortigern and drives back Saxons.
449–455	Vortimer killed; Vortigern restored; return of Hengist. Massacre of nobles. Vortigern flees.
455–457	Ambrosius arrives; defeats and kills Vortigern. Made king. Defeats Hengist.
457–460	Rebuilding programme.
Late 460s	Ambrosius killed; Uther quells North. Octa and Eossa imprisoned.
c470	Birth of Arthur.
485–494	Uther poisoned; Arthur crowned. Octa and Eosa escape and are killed. Period of Arthur's battles.
495–506	Arthur's peaceful reign and rise of chivalry.
506–515	Arthur's Gallic campaign, culminating in imperial coronation.
516–520	Arthur's second Gallic campaign and march on Rome; Mordred's treachery; Arthur's return and fall at the battle of Camlann.
523	Death of Arthur in Avalon (Geoffrey cites 542).
520–532	Reigns of Constantine, Cynan and Vortipor.

This timeline relates only to Geoffrey's narrative chronology and, of course, takes no account of individuals mentioned who existed at other times. The main difference between this chronology and the previous summary in Table 14 is the appearance of Uther. Geoffrey has Ambrosius killed after a short reign, whereas the assumption from the writings of Gildas and Nennius is that Ambrosius was the main British opponent to the Saxons during the 460s and 470s. Geoffrey also gives an earlier death for Hengist – indeed, his date for the death of Octa coincides with the *ASC*'s suggested date of 488 for Hengist's passing.

Whichever way we look at it, albeit from very shaky sources, Arthur's reign fits into the period 490–520. That does not mean that all of the events attributed to Arthur also have to fit into that period. Geoffrey's whole story from Vortigern to Arthur is clearly culled from a host of fragments and incidental sources which Geoffrey, in his desire to create a powerful narrative and a propaganda tool, together with his general misunderstanding of events, chose to piece together in a sequence that suited his purpose. In so doing he created the story of Arthur, and whilst we should not immediately dismiss everything that he says, because it does have a frustrating internal logic, neither should we accept anything. We must, however, admire Geoffrey's skill and imagination in creating a legend that has lasted a thousand years.

6. Conclusion

Geoffrey has clearly used six or seven different narrative sources, which he has interspersed with elements from Gildas, Nennius and the *Welsh Annals*.

(1) A chronicle, perhaps from Brittany, which traces the immediate post-Roman period, including the stories of Constantine and Ambrosius.

(2) A Welsh chronicle (linked with Nennius) for the story of Vortigern.

(3) A chronicle, also probably Breton, which is the story of Uther. This may be the same as (1).

(4) A northern chronicle of the sixth or seventh century, which traces the war between the Men of the North and the Saxons in the period 550–600. This may be the same one that Nennius knew and could have been written by Rhun ap Urien.

(5) Another northern chronicle – or the same as (4) – tracing the Viking invasion of Britain in the eighth and ninth centuries.

(6) A Gallic or Breton chronicle about the campaigns of Clovis and the Franks.

(7) A further chronicle, probably Welsh, which traces the battles between Arthur and Mordred.

Any of the above may not necessarily be a single or even a lengthy document. More likely they are fragments, perhaps of poems, annals and folktales. It is evident from the flow of Geoffrey's narrative that he was joining together accounts which he interpreted as relating to Arthur, but not necessarily the same Arthur. He also developed parallels with the reign of Henry I.

What seems evident from Geoffrey's account is that, despite his almost seamless narrative, the Arthur who fights the battles in the North is not the same Arthur who fights in Gaul, and neither is necessarily the Arthur who is the son of Uther and who meets his fate at Camlann. This suggests three, possibly four, prototypes for Arthur.

(1) An Arthur who was descended from the daughter or wife of Emyr Llydaw in Gwent (Llydaw being mistaken for Brittany), who lived in the late fifth century. This could have been the seventh-century Arthur of Gwent by name but not necessarily by reputation as Geoffrey makes no reference to the Welsh tradition after Vortigern.

(2) An Arthur whose name was miscopied from Arddun, the child of Eliffer (Eleutherius) of the North, and who lived in the mid-sixth century. This name may subsequently have become fused with Elifer's father Arthwys (Arthur of the Pennines).

(3) Clovis, the king of the Franks, whose life parallels Arthur's.

(4) A later hero who fought the Viking invaders in the eighth and ninth centuries. The obvious contenders for this are Alfred the Great and Athelstan, whose battles against the Vikings have some similarity to Arthur's.

Since the crucial element is who Geoffrey believed fought at Badon, I suspect he found this in his Northern Chronicle, which he tried to blend with the elements in Nennius and Gildas. If it were ever possible to prove that either Arthwys ap Mar or Eliffer fought at Lichfield and Caer Faddon, then we would have found Geoffrey's Arthur.

10

THE REAL KING ARTHUR – THE TWENTY CLAIMANTS

1. The ground rules

We have now covered all of the surviving historical and quasi-historical texts that relate to Arthur. This means that in the last nine chapters we have touched upon the real Arthur – or Arthurs, because I believe it has become very evident that we are not dealing with one individual. The old tales retold by Nennius, those in *The Mabinogion*, and those by Geoffrey of Monmouth are a potpourri of historical characters, most of whom are known only by name. It was from these stories that the Arthur we have come to know grew in the telling, becoming the Arthur of Thomas Malory, but so far removed from the original as to be scarcely recognizable.

Which, of course, raises the question: will we recognize Arthur when we find him? What are the ground rules by which we can identify him? What key fact allows us to point at a figure in the line-up and say, "That's him"?

I said at the very start of this book that we have to find the right person in the right place at the right time. All of this exploration through the dim and often very vague pages of lost history has been about teasing out people's identities, and establishing when and where they lived. We have covered close on a thousand names and whilst this is only a very small fraction of all those living in the fifth and sixth centuries, it is a high proportion of the movers and shakers.

There is really only one criterion. The original Arthur, the one from whom all else flowed, has to be the victor of the first battle of Badon. Although we have not conclusively identified the site of Badon we have, thanks to Gildas, managed to fine-tune the date of Badon to between 493 and 497.

However, there is one strong caveat. Gildas, the one person who could have told us who was the victor at Badon, chose not to. As a consequence, we do not know who the victor was. However, what makes legends grow are not the facts, but what we *believe* to be the facts. So whilst the victor of Badon is the real origin of the Arthur legend, he does not have to be the original Arthur. Someone else may very rapidly have become associated with Badon so that the legend grew around him.

This happens quite often. Take, for instance, the Gunpowder Plot. If we were asked to name the chief conspirator, I suspect most of us would immediately name Guy Fawkes. But the mastermind was not Fawkes at all, but Robert Catesby. We know this because the details are fully documented, but that still doesn't stop us remembering Guy Fawkes above all others and, if it had happened many centuries earlier and all documentation was lost, we'd probably only remember Fawkes.

In the case of Arthur, history has been revised and rewritten so many times that virtually all we are left with is the version people wanted to remember. In that case, identifying the real Arthur may not mean identifying the victor of Badon, but identifying the person everyone *thinks* was the victor of Badon.

How, you may ask, do we know who they thought was the victor of Badon?

Because they told us. Gildas didn't directly, but gave us some clues. Nennius told us he was the victor of eleven other battles. *The Dream of Rhonabwy* tells us his chief counsellor was Caradoc Vreichfras, who is closely associated with Ergyng, and that his bishop was Bedwin, also named in the first of the Triads, which link Arthur, Bedwin and Caradoc with Celliwig in southern Gwent. However, the story places the battle of Caer Faddon in Powys, which though this may not be the original Badon, may be the one they associate with the victor. Geoffrey makes him the son and successor of Uther, the brother of Ambrosius. Uther and Ambrosius were allegedly the children of Constantine of Armorica, but we have surmised that this is not the Armorica known today as Brittany, but Llydaw in Ergyng.

Those are just some of the secondary pointers which help us home in. But let us first examine all of the contenders once again in chronological order to refresh our memories, and see whom we can eliminate. The dates given are as per the tables in Chapter 3.

2. The contenders

1. Lucius Artorius Castus (140–197)

He seems a rank outsider, but there is much about him that may have contributed to the legend. Littleton and Malcor put forward a compelling argument that the Sarmatian folktales of the Iazygian soldiers captured by Castus in Brittany and settled in Ribchester (Bremetennacum) could have contributed to the later Arthurian legend, particularly the story of returning Excalibur to the Lady of the Lake. They propose that Castus's campaign in the North reflects Nennius's sequence of battles, though their case for Dumbarton as Badon is perhaps the weakest element. Castus's exploits in Armorica possibly became associated with the character of Riothamus. Whilst Castus cannot be the original Arthur of Badon, his activities could certainly have encouraged the initial development of the legend.

2. Riothamus (430–500)

The idea that Riothamus might have been Arthur has apparently been around since at least 1175, when a monk at Orcamp Abbey in France made the connection. This Riothamus has become identified with the King Arthur recorded in the biography of Goeznovius by the Breton monk William, written in 1019, who stated that Arthur fought in Gaul. The current champion of the idea is Geoffrey Ashe in *The Discovery of King Arthur*. As Riothamus is another of those names that double as titles, and means "over king", he could as easily be Arthur, based on Ardd-ri, or "High King." Others have suggested that he was Ambrosius.

Because we have only a brief glimpse of Riothamus, and that entirely in Gaul and, for that matter, as the loser of a battle, not as a victor, he hardly stands out as a hero who would form the basis of legend. He might be equated with the Breton King Iahann Reeth, a name that may have been conflated with the later ruler Ionas Riotham.

The main problem with Riothamus also being Arthur of Badon, however, is one of timing. If Riothamus were Arthur, he would have to have been old enough to command troops in 469, and go on to be victorious at Badon around 493–497, and fight at Camlann in 514–518. His activities in Gaul could certainly have added further fuel to the flames of legend, but he is unlikely to be the victor of Badon.

3. Ambrosius Aurelianus (430–500)

This idea took root because Gildas, who was the first to name the battle of Badon, makes no mention of Arthur at all, but does name Ambrosius in the lead-up to the battle. Let's look again very closely at his wording. The relevant sections are §25 and 26 of *De Excidio*. Halfway through §25, after having said that under Ambrosius the British regained their strength and fought back against the Saxons, Gildas writes "*ex eo tempore*" which can be translated as "from that time on" or "after a given time". The phrase even appears in the Bible

(Genesis 47:26) where it is translated as "from that time". This gives the impression that at least some time has passed. It is not soon after, or presently. This sense of time is emphasized when he talks in the next section about the victories shifting between the British and the Saxons, "*usque ad annum obsessionis badonici montis*" which translates literally as "all the way to the year of the siege of Mount Badon". "All the way" is not a few months or even a few years. These two phrases make it clear that Gildas was talking about a span of some years from when Ambrosius took command to the eventual victory at Badon.

That alone does not rule out Ambrosius being the commander at Badon. The evidence shows that Ambrosius took command a few years after the Saxons had been driven home by Vortimer. Since Vortimer was dead and Vortigern disgraced, there was no other commander in charge until Ambrosius took control. We know that this has to be after 455, probably after 460 (*see* Table 14), but not long after. Ambrosius's campaign may even have run into the 480s, but to have one commander leading a battle campaign, no matter how intermittent, for thirty years is expecting much. Ambrosius is unlikely to have been born later than 435, which would make him fifty-eight in 493 and nearly eighty at the time of Camlann. Ambrosius could still have been the victor of Badon, but he is unlikely to have been the Arthur of Camlann.

Ambrosius's dates coincide almost exactly with those of Riothamus, leading many to suggest that they are one and the same. If he had returned to Britain to continue his battles, this might explain why Riothamus is not heard of again in France. Frank D. Reno, in *The Historic King Arthur*, takes that extra step by making Ambrosius/Riothamus/Arthur all the same person, resulting in a rather aged Arthur. Reno suggests a birth year for Ambrosius of 422 and that Arthur died in 518, making him ninety-six. It is hard to imagine how he could have achieved anything at Camlann, let alone attempt to do battle with Mordred.

The only way that Ambrosius could be Arthur is if Ambrosius's campaign were shorter than Gildas implies, and therefore all of the preceding dates are shifted. This is a case to be argued, because we have already suggested that the main Saxon invasion, the second or third *adventus*, was not until the 470s, even the late 470s. We might imagine a campaign running from, say, 477 (Aelle's arrival) to 493, just sixteen years, which would not contradict Gildas. Still long, but perfectly manageable for one significant Roman. If Ambrosius was in his late twenties at the start of this, he would be forty-three at Badon and sixty-four at Camlann.

However, this causes problems at the start of the fifth century. If Ambrosius was not born until 450, his father by then would have been in his sixties at least and though this is possible, it seems unlikely. This scenario would also rule out any possibility of Ambrosius being Riothamus.

So whilst we cannot rule out Ambrosius as being the victor of Badon, it is not realistic for him to have continued the Golden Age usually attributed to Arthur. Ambrosius must have handed over power to someone, and this leads us to our next contender or contenders.

4. Pascent (430–500)

If Arthur was Ambrosius's successor, we must consider Pascent, because Nennius tells us (§48) that when Ambrosius became king he installed Vortigern's eldest surviving son, Pascent or Pasgen, as ruler of the "provinces" of Builth and Gwrtheyrnion.

The use of the word "provinces" is intriguing as it has echoes of the old Roman term for one of the divisions of Britain. One might expect Ambrosius, upon becoming the High King (or, a true Roman, the vicarius), to appoint governors to the former Roman provinces.

If Ambrosius were mounting a retaliatory campaign against the Saxons he would have needed strong, trustworthy provincial governors and a reliable right-hand man. Pascent's descendants went on to rule Gwrtheyrnion and later Powys, so we must assume that Pascent was a reliable supporter of Ambrosius and not the rebel whom Geoffrey of Monmouth portrays.

So Pascent must be a part of the Arthur story, as he was one of the legitimate "kings" alive at that time. However, he was of the same generation as Ambrosius and would have been too old to fight at Badon, so I do not regard him as a serious candidate for Arthur. He may well have done the solid work of governing Britain while Ambrosius led the battle campaign, but administrators are never remembered.

It is the generation after him that is of more interest.

5. Cadell and Riocatus (both 460–530)

Ambrosius must have looked for a successor, not in Builth and Gwrtheyrnion where Pascent's line continued, but in Powys, which had been his central power-base, governed from Wroxeter. When Ambrosius died he had to hand that over to someone.

We know that Ambrosius had children, because Gildas refers to his descendants unfavourably. It is possible that they did not survive him and, whilst his grandchildren may have subsequently carved out their own territory (Aurelius Caninus being one possibility) they do not seem to have re-established themselves, otherwise their ancestry would have been celebrated. Certainly there is no case to make that Arthur might have been Ambrosius's son. Not even Geoffrey says that though we will return to the question of Uther Pendragon and his family shortly.

Because the early pedigrees of Powys are in such a mess it is difficult to untangle the succession. Regardless of any later power struggles, it is clear that someone had to rule Powys after Ambrosius. I have presented my own interpretation of this in Table 10, where I suggest that Ambrosius passed the succession on to Cadell. He was the son of Categirn, who had died fighting the Saxons, and was thus Pascent's nephew and Riocatus's cousin. Both Cadell and Riocatus were grandsons of Vortigern.

Cadell has his own origin tale, as related by Nennius (*see* Chapter 6). It's a standard rags-to-riches folktale which may have some basis in reality. It is possible that, with Vortigern disgraced, Cadell had nothing to inherit and so may have lived initially as a scullion. His name, in its original form, Catel, means "cattle". He may well have been fostered, as was the Celtic custom, but to a poor family.

Of interest is the connection between Cadell and Germanus. Most scholars believe that in this tale Germanus has become confused with the Irish monk Garmon. Garmon, or Harmon as his name also appears, has several churches dedicated to him throughout Wales, and a small village of St Harmon still exists in mid-Wales near Rhayader. Baring-Gould allocated Garmon the dates 410–475 and though very conjectural may at least give us an approximation. The last ten years of his life were spent as Bishop of Man. It is possible that Garmon served as a mentor for the young Cadell, who may have been raised in the church. Cadell was probably born in the early 450s, and thus may have received Garmon's blessing around the age of twenty-one in the early 470s. He could have succeeded Ambrosius in the 480s and still only have been about forty at the time of Badon. His nickname, *Durnluc*, is usually translated as "gleaming hilt" or "hilt of light", significant with regard to Arthur's Excalibur.

The concept of the ruler of Viriconium, the last major city in Britain, wielding a bright sword and living in an area with which all of the battles have been associated, including Badon (at Caer Faddon), is a compelling one. There is certainly a sufficient case for Cadell to be considered as a serious contender as one of the characters behind the historical Arthur.

His cousin, Riocatus, may also be significant. We know that in his youth he entered the church and rose to the rank of Overseer by the year 475, when Sidonius mentions him in a letter to Bishop Faustus in Armorica. This suggests Riocatus is quite senior and so may have been in his thirties or even forties by this time. We do not know what became of him, or whether he even left the Church to take up the kingship of Gwrtheyrnion, but even if he stayed in the Church it would not stop him being present at Badon, perhaps in his fifties by then. The *Welsh Annals* comment that "Arthur carries the Cross of Our Lord Jesus Christ for three days and three nights" emphasises the religious angle, and the distant echoes of the Alleluia Victory suggests someone, perhaps Riocatus, was reprising the role of Germanus. There is also the similarity to the earlier battle at Guinnion, where "Arthur carried the image of Holy Mary" according to Nennius. Guinnion and Badon were clearly holy battles. If Riocatus was not Arthur himself, could he have been his holy representative against the pagans?

Someone who was alive at the time of Badon, who was called "king of battles" but was not himself a king, has much in common with Nennius's meagre description of Arthur. And Riocatus, like Cadell, was in the right place to have been able to fight a sequence of battles along the southern or western frontier.

6. Owain Danwyn (450–530) or Cynlas (480–560)

Owain Danwyn or "White Tooth" is put forward as a contender for Arthur by Keatman and Phillips in *King Arthur – the True Story*. I have already discussed their basic premise in Chapter 7 and have little to add here. Owain was contemporary with Badon and may well have fought there, but he was a minor ruler at Rhos. Although he lived at the right time, there are no other factors that would make him a likely candidate for Arthur.

On his website,* Mark Devere Davis puts forward several arguments to suggest that Owain's son Cynlas was Arthur. Most of these, like the proposals for his father, revolve around him living at the Fortress of the Bear, and make several other links with "bear" imagery. Davis highlights that Cynlas lusted after his wife's sister, a charge that was also brought against Arthur in later legend (with three Gueneveres). Davis also highlights Gildas's odd comment that Cynlas possessed "arms special to himself", which is suggestive of Excalibur.

From Gildas's tirade against Cynlas, it is apparent that he was a vicious despot who would not have been remembered as the heroic Arthur of Badon, or as a hero of any kind.

---

* *See* www.angelfire.com/md/devere/urse.html.

7. The Pendragons: Brychan (430–500) and Dyfnwal (455–525)
If we accept the date for Badon as being in the mid-490s, then
according to Table 16 the Pendragon was probably Brychan of
Brycheiniog. Dyfnwal Hen would have been Pendragon at the
time of the *Welsh Annals* date for Badon in 518. Neither Uther
nor Arthur appears in the list of Pendragons as detailed by
Laurence Gardner.

We know little about the real Brychan. Legend attributes
him with thirty-five children, highlighting his patriarchal status. There is doubtless much confusion between the original
Brychan of Brycheiniog and his son, or grandson, Brychan of
Manau.

Most of Brychan's children entered the church; indeed, he is
included in the Welsh Triad of the "Three Saintly Families" of
Britain. According to legend, Gwynllyw of Gwent abducted
one of Brychan's daughters, Gwladys, and Brychan pursued
him in a violent fury. It needed Arthur, Cei and Bedwyr to stop
the bloodshed. Although Arthur was probably added to this
story later, it shows that there is no tradition suggesting that
Brychan and Arthur are one and the same. Brychan did have a
son called Arthen (460–530), the first example of an Arth-
named child of a Pendragon. But he too entered the church.
Cefn Arthur is on an old drovers' road near Llandovery.

As we have seen, Dyfnwal was a warrior who was a constant
threat to those tribes south of the Wall. There is a pattern of
battles related to Nennius's list that could represent an offensive against the Gododdin and Angles, and could place Badon
in the north at Bowden Hill, near Linlithgow. Though this
clearly had been the site of an ancient battle, nothing has yet
suggested one as old as Badon, and the debris found there by
the eighteenth-century antiquarian Sir Robert Sibbald is
doubtless related to one of any number of battles in this area
during Scotland's conflicts with England. Dyfnwal was ob-
viously a powerful warrior, and he must have left behind
significant memories, some of which may later have attached
themselves to the Arthurian legend.

8. Vortipor (470–540) or Agricola (440–510)

Vortipor of Dyfed was a contemporary of Dyfnwal and may have operated in the same role in Wales as Dyfnwal did in the north. Vortipor was known as the "Protector". The title was not unique in Britain – Coel Hen had also used it, but probably with direct authority from Rome. With Vortipor, whilst he may have been pro-Roman, the title seems more one of conceit than of rank.

Vortipor is one of the kings singled out for criticism by Gildas who calls him the "bad son of a good king" and "spotted with wickedness". He may have been a better ruler in his youth but in his old age, when Gildas was writing, he was "defiled by various murders and adulteries". This included "the rape of a shameless daughter". Gildas does not say whether this was Vortipor's own daughter or "daughter" in a symbolic sense, such as a "daughter of Eve" or "daughter of the church". Others have interpreted it as a step-daughter. We know that later legends give Arthur an incestuous relationship with his sister, of which Mordred was the offspring. Arthur is not always the hero we like to imagine. Geoffrey of Monmouth portrays him as proud and vain in later years, defying Rome.

Since Gildas thought so ill of Vortipor, yet wrote of Badon as such a victory, does that mean that Vortipor could not have been the victor of Badon? Perhaps, but the opposite is as likely. If Gildas were going to castigate Vortipor then he would hardly want to name him as the victor of such an important battle. It would be surprising if Vortipor, as Protector, did not fight at Badon, which was the decisive battle against the Saxons. Perhaps Vortipor had not called himself the Protector at that stage. After all, if his father were still alive, and in his mid-fifties, he probably also held the title – or at least the role – of Protector, and Gildas did at least praise him as a "good king".

We can almost certainly determine the coalition of kings. If the battle were in the south, then it probably involved Cadwallon Lawhir, Cadell, Rhain ap Brychan and perhaps

Caradog Vreichfras. Agricola (Aircol) would have been the senior king though, because of his age, he may not have been involved in the majority of the fighting. That could well have been left to Vortipor as the *dux bellorum*.

Nennius tells us that Arthur fought "along with the kings". Gildas also calls Vortipor's father a king, but if Agricola also held the rank of Protector, he may have been regarded by later generations as over and above the kings.

In fact something like that may well have been felt by his son. Vortipor is, after all, a title, very similar in derivation to Vortimer – both names are rendered as Gwerthefyr in Welsh – and means "Over King". We do not know Vortipor's given name. His great-grandson was called Artúir, so we cannot dismiss the possibility that the name recurred in other generations, especially as his 4 x great-grandfather also bore the prefix in Artchorp. Vortipor's title in Irish was Gartbuir, and it may just be possible that the Gaelic *b* was misread as an *h*, when written as *Gartbuir*.

Certainly if Agricola was the senior "Protector", he would have been in command at Badon, and the only reasons why he and Vortipor would not be present would be if Badon was in the north or happened later than the 490s.

Vortipor has perhaps one other surprise in store. In *Bloodline of the Holy Grail* Laurence Gardner makes several points about Artúir of Dyfed. I treat these separately below, but one is more relevant here. Gardner suggests that it is Artúir of Dyfed who died at Camlann in 537 or 538. Artúir lived too late for this, but Vortipor could well have died at around that time, and he is quite likely to have died in battle, despite his age. Our revised date for Camlann is 520, but this is based on its relationship to Badon. Supposing the Camlann entry in the *Welsh Annals* is correct at 538, Vortipor would then be in his mid-sixties. There is some suggestion that Vortipor was in battle against his neighbour Ceredigion. That territory was between Demetia and Gwynedd, and Vortipor may have invaded Ceredigion many times in conflict against Gwynedd.

One of the likely locations for Camlann is in northern Ceredigion on the border with Gwynedd. Vortipor would have passed through here on his way to Gwynedd and that may be where he was ambushed and killed. We do not know Vortipor's fate but it was always more likely to have been in battle than peace. We do not know if he was killed by a nephew, but a family rivalry may well have been involved, if Vortipor had disposed of his wife and raped her daughter.

9. Cerdic (480–550) or Caradog (445–515)

This case is put forward by John C. Rudmin in "Arthur, Cerdic and the Formation of Wessex" available on the Celtic Twilight website.[*] Rudmin's argument is that Arthur, Cerdic and Caradog Vreichfras are all based on the same individual and he cites a number of comparisons. One of these is that Caradog's wife was Guignier, sister of Cador of Cornwall and, as we have seen, Arthur's future wife Guenevere had been raised in Cador's household. However, Guignier is a later addition to the Caradog legend. In the Welsh tales, Caradog's wife was Tegau Eurfron, though the stories about them are similar, further examples of how common characters (such as Cador) were thrown into the melting pot of legend. There may be more of a case to argue that Cerdic and Caradog are the same, or at least related, as we have explored, but it requires some manipulation to bring Arthur into that equation.

Caradog Vreichfras may well have fought at Badon, which is probably why he features so strongly in the later tales. Cerdic is unlikely to have been involved, on either side. If anything, Cerdic benefited from the collapse of Arthur after Camlann which, if it was in 538, saw Cerdic establish the West Saxon kingdom.

10. Urien of Rheged (c535–591)

There is a strong likelihood that Urien's battles against the Angles became fused in the folk memory with some of

---

[*]   See http://gorddcymru.org/twilight/index.htm.

Arthur's battles. Urien is known to have scored a sequence of victories against the Saxons in a well-known battle list. Even though Badon was a victory for Arthur, Camlann was a defeat and betrayal, and Urien's death at Lindisfarne, betrayed by Morcant, would have echoed down the years. The *Northern Chronicle*, probably kept by his son Rhun, would have honoured Urien's victories along with others of the north (especially Arthwys, Eliffer and Peredur).

11. Athelstan (895–939)

The unsung hero of English history. While Alfred's greatness is rightly celebrated, that of his grandson, who ruled the English from 924 to 939, is often overlooked. Yet it was Athelstan who united Britain as none had previously. The main parallel with Arthur is that Athelstan had to conduct a campaign in the North to suppress both Welsh hostilities and the Norse in York. He also quelled a Cornish revolt under their king Hoel. He achieved a period of peace and prosperity in England never previously experienced. Although this is not the same as the post-Badon Pax Arthuriana, it does have parallels with Geoffrey's portrayal of how Arthur achieved peace. Also, after the Scots broke the treaty arrangement in 934, hostilities broke out which caused Athelstan first to devastate Scotland, just as Geoffrey described Arthur doing in his campaign, and then to meet a combined army of Scots and Vikings at Brunanburh in 937. All agree that this battle was the most decisive of all Saxon victories, and yet, like Badon, no one is really sure where Brunanburh was fought. All this happened two hundred years before Geoffrey wrote his *History*, but considering his ability to confuse facts from any period, he may well have encountered a document about Athelstan's northern battles and, not knowing its origin, incorporated elements of it into his tale.

I shall now work through all of the individuals with any likely Arth- prefixed name, including some we have not yet discussed who I feel need to be mentioned if only to be dismissed.

These are also presented in date order for the fifth and sixth centuries.

12. Arthwys ap Mar (450–520)

One of the Men of the North. He does not appear in all of the genealogies, but when he does he is always cited as the son of Mar, grandson of Ceneu and great-grandson of Coel, which would place his lifetime in the 480s. The name sometimes appears as Athrwys, which means his name may have been derived from *Athro*, the root word for "teacher" or "master".

It is frustrating that we do not know enough about these Men of the North. We can perhaps learn a little about Arthwys through his sons, the most famous of which was Eliffer of the Great Host. Eliffer (or Ele*uther*ius) was the father of Gwrgi and Peredur and his wife, Efrddyl, was the sister of Loth, highlighting at least two names closely linked with the Arthur of legend. Eliffer's sons were renowned heroes fighting the Angles, and doubtless Eliffer's "Great Host" or Warband was equally involved in such conflict, so we may imagine Arthwys was, too. As previously noted one Welsh Triad erroneously credits Eliffer with a "son" called Arthur Penuchell, the "wingheaded". The manuscript was held at Oxford and could well have been seen by Geoffrey.

It is possible that in Geoffrey's day, and certainly in Nennius's, there was a manuscript, now long lost, which told a Chronicle of the Northern Wars. This may well have recounted the exploits of Arthwys and Eliffer, some of which influenced Geoffrey's *History*. We have no way of knowing, but the number of sites in the North that could relate to Nennius's battle list is sufficiently tempting to suggest that there was an Arthur of the North, probably resident in Elmet, whose exploits against the Angles were long remembered. It may be this Athrwys whose death is mentioned in stanza 19 of *Y Gododdin*. Because the *Gododdin* integrates various heroics there is no reason to presume this death happened at the battle of Catraeth, as Arthwys ap Mar lived a century earlier, but it may tell us that he died in battle.

Arthwys is the best situated to fight a campaign along the eastern frontier which, because of its association with Gildas's "partition", is the one most likely to be connected with Badon. Though it cannot be wholly discounted, Arthwys is unlikely to have fought as far south as Liddington, but if his territory were in Elmet, it would have been possible for him to bring reinforcements to a siege around the Breidden Hills or the Wrekin in Powys. In fact, if the Saxons had advanced that far west by the 490s, it would have been a certainty that the British in Powys would have looked to their northern cousins for aid. Just possibly, despite the other great and powerful at Badon, it was the northern prince who saved the day and entered legend. It may even be just as Geoffrey described it, with Arthwys pursuing the Saxons from Lichfield to a last-ditch battle in Powys.

13. Arthfael ap Einudd (480–550)

Arthfael appears in the *Life* of St Cadog, who lived in the early sixth century. He is identified as a king of Glamorgan who granted Cadog land at what is probably modern-day Cadoxton, near Neath. His son Gwrgan the Freckled is also mentioned in Cadog's *Life*, when Cadog gives Gwrgan a sword given to him by Rhun ap Maelgwyn. Arthfael ruled close to Mynydd Baidan, where Blackett and Wilson identify Mount Badon, and he was almost certainly alive at the time of the battle. Arthfael is a contemporary of Arthmael (St Arthmel), and their names are ostensibly the same, but there is no record that Arthmael ever ruled, even as a sub-king. The genealogy in which Arthfael appears is clearly corrupt and has probably picked up more than one pedigree. Despite this and the fact that Arthfael is a fairly common name amongst the later kings of Gwent, Lifris, who wrote the *Life of Cadog* around the year 1100, still made the connection between Arthfael and his son Gwrgan, suggesting that there may be something tangible behind the story. Unfortunately, no more is known.

14. Saint Arthmel (482–552)

Proposed by Chris Barber and David Pykitt in *Journey to Avalon*. Their idea is not so much who Arthur was but whom he became. The chronology only works if the dates in the *Welsh Annals* are correct for Badon and Camlann. It is also surprising that someone allegedly so well known could change identity so successfully and not be remembered by so many other notable holy men in Brittany, not least Gildas himself. Brittany had its own memories of Arthur, and centuries later his name evolved into Arzor. If the Bretons knew Arzor was really Arthmael, that would surely have found its way into the later legends.

15. Arthfoddw ap Boddw (540–610)

Suddenly there is a time leap. Despite the admitted roughness of our chronology, we have had a cluster of Arth- names in the mid-to-late fifth century, though no true Arthurs; but now there is none until the mid-to-late sixth century. Curiously, it is a gap that exactly encompasses the time of Arthur of Badon who, based on the limited evidence we have, must have lived from about 470 to 520, or to 540 if the later Camlann date is correct. The first new Arth- name seems to occur within a year or two of Arthur's death. Even more curiously, the first known is Arthfoddw, a name that means Arth the lucky or Arth the fortunate. Could Boddw of Ceredigion have named his son after Arthur in the hope that he would be fortunate? If so, then there must be another Arthur that we are missing or one whose real name we do not know. This is the gap filled precisely by Vortipor, Cadell and Riocatus.

We know nothing else about Arthfoddw. He is a name in the pedigrees of the rulers of Ceredigion. It may be pertinent that he chose to pass a similar name on to his son Arthlwys, of whom more below. That is the only example we have of successive generations with an Arth- name. It suggests to me that we have already passed the Arthur of Badon and that his name had left an impression.

16. Artúir ap Pedr (550–620)

We have at last reached the first individual whose name is genuinely "Arthur". The grandson of Vortipor, Artúir ruled Dyfed at the end of the sixth century. We are thus clearly a whole century after Badon so this Arthur can have no direct connection with the original historical Arthur.

Yet stories may have attached to him that later became grafted on to the composite Arthur of legend. We have already encountered several, most notably the hunt for the boar Trwyth. Stripping the story brings us back to a probable historical event, a series of battles against a brigand and his men who came from Ireland and first laid waste to parts of Dyfed before moving on to Gwent. The Gwent episode may relate to an entirely different historical event. The rulers of Dyfed were of Irish descent and they must have spent much of their time defending their lands from further Irish raiders. Also present in Arthur's court, in the tale of *Culhwch and Olwen*, are several survivors from lost lands, such as Gwenwynwyn, recorded as Arthur's champion, and Teithi the Old. The lost lands are believed to have been off the coast of Dyfed or Ceredigion, and perhaps to the north in Morecambe Bay. These locations could all be plausibly associated with the court of Artúir of Dyfed. Neither of them is of great significance in the later story of Arthur, and it is hard to imagine that Artúir of Dyfed played much part in fighting against the Saxons who, by his reign, were becoming firmly established in "England" and were enclosing the British into Wales.

In *Bloodline of the Holy Grail* Laurence Gardner tells us some unusual facts not recorded elsewhere. He tells us that Artúir of Dyfed was installed by Dubricius in 506. Dubricius was alive then but Artúir of Dyfed was not even a gleam in his father's eye. No matter how we play around with the dates in the Dyfed pedigree – probably the most reliable of all of them – it would be impossible to have Artúir of Dyfed alive earlier than 530. Also Dubricius is most unlikely to have installed a king in Dyfed since, as we have seen, his territory was soundly in Ergyng. The bishop of Dyfed was Dewi (St David), whose dates are even more fluid than Dubricius's. In fact, opinion is shifting towards there having been two holy men called Dewi in Wales during the sixth century. The lesser-known Dewi of Ergyng (who gave his name to Dewchurch, Dewsall and others), lived from perhaps 480 to 550 and was the companion of Dubricius and Gildas. The second, more famous St David of Dyfed lived from around 520 to 590 and could quite possibly have inaugurated Artúir of Dyfed as king, perhaps in the 580s. Whether the earlier Dewi or even Dubricius enthroned a previous king of Dyfed, I have no idea, but 506AD would be a perfectly acceptable date for the accession of Vortipor, or *Gartbuir* as he may be remembered.

Gardner also tells us that Artúir of Dyfed's sister Niniane had married Ambrosius as part of a treaty to stop Dyfed's incursions into Powys. We know Niniane, also known as Nimuë or Vivien, from the later legends as the lover of Merlin, as she has also been equated with the Lady of the Lake. Gardner makes her the mother of Merlin. If these elements are true they would again apply to an earlier ruler, such as Vortipor, as might Arthur's involvement at Camlann, which I have already discussed under Vortipor.

Nevertheless, with Artúir of Dyfed we start to see how some of the exploits of a real Arthur come together with the Arthur of legend and also show how both could be linked to a possible earlier "Arthur" in the form of Vortipor/ *Gartbuir*.

17. Artúir mac Aedan (560–596)

This historically attested character was recorded by Adomnán in his *Life of Columba,* written less than a century after the real events. Columba had, apparently, correctly foretold that Artúir would not succeed Aedan as king of the Dál Riatan

Scots. Artúir met his fate in battle against the Picts, probably in 596. Laurence Gardner, though, who believes Artúir was the original Arthur, gives the date as 603. He believes that Artúir fought at both Camelon, near Falkirk, and Camboglanna on Hadrian's Wall. The battle at Camboglanna was savage, resulting in a rout that spilled over into a second battle at Degsaston [Dawston]. It was there that Artúir died, along with hundreds of his fellows. This was the decisive battle for the English that saw Athelfrith's domination of the north and the capitulation of the British and Scots. Aedan was a broken man after that.

Gardner makes Aedan the Pendragon of Britain and thus claims that Artúir is the only "Arthur" to have been born to a Pendragon. This is true if we exclude Arthen ap Brychan, previously cited. Although the exploits of Artúir are not fully recorded, many of his father's are, as he was, according to the authors of the *Biographical Dictionary of Dark Age Britain*, "one of the greatest warlords in the British Isles during the early Middle Ages". Although of Irish stock on his father's side, through his mother and grandmother he was of British stock and could claim descent from Dyfnwal Hen, so he was arguably more British than Irish. Aedan's wife was also British, which makes Artúir at least three-quarters British.

Aedan undertook several exploits in which Artúir would have been involved. He fought against his overlord Baetan mac Cairill in Ulster in 574, when Gardner maintains Artúir would have fought at Dun Baetan. Aedan then led a campaign against the Orkneys in 580, and conquered the Isle of Man in 582, a sequence of battles that closely follows Arthur's own, according to Geoffrey of Monmouth. It was not until the 590s, with his battles against first the Picts and then the Angles, that Aedan's golden touch began to fail, and it was at this time that Artúir died. Of course Geoffrey conveniently ignores this and moves on to another chronicle to explore Arthur's later adventures. But it seems likely that Geoffrey was influenced by Artúir mac Aedan's exploits as part of Arthur's early conquests. Some of these may translate into the battles in Nennius's list, especially those in Glen Douglas in Lennox.

Artúir ultimately failed in his battles against the Picts and there was no heroic accession to the throne. Artúir, therefore, also fits the criterion of a battle lord who fought alongside kings. Yet his victories were not his own, but his father's, and they did not herald a period of peace between the British and Saxons as achieved at Badon. We know that Artúir was a contemporary of Myrddin, whom Geoffrey called Merlin. Whilst this begs a comparison with the original Arthur, it really opens up a false trail, as Myrddin had nothing to do with Geoffrey's Arthurian Merlin. The relationship provides a likely clue as to why Geoffrey confused the two.

Artúir is clearly one of the figures behind Arthur, but he's not the major one.

18. Arthlwys ap Arthfoddw (570–640)

Listed only for completeness. His father is included above, and the fact that Arthlwys inherited the Arth- prefix emphasizes the growing significance of the name.

19. Artúir ap Bicor (590–660)

As discussed in Chapter 8, this Artúir immortalized himself through a lucky slingshot throw in killing the Irish champion Mongan, and with the Arthur name now gathering interest this exploit was yet another to add to the list of achievements. If the episode had reappeared in the legends it would have meant something, but as it didn't, we can only conjecture that Artúir's moment of fame, sufficient for him to be remembered in the Irish Annals, served to feed the rumour mill even more on the growing legend of Arthur.

20. Athrwys ap Meurig (610–680)

Of all the "Arthurs", this one is both the most promising and the most frustrating. Athrwys was a ruler of Gwent sometime in the seventh century, or possibly earlier. Blackett and

Wilson, in *Artorius Rex Discovered*, date him 503–579, a century earlier than the date given in Table 8, whilst Barber and Pykitt, in *Journey to Avalon*, date him even earlier, 482–562. Since everyone has used the same pedigree, the difference is due to methods of dating. We know that his great-grandson Ffernfael died in 775, a date unlikely to be wrong, as the *Annals* in which that is recorded were brought into their final form only fifty years afterwards. Even if Ffernfael lived till he was ninety, and was thus born in 685, and each respective father was fifty when their son was born, we could only push Athrwys's birth back to 535. There may be a missing generation but, in all probability, Athrwys was a seventh-century ruler, perhaps born as early as 600 or 590 at a push, but no earlier.

Although I have used the name Athrwys here, he only appears in one pedigree under that name. Elsewhere he is listed as Atroys, Adroes, Athrawes and Adros, scarcely names to cause confusion with Arthur.

Bartrum notes that whilst he appears frequently in the *Book of Llandaff* as a witness to charters and grants, he is never identified as a king. Possibly his father Meurig lived to a great age, as seems the case with several of the rulers of Gwent, and thus outlived Athrwys. This would support Nennius's remark that Arthur fought alongside kings but was not apparently king himself. Perhaps Athrwys served as regent in his father's old age, and was thus king in all but name, and he may have served as a sub-king of Ergyng.

There is a deed in the *Book of Llandaff* apparently witnessed by "*Athruis rex Guenti regionis pro anima patris sui Mourici*", and though the grant may be accurate the other witnesses all date from the time of Dubricius, a hundred years earlier. The *Book of Llandaff* was not compiled until 1108, when the abbey needed to establish its rights over lands being appropriated by the Normans, and though it was drawn together from surviving documents doubtless much creativity was exercised in trying to reconstruct the more ancient and lost ones. It suggests that Athrwys was believed to be a contemporary of Dubricius and no one really knew which century that was.

Does all this necessarily matter? It certainly does, because Arthur of Gwent lived in the century or two before the tales of *The Mabinogion* and the *Welsh Annals* and other old documents were being created. He was the Arthur freshest in people's collective memories. He was far enough back for all history to be blended together (200 years might as easily be 400 in folk memory) but recent enough that the oral tradition remembered him fairly freshly. Thus all memories of Arthur could be pinned on to him.

However, Athrwys ap Meurig had to have been a memorable king in his own right in order for the blurring of memories to work. It would be no good if he were remembered as a coward or an imbecile. The memory of Athrwys ap Meurig could most easily be confused with Arthur of Badon if they had done something similar – something remarkably similar.

The clue to this may lie in the fact that at the time that the Arthurian legends were coming together, in the late eighth century, there was another Athrwys ruling Gwent, the great-great-grandson of Athrwys ap Meurig. This later Athrwys was the son of Ffernfael and ruled from about 775 to 800. This was when Offa ruled Mercia. At that time no other ruler in Britain mattered. Offa was the great king, the first to style himself "King of the English", with designs on becoming emperor. He had come to power in 757 and defeated the Welsh at Hereford in 760. It is believed that as part of the peace treaty Ergyng was taken over by Mercia, perhaps still administered by Ffernfael ap Ithel, but subservient to Offa. After Ffernfael's death in 775, it seems that Ergyng passed completely to the English. From 777 onwards Offa instigated a further series of raids into Wales, this time in retaliation for an offensive from Powys under Elisedd. Having asserted his authority Offa instigated the construction of the great earthwork known as Offa's Dyke and the building of this must have run throughout the reign of Athrwys ap Ffernfael. Although the Dyke did not run continuously into the south, as the Wye effectively formed the border, it was particularly strong around the border with Gwent. The ditch of the Dyke was on the western side, meaning it was there to stop the Welsh getting out. Wales was being hemmed in.

We know next to nothing about Athrwys ap Ffernfael, yet he may well be the key to the Arthurian legend. Here was a king who had lost part of his kingdom and was now being further humiliated by the greatest king Britain had known and was powerless to respond. What better way to save face than to revel in the glories of the past and to remember the great deeds of his ancestors?

What great deeds?

Well, there was one of great significance and that was the battle of Tintern Ford or, to give it its proper name, Pont y Saeson ("Bridge of the Saxons"). Tintern had once been a royal fortress, and in the days of Tewdrig ap Llywarch it was one of the glories of the kings of Gwent. The story, as told in the *Book of Llandaff,* says that Tewdrig had ruled for many years and was old and tired. He wished to retire into the church and pass the governance to his son Meurig. Not long after, however, the Saxons invaded Ergyng and Meurig was under pressure. Tewdrig, who had a vision in which an angel told him he would be victorious but would himself be killed, came out of retirement, buckled on his sword and led his army to one last victory. It was the greatest victory of them all. As Archenfield Archaeology report, "This stopped their advance and South Wales was never again to be seriously threatened by the English people."* This battle has strong resonances of Badon, perhaps even of Camlann, because, as prophesied, Tewdrig was injured by a lance and died three days later. He was buried at Matharn near Chepstow, close to Caradog Vreichfras's palace at Caldicot. Caradog could even have been present at that battle.

* *See* www.archenfield.com/history_earlymedieval.htm.

The battle of Tintern was as important to the kings of Gwent and Ergyng as Badon had been a hundred years earlier. Could Athrwys of Gwent have been at the battle of Tintern? If so, maybe some of the glory of that battle passed to him and over time, Tintern and Badon merged in the collective memory.

There has always been a problem dating this battle. Amazingly, it does not feature in the *Welsh Annals*, which may be a point in favour of arguing that by the time those *Annals* were compiled, memories of Tintern and Badon had started to blur. John Morris in *The Age of Arthur* suggested the battle may have happened in 584. After their victory at Dyrham in 577, when the Saxons defeated the rulers of Gloucester, Cirencester and Bath, the Saxons invaded the Severn Valley. The *ASC* reported a setback in 584 when Cutha was killed at Fethan Lea. The identity of that battle site has not been resolved to everyone's satisfaction. Both Stoke Lyne in Oxfordshire and Stratford-upon-Avon have been suggested and Tintern can't be ruled out. However, other dates have been suggested. Sarah Zaluckyj in *Mercia* cites 597, whilst Hereford's own archaeological studies suggest around 620 or as late as 630.

It is unlikely to have happened much after the succession of Penda of Mercia, whose rise to power began in 626. The evidence suggests that Penda had an alliance with various Welsh princes, which he called upon as he fought his way to Mercian control. The battle would probably have been after Chester, which had been an overwhelming victory for the Northumbrians against the British. That defeat had been one of the factors that caused the Welsh to ally with Mercia. Chester also frustrates dating, but the prevailing view is that it happened in 615. The West Saxons were heavily on the offensive in the late 620s. Penda managed to defeat them with British help at Cirencester in 628. In all likelihood a West Saxon defeat by the Welsh at Tintern happened just before then, perhaps with Penda's help, in around 626. It could have been slightly earlier. It's unlikely to have been later.

If we suggest 626x628, that fits in remarkably well with our pedigrees in Table 8. Despite the problem in dating the Gwentian kings, that date exactly fits the life-span for Tewdrig. It would also suggest that his grandson Athrwys could have fought at the battle. He was probably around twenty and it might have been his first major conflict.

Perhaps thereafter Athrwys fought alongside Penda. Perhaps some of Nennius's battle list relates to Penda's climb to power between 626 and 633. Penda had combined forces with Cadwallon of Gwynedd who was on a personal vendetta of revenge against Edwin, king of Northumbria. Cadwallon and Edwin had apparently been childhood friends but when Edwin defeated Athelfrith and became king in 616 all that changed. Cadwallon succeeded to Gwynedd around the year 620. In that same year Edwin conquered and extinguished the British enclave of Elmet near Leeds, and doubtless refugees settled in Wales. This was probably the spark that lit the fire, as Cadwallon is supposed to have fought Edwin soon after and was soundly defeated. Geoffrey of Monmouth places the battle at Widdrington, near Morpeth in Northumberland, but it is unlikely that Cadwallon would have undertaken a battle so far from his base at that stage. Edwin continued the campaign through North Wales and into Anglesey. Cadwallon was driven to the very tip of the island and had to flee to Ireland (or possibly Brittany) where he remained in exile for seven years.

He returned in about 629 and it was then that his campaign of revenge began. An elegy to Cadwallon, *Marwnad Cadwallon*, talks of fourteen major battles and sixty musterings. The battle list is longer than Arthur's and includes a battle at Caer Digoll in Shropshire, close to the site for Caer Faddon in *The Dream of Rhonabwy*. At what stage Cadwallon and Penda joined forces is not clear. It may well have been from the start, with the mutual objectives of the extermination of Edwin and the conquest of Northumbria.

The culmination of the campaign happened on 12 October 632 at Hatfield, which is almost certainly Hatfield in

Yorkshire, north of Doncaster – possibly the place that Geoffrey cited in his *History* for Ambrosius's defeat of Hengist. Here Penda and Cadwallon slaughtered the forces of Edwin of Northumbria, including Edwin himself and most of his family. The two did not leave it there. They went on a rampage through Northumbria, laying waste to the land, for a whole year. However, Cadwallon was caught by surprise at Heavenfield, near Hexham, by Hadrian's Wall and was killed by Oswald, son of King Athelfrith who had defeated the British at both Chester and probably Catraeth.

Had Cadwallon survived, the future of the British may have been very different. Cadwallon could have reclaimed much of the North for the British, but with his death the British resistance crumbled. The year 632/3 was their final triumph.

Perhaps Athrwys of Gwent was involved in it all. We know that Cadwallon had a huge force with him. The campaign could not have been supported by Penda's men alone. Cadwallon no doubt mustered British men in the North, but he needed large reserves to sustain his campaign for a whole year so far from Gwynedd. With Tewdrig dead and Meurig king, Athrwys was heir apparent but doubtless looking for battle experience. If he had helped in the victory at Tintern he now helped in the destruction of a kingdom.

We don't know if Athrwys was involved, but it would surprise me if he weren't. Cadwallon could not have achieved this with a force from Gwynedd alone, or even with the men of Powys. Gwent had already shown its prowess by defeating the Saxons at Tintern, and surely Cadwallon would have wanted some of that prestige for his army.

This is not to say that the legend of Arthur is based on the campaign of Cadwallon. Not at all. But when, in the late eighth century, the Welsh looked back to that final Golden Age when they proved they could defeat the English, might not some of the memory of Badon have blurred with Tintern and the name of Athrwys become associated with past glories?

It is only a proposal, but it would explain why Athrwys ap Meurig, who lived over a hundred years after Badon, and well beyond the traditional Arthurian period, might in any way be regarded as a candidate for the original Arthur. It explains why Arthur is shown as ruling from Caerwent (or Caerleon, as Geoffrey believed) and from Gelliwig, because that was Arthur of Gwent's base. It explains why so many of Arthur's court in *Culhwch and Olwen* and *The Dream of Rhonabwy* are people of Gwent, such as Bishop Bedwin and Caradog Vreichfras. Doubtless both were involved in the battle of Tintern and the subsequent campaign of Cadwallon. It would explain the second half of the pursuit of the Boar Trwyth which takes place through Gwent. The victory at Tintern is close to the eventual expulsion of the Boar at the estuary of the Wye. It would also explain how Arthur's campaigns seem to shift between Wales and the North.

This does not mean that Geoffrey confused Cadwallon's campaign with Arthur's. The memories and histories of these still remained separate, but in Gwent the emphasis may have changed so that Athrwys's role became more significant, and over a relatively short period this change became fused with earlier tales of Saxons vanquished by the British. Athrwys, now treated as the victor at Tintern, also became the victor of Badon by association and was so recorded in the *Welsh Annals*, the two histories merged and any written record was lost.

3. Rebuilding Arthur

The composite Arthur had been created, and continued to grow. It ought to be possible to show how this recomposition took place. I've already covered much of this above, so let's summarize it here. At this stage I am talking only about the Arthur from *The Mabinogion* and Geoffrey's *History*, and not the later Arthur of the romances, which is a whole other story. The suggestions included here are hypothetical but all are based on clear deductions made throughout this book.

Table 19 The composite Arthur story as per Nennius, Geoffrey, etc.	Possible original historical episode
Uther disguised as Gorlois seduces Ygerna (*Geoffrey, viii.19*)	None. Pure legend, possibly based on the Irish legend of Manannan ap Lir's seduction of the wife of Fiachna and the birth of Mongan. The character of Uther as Arthur's father may be influenced by Eliffer/Eleutherius of the North.
Arthur ascends throne at age fifteen, crowned by Dubricius (*Geoffrey, ix.1*)	Both Artúir mac Aedan and Athrwys ap Meurig may have been inaugurated into a command around the age of fifteen, Artúir as Wledig under Aedan and Athrwys as sub-king of Ergyng. However, probably the only ones who could have been inaugurated by Dubricius were Cadell or Caradog.
Arthur's battle campaign against the Saxons (*Nennius §56; Geoffrey ix.1–3*)	Most recently Athrwys ap Meurig's involvement with Penda against Edwin but influenced by the campaign of Aircol's alliance in the fifth century and that by Arthwys ap Mar and Eliffer, plus Urien of Rheged against the Angles or Aedan and Artúir against the Picts and Angles. Possible influence by later campaigns of Alfred and Athelstan against the Danes.
Battle of Badon (*Gildas §26; Nennius §56; Geoffrey ix.4*)	Most recently Athrwys ap Meurig at Tintern, but originally the confederate kings under Aircol with Arthwys ap Mar's victory at either Breidden Hill (or the Wrekin) or Liddington Castle.
Arthur's follow-up campaign against Irish, Picts, Islay (Man?) and Orkneys (*Geoffrey ix.5–10*)	Aedan mac Gabhran's campaign in which Artúir mac Aedan was probably involved. May also be influenced by Athelstan's battle against the Scots.
Arthur's twelve years of peace (*Geoffrey ix.11*) More likely a generation of peace	Followed Gwent's victory over Saxons at Tintern, but originally the victory by Aircol's alliance and Arthwys at Badon.
Hunt of the boar Trwyth (*Culhwch and Olwen*)	Dyfed episode drawn from Vortipor's or Artúir of Dyfed's battles against Irish raiders; Gwent episode probably based on Athrwys ap Meurig's forays against Saxons, or an earlier campaign to push Gewisse out of Ergyng.
Arthur's campaign against "Norway" and Gaul (*Geoffrey ix.11*)	Trigger for "Norway" was Athelstan's campaign at York and for Gaul was empire building by Henry I; Gaul's seed may have been influenced by Lucius Artorius Castus's campaign in Brittany, and possibly by Magnus Maximus's imperial campaign, but also merged with tales of Clovis and Ferreolus.
Arthur's special coronation (*Geoffrey ix.12–13*)	Probably invented by Geoffrey based on coronation of Norman kings, especially Stephen's, which he probably witnessed. But may have drawn origin from special coronation of Edgar at Bath in 973 or Offa's special ceremony in 787.

Arthur's campaign against Rome (*Geoffrey ix.14–x.13*)	Immediate trigger was excommunication of Henry I, but probably drew upon the imperial campaigns of Magnus Maximus and Constantine.
Treachery of Mordred (*Geoffrey xi.1*)	May have been premature death of Athwrys ap Meurig caused by involvement with his second cousin Medraut. Earlier betrayals, such as Urien's by Morcant, may also have influenced.
Battle of Camlann (*Geoffrey xi.2*)	We do not know where Athwrys ap Meurig died and there might well once have been a Camlann in Gwent. Otherwise may have been influenced by death of Artúir mac Aedan at Camboglanna, the possible death of Vortipor or Artúir of Dyfed at Camlan, or the slaying of Arthwys ap Mar, maybe also at Camboglanna.

4. The solution?

We have reached the end of our quest and it has been one of diversion and confusion, smoke and mirrors, deception and uncertainty. In Table 19, I bring together the various elements of the legend and the early records in an attempt to show how all of these may have originated. It may help you draw your own conclusions about the origins of the Arthurian tales. There is no doubt in my mind that the Arthur that we know was a composite consisting of several historical characters, some of whom we can guess at. So much has become confused and blurred over time that it is probably impossible to gain any certainty over the real Arthur, but having immersed myself in the history and legend for so long, I cannot help having my own ideas and suggestions. So whilst I leave the final answer open-ended for you, the reader, to consider, let me throw in my own theories.

I said at the outset that to find Arthur we needed to identify who was the victor of the battle of Badon and to do that we needed to know when that happened, where it took place and who was present. Have we done enough to answer those questions? Authoritatively and completely, no we haven't. I don't think that's possible with the data available. Otherwise, discovering the identity of Arthur would have been achieved long ago. But I think we can come close. Close enough that whilst Arthur still lurks in the shadows, it's possible to put one or two names to him.

Dating Badon was the first question, and we have followed through various chronologies to see where these lead us. Although the *Welsh Annals* give a date of 518 for Badon, other data called this into doubt and meant we had to consider all of the years leading up to Badon.

The story of the period from the withdrawal of Roman administration in 410 to the time of Badon was one of battle, plague and famine mixed with years of plenty. The contrast between the two suggests that Gildas and others may have exaggerated the problems in order to make their point, and it was these exaggerations that remained in the memory rather than the broader picture. The suggestion was that no sooner had Roman authority gone than Britain was inundated by Picts, Irish and Saxons in carnage that lasted until Badon. Yet underneath that story we catch glimpses of a Britain which is prosperous. After all, Constantius, in his *Life* of Germanus, written in about 480AD, referred to Britain in the 420s as "this most wealthy island".

The story that emerges is not one of Britain devastated by invaders but of a land able to protect itself against occasional incursions by Picts, Irish and Saxons with those incursions initially confined to northern Britannia, the old province of Britannia Secunda, and perhaps also the mysterious Valentia.

The *Gallic Chronicle* suggests that Britain remained nominally under Roman rule until at least 441AD, by which time the Saxons held sway. We know from Stephen Oppenheimer's research that the Britons living in eastern "England" were predominantly of Germanic bloodstock, and so genetically different from those in Wales and Scotland, even though we may group them all together as Celts, by culture. This would mean that those Saxons who came to Britain from Saxony, Frisia and Angeln would have found it easier to blend in with those living in the east than elsewhere in Britain so that, as the fifth century developed, the culture in Britain shifted from

Roman to Saxon. It was not a wholesale Saxon conquest of Britain. Instead, Germanic chieftains and warlords, displaced from their native homes, took advantage of the Saxon settlements in Britain to establish new territory.

This must have created a rift amongst the ruling elite in Britain between those who wanted to preserve the Roman ways and those prepared to work with the Saxons. This almost certainly led to internal struggles and civil war. The battle between Ambrosius and Vitalinus in 437AD was part of that. Both Ambrosius and Vitalinus, and their successors, the second Ambrosius and Vortigern, had their power-base in south-west Britain, in Britannia Prima, and I suspect that their conflict was for authority in that province rather than for the whole of Britain.

Doubtless, their internal struggles reduced their ability to protect the rest of Britain so that we find Saxon and Angle warlords establishing themselves in eastern Britain. Soemil took command at Deira probably in the 440s, Wilhelm in East Anglia soon after. Cerdic's ancestor, Gewis, must also have made inroads into southern Britain around this time. I think it would be fair to assume that by the time Vortigern asked for help from Hengist, the Saxons were already well established along the eastern coast of "England".

Whether Vortigern really employed Hengist to help fight against the Picts or whether in fact he was employing Saxon mercenaries to fight against other Saxons remains unclear, but either way it's almost certain that by around 450 the prosperous areas of southern Britain were coming under threat. Vortigern had doubtless been happy to leave the descendants of Coel and Cunedda to fight the Picts in the north of Britain, or the Irish in North Wales, providing the wealthy lands of southern Britain were left alone, but once these came under threat he had to do something. But his plan backfired. Vortigern retreated to his power-base and it was left firstly to his son, Vortimer, and then the son of his old enemy, Ambrosius, to protect the south. Vortimer's battle campaign in the 450s, was, I am sure, in eastern England, mostly in Lindsey, and it was successful for a period, though Vortimer was killed.

But the Saxon threat returned. The 460s saw Ambrosius's campaign supported perhaps by Aircol of Dyfed and possibly Brychan and Pascent. They managed to hold Britannia Prima, but by the 480s the Saxons were dominating eastern England. Octa, who may or may not have been a son of Hengist, and who had established himself in Lindsey, came south to Kent and joined forces with Aelle, who now had a strong base in Sussex.

By this stage the British are fighting on two fronts. There are the northern British in their kingdoms in Rheged, Strathclyde, Gododdin and Elmet fighting the Angles of Deira and Bernicia. In the south, the British of Powys, Gwent and Dumnonia are fighting the Saxons and Angles in what is becoming East Anglia, Essex and Sussex. Amongst these conflicts may be some or all of the battles listed by Nennius. Whilst they are presented as a single sequence, they may have been a series of British victories spread across Britain and between different forces.

Whatever the circumstances, the decisive battle was at Badon Hill. It was such a decisive battle that Gildas recalled that even after forty-four years all "external wars" had stopped and there was a "calm of the present". Since Gildas distinguishes between "external" wars and "civil" wars, he must be referring to battles with the invading forces, including the resident Saxons, as distinct from between the British (of whom Gildas was one), where conflict evidently continued.

So, in order to date Badon, we look for a period of at least forty-four years where there was no significant series of battles between British and Saxon forces. Here records are limited to the *Anglo-Saxon Chronicle* and its data are suspect because not only are the dates themselves confusing, with repetition of data, but the Saxons would focus on their victories and ignore British victories. Thus the *ASC* makes no mention of Badon.

Whilst the *ASC* records various Saxon and Angle victories during the late fifth century it then goes quiet for some years

with the only activities attributed to Cerdic. The dates relating
to Cerdic in the *ASC* are all suspect, because of repetition and
contradiction, but the likeliest dates that emerge are either 529,
based on internal chronology or, more likely, 538, based on
other internal chronology corrupted by the Easter cycle of
records. The *ASC* also records that in 547 Ida became ruler of
the northern Angles, though that date is also suspect. I calculated that Gildas wrote *De Excidio* some time in the 540s, but
even if we ignore that for this current purpose, we can deduce
from the *ASC* that there were no Saxon victories between 491,
the date of Aelle's victory at Anderida, and Cerdic's accession,
which was either in 529 (thirty-eight years later) or 538 (forty-
seven years later). Similarly, in the north, there is no record of a
Saxon or Angle victory prior to Ida in 547, and Gildas's forty-
four years would take us back to 503, and even earlier if Gildas
was writing prior to 547.

Badon, therefore, had to be earlier than 503 and later than 491
and the other factors I explored narrowed it down to between
493 and 497. It is perhaps pertinent that Fergus was able to
establish himself as ruler of the Scottish Dál Riata in 498,
probably taking advantage of the period of peace after Badon.

At that time the leading British chieftains in the north of
Britain were Dyfnwl Hen of Strathclyde, Brychan of Manau,
Merchiaun of Rheged and Arthwys of the Pennines (probably
Elmet). The leading figures in the south were Cadwallon of
Gwynedd, Vortipor of Dyfed, Caradog Vreichfras of Gwent,
Cadell of Powys and Riocatus of Gwrtheyrnion. There are
others in the genealogies, and though I accept that the dates
accorded them are prone to some generational shift, the
chances are that it was amongst these we will find the "kings
of Britain" alongside whom Arthur fought, according to
Nennius's old papers. This does not mean that Arthur is
necessarily in addition to the above. There is no way of
knowing that all of the above were "kings" at the time of
Badon, though they were certainly senior amongst the patriarchal families and may subsequently have become kings.

The one name that stands out is Arthwys of the Pennines, not only because his name is the closest to Arthur (though we must remember that the Arthur of Badon may not have been called Arthur), but because if his territory was central Britain, as far south as Elmet (Leeds), then he was in a position to have fought in either a northern campaign or a southern one. Although the sites for Nennius's battle list might be all over Britain, it is unlikely one *dux bellorum* could have sustained a sequential campaign across the whole of Britain. It had to be focused.

Let us for the moment assume it was one campaign, under one commander. Although the Angles had been settling in northern Britain since the time of Soemil, in the 440s, there is no specific record of major conflict with the British in the north. The northern battles were chiefly the British against the Picts and/or the Irish. The records of Nennius and Bede make it clear the enemy at Badon was the Saxons. Gildas is more ambiguous, referring only to "enemies", but the whole inference of his diatribe is that these enemies were the heathen Saxons.

This suggests to me that Badon was not in the north. It was either along the frontier that was drawn up after Badon, and which I equate with the Roman roads of Dere Street and Ermine Street, or it was further in the south, closer to the borders of the old province of Britannia Prima. Referring back to Map 7 there are no obvious sites for Badon along the Dere/Ermine Street frontier. All the suggested candidates such as Bowden Hill near Linlithgow, Bowden in the Eildon Hills or Bowden in County Durham are too far north for a climactic battle when so much activity was in the south.

I singled out Liddington Castle in Wiltshire as the most suitable site, though other close contenders were the Wrekin in Shropshire near the Roman fort of Viriconium or Caer Faddon near Welshpool (remembered in *The Mabinogion* as the site of Badon). These are all around the borders of Britannia Prima and are easily accessible by the Roman road system. They also all incorporated major hill forts and were close to old Roman cities that had survived well into the fifth century (Viriconium, Cirencester and Bath).

Moreover, the sites of Nennius's other battles, as listed in Table 15 and shown on Map 8 as the southern frontier and part of the western frontier, suggest sites that would fit in closely with battles fought to protect the border of Britannia Prima with occasional forays by either side beyond that frontier. It is possible that some of the pre-Badon battles were along the eastern frontier but there just aren't enough identifiable sites to make this a continuous battle front.

So, if my deductions are right, this has given us a date – around the mid-490s, and a location – in the central south-west, possibly in Wiltshire or Shropshire. We also have some possible names for rulers or commanders, which are worth repeating:

Arthwys of the Pennines and his son Eliffer
Caradog Vreichfras of Gwent
Cadell of Powys
Cadwallon Lawhir of Gwynedd
Geraint of Dumnonia
Riocatus of Gwrtheyrnion
Vortipor and his father Aircol of Dyfed

This is a formidable coalition of kings and princes. Remember that Arthwys's son, Eliffer, was renowned for his "Great Host" of warriors. Caradog, whose nickname means "Strongarm", is remembered in *The Mabinogion* as being present at Badon. Cadell had the epithet *Durnluc* meaning "gleaming hilt", perhaps a hint of Excalibur. Cadwallon was *Lawhir* or "Longhand", tall and powerful. Riocatus's name means "king of battles". Vortipor was "the Protector", a name which in Irish was written as *Gartbuir*, easily mistaken as *Arthuir*. These all lived at the time of Badon. What more of an army of heroes could you want?

It is evident from this that the later rulers, Artúir of Dyfed and Athrwys of Gwent, could not be Arthur of Badon, because they lived up to a century later, but their reputation in Welsh legend would benefit from the association of names. Athrwys of Gwent may even have strengthened the association of the name Arthur with Badon because of his own involvement with the victory of the Welsh over the Angles at Tintern, a battle which subsequently blended into the folk memory as one as significant as Badon. Likewise Artúir mac Aedan could not be the Arthur of Badon even though his prominence in the north passed into folklore and caused his name to be associated with many local legends and geographical features. Moreover, it was Artúir mac Aedan who was a contemporary of Myrddin the Bard and thus caused Geoffrey of Monmouth's erroneous association in the first place.

I suspect that when this army marched to Badon it went from Caerleon, because the concentration of later legends linking Arthur and the battle with Gwent and Ergyng are so insistent that there has to be some connection. It may well have met with the armies of Arthwys and Eliffer at Viriconium, if the battle was at the Wrekin or Caer Faddon, but equally Caerleon would be a strong marshalling point for a march to Liddington, via Cirencester. Or they may have gathered at the hill fort at Cadbury, which was reinforced at this time, and is named after Cadwr of Dumnonia, who might also have been present. If the battle was fought against Aelle and Oisc then it is more likely to have been at Liddington.

It is a theory built on very vague circumstantial evidence, I freely admit, but it's one that does not conflict with known historical and archaeological evidence or with folklore or legend.

After Badon the victors would benefit from a generation or more of peace with the Saxons, who were retained behind an eastern frontier. This allowed some to fall into evil ways, to be castigated by Gildas.

If Vortipor was Arthur, then he was a tarnished hero, but his title *Gartbuir* may have been read by later chronicles as

Arthuir, enough to connect a name. Cadwallon carved out a strong reputation in his own right and he would never have become confused with Arthur. Caradog was always seen as Arthur's viceroy and doubtless ruled Ergyng for many years after Badon in great glory. Geraint was remembered in song as a great hero, and was compared to Arthur, so could not have been him. Riocatus may have been at Badon, though one would have expected Dubricius to be the leading bishop present, despite the resonance and temptation of Riocatus's name as "king of battles".

That leaves Arthwys of the Pennines and Cadell of the Gleaming Hilt. Arthwys was definitely in the right place at the right time and with his son's "Great Host" could have marshalled a formidable army. Cadell became the ancestor of the rulers of Powys and his line ruled for the next 300 years. He won back this kingdom after having lost everything.

Could the activities of Arthwys and Cadell have been the start of the Arthurian legend? After this quest through the dark corridors of history it strikes me as entirely possible.

That's my conclusion. What are yours?

BIBLIOGRAPHY

The following lists the major works and websites I consulted in the preparation of this book and which are cited in footnotes in the main text.

Books and other texts

Alcock, Leslie (1971), *Arthur's Britain*, London: Allen Lane.

Alcock, Leslie (1987), *Economy, Society & Warfare Among the Britons & Saxons*, Cardiff: University of Wales Press.

Ardrey, Adam (2007), *Finding Merlin, the Truth Behind the Legend*, London: Mainstream.

Arnold, Christopher J. and Davies, Jeffrey L. (2000), *Roman and Early Medieval Wales*, Stroud: Sutton.

Ashe, Geoffrey (1987), *The Landscape of King Arthur*, Exeter: Webb & Bower.

Ashe, Geoffrey (1997), *The Traveller's Guide to Arthurian Britain*, Glastonbury: Gothic Image.

Ashe, Geoffrey (2003), *The Discovery of King Arthur*, revised edition, Stroud: Sutton.

Barber, Chris and Pykitt, David (1993), *Journey to Avalon*, Abergavenny: Blorenge Books.

Barber, Richard (1972), *The Figure of Arthur*, Cambridge: D. S. Brewer.

Barber, Richard (1993), *King Arthur, Hero and Legend*, new edition, Woodbridge: Boydell Press.

Barnwell, P. S. (1992), *Emperor, Prefects & Kings, the Roman West, 395-565*, London: Duckworth.

Barron, W. R. J., editor (2001), *The Arthur of the English*, Cardiff: University of Wales Press.

Bartrum, P. C. (1966), *Early Welsh Genealogical Tracts*, Cardiff: University of Wales Press.

Bartrum, P. C. (1993), *A Welsh Classical Dictionary*, Aberystwyth: National Library of Wales.

Bassett, Stephen, editor (1989), *The Origins of the Anglo-Saxon Kingdoms*, Leicester University Press.

Blackett, Baram and Wilson, Alan (1985), *Artorius Rex Discovered*, Cardiff: King Arthur Research.

Blake, Steve and Lloyd, Scott (2000), *The Keys to Avalon*, Shaftesbury: Element.

Blake, Steve and Lloyd, Scott (2002), *Pendragon*, London: Rider.

Breeze, David J. (1982), *The Northern Frontiers of Roman Britain*, London: Batsford.

Bromwich, Rachel, Jarman, A. O. H. and Roberts, Brynley F., editors (1991), *The Arthur of the Welsh*, Cardiff: University of Wales Press.

Bruce, Christopher W. (1999), *The Arthurian Name Dictionary*, New York: Garland.

Cameron, Kenneth (1996), *English Place Names*, London: Batsford.

Carroll, D. F. (1996), *Arturius – a Quest for Camelot*, Goxhill: privately published.

Castleden, Rodney (2000), *King Arthur, the Truth Behind the Legend*, London: Routledge.

Chambers, E. K. (1927), *Arthur of Britain*, London: Sidgwick & Jackson.

Coates, Richard (1989), *The Place-Names of Hampshire*, London: Batsford.

Coe, Jon B. and Young, Simon (1995), *The Celtic Sources for the Arthurian Legend*, Hampeter: Llanerch.

Coghlan, Ronan (1991), *The Encyclopedia of Arthurian Legends*, Shaftesbury: Element.

Crawford, O. G. S. (1935), "Arthur and His Battles", *Antiquity*: 35.

Dames, Michael (2002), *Merlin and Wales, a Magician's Landscape*, London: Thames & Hudson.

Dark, Ken (2000), *Britain and the End of the Roman Empire*, Stroud: Tempus.

Dark, K. R. (1994), *Civitas to Kingdom*, Leicester University Press.

Davidson, Hilda Ellis (editor), Fisher, Peter (translator) (1996), *Saxo Grammaticus: The History of the Danes, Books I–IX*, Cambridge: Brewer.

Davies, Hugh (2002), *Roads in Roman Britain*, Stroud: Tempus.

Davies, Wendy (1982), *Wales in the Early Middle Ages*, Leicester University Press.

Dillon, Myles and Chadwick, Nora (1967), *The Celtic Realms*, London: Weidenfeld & Nicolson.

Dornier, Ann (1982), "The Province of Valentia", *Britannia*: 13.

Dumville, David N. (1993), *Britons and Anglo-Saxons in the Early Middle Ages*, Aldershot: Ashgate Publishing.

Ellis, Peter Berresford (1993), *Celt and Saxon, the Struggle for Britain AD 410–937*, London: Constable.

Evans, Stephen S. (1997), *Lords of Battle*, Woodbridge: Boydell Press.

Fairbairn, Neil (1983), *A Traveller's Guide to the Kingdoms of Arthur*, London: Evans Brothers.

Fraser, James E. (2009), *From Caledonia to Pictland, Scotland to 795*, Edinburgh University Press.

Gardner, Laurence (1996), *Bloodline of the Holy Grail*, Shaftesbury: Element.

Garmondsway, G. N., editor and translator (1972), *The Anglo-Saxon Chronicle*, London: Dent.

Gelling, Margaret (1984), *Place Names in the Landscape*, London: Dent.

Gelling, Margaret (1992), *The West Midlands in the Early Middle Ages*, Leicester University Press.

Gidlow, Christopher (2004), *The Reign of Arthur, from History to Legend*, Stroud: Sutton.

Gilbert, Adrian, Wilson, Alan and Blackett, Baram (1998), *The Holy Kingdom*, London: Bantam Press.

Giot, Pierre-Roland, Guignon, Philippe and Merdrignac, Bernard (2003), *The British Settlement of Brittany*, Stroud: Tempus.

Glennie, John S. Stuart (1869), *Arthurian Localities*, reprinted Llanerch, 1994.

Goodrich, Norma Lorre (1986), *King Arthur*, New York: Franklin Watts.

Goodrich, Norma Lorre (1988), *Merlin*, New York: Franklin Watts.

Goodrich, Norma Lorre (1992a), *Guinevere*, New York: Harper-Collins.

Goodrich, Norma Lorre (1992b), *The Holy Grail*, New York: HarperCollins.

Green, Miranda J. (1992), *Dictionary of Celtic Myth and Legend*, London: Thames & Hudson.

Higham, N. J. (2002), *King Arthur, Myth-Making and History*, London: Routledge.

Hill, David (1981), *An Atlas of Anglo-Saxon England*, Oxford: Blackwell.

Hogg, A. H. A. (1975), *Hill-Forts of Britain*, London: Hart-Davis, MacGibbon.

Holmes, Michael (1996), *King Arthur, a Military History*, London: Blandford.

Hood, A. B. E. (1978), *St. Patrick, His Writings and Muirchu's Life*, Chichester: Phillimore.

Ireland, S. (1986), *Roman Britain: A Sourcebook*, New York: St. Martin's Press.

Johnson, Stephen (1980), *Later Roman Britain*, London: Routledge & Kegan Paul.

Jones, Michael E. and Casey, John (1988), "The Gallic Chronicle Restored", *Britannia*: 19.

Kennedy, Edward Donald, editor (2002), *King Arthur, a Casebook*, London: Routledge.

Kirby, D. P. (1991), *The Earliest English Kings*, London: Unwin Hyman.

Koch, John T. (1997), *The Gododdin of Aneirin*, Cardiff: University of Wales Press.

Koch, John T. with Carey, John, *The Celtic Heroic Age*, 4th edition, Aberystwyth: Celtic Studies.

Lacy, Norris J., editor (1996), *The New Arthurian Encyclopedia*, New York: Garland.

Lapidge, Michael, Blair, John, Keynes, Simon and Scragg, Donald, editors (1999), *The Blackwell Encyclopedia of Anglo-Saxon England*, Oxford: Blackwell.

Littleton, C. Scott and Malcor, Linda A. (2000), *From Scythia to Camelot*, new edition, New York: Garland.

Loomis, Roger Sherman, editor (1927), *Celtic Myth and Arthurian Romance*, New York: Columbia.

McClure, Judith and Collins, Roger, editors (1994), *Bede, The Ecclesiastical History of the English People*, Oxford University Press.

McKenzie, Peter (1999), *Camelot's Frontier*, Morpeth: Longhirst Press.

Matthews, John (1991), *The Song of Taliesin*, London: Aquarian Press.

Matthews, John and Stead, Michael J. (1995), *King Arthur's Britain*, London: Blandford.

Millar, Ronald (1978), *Will the Real King Arthur Please Stand Up?*, London: Cassell.

Mills, A. D. (1991), *Oxford Dictionary of Place Names*, Oxford University Press, reprinted 2003.

Moffat, Alistair (1999), *Arthur and the Lost Kingdoms*, London: Weidenfeld & Nicolson.

Moorhead, John (2001), *The Roman Empire Divided, 400–700*, Harlow: Longman.

Morris, John (1973), *The Age of Arthur*, London: Weidenfeld & Nicolson.

Morris, John (1980), *Nennius, British History and the Welsh Annals*, Chichester: Phillimore.

Morris, John (1995a), *Arthurian Sources, Vol. 2, Annals and Charters*, Chichester: Phillimore.

Morris, John (1995b), *Studies in Dark Age History*, Chichester: Phillimore.

Muhlberger, Steven (1983), "The Gallic Chronicle of 452 and Its Authority for British Events", *Britannia*: 14.

Myres, J. N. L. (1986), *The English Settlements*, Oxford: Clarendon Press.

Oppenheimer, Stephen (2006), *The Origins of the British*, London: Constable & Robinson.

Padel, O. J. (2000), *Arthur in Medieval Welsh Literature*, Cardiff: University of Wales Press.

Phillips, Graham and Keatman, Martin (1992), *King Arthur, the True Story*, London: Century.

Reid, Howard (2001), *Arthur, the Dragon King*, London: Headline.

Reno, Frank D. (1996), *The Historic King Arthur*, Jefferson, C: McFarland.

Reno, Frank D. (2000), *Historic Figures of the Arthurian Era*, Jefferson, C: McFarland.

Riton, Joseph (1825), *The Life of King Arthur*, London: Nicol.

Rivet, A. L. F. and Smith, Colin (1979), *The Place-Names of Roman Britain*, London: Batsford.

Roberts, Brynley F. (1971), *Brut y Brenhinedd*, Dublin Institute for Advanced Studies.

Roberts, Peter, translator (1811), *The Chronicle of the Kings of Britain attributed to Tysilio*, facsimile edition, Llanerch, 2000.

Salway, Peter (1981), *Roman Britain*, Oxford: Clarendon Press.

Skene, W. F. (1988), *Arthur and the Britons in Wales and Scotland*, Lampeter: Llanerch.

Snyder, Christopher A. (1996), *Sub-Roman Britain*, Oxford: Hadrian Books.

Snyder, Christopher A. (1998), *An Age of Tyrants*, Stroud: Sutton.

Snyder, Christopher A. (2000), *Exploring the World of King Arthur*, London: Thomas & Hudson.

Stafford, Pauline (1985), *The East Midlands in the Early Middle Ages*, Leicester University Press.

Stobie, Denise (1999), *Exploring King Arthur's Britain*, London: Collins & Brown.

Swanton, Michael, editor and translator (1996), *The Anglo-Saxon Chronicle*, London: Dent.

Thomas, Charles (1981), *Christianity of Roman Britain to AD500*, London: Batsford.

Thompson, E. A. (1984), *Saint Germanus of Auxerre and the End of Roman Britain*, Woodbridge: Boydell Press.

Thorpe, Lewis, translator (1974), *Gregory of Tours, the History of the Franks*, London: Penguin.

Tolstoy, Nikolai (1985), *The Quest for Merlin*, London: Hamish Hamilton.

Turner, P. F. J. (1993), *The Real King Arthur*, Alaska: SKS.

Vince, Alan (1993), *Pre-Viking Lindsey*, City of Lincoln.

Walker, Ian W. (2000), *Mercia and the Making of England*, Stroud: Sutton.

Wildman, S. G. (1971), *The Black Horsemen*, London: Baker.

Williams, Hugh, translator (1889), *Two Lives of Gildas*, reprinted Felinfach: Llanerch, 1990.

Williams, Hugh, translator (1901), *Gildas*, London: David Nutt.

Williams, Sheridan (1996), *UK Solar Eclipses from Year 1 to 3000*, Leighton Buzzard: Clock Tower Press.

Wilson, Roger J. A. (2002), *A Guide to the Roman Remains in Britain*, 4th edition, London: Constable.

Winterbottom, Michael, editor, translator (1978), *Gildas, The Ruin of Britain and Other Works*, Chichester: Phillimore.

Wood, Ian (1994), *The Merovingian Kingdoms, 450–751*, Harlow: Longman.

Yorke, Barbara (1990), *Kings and Kingdoms of Early Anglo-Saxon England*, London: Sealby.

Yorke, Barbara (1995), *Wessex in the Early Middle Ages*, London: Leicester University Press.

Zaluckyj, Sarah (2001), *Mercia*, Almeley: Logaston Press.

Websites

Arthuriana, run by Southern Methodist University, Dallas, Texas 75275-0432, USA. Website: smu.edu/arthuriana/arthursubs.htm

Britannia, run by David Nash Ford. Website: www.britannia.com/history/ebk/

The Camelot Project, University of Rochester, designed by Alan Lupack, website: www.lib.rochester.edu/camelot/cphome.stm

The Heroic Age on-line journal. Publisher and Editor-in-chief, Michelle Ziegler. Website: http://members.aol.com/heroicage1/homepage.html

International Arthurian Society (IAS) founded by Eugène Vinaver, Jean Frappier and Roger Sherman Loomis in 1948. It publishes an annual *Bibliographical Bulletin*. Website: http://www.st-andrews.ac.uk/~iasbb/

King Arthur Forever website run by Michael Torregrossa: http://kingarthurforever.org/

Vortigern Studies "Faces of Arthur" sub-site, run by Robert Vermaat at: www.geocities.com/vortigernstudies.org.uk/

INDEX

To avoid duplication the titles of stories and romances are entered under their English name wherever practical. Individuals known by a variety of names are entered under their most common form of name (e.g. Guenevere, Gawain).